EVERYONE'S SUPPORT SYSTEMS

A Complete Guide to
Effective Decision Making
Using Microcomputers

EVERYONE'S SUPPORT SYSTEMS

A Complete Guide to Effective Decison Making Using Microcomputers

Chantico Publishing Company, Inc.
Edited by

Dr. Robert S. Snoyer

Glenn A. Fischer

BUSINESS ONE IRWIN
Homewood, Illinois 60430

© RICHARD D. IRWIN, INC., 1993

Sponsoring editor: Susan Stevens, Ph.D.
Project editor: Susan Trentacosti
Production manager: Mary Jo Parke
Jacket designer: Annette Vogt
Compositor: Carlisle Communications, Ltd.
Typeface: 10/12 Times Roman
Printer: Arcata Graphics/Kingsport

Library of Congress Cataloging-in-Publication Data

Everyone's support systems : a complete guide to effective decision
  making using microcomputers / Chantico Publishing Company, Inc.:
  edited by Robert S. Snoyer and Glenn A. Fischer

    p. cm.

  ISBN 1-55623-874-6

  1. Decision support systems.   2. Microcomputers.   I. Snoyer,
Robert S.   II. Fischer, Glenn A.   III. Chantico Publishing Co.

T58.62.E94   1993   92–25389
658.4'03—dc20

Printed in the United States of America
1   2   3   4   5   6   7   8   9   0   AGK   9   8   7   6   5   4   3   2

TP

Acknowledgments

This book is one in a series developed through the efforts of the Profit Oriented Systems Planning Program Organization (POSPP). The membership of this group represents organizations at all levels of participation in the development and implementation of automation technology within industry, commerce, and government. This book represents the experiences of these organizations' members and participants, who are outstanding practicing professionals specializing in the subject area, as well as the contributions of consultants, manufacturers, and the academic council of POSPP/Chantico.

The materials provided by the membership have been compiled and edited by Chantico Publishing Company. The material represents a broad range of experiences as well as the theoretical basis for these activities. Participating individuals and companies are:

Name	Title	Company
Using Organizations		
Douglas LaFontaine	Manager, MIS Applications Development	Chrysler Corp.
David Roberts	Account Manager	General Motors Corporation
Lynn G. Trimpey	Director of Systems and Operations	ConAgra, Inc.
Edward Tomlinson	Vice President, Systems Planning and Integration	Beneficial Corporation
William Boos	Director of Marketing Systems	IBM Corporation
George Houdeshel	Director of Operations, Management Information, Decision Support Systems	Lockheed Aeronautical Systems
Bobby J. Culpepper	MIS Manager	Phillips 66 Corp.
Grady Baker	Executive Vice President	Georgia Power & Light
Carl Peterson	Vice President, Corporate Planning & Information	National Westminster Bank
James Tunis	President	Lincoln National Information Services, Inc.
Karen Baughman	Senior Director, Financial Development Intra-Company and Support Services	CSX Technology

Name	Title	Company
Academic Institutions		
Dr. John F. Rockart	Director, Center for Information Systems Research	Massachusetts Institute of Technology
Michael S. Morton	J. W. Forrester Professor of Management	Massachusetts Institute of Technology
R. H. Sprague, Jr.	Professor & Chairman, Decision Sciences Department	College of Business Administration, University of Hawaii
David W. DeLong	Research Associate	Harvard University Graduate School of Business
John C. Henderson	Former Associate Professor, Management Science	Center for Information Systems Research, Massachusetts Institute of Technology
Consultants		
Bernard Bowler	Director of Integrated Office Software	IBM Corporation
Daryl C. Youngman	Director	Washington University of St. Louis
Wayne Burkan		Comshare Corp.
Craig Barlow		Comshare Corp.
David Friend	Chairman	Pilot Executive Software, Inc.
Alan Greif	Principal	Booz-Allen & Hamilton, Inc.
Harry Rodenhi	Vice President, Consulting Services	Decision Support Technology, Inc.
Alan Paller	President	AUI Data Graphics

Dr. Robert S. Snoyer

Glenn A. Fischer

Contents

INTRODUCTION   1

Chapter One
EFFECTIVE COMPUTER SUPPORT FOR
EXECUTIVES   6
Decisions that Matter, 6
The Need for Management Support Systems, 7
Corporate Culture and Individual Attitudes, 11
The Strategic Value of Management Support Systems, 14
Structured and Unstructured Decisions, 17
Implications for Executive Action, 20

Chapter Two
THE SPECTRUM OF MANAGEMENT
SUPPORT SYSTEMS   23
Terms Used for Management Support Systems, 23
Comparison of Management Support Systems, 26
The New Technology and the Old Technology, 32
System Development for MSS, 44
Comparison of Traditional and Prototyping SDLC, 47
Management for MSS Development, 50
The Benefits of Management Support Systems, 57

Chapter Three
ORGANIZATION AND INFORMATION
DELIVERY ISSUES   59
The Movement toward End-User Computing, 60
Information Center Support for MSS, 64
Information Display for Executives, 68
Organizing for Management Support Systems, 77
Implementing Group Decision Support Systems, 80
Establishing an Optimum Balance, 87

Chapter Four
EXECUTIVE INFORMATION SYSTEMS   89
Meeting the Individual Needs of Executives, 90
The Organizational Impact of EIS, 92
Components of an Executive Information System, 95
Implementing an Executive Information System, 96
Information Requirements and Data Acquisition, 101
Tracking Critical Success Factors, 108
Key External Factors, 109
Data Access Challenges, 110
Micro-to-Mainframe Connections, 112

Chapter Five
DECISION SUPPORT SYSTEMS (DSS)   115
When to Use Decision Support Systems, 115
An Integrated View of DSS, 117
Level of Support Provided by a Decision Support System, 120
The Role of Assumptions in DSS, 122
Building Blocks for a DSS, 123
Typical Uses of Decision Support Systems, 125
Review of DSS Activities, 125

Chapter Six
DATA MANAGEMENT ISSUES   128
Data Management for DSS and EIS, 128
Data Management Alternatives, 130
Problems with the Volume of Data Requests, 133
Data Requirements for a Subject Perspective, 134
Responsibilities for Data Management, 137
Data Access Requirements, 139
Database Administration, 144
Data Security Considerations, 146
Disaster Preparedness and Recovery, 152

Chapter Seven
SYSTEM MODELING ISSUES   159
The Use of Computer Modeling, 159
Types of Computer Models, 161

Initiating Model Development, 162
Viewpoint Modeling, 164
Model Development Time, 167
Developing the Model, 170
Data for the Model, 172
Study Reports, 174
Debugging and Documenting the Model, 175
Model Investigation, 178

Chapter Eight
SPECIAL AND FUTURE MANAGEMENT ISSUES   180
Computer Resource Management, 180
Data Management Trends and Relational Database
Systems, 189
Data Ownership and Data Sharing, 197
Effective Use of Quality Assurance, 216
Security and Disaster Recovery Requirements, 224

Chapter Nine
SPECIAL AND FUTURE TECHNOLOGY ISSUES   230
Application Prototyping and Fourth-Generation
Languages, 231
Definition of Application Prototyping, 231
Artificial Intelligence and Expert Systems, 245
Advanced Use of Graphics, 254
Microcomputer Networking and Local Area Networks, 272
Document Image Processing and Optical Disks, 283
Use of Teleconferencing and Corporate Videotex, 292
Future CD ROM Availability, 306

Chapter Ten
EVALUATION AND SELECTION OF
MANAGEMENT SUPPORT SYSTEMS   313
Defining Objectives and Needs, 314
The Selection Committee, 317
Use of Checklists in Evaluation, 319
Areas of Software Package Evaluation, 320
Checklists for Comparative Evaluation of Software
Packages, 325

Use of Metrics in Software Package Comparison, 337
Request for Proposals, 343
Vendor Presentations, 350
Justifying the Purchase, 360
Product Performance Benchmarks, 363
Selection and Test of The Primary Product, 368
Making the Final Selection, 370

Chapter Eleven
MICROCOMPUTER MSS SOFTWARE   377
MSS Modeling Packages on Microcomputers, 377
The Spreadsheet Package, 379
Integrated MSS Packages, 382
Checklist for Evaluating Spreadsheet Packages, 384

Chapter Twelve
SOME FINAL THOUGHTS   387
Security Considerations, 387
EIS for Use by Top Executives, 388
Computer Hardware and Network Considerations, 389
Software Tools, 390
Database Considerations, 391
Role of Standards, 392
Role of MIS or the I/S Organization, 393
The End, 394

Index   395

Introduction

You have probably heard the expression "You can't tell the players without a score card." The jargon used by computer people often sounds or looks like confusing gibberish filled with acronyms and technical terms seemingly aimed at making the subject unintelligible to the ordinary person. Most would agree that this is true of information and support systems.

You need only select one word from each column in the following chart and you will build a list of impressive technical terms along with their associated acronyms.

Column 1	Column 2	Column 3
EXECUTIVE		
	INFORMATION	
MANAGEMENT		SYSTEMS
	SUPPORT	
DECISION		

This book will clarify and simplify the whole matter of decision support systems. It will give knowledge and understanding to managers and other users to whom computers and computer systems are simply a means to an end. Information technology (IT) workers and computer experts will find it equally useful. The information in this book will enable them to use the terminology correctly, improve their ability to communicate more effectively, and aid them in the development of systems.

This book covers various types of automated systems utilized in the support of decision making at all levels of an organization. It represents a broad range of experiences as well as the results of considerable proven research into these activities. Basic to the material are the authors' participation in Profit Oriented System Planning Program special meetings, and roundtable discussions on the subject. Participants in these meetings and discussions were senior operating executives, academic researchers, and consultants.

The purpose of this book is to describe a number of processes for automating the efforts of knowledge workers, executives, and line-management and other professionals within an operating organization by embedding computer-based

1

technology into the decision-making and planning processes. There is a method for making information about the decision-making and planning processes available to interested managers and others. This is achieved by building and using systems that are designed to work vertically (from executive to functional staff) and horizontally (from peer to peer and across functional areas).

This book is unique in that it explores executive information support systems and decision support systems from the perspective of both short-term and long-term benefits. This is particularly true when these systems are expanded to become "everyone's information systems." When this is accomplished, they turn into heavily utilized, cross-functional tools. Usage may vary, from short-term decision support for a particular issue, or for long-term support of an organizational group consisting of a variety of knowledge workers and project management. This can occur regardless of geographical location or organizational position.

Everyone's Support Systems covers all aspects of preparing a foundation that can be successfully broadened. It also outlines how these systems augment each other and how they support the human resources of an organization.

Some of the key issues addressed are:

- The impact of the current organizational trend of moving toward flatter organization control and cooperative processing efforts.
- How to optimize business processes by the use of information technology to meet strategic and competitive goals.
- How to identify and gain the leadership necessary for successful implementation and use.
- How to design systems that monitor business needs, analyze trends, and help with planning.
- How to anticipate and accommodate the organizational, functional, and human-resource impacts of these systems.
- What the data management issues are and how to resolve them successfully.
- The best methods for justifying the various types of support systems.

Following is a brief summary of the chapters in this book:

Chapter One: Effective Computer Support for Executives

This chapter points out that the book provides a management baseline the executives can use to evaluate an organization's decisions in the use of management support systems (MSS). It emphasizes they should be used for decisions that matter. It notes that the new agenda for MSS has gone beyond decision support systems (DSS) and calls for a refocus on the enhancement of support capabilities and the exploitation of nontraditional techniques. The strategic value of MSS is discussed. A distinction between structured, semistructured, and unstructured decisions is made. The implications for executive action are noted.

Chapter Two: The Spectrum of Management Support Systems

Popular terms for MSS used in the literature are noted. The interlocking and overlapping types of support available today are explained, and a comparison is made between DSS and EIS (executive information systems). Differences between old and new technologies are noted. The benefits of MSS are listed.

Chapter Three: Organization and Information Delivery Issues

The implications of new end-user computing methods for executives are discussed. The modes of information delivery and the personnel involved are noted. Possible methods of organization are reviewed, pointing out that MSS must rely on Operations, Telecommunications, and Control. The Information Center is suggested as an excellent way to expedite the development of MSS, and information display considerations are listed. The use of group decision support systems (GDSS) for organizational efforts is summarized. It is pointed out that there must be an optimum balance obtained between effectiveness, efficiency, and control.

Chapter Four: Executive Information Systems (EIS)

Executive information systems (EIS) are defined as systems designed for the two top levels of management, to enable them to make sense of the available information for monitoring and for status access. The development and exploration of models for obtaining insight are noted, with the possible organizational impact of such systems. The components of an EIS are defined, and the problems encountered implementing the system and obtaining useful data are discussed. Tracking with Critical Success Factors (CSF) and Key External Factors (KEF) is reviewed. Problems of data access and micro-to-mainframe connections are discussed to point out key areas of management consideration.

Chapter Five: Decision Support Systems (DSS)

Decision support systems (DSS) are described as computer-based information systems developed to improve the decision-making process in an organization. An integrated view is given of DSS to show its current direction. Basic information is provided on the level of support provided by a DSS, the role of assumptions, and the use of building blocks. The long use of DSS has proven its value in identifying problem objectives, developing and examining alternatives, and choosing an optimum solution. Some typical uses of DSS are listed.

Chapter Six: Data Management Issues

There is a need to understand how information is handled in EIS and DSS systems, and to establish the necessary controls over its use. Data management alternatives of local data management, on-line extract files, and on-line active databases are discussed. The new responsibilities and roles in data management are noted, and the new problems of database administration are briefly reviewed. The necessity of attention to data security and disaster preparedness is discussed.

Chapter Seven: System Modeling Issues

Computer modeling is described as the development and use of a computer program to simulate a business situation. Considerations in model development and estimation of model development time are reviewed. Steps for developing a model are outlined. Some investigative possibilities of models are described, including "what if" analysis, goal seeking, sensitivity analysis, and risk analysis.

Chapter Eight: Special and Future Management Issues

Different levels of computer resource management and possible types of services are reviewed. General considerations of departmental and centralized computing are listed. New data management trends are noted; in particular, the movement toward relational database systems. Some seldom-considered aspects of data ownership and data sharing are discussed. The effective use of Quality Assurance (QA) is discussed. Policies are suggested to cover user responsibilities for data protection.

Chapter Nine: Special and Future Technology Issues

A number of technological advances relating to management support systems are described. These include application prototyping, fourth-generation languages, artificial intelligence, expert systems, advanced use of graphics by managers, and management considerations of microcomputer networking and local area networks. New technologies that are becoming useful for MSS are discussed, including document image processing, optical disk memories, teleconferencing and corporate videotex, and CD ROM.

Chapter Ten: Evaluation and Selection of Management Support Systems

There are many management support tools designed for senior decision makers. Properly chosen, MSS software can be one of the most beneficial purchases a corporation can make. The selection process should be systematic and should include business and technical considerations. A nine-step software selection process is outlined. Points are made relative to requests for proposals, vendor presentations, and cost justification.

Chapter Eleven: Microcomputer MSS Software

The varieties of micro-based management support software are reviewed, with their limitations. The spreadsheet package is briefly described, and the usefulness of windows is noted. A checklist is provided for evaluating spreadsheet packages. Considerations include:

Which new technologies offer the most promise in meeting an organization's goals.

The effect of these systems on security and business (disaster) recovery.

Selection criteria when purchasing these systems.

Preferred techniques and where they are useful.

Chapter Twelve: Some Final Thoughts

Computers, especially microcomputers, are rapidly becoming a way of life in America. Chapter Twelve outlines some of the implications, considerations, and issues as the 1990s rush into focus. Some sage advice is offered regarding "everyone's support systems."

Chapter One

Effective Computer Support for Executives

The purpose of this chapter is to assist managers in understanding, selecting, implementing, and controlling management support systems. Executives find direct and confidential access to available information to be competitively useful. A system is a true management support system if it deals with decisions that matter. The information needs of executives can be effectively met by systems that monitor their business, analyze trends, and help in planning future directions.

The area of activity for using the computer for management analysis is rapidly broadening. The scope of decision support systems (DSS) alone is too limited and no longer represents a broad enough view. The new agenda in management decision support is the enhancement of support capabilities.

System approaches and selections for management support systems (MSS) are specific to each organization. They fundamentally depend upon the particular corporate culture. Required executive information and computing capabilities are unique to each individual.

Strategic information systems are systems developed in response to business initiative. An executive information system (EIS) or DSS may offer a strategic advantage, gained as a result of executives going through the analytical process and receiving value-added data in the reports.

The information needs for structured, semistructured, and unstructured decisions are described. The types of decisions may be operational, tactical, or strategic. The most valuable information from MSS is exceedingly time-sensitive.

Finally, the action-oriented implications for senior management are noted.

DECISIONS THAT MATTER

The purpose of this book is to help executives, managers, and information services personnel understand the varieties of computer-based management support systems (MSS) that are available, and to:

- Aid in the use of MSS in decision making and management control.
- Clarify the often fine and artificial distinctions found in professional and sales literature.
- Show the natural operational relationships between the various available decision-analysis and support systems.
- Elucidate the organization, selection, implementation, and control of such systems.

This book is not a theoretical exposition of EIS, DSS, and similar systems, or an editorial favoring specific directions to take. Its prime value is the provision of a *management baseline* the executive can use in the evaluation of the organization's decisions regarding the use of such management support systems. It is profuse with lists of key points, comparisons, and checklists, and is therefore a practical tool to work through an obscure area of data processing. Those concerned with information services functions will be able to use it to enhance their organization's use of new computer technologies to further their goals.

Several writers have said that a system is a true executive information system if it deals with decisions that matter. If any MSS meets such a criterion, it can be claimed that it is a management support system, and that it is of strategic value to an organization.

There are many approaches to developing information systems that support management. The approaches that have proven most useful and efficient are emphasized in this book to enable Information Services staff to provide *effective computer support for their executives.*

THE NEED FOR MANAGEMENT SUPPORT SYSTEMS

Most information that executives receive comes from informal sources, but much is routinely supplied by the regular production of the computer application systems in their organization. These data normally include most of the numbers that show whether the operation is running profitably or according to plan, and they are the source of all internal information relative to trends in the operation. Staff personnel can usually take these computer reports and generate reports that are simplified, showing the movement of key indicators, then produce short-term projections of those indicators. Because such computer applications are usually developed specifically for structured operational decisions, rather than for unstructured executive analysis and planning, they are never completely adequate for top executive analysis, planning, and information needs.

Senior management requires information for three areas of activity: monitoring the business, analysis of trends, and planning future efforts.

1. *Monitoring the business* is accomplished routinely, and in detail, by lower levels of management. Whenever problems arise, however, or specific activities are of executive concern, senior management personnel need frequent and regular information on the movement of key indicators, or about anything else that comes to their minds. The voluminous flow of historical reports and analyses generated from the computer may contain the desired information, but it is difficult to scan. Executives need specific extracts of immediate, current interest. In the past, some of these requested extracts were appended to regular reports, or were prepared on request by analytical staff, possibly using DSS approaches. Now, and in the future, managers expect to be able to key in simple inquiries and get up-to-the-minute numbers on specific factors of interest.

2. *Analysis of trends* is not always easily accomplished using large piles of output reports. Certainly, staff personnel can produce trend analyses and report on them regularly. The types of trend analyses that management requires, however, frequently are on new approaches in areas that have not yet been analyzed by staff. Questions come up in discussion, or in their minds, and they would be interested in a simple response. It may be a complex area relative to the existing application programs, and it may involve interaction with external data. Their information need may be for straightforward extraction of new data structures, with possible manipulation of information in simple statistical projections or time series analyses.

3. *Planning future directions* in an informal way to get a feel for the most likely effects from present decisions is a regular information need of executives. These will normally be relatively short-range projections, because that is all most data can realistically support with simple analyses. Senior managers will want to use these short-range projections, however, and compare them with extrapolations in their minds to estimate their validity. The type of information manipulation capability required by executives is selective extraction of data with simple display, and a straightforward means of showing trends, either in tabular or graphic form.

The information needs of executives thus start with some type of database that can be accessed without requiring a lot of requested data transformations. Individual linear files of data would not be satisfactory for such data access. Because the information requirements of an executive range widely across an organization, the problems of making data readily available are considerable. Few organizations have a unified database covering all the areas that may be of executive interest. At present, the most practical way of preparing information for executive access is to produce an extract database of the types of information that are most likely wanted. Of course, this approach could not possibly cover all the types of inquiries that an executive may want to make. On the other hand, it can be made easily accessible, it can be adapted to new areas of executive interest, and it can be established on a personal computer that will offer rapid access to the executive.

The information needs of executives also tend to be nonrepetitive and ever-changing. They arise from concern about meeting plan targets, from concern about operational problems expressed by subordinates, and from new ideas about changes in direction that may be taken. There is no way systems analysts can predict, or the managers themselves can state, what information needs will be in the near future. They can only state the types of information needs that they currently have or required recently. This should be sufficient for developing the information access database that will satisfy a senior manager in many instances, particularly around planning time or during planned financial discussions. It will certainly indicate the level of data that must be available and the data consolidation that would be appropriate. The database then will need constant management by a staff person, and there will be a learning situation on the parts of the senior manager and the responsible analyst involved. Some queries will be quickly satisfied; other queries will prove more difficult; and experience will show whether a major effort should be put into extracting and maintaining other types of data.

Senior executives usually do not make decisions based on the detailed information generated by computer systems. Rather, they usually base decisions on personal contacts and on their feelings about the validity of recommendations from subordinates. They need regular operating reports and the results of routine computer analyses they may have requested, but these numbers simply give a foundation for their personal judgment about the direction the organization is taking. Senior executives usually are interested in the results of complex statistical analyses and numerical models, but do not rely on them for decisions. Such results, after all, are based on historical data and technical forecasts. Top management bases decisions more on its own experiences in similar situations, its own intuition about projections, and constantly developing understanding that arises from discussions with subordinates. Extensive fact-finding is summarized by staff, with technical projections made about the consequences of alternatives. They base day-to-day decisions on personal experience combined with up-to-date knowledge of what is happening that may come from computer reports.

Some senior executives handle decisions directly and centrally with staff consultations. Other executives prefer broader consultation, shared decision making, and common agreement on the decisions that are reached. Still others delegate as much executive responsibility as possible, after reaching agreement on a plan of action. All of these decision-making approaches require the routine availability of operating results, and a number of summaries and analyses generated from those results. In modern business it simply is assumed that computer-generated reports will be sufficiently available to whichever level of management will use them for analysis. The following considerations are not always assumed, but should be objectives of an executive information support system:

- Information support for all levels of management, with data integration and control between management layers.

- Computer support for all phases of the decision-making process.
- Systems that can be controlled by end users to meet changing requirements.
- Information support for independent and interdependent decision making by various staff levels, including individual, group, and organizational analyses.
- Simplicity of use, so executives can truly interact with the data if they desire to examine it on a terminal.
- Support for structured and unstructured decision making.

Enhancement of Support Capabilities: The New Agenda

This book deals with management support systems (MSS), rather than decision support systems (DSS) only, because use of computers for management analysis is rapidly broadening. DSS are usually thought of as package programs that are put on a micro or mainframe, and used with personal files of data or selected data extracts. This is no longer a sufficient view, because complex central systems are now often used, the terminals or micros are networked, and there may be on-line interaction among a small management analysis and review system and main-frame systems. As managers become familiar with computer use and find they can get reasonable and valuable answers from smaller systems, they will want access to more complex systems, either run by subordinates or used with simple instructions by themselves.

At DSS '87, the Seventh International Conference on Decision Support Systems, sponsored by the College on Information Systems of The Institute of Management Science, the trend continued toward more interest in the Emerging Technologies track and the Executive Information Systems track than in the DSS Practices and Methodologies track. This turning point in the DSS field was emphasized by Dr. Peter G.W. Keen, a DSS authority since 1972, in his keynote address. Some of his points were:

- After 15 years, the subject of DSS is dead. We should declare a victory, because our mission has been achieved in the acceptance of DSS. We must now refocus, raise our targets, and attack *decisions that matter* creatively, as individuals and in organizational groups.
- DSS is an artificially narrow subset of a broad field. We must break down the artificial barriers and extend the systems environment for managers. The DSS experience base is invaluable, but the new agenda is *enhancement of support capabilities*. Give managers new targets, technologies, and techniques for effectiveness. We must no longer look at management support systems in a self-limiting way. Using new hardware/software, methods, and approaches, a move must be made away from the limited domains of simple decisions. There are many alternatives to consider.

• The innovative force in DSS in the 1970s was a radical concept of the role of computers. Many useful systems were developed. They now have become bland and have become the trivia of the late 1980s, because of overdominance of software packages and the trivialization of support to managers.

• Nontraditional techniques, such as document-based transmission (videotex), telecommunications systems, and power tools such as expert systems, need to be exploited.

• Techniques need to be improved, making use of newer hardware and software advances and not simply staying with spreadsheets.

• DSS, EIS, MIS, management science, end-user computing, expert systems, and office technology cross over into one another. Their interacting advantages are waiting to be exploited.

CORPORATE CULTURE AND INDIVIDUAL ATTITUDES

The major problem in the effective development of EIS and DSS systems is the lack of understanding about them. Few managers want to start on new approaches to managing a business unless the approach is well understood by others and by higher management. Unfortunately, the classic warning of Machiavelli in *The Prince* is appropriate to apply to selling the idea of executive information systems to senior managers, expecting them to appreciate terminals on their desks: "Nothing is more difficult to take in hand, or more perilous to conduct, than to take the lead in the introduction of a new order of things." If the idea of using equations and computers to produce acceptable answers to business problems is strange to management, then it will take a great deal of successful demonstration and a prolonged sales effort.

The development and implementation of EIS and DSS systems is not difficult for computer professionals. The problem of management understanding about them may be the only real problem. Most managers simply do not appreciate what it takes on their part to develop and implement such a system, and how the effort should be controlled and used. Despite widespread acceptance in computer circles, the concept is still too new to many managers, and there are relatively few who know what to expect from such a project. They may have read articles or received a brief training course on the concepts involved, but they often still do not know how it will fit in with their work and their style of management. This is not active Machiavellian resistance; it is basically confusion and lack of understanding of the operation and usefulness of these new computer-oriented management support systems. In addition, the approach may not fit into the manager's ideas about the corporate culture.

The corporate culture is essentially the management style of an organization. It puts firm bounds on what is expected from managers. If managers step out of the type of work that is expected of them by the corporate culture, they take great risks of their efforts being rejected. Many managers cannot visualize themselves sitting at a terminal and using computer output to arrive at substantive decisions. They are not comfortable with the analysis, design, implementation, and use of such systems. They do not want to become familiar with such things, or spend time pressing keys. They like to leave the analytical work to subordinates and even may fear staff misuse of such a system. This is a real problem and can be handled rapidly only by starting with such systems at the top, then working down. If senior management does not see that EIS and DSS systems might be useful to their organization, then this particular game may be lost before it is started. This is a particularly critical point.

If a top manager accepts the EIS approach and has staff working actively on it, there is a reverse implementation problem that is more readily handled. If a senior manager has a successful EIS system operating, it will literally force most managers below to get similar computers or terminals in order to have access to the same information files. If they do not keep up with the technology, they will not be able to answer the questions posed to them with sufficient promptness, and they will not know exactly what figures their boss is using. This will cause a heavy demand for systems installation. While the initial system may have been readily justified for the senior manager, it may be difficult to fit 20 or 30 or more systems into the current operating budget. The users may pay for their own systems, but the support requirements will multiply rapidly. At the time of the proliferation of EIS systems, it is helpful to reach an agreement regarding its strategic value to the corporation, and to agree on a special budget.

Another useful approach is to develop a chargeback policy that will allow the rapid installation of systems without too great an effect on the Information Services budget.

The existing corporate culture, therefore, will have a material effect on the introduction and development of EIS and DSS systems. If the notions are foreign to the thought processes of management, the only reasonable way to proceed is to start with DSS systems at the lower analytical levels. Their successful use will then filter slowly upward. This is a good approach, because if the use starts at the top before those at lower levels are familiar with the new way of thinking, a difficult problem can be caused. If the pressure is on because a senior manager has installed a successful system, opposition and resentment can build up. Key managers at lower levels may not want to become so dependent on Information Services help and may start their own information groups to retain their power. This change can be softened by cooperatively supplying a great deal of support and hand-holding, and by giving one-on-one instruction to the managers.

Another problem understood by Information Services, but possibly not obvious to operational managers, is the large amount of hardware and software

FIGURE 1–1
Problem Diversity

High		
	Open to new approaches	High interest in support systems
	Little interest in new approaches	Possible niche applications
Low		
	Low	High

Source: Adapted from Gary K. Gulden, Index Systems, Inc.

capabilities required to develop and support such systems. The special requirements of EIS make them heavy users of machine cycle, and they are often given high priority-interrupt status. Many software packages on the market are not calculation-efficient and can barely meet the types of functional requirements necessary. This makes them inefficient in operation and expensive to use. The technology selected must be integrated, transparent to the users, and fast to run. These are technical problems, but they must be faced early in development of MSS and DSS systems and can be solved adequately only by professional systems and programming staff.

Figure 1–1 is adapted from a talk given by Gary K. Gulden of Index Systems, Inc. It shows that when there is a stable management, with few recent position changes and little diversity in the problems facing management, there is little interest in new approaches for problem solving and solution optimization. When the same management is faced with diverse problems and new challenges, there may be possible niche applications of known computer solutions that can be introduced and will be accepted willingly. Similarly, when new management appears in a group, even though the old problems still may be the same, there is always a possibility that the new people will be open to new computer approaches to aid in the solution of problems. The best possible case is when there is new management and a new diversity of problems to solve. Such an organization is ripe for the introduction of a variety of computerized management support systems.

Finally, individual attitudes are frequently colored by a technical problem that can have political ramifications in the installation of EIS and DSS systems. This problem can be highly sensitive and cause managers to make it difficult for others to make reasonable calculations. This critical issue is *ownership of data;* it will be discussed further in Chapter Six, "Data Management Issues."

David W. DeLong and John F. Rockart[1] point out that the ownership question can have serious political implications in any organization. The point of disagreement is whether to allow senior managers to have ready access to unfiltered operations data. With on-line access to operational reports, senior managers can get information two days after the monthly books close, instead of the traditional 20 days. Divisional executives may have to install their own EIS systems so they can be aware of information the senior executives are examining, and be prepared for questions. Such reactive development of systems is not popular, however. It is preferable to deal with this critical problem before a system is installed, so that cooperative decisions can be made on how to handle it.

In most organizations with large systems, there is a database manager who is competent to address the problems of data ownership and data distribution on a technical level. This person should surface the problems of ownership and control of data in the computer files and describe how they can be accessed. Decisions can then be made as to who gets what data, and when they may have access to it. The problems of possible alteration of data are most critical to address. Different reports to management can easily show different figures for the same items if agreement has not been reached as to who may modify or update data.

THE STRATEGIC VALUE OF MANAGEMENT SUPPORT SYSTEMS

Strategic information systems are computer systems that implement business strategies. They are those systems where Information Services resources are applied to strategic business opportunities in such a way that the computer systems have an impact on an organization's products and business operations. Strategic information systems are always *systems developed in response to corporate business initiatives.* In several well-known cases, the ideas came from Information Services people, but they were directed at specific corporate business thrusts. In other cases, the ideas came from operational people, and Information Services supplied the technological capabilities to realize profitable results.

Most information systems are looked on as support activities to a business. They mechanize operations for better efficiency, control, and effectiveness, but they do not in themselves increase corporate profitability. They simply are used

---

[1]David W. DeLong and John F. Rockart, "A Survey of Current Trends in the Use of Executive Support Systems," CISR WP #121, Center for Information Systems Research, M.I.T. Sloan School of Management, November 1984.

to provide management with sufficient dependable information to keep a business running smoothly, and they are used for analysis to plan new directions. Strategic information systems, on the other hand, become an integral and necessary part of a business and directly influence market share, earnings, and all other aspects of marketplace profitability. They may even bring in new products, new markets, and new ways of doing business. They directly affect the competitive stance of an organization, giving it an advantage against competitors.

Strategic systems are systems that link business and computer strategies. They may be systems where a new business thrust has been envisioned, and its advantages can be best realized through the use of information technology. They may be systems where new computer technology has come on the market, and planners with an entrepreneurial spirit perceive how the new capabilities can quickly gain competitive advantage. They may be systems where operational management people and Information Services people have brainstormed business problems and realized that a new competitive thrust is possible when computer methods are applied in a new way.

The question then arises, "Is there a strategic advantage to an EIS or a DSS?" John VanOpdorp of the Sloan School of Management said the answer may be yes or no. If a system simply profiles available reports, there is no direct strategic value in the system itself. It is unlikely that there will be any sustainable business gains from the MSS. If its use leads to business value, however, the action of *going through the process* can be profitable to an executive. A good MSS can promote more effective and efficient management of a firm. It has the primary benefits of consistency of data, efficiency and flexibility of use of the data, and clearly improved understanding of the information. The MSS is a value-added feature in that it improves the content, format, and timeliness of the information supplied. If the EIS is used in a manner that supports the management style and philosophy of an executive, it can have a measurable strategic advantage.

Norman F. Rickeman of Arthur Andersen & Company points out that executives want *results* that affect real and perceived positive growth or change. An EIS can meet real needs of executives, partly because what gets measured gets done. The traditional I/S approaches have seldom met their strategic information needs, but a flexible and creative system can link strategies to results. If an MSS system is in place and is a good delivery vehicle with workable solutions, then it may be used by a CEO. If the CEO likes it, and claims that it helps, then it is not only justified, it probably provides a strategic advantage.

David Gleason of Pilot Corporation says an EIS is any system that is specifically useful to executives and is used by them. This covers a wide range of possibilities. He points out that executives are the most demanding systems users in a corporation, and the older methods of information delivery and production of graphs are too slow. Senior executives expect information as a strategic resource, and the flexibility to use the information to deal with change. Some type of MSS, EIS, or DSS is imperative because:

- Executives expect more from a computer than from reports from transactional systems.
- An EIS can be a mechanism for strategic organizational change.
- Numerous executives are getting benefits from EIS now.

Executives generally do not have trouble getting information to analyze strategic decisions. They find great advantage, however, in getting information by direct access rather than on a reporting schedule, and in getting it *confidentially*. The value of executives getting the data they want when they want it, and without asking others to provide it, is that such systems and data aid in strategic planning.

There is general agreement that strategic systems are those information systems that may be used *for gaining competitive advantages*. How is a competitive advantage gained? Different writers list different possibilities, but none of them claims that there may not be other openings to move through. Some of the more common ways of thinking about gaining competitive advantages are:

1. *Deliver a product or a service at a lower cost.* This does not necessarily mean the lowest cost, but simply a cost related to the quality of the product or service, and that will be attractive in the marketplace and yield sufficient return on investment. The cost considered is not the data processing cost, but the overall cost of all corporate activities for delivery of that product or service. There are many operational computer systems that have given internal cost savings and other internal advantages, but they cannot be thought of as strategic until those savings can be translated to a better competitive position in the market.

2. *Deliver a product or a service that is differentiated.* Differentiation means the addition of unique features to a product or service that are competitively attractive in the market. Generally such features will cost something to produce, and they will be the selling point, rather than the cost itself. Seldom does a lowest-cost product have the best differentiation. A strategic system helps customers perceive they are getting some extras for which they are willing to pay.

3. *Focus on a specific market segment.* The idea is to identify and create market niches that have not been adequately filled. Information technology is frequently able to assist in providing the capabilities for defining, expanding, and filling a particular niche or segment. The application would be quite specific to the industry.

4. *Innovation.* Use computers to develop products or services that are new and appreciably different from other offerings. Examples of this are automatic credit card handling at service stations and automatic teller machines at banks. Such innovative approaches not only give new opportunities to attract customers, they also open up entirely new fields of business so that their use has an elastic demand.

Almost any EIS or DSS may be called strategic if it aligns the computer strategies with the business strategies of an organization, and if there is close cooperation in its development between Information Services people and executives. There should be an explicit connection between the organization's business plan and its systems plan to provide better support of the organization's goals and objectives, and closer management control of critical information systems.

Strategic systems thus attempt to match computer resources to strategic business opportunities where computer systems will have an impact on products and business operations. Planning for strategic systems is not defined by calendar cycles or routine reporting. It is defined by the effort required to impact the competitive environment and strategy of a firm at the point in time at which management wants to move on an idea.

STRUCTURED AND UNSTRUCTURED DECISIONS

The information needs of executives are for unstructured or semistructured decisions. The types of decisions they need to make are not completely programmable in advance. They require the extraction and display of information, which is then studied to determine the need and the rules for the next extraction or manipulation of data. The information needs of executives are, therefore, met by a facility to locate and gain access to data, and to manipulate it with relatively modest functions to test ideas and theories about trends and expected results. The rules for executive decisions are constantly changing, and the importance of different data elements is completely variable over time.

Herbert Simon of Carnegie Tech originated the idea of *structured and unstructured decisions* after considerable work with highly structured linear programming applications and from trying to fit the method into business problems. The difficulty is that the rules are preset before a linear program is run. Business executives do not make many decisions by sticking to a rigid set of rules. Structured decisions are conclusions from analyses that have been previously discussed and are understood by those involved. They use defined input data and produce an expected form of results. We can tell a subordinate, or a computer, what to analyze in advance. The subordinate, or the computer, will then carry out a fixed set of calculations in a predetermined way and arrive at the desired results. Many structured decisions are of great use and have been highly profitable when put on a computer. They are the base of the vast majority of operating computer systems. They may give specific, controlled accounting figures. They may give answers to an estimated set of input data, such as linear programming approaches. They may give ranges of expectations, such as statistical calculations. In all cases, in a structured decision process, specific data will always be entered in a similar, expected way, and the form of the result will be known in advance.

If the decision is structured, it can be readily programmed; thus a subordinate can be delegated the responsibility of handling it. Structured decisions are the essence of most information systems that are currently programmed and running on large computers. COBOL is the best example of a completely structured programming language. Nearly all application analysis and programming in routine use has an integrated structure. One good reason for this is that as more programs can be handled in a completely defined structure, the more efficient they will be in routine operation and maintenance.

Unstructured decisions are vague, or loosely defined, until they have been accepted. They may involve a search for a profitable area in business projections, or a qualitative selection without arbitrary standards, or getting a feel for the effect of the variability or sensitivity of data. *Most senior management decisions are unstructured.* In a manager's organization there is a loosely defined competition for time, money, and assignment of resources. Managers may have an intuitive feeling for what may be best and are interested in any analyses or data that may show similar directions to the ones they favor.

At lower levels in an organization, decision support systems are usually designed to provide structured answers on demand. These answers are frequently accepted without further analysis. Usually the decision rules are thoroughly tested before they are used, and once they have been agreed upon, they are followed routinely.

At middle levels in an organization, decision support systems usually are semistructured and used in a more advisory capacity. The results are reviewed carefully against knowledge and recent experience, and the answer received may be accepted, modified, or rejected. A manager is assured that at least a certain calculation was performed against specific, known, recent data, and that the result was calculated in a consistent way. The manager then has the option of modifying the system or the data, and of changing the structure of the decision-making algorithm. The system may be changed repeatedly until it gives more reasonable or sensible results, in the opinion of that manager at that time. There also may be a considerable analysis undertaken to examine the sensitivity of the system to changes in data or analytical method. The system may be fine-tuned or even dramatically changed at the request of the manager using it. Thus middle-management decision support systems are frequently treated as unstructured systems.

These broad, middle-range decision support systems are usually run with the capability of analytical modifications and with some record trail kept of the changes that were made in the study. It becomes clear that there are two statements that can be made about decision support systems that are used for analysis rather than direct operations:

- Neither the system alone nor the manager alone could do as good a job of optimizing the results as can the two combined.

- There is frequently no sharp line between structured and unstructured systems, since the degree of management input may vary from time to time.

When decision support systems are used by senior management, they become *executive information systems* and are used completely unstructured. Executives are not interested in routine results, because subordinates can handle those. They may want to watch a specific output report for a period of time to see whether a planned improvement occurs, but they then lose interest in those figures. They only want to pick out specific pieces of data, or certain trends, to test ideas and theories they have and confirm or reject their experiential feelings. If they think the information obtained in an unstructured way should be analyzed further, they will tell their subordinates to do the analysis. If they have trouble getting a rapid response from the computer system, they will simply turn to the telephone and get a rapid response from their analysts. The purpose of executive information support systems is to give quick answers to completely unstructured decisions, if possible.

Artificial-intelligence (AI) methods are not the simple answer to senior management needs. They are exceedingly helpful for staff personnel to make wide-ranging searches of miscellaneous data and to reach conclusions that may be unexpected or difficult to obtain otherwise. Most AI systems depend upon a predefined knowledge base, however, while senior management decisions are based on knowledge and feelings far beyond the range of the available knowledge base in the computer files. AI approaches provide extensive tools to search for unusual combinations of data, and to discover unexpected relationships. They are of great advantage to senior staff analysts because they are directly useful for formulating unstructured decision resolution. But they are structured in the sense that their knowledge base is always fixed by the hardware memory it occupies. Because they are tied to a fixed knowledge base, they do not have the same extent of "unstructuredness" present in the minds of managers during discussions about critical decisions. Executive management is a highly personalized action, and feelings are always present that are currently impossible to express objectively.

Decisions also can be usefully categorized by the type of decision in terms of impact on the organization. These categories include:

1. Operational.
2. Tactical.
3. Strategic.

Operational decisions tend to be structured decisions involving lower to middle management of an organization. They relate to the efficiency with which an organization accomplishes its mission. Examples of operational decisions include purchasing decisions among alternate vendors, scheduling of operations, whether or not to work overtime, and so forth. Operational decisions are often best supported by a classical transaction-driven system, such as an on-line dispatch system for a transportation company, or an airline reservation system. However, the potential use of DSS in operational decision making should not be ignored. A simple computer model that balances overtime costs versus added personnel might improve an organization's bottom line.

Tactical decisions are directed toward managerial control and are concerned with assuring the effectiveness of an organization in achieving its mission. A typical tactical decision is semistructured with a medium-term impact. A good example of a tactical decision was that made by Chrysler Corporation in the design of the K car, when its length was limited to 171 inches to gain transportation efficiencies using the railcar distribution system. Tactical decisions are typically made by middle to upper management. They may be aided by classical MIS systems (such as a marketing information database, or an inventory control system for a distribution company) or by innovative decision support systems. An example of a DSS in support of a tactical decision would be an analysis of the price sensitivity of a new or old product.

Strategic decisions involve setting policies, choosing objectives, and selecting resources. Typical strategic decisions are unstructured and have a long-term impact on an organization. An example of a strategic decision was Sears' decision to expand beyond the catalog business while Montgomery Ward stood pat. Another example of a strategic decision would be a decision to merge with or acquire another company. Decisions of a strategic nature can be enhanced substantially by a properly implemented DSS. For example, a DSS used by a property management company allowed management to make the strategic decision to sell part of the business. It identified the real costs and potential profits of the business. Management's understanding of the probable results of various scenarios was enhanced by "what if" examination. Thus management was able to use a DSS to clarify its thinking and, ultimately, to make a policy decision.

IMPLICATIONS FOR EXECUTIVE ACTION

Considering recent advances in information extraction and analysis, John Rockart has pointed out six major, action-oriented implications for senior management in the information services area. These are:

1. *The process of executive information support requires attention by top management today.* There is sufficient knowledge to build acceptable systems, and much of the technology is available today in packaged programs and specialized terminals. There are always economic and competitive pressures, and

improved information support for top management is desirable and possible. The real problem, however, is that most Information Services people have been unsuccessful in approaching top management for discussions that will lead to action in this area. Techniques available to support managerial processes are new and different, and there must be a determined effort to make top management aware of the possibilities. Nothing will happen unless the initiative to move is finally taken by the executives.

2. *Top management can take advantage of information support without direct access to a computer.* Some senior executives will want a computer or a terminal in their office; many others will be satisfied to state the problems to their analytical staff and have them get the information. Information support of an executive office through functional staff has the great advantage that extra complication is possible, and all inquiries need not be made in a completely simplified manner. Data translation and analysis can be performed as long as the response is swift and accurate. Special facilities must be prepared to enable such inquiries.

3. *Because executive information support systems are designed to evolve, the entry price can be relatively modest.* The price has already been paid in most organizations in the development of large operational systems, and extensive data files and databases. The ongoing data processing operation is supplying most of the data required and holding it in available form. New microcomputers and data extraction packages are available at relatively reasonable costs. The staff problem is to build a prototype system, probably as an extract database on a smaller computer, and be ready to maintain and modify it. Senior management will then have access to limited but accurate and useful databases, and will be able to experiment with the possibilities offered.

4. *To take full advantage of this potential, top management must get involved in systems design.* Systems analysts have traditionally had difficulty in determining the needs of senior management, mainly because those needs are seldom stable and vary regularly. If the technical people try to develop their concept of what their manager wants, there will likely be no interest in it. Top management must assist the analysts in the design of the system and present their feelings about the access methods offered. This analysis is best approached by preparing a nontechnical menu of all the possibilities that appear to be reasonable, including data files, data access, equipment, and support, and letting the senior manager make initial selections on an experimental basis. If the parameters do not prove adequate, the system can be modified or fine-tuned. This is an unknown area, and there will not be much satisfaction until the executive has had some useful experience with the system and has fit it to the desired management style.

5. *A new information support organization must be established to aid line executives and key staff in using the system.* This is an ideal application for an Information Center staff. They have had experience working with managers, explaining technical possibilities, and making specific data files available. They

will be completely oriented to servicing requirements with available information and processes, rather than constructing new and complex approaches. They will be prepared to support an existing system continuously.

6. *The organizational implications of executive information support systems must be given careful thought.* A change in the types of information available to top management may have a profound impact of the status reporting of subordinate management. Line management personnel may perceive a significant change in the distribution of power because of their loss of control over information reporting.

Chapter Two

The Spectrum of Management Support Systems

Many of the terms used for the large variety of Management Support Systems (MSS) available are listed and discussed in this chapter. The overlapping spectrum of the types of support offered by EIS, ESS, DSS, MCS, MIS, and OSS are diagrammed and explained. The distinction made between executive information systems (EIS) and decision support systems (DSS) is clarified, and the types of systems are compared.

The differences between the new technology of MSS and the older technology of MIS are reviewed, together with types of controls and the new system development life cycle. The architecture for on-line control versus independent operation will have some constants, but there are critical capabilities that must be considered. These considerations include the ability to grow with strategic applications, the quality of systems and software, the availability of information, cost-effective operation of computers, and communications and network compatibility.

The new approaches to system development for MSS strongly favor the use of prototyping development. This is discussed and compared with the older system-development life-cycle technology.

A number of considerations for new problems in the management of MSS development are also discussed, including training, consultation, departmental control, standards, security, and communication with the professionals in Information Services. The benefits derived from management support systems are outlined.

TERMS USED FOR MANAGEMENT SUPPORT SYSTEMS

In discussing the differences between various types of MSS, many authors and professors have felt free to introduce their own naming systems, and to describe in detail the differences between their new ideas and the older ideas about MSS.

This is certainly admissible, but it has caused a profusion of variations in the names of types of systems, and some artificial distinctions have become publicized. Most managers are merely concerned with what MSS can do for them operationally and are pragmatic in the mixing of system capabilities and structures to suit their specific business needs. It is also true that, in practice, even the most simple and effective MSS is basically dependent on an older complex of operational MIS systems for the supply of routine, controlled, and trustworthy data about an organization's operation.

It will be helpful, therefore, first to list, define, and compare some of the many different terms used for MSS that may have been intended for different organizational levels and for a variety of management reasons. The literature, particularly from vendors of new systems and from universities, has new terms frequently introduced to make specific sales points or to create differentiations that are not necessarily related to corporate reality. Many papers have been written that carefully distinguish between MIS, ESS, and DSS, for example, without touching on their common base of corporate information and their many similarities.

Of course, there are numerous differences between the structure and use of many of the systems. There are also many constants and similarities from management's viewpoint. The differences were clearer in past generations of software systems, where there was little direct connection between them. In the current trend toward shared relational databases; controlled, off-loaded summary files for analysis; and communications networks in both local and wide areas, system overlaps are becoming broader, and many claimed differences are becoming artificial. This is of considerable help to systems analysts and programmers who must draw together their various systems to share data.

Following are some of the terms for systems that are related or overlap:

Decision support systems (DSS) (Michael Scott Morton, 1979).

Executive information support systems (John Rockart, 1981).

Executive information systems (EIS).

Executive support systems (ESS).

Professional support systems (some IBM manuals).

Management control systems (MCS).

Management information systems (MIS).

Information systems (I/S) (abbreviation also used for an information services department).

Operational support systems (OSS).

Management science/operations research systems (MS/OR) (1950s).

End-user computing systems (EUC Systems).

Office automation systems (OAS).

Expert systems and artificial intelligence (AI).

Economic modeling and forecasting.

The systems referred to by these terms may be quite distinct or may interact with other types of systems. Some, such as forecasting, may be commonly incorporated into others or used as stand-alone systems. Insofar as these systems supply information to management for decision making and control, they all can be considered as variations of management support systems. They offer interlocking and overlapping types of support to management. Some of them, such as MIS, I/S, OSS, and OAS, are designed principally for routine operational support rather than direct, individual management support. However, DSS advocates frequently are unaware that many of these larger, highly controlled, operational management information systems (MIS) contain small subreports completely devoted to specific management information that has been requested for individual management support. For many years, in any rational Information Services organization, higher-level managers have not been faced with stacks of computer output paper, but have been given summarizations and calculations they specifically requested in the form of tear-off sheets or briefing books related to financial and operational systems. Operational summaries and general ledger summaries have been commonplace for years. Relatively new is their availability on CRT screens in top-floor offices, and the capacity to make further inquiries in a relatively simple way by using the newer fourth-generation languages and specialized data-access methods.

In particular, information centers (ICs) have been in the forefront in recent years setting up *extract databases* in intermediate files so they are readily available to analysts and managers for random review and the printing of simple reports. The ICs also have aided direct, on-line inquiry of many files. The IC approach has greatly facilitated the use of DSS and EIS tools by a wide range of managers and their staffs. Information Services seldom has been loathe to support management requests for information in the past. They simply have been faced with great, almost insurmountable difficulties in giving reasonable response time to special requests while keeping the rest of their work going at the same time. They have far more tools in their tool kit for management inquiry than most DSS analysts realize. The Information Center movement has accomplished a remarkable task in interpreting management requests for information to I/S, and in facilitating the extraction of the necessary data files to an available location, with user-friendly tools to take advantage of the data.

Fourth-generation languages (4GLs) are not foreign to professional systems analysts and programmers; they are simply not efficient enough for large systems. Most I/S staff are familiar with their use and possibilities and can be of great assistance in bridging complex COBOL or other files with simpler, flat extract files that are easily used for DSS and EIS.

COMPARISON OF MANAGEMENT SUPPORT SYSTEMS

Figure 2–1 shows the interlocking and overlapping types of support available today. There are many commercial products in all the areas of this figure, although some are decidedly better than others in giving interlocking support. This diagram was adapted from a similar one developed by Gary K. Gulden of Index Group, Inc. Its clear message is that though many of these various systems stand

FIGURE 2–1

Interlocking and Overlapping Types of Support

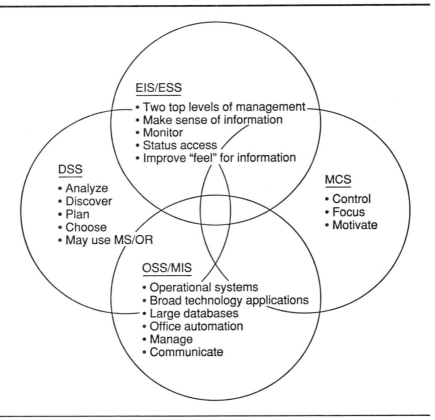

End-User Computing, 4GLs, Expert Systems, Natural Languages, and External Data Access are in all segments.

Source: Adapted from Gary K. Gulden, Index Group, Inc.

alone and are operated independently, their greatest corporate value in validity, efficiency, and effectiveness comes from the coordination and sharing of information. Bridges are available today between levels of all such systems and should be employed.

Executive information systems (EIS) or executive support systems (ESS) are terms used in the literature for MSS designed for the use of the two top levels of management. Their purpose is to make sense of the available information extracted for management or made available to them for search. They are used principally to *monitor* and to provide *status access*. Some managers prefer to look at a variety of information to improve their "feel" for the meaning of the information.

Decision support systems (DSS) cover a wide range of systems used by professionals for analysis and study. As some of them become tested and fine-tuned, they may be used at any level of an organization to provide data for operational control. In their myriad uses, they may be designed for analysis, to search data to discover trends and anomalies, and to make choices among various possibilities. They are commonly used in planning to determine the sensitivity and approximate the probable outcomes of decisions. Many DSS use data as subsets: statistical and forecasting programs, management science models, or operations research analyses.

Management control systems (MCS) is a less-used, generic term for those systems specifically designed to provide data for routine financial or operational control of any part of an organization. Whereas most large applications on a computer are concerned with gathering and reporting data, and producing summarized information from it, MCS systems are designed to produce reports that highlight special areas to which management wishes to draw regular attention while a problem is being solved. They are systems that use extracted data to allow ongoing control, focus on a particular area, or motivate operational personnel to pay more attention to an area.

Management information systems (MIS), or operational support systems (OSS), include the bulk of applications systems run on a computer. They must be included in any discussion of MSS because management relies on them for the operation of an organization, and they are the systems most commonly used to provide management with control data and decision information. In the larger view, DSS and EIS are simply subsets of the numerous computer systems used by management.

Because DSS and EIS are specifically designed to answer particular questions, they may provide the clearest and simplest way of getting certain information to management. They can be very effective in this process, but they are not the only ways of supplying management with needed information. In fact, OSS and MIS are so numerous, so large, and so full of useful information that they are actually the most common MSS in use. They are not the most focused way of getting the information, however, or the most effective way of supplying the information. Therefore, the bulk of this book is concerned with describing and explaining decision support systems (DSS) and executive information systems (EIS and ESS). They are efficient, effective, and can be used with the necessary control.

This categorization of management support systems is primarily concerned with the external aspects of the systems and not with their internal structures, which can be very similar or very different. End-user computing (EUC) may be strongly into DSS, but may use any of these four types of support systems. The newer 4GLs, expert systems, and natural languages may be used in any of these types of systems, although 4GLs usually will be in DSS, expert systems usually will be employed by MCS, and natural languages often are reserved for EIS. External data access, or access to files that are not in the used computer, may be a feature of any of the approaches. Usually, however, the MIS are designed to gather all the data files in use at one location.

There is a marked difference between executive information systems and decision support systems in any given organization. Among organizations, however, there is a spectrum of systems and an overlapping of the naming of them. The two approaches blend into one another, depending upon whether or not the senior executive likes to (1) access information directly from files on a terminal, (2) make brief "what if" calculations, (3) compare external information directly with internal information, or (4) rearrange data and make simple projections.

In the past, literature in the field has called the whole spectrum, from detailed data analysis to simple data review, decision support systems (DSS). John F. Rockart of the Massachusetts Institute of Technology[1] was one of the first to perceive that analytically oriented executives desire the personal use of a terminal for access to and analysis of data in the computers. This desire calls for a different type of system than the average DSS, but is qualitatively a subset of it. The two types of systems will first be defined, then some of the differences will be analyzed.

Decision support systems (DSS) are computer-based information systems developed specifically to assist responsible individuals in making optimized decisions. Most DSS are analytical computer-based systems. They provide pertinent information on demand that may be based on incomplete or estimated data and may have widely dispersed information sources. Because the tasks are usually not well-defined and the questions are exploratory, DSS usually are interactive information-handling systems with simple languages, to allow rapid so-

---

[1]John F. Rockart and Michael E. Treacy, "Executive Information Support Systems," Center for Information Systems Research, MIT, April 1981; "The CEO Goes On-Line," Center for Information Systems Research, MIT, CISR no. 67, April 1981.

lutions to specific information analysis problems. They may be used for planning, management control, or operational control. They generally use planning and modeling software that covers database systems, data inquiry and retrieval, model creation and execution, statistics and forecasting, econometric analysis, report generators, and computer graphics.

The primary aspects of a DSS are:

- *Flexibility in use,* with the ability to manipulate variables that affect an organization.
- *Ease of use,* so people may use the systems irregularly with relatively little training.
- *Modeling and analysis* capabilities to match the technical level desired by the user.
- *Tabulation and graphics* capabilities, allowing structures on demand and rapid report production.
- *User control* of the system, algorithms, and output.

Some decisions that managers and other individuals make routinely are incompatible with computer methods, but many other decisions can be facilitated by the computer's ability to manage databases, run simulation and statistical models, handle rapid inquiries, and provide individualized output.

Executive information systems (EIS) are principally computer-based query systems. They are information systems developed to supply senior executives with appropriate information on demand, in response to irregularly structured inquiries. They usually consist of an extract database with simplified access methods. They are principally data inquiry and retrieval, with some report generation and graphics capability. Executives usually desire one or more of three modes of access to the information:

1. *Status access:* Ready access to automated reports that give the current status of various operations or projects. Executives frequently change the areas where they want status access.
2. *Personal analysis:* Ability to look through certain data files and manipulate the figures, reporting them in various ways.
3. *Model-based analysis:* Ability to invoke specific calculation models with ready access to the required data. This may involve making simple projections or adding data from external sources.

The primary aspects of an EIS are:

- Specific database, usually an extract database, to which the executive wants irregular access.

- Limited flexibility with a prearranged level of manipulation capability.
- Simplicity of use with little time involved in reading instructions or preparing the inquiry commands.
- Limited, predefined analytical capability.
- Elementary tabulation and graphics capabilities.

An executive information system may be considered a specialized type of DSS in which there is limited and relatively simple use, very high priority when used, considerable backup organizational support, and constantly changing requirements.

EIS systems are not normally used to arrive at decisions, but are used simply to review information in various formats and structures to aid in the decision-making process. The output from DSS that is handled by lower-level management may be critical input to an EIS system. Although considerable time and effort are normally put into the use of typical decision support systems, senior management usually is not inclined to spend much time with an EIS system. Both approaches, however, require just as much development and maintenance effort by technical specialists. In addition, the EIS approach normally requires continuous technical supervision to assure the satisfaction of the senior executive user.

Packaged DSS systems are of great use to the majority of management analysts who can adapt their inquiries and approaches to the structure of the package and still get the information they desire. EIS systems usually are modified and carefully tailored to suit the particular requirements of the senior manager. The need is for greater flexibility and simplicity in processing assistance and output formatting.

Decision support systems differ from most computer-oriented approaches to problem solving because they are used to help make decisions that are not based just on the results of a computer algorithm, but allow a combination of those results with management understanding and initiative. EIS systems are even more unstructured, in that they essentially supply input to the senior executive's thought process. DSS are a data-rich extension of the traditional techniques of operations research and computer simulation. They allow the decision maker to use packaged approaches to all phases of problem solving, including problem formulation, choosing the relevant data, picking the approach to be used to generate the solution, and evaluating the solutions presented. They are "what if" systems with a large number of capabilities that are readily available.

Figure 2–2 gives a brief summary of the two ends of the spectrum of systems discussed and offered on the market today. Some vendors are selling the idea of relational databases and artificial intelligence. Both may be excellent for technical managers. Other vendors are claiming simplified languages and greatly improved graphics output. Such features are best for senior managers. Some executive decision makers want to do their own number-crunching on the data

FIGURE 2–2

Comparison of Management Support Systems

Features	Decision Support System	Executive Information Support System
Problem-solving expertise required	Analytical and technical managers need detailed training for problem solving	Senior management staff wants only brief training for specific uses
Communication with the computer	Simplified processes that can have familiar problem complexity, but *not* language complexity	Simplified processes for rapid responses
Data management software	Need to investigate and extract large quantities of data from different internal and external sources	Need to extract and review specific or summarized data from defined sources
Business-planning software	Tabulation and statistical programs with consolidation and summarization capabilities. Operations research methods	Tabulation, summarization, and consolidation in simplified formats
Algorithmic capability	Mathematics, statistics, forecasting, time series analysis, and other techniques	Simplified statistics and forecasting
Communications	Ability to collect data from diverse sources and transmit to others	Ability to collect data from specified files and some external sources
Personal-computer usage	Micro-to-mainframe connections for large consolidations and maintenance of databases, plus local-area-network (LAN) interaction	Connection to extract database, some external sources, and some subordinate equipment
Output	Presentation-quality portrayal of results in tabular or graphic form on paper, slides, or transparencies, including color	Tabular or graphic portrayal for review

from large files, while others simply want projection systems and statistics that give them a feeling for the data. All decision-oriented executives want to match their knowledge and intuition to the computer numbers before concluding that a decision has been made. They want to get some feel for the range and sensitivity of projections before claiming them as their own.

THE NEW TECHNOLOGY AND
THE OLD TECHNOLOGY

There is another differentiation that can be made between the various approaches to management support systems. This is between the systems developed under the old systems technology, which is still valid for many cases, and the systems developed under the new systems technology. There are good reasons for using one or the other approach, but there are wide differences in their use. Interestingly, when the fully designed (old) systems are put together in a stepwise manner using prototyping, the two technologies overlap.

The old technology is the use of the full system development life cycle (SDLC) with complete system definition as an early phase, and an architecture that is basically on-line to the central computer. The new technology is the experimental and analytical use of data files to produce management reports without a full range of controls on either the definition of the system or the data used in its operation, and an architecture that is a loosely coupled network of microcomputers. This latter approach is the way most analysts and managers develop their DSS, EIS, and similar systems. They draw on the controlled MIS systems, but they do not share their careful control in development. They may use on-line programs, particularly for access to internal and external databases, but most of their work is done on the freestanding personal computer.

There are three areas of differentiation that can be observed readily between the old and new technologies. These are:

1. *Architecture:* On-line control versus independent operation.
2. *System Development:* Standard SDLC versus prototyping.
3. *Management:* Central control of development versus departmental control.

Architecture for MSS

There always will be massive on-line database systems with hundreds or thousands of terminals or simple PCs connected to the central computer under central control. This architecture has proved to be extremely effective for centrally controlled applications, particularly those that deal with money or corporate operations. This can be thought of as the old technology, because it has existed for some time. Newer features constantly are being added to such systems. New management support systems, however, more frequently are on departmental computers with attached PCs, or on freestanding PCs. The reason is obvious. They are simpler and faster to install than the older, massive systems, and they remain under the control of local management.

There are common requirements, or critical capabilities, that are present in architectural and management approaches. They will have different levels of importance in different organizations, but they all should be considered in deciding which route to take for management support systems. These critical capabilities are in addition to the specific considerations for software, hardware, data control, and communications. In most organizations there will not be a rigid policy for MSS for either of the approaches to architecture. There always will be a variety of requirements that will indicate which alternative should be emphasized. While plans and controls are developed for specific MSS that are of current interest, other alternatives should not be neglected, because departmental needs for management information will change over time.

There are some critical capabilities, therefore, that are constant over the whole spectrum of management support systems, and over the two different approaches to information management and delivery; and other capabilities that differ markedly. These critical capabilities that must be considered are:

- Strategic planning and the ability to grow with the selected architecture.
- High-quality systems and software for the users.
- Availability of corporate information and shared data, as needed.
- Cost-effective operation of the computers.
- Communications and network compatibility for data interchange.
- Availability of the desired systems and helpful vendor relationships.
- One station, or PC, for each user, with all the required functions.

Attention to these requirements can greatly increase the chances of a successful management support system.

Strategic Planning and Ability to Grow

Information Services is concerned with the rapidly developing ways of thinking about strategic information systems. I/S planners are taking a new view of the business process and their role in it. There are new opportunities to be gained through computing processes if the end-users are working on strategic applications that can directly affect an organization's competitive position. There should be a planned effort to understand these new concepts, assess the company's position, and identify and select appropriate methodologies. The significance of thinking about strategic systems has two critical areas.

The first critical area is the possibilities of strategic systems. New ways of thinking about corporate possibilities of the use of information systems should be central to Information Services. The staff must reevaluate its position, direction, and management style to help provide the directions and methodologies to develop the business-related plans required by the organization. They must put a higher value and priority on supporting the systems and computer work that will impact the company's strategic position. Obviously, I/S staff members are in no position to be "gatekeepers," and to make decisions about which users to support and which to leave alone. They are in a position, however, to help identify systems with strategic possibilities and to give higher priority to their support for those systems. The possibilities are limitless, the stakes are high, and there are sometimes opportunities for staff to give support to this new area.

The second critical area is the planning of the computing system. Three types of computing systems can be planned to give the central services required: connection to the central mainframe, a departmental processor, and stand-alone microcomputers. These approaches have their advantages and disadvantages, and the selection is frequently made on the basis of one or two major uses. Start-up costs are involved, and a department must be in the position of satisfying most of the budget. If it appears that there are strategic system opportunities being considered, these systems should dictate the course to be taken. For example, if the operational users can show strategic possibilities for a system, and it relies heavily on access to voluminous databases, then direct connection to the central mainframe should be favored, even if it means a considerable expansion of central-computer resources. Such a system would be feasible only if adequate security controls could be put in place to protect the mainframe database. A possible answer would be to go to dumb terminals or to personal computers with limited capabilities. In any case, if the strategic system requires access to the central database, then the required systems to facilitate the process should be acquired.

In another example, the strategic possibilities may require considerable analytical power in the personal computer terminals, and the handling of highly sensitive information. In such applications, departmental processors with downloaded databases are indicated. The necessary controls can be put on the downloading of the data, then complete departmental freedom can be allowed with their analytical operations on the database. In this case, the budget would be expended on the acquisition of a departmental processor and the necessary software for it.

In a third example, the strategic impact may be in giving company representatives their own personal computers for independent use in the field, or in giving investment analysts powerful micros so they can work independently. In this example, the obvious development costs would be in the selection of the micros to be used and the development of stand-alone programs on them.

Strategic system opportunities are not obviously available to every group whenever they want such systems to surface. It is reasonable to expect that there may be such opportunities, however, and I/S planners must take a new view of the business process and their role in it. They must look constantly for new possibilities for the use of information technology. Instead of viewing their business clients as individual and independent computer users, they must view business as a related chain of activities and try to examine the *value-added* elements of the information content of possible products or services. Business systems then are no longer considered as freestanding computer applications, but are part of the business cycle, from business planning and organization through production, distribution, marketing, and service. At any point in this chain there may be real opportunities for I/S-supported systems to provide information technology for a competitive advantage.

Strategic systems are a complex subject because they differ widely in form and content. They are completely individual for each organization. Also, they are seldom obvious and are not always planned at the time the style of computing for an organization is being planned. If they are being considered, however, they are important enough to swing the decision about the type of computer service to be supplied. Most strategic systems are specific in their requirements, while other users can fit easily into a different variety of database availability. The main point to be considered is that, once identified, strategic systems should carry great weight in the selection of an alternative for MSS computing. If none have been identified, it is always possible that a strategic system use may turn up. The lesson, then, is that planning should take into account the chance of considerable growth in the services desired. Plan for a system offering that can be expanded. Leave open the capability of "growing with the system." Mainframe memory can be purchased, departmental computers can be enlarged, and more PCs can be acquired, but can the operating and application systems that are being considered expand with increased system requirements?

Obviously, the process of strategic planning is complex, and it would not be started simply to determine whether or not to use centralized or departmentalized computing for MSS. It may be underway in the organization, however, and if it is, then the results of the strategic planning process should be the critical determinants of system selection. Making the choice is not simply a technical job. It is the convergence of business and systems planning, and, in the case of end-user computing, the business interests are more important. If there is any possibility of aiding a strategic corporate thrust with the selected computing system, that should take precedence.

Typical situations relative to strategic planning and growth are:

1. *Connection to the central mainframe.* There will be a close tie to central I/S planning, and strategic opportunities being considered may be readily available. Planning for the terminals will be associated directly with planning for the central computer.

2. *Departmental processor and PCs.* If strategic opportunities are being studied in a department, it is likely that the use of PCs will be considered. Planning will be limited to the department, however, and other strategic thrusts and planned programs may not be known.

High-Quality Systems and Software

It is true that the success of any approach to supplying resources for MSS computing will rest on the quality of the systems and software provided. The best-planned system can be a disaster if the software is difficult to use, the hardware is ineffective, and there is frequent system downtime. There are two processes that assure high-quality systems and software: select systems and software on the basis of defined functional requirements; and put the development and operational phases under formal quality control.

Selection of systems and software is discussed later in this book. The economics of the acquisition of necessary resources may drive the selection in a particular direction. What is looked for is the best match of functional requirements at an acceptable cost. There are many considerations in hardware and software acquisition, and any of them may be a deciding factor in the final decision.

The use of formal quality control over the development and operational phases of the computing arrangement will depend upon the staff available and the procedures in place in the organization. If there is a quality assurance staff, and quality-control procedures are used in routine system development work, they should be consulted about the selection and introduction of a distributed computing system. This is particularly important because there will be a number of new users and new departments involved in the process, and it should be done right.

Quality assurance is usually a staff function in Information Services that analyzes, develops, and implements control and review systems in all areas of information analysis and production. I/S quality-control staff does not necessarily perform the full quality review work itself, but develops methodologies and oversees them. It is partly intended to raise corporate consciousness of quality information products. The approach is targeted at ensuring that products meet the level of quality described in specifications and also meet a prescribed level of service.

This is a critical capability required for establishing any distributed processing service. If any of the types of proposals cannot be judged and followed as to their quality, there may be an inherent problem right from the start. For example, if a large number of stand-alone personal computers is being considered for MSS work, the biggest problem may be the ability to control the quality of the products produced. It is obvious that the data-handling capabilities of personal computers are such that outside controls are difficult to maintain, corporate data can deteriorate in quality by the addition of other numbers, and security controls may be lax. Thus the alternative of using stand-alone personal computers should be considered only if such quality considerations are felt to be unimportant. As another example, when data quality and integrity on the mainframe are considered to be most important, direct connection to the central computer is not indicated. There would be too many problems of quality control of the stored data.

Quality assurance is a pragmatic approach to management problems. It depends upon particular situations, the availability of staff, and whether detailed quality control is considered necessary. It depends completely upon an organization's needs and objectives. If management expresses a need to have uniform attention to quality, to control operations in specific areas, or to have assurance that legal requirements are met, then the alternative selected must be compatible with all the security and control objectives that have been listed. If, on the other hand, the objectives are simply to encourage quality awareness in individual departments, leaving the controls up to them, then there will be little effect on the decision.

Following are some of the quality management capabilities that may be desired:

- Ability to intercept the information path and review the computation.
- Ability to follow specific quality standards and procedures.
- Ability to install recommended audit controls.
- Ability to obtain uniform attention to quality by all users.
- Use of system development standards.
- Use of test and analysis tools.
- Ability to gather statistics on production operation.
- Review by experienced systems personnel.

Typical variations in quality management capabilities are:

1. *Connection to the central mainframe.* Most of these capabilities are attainable with connection to the central mainframe. It is likely that a Quality Assurance group has already reviewed the application systems in use, and there certainly will be production statistics and trouble reports gathered on the central computer's operation. Audit controls likely will be in force also.

2. *Departmental processor and PCs.* Most of these capabilities are attainable with the use of a departmental processor. They are isolated readily and identified in the departmental environment. It is efficient from a control viewpoint to train departmental personnel, institute departmental quality controls, and follow computational activity on a departmental processor. It is a readily defined computing area that likely will have similar control problems throughout.

Availability of Corporate Information and Shared Data

The *principles* of data management of MSS on PCs are identical to those for larger computer systems, but the size limitations of microcomputers make the *practice* of data management a minor subset of the records management systems in big central computers. One of the realities of microcomputing is that the sizes of the files are smaller, the instruction set is more limited, and fewer peripherals are available. Access to the large database may be provided for the small systems, but control of the large databases remains with the mainframe computers. There are also practical limitations with micros in areas such as the size of names and fields used, the number of fields, the size of records, and the practical number of records that can be handled.

Further information about data management and the availability of shared information is given in Chapter Six, "Data Management Issues." The subject of computer resource management, or the management of the various configurations for making corporate information available and sharing it, are discussed in the section on computer resource management in Chapter Eight.

Except for straightforward decision-support calculations using files that are organized in a simple way, most data should be organized in a database for the requirements of management, updating, control, and sharing. Users at all levels of computing should be given help in setting up standard database files that will provide them with the level of capability they need. There is a wide range of database systems to choose from. The level of sophistication chosen will depend upon the requirements of the application, the amount of data sharing that is expected, and whether there will be a connection between PCs and the mainframe database. "Local data management" does not preclude a connection with other computers; it simply means that a group separate from Information Services will plan and organize its own data files, and be responsible for the control, updating, and security of those files.

Systems, standards, and procedures that pertain to data access requirements, data management software, and the selection and use of database management systems are equally appropriate for data files maintained locally, data files shared within a department, and data files downloaded from the central computer. Microcomputers are powerful processors, and management principles learned on central computers should be applied to the management of PC data files.

The use of on-line extract files, or replicated production data, on departmental computers is popular for MSS data management because it makes data available from the large data files on the central computer, yet its use and security can be controlled. With well-managed file extraction there is little possibility of contaminating the data in the central files. A specific support group can manage such an operation and supply agreed data files that are extracted at intervals from the mainline systems in the central data files. The imposed controls can be rigid in the extract phase, but looser in the usage phase. Multiple users usually have free access to the extract files, but there is never uploading of data without tight controls.

Connection of the central mainframe to on-line active databases by analysts is obviously necessary for DSS to analyze some transactional systems and will be the future direction of many other systems. When adequate controls have been installed, multiple users can use multiple applications. The applications can be open-ended with continuous revision and expansion. On-line active databases can be of critical importance to the organization, but the problems of management and data control need careful analysis. Normally, the users get read-only access to specific files. A real and frequent problem of this approach is the possible degradation of performance of the central computer when many personal computers have access to the files.

Some considerations for data management alternatives are:

1. *Connection to the central mainframe.* These are on-line active databases, or production files, that are used. The applications are open-ended, and new reports may be generated. The data files may be continually expanding, and data elements may be updated during use. There may be multiple users with multiple applications. A big advantage of this alternative is that it is controlled by the corporate data dictionary.

2. *Departmental processor and PCs.* Information is extracted on-line periodically and downloaded to the departmental processor for use. Agreed data files are extracted at specified intervals, not continuously. In this case, the central data files are updated and maintained centrally with rigid controls. The extracted files are under the control of a support group, such as an Information Center or the departmental users. The central files rely on the corporate data dictionary so it also can be used for the extracted files. Controls on the extracted files are usually less rigid.

Cost-Effective Operation

The cost-effectiveness of an MSS/DSS operation will be difficult to determine until the system has been in place and its popularity has become apparent. Successful computer methods have the tendency to proliferate rapidly as more and more people hear about them; and while they may be economical on a smaller scale, they can be costly on a larger scale. It is important, therefore, when considering a planned approach to computing, to look at its cost-effectiveness if there is widespread use of the method.

First, there must be management of the organization's *information resource.* Organizational information is a valuable resource in and of itself. If the installation of a number of personal computers or terminals is considered a critical link in the overall handling and management of data, reports, and information, it should be given enough management attention to help assure an orderly flow of information so that the decisions made will be optimum for the organization. The use of personal computers must not be allowed to fragment the handling of information, which can lead to a loss of control through inadequate supervision and a more costly process of getting needed information. Captured, controlled, and systematically stored information involves considerable cost. This is well understood by the central computer operation. Users are mistaken if they believe they can develop equivalent data more cost-effectively. Certainly, they can develop smaller files of specialized data cheaper than if the data were put on a central computer. But as soon as they wish to enlarge those files and combine them with other files, the departmental or the central computer has a distinct cost advantage.

Second, there can be no understanding of cost-effectiveness unless a particular group's service objectives are carefully defined in advance and will be met by the selection of a particular system of operation. Management's objectives for the operation must be always in the forefront. There are trade-offs in the use of PCs or terminals, and they must be used where they are most effective and for the jobs where they are best suited. If a PC is most helpful for one program, but a terminal to a central computer is best suited for another, then the uses must be balanced and a decision made on an economic basis. Benefits are maximized if PCs are employed correctly where they are most useful, and not forced in where they are of only marginal use. Planning and management control are absolutely necessary to obtain the benefits that can be realized from the systems.

Analysis of the cost of a system installation may lead to a balance between the controls on and operations of the central large systems and the possibly separate sets of data and controls on the PCs. The data needed on the smaller systems may be in different forms than in the central data dictionary. If there is to be any interchange of information, common interfaces must be established and the problems of data sharing solved. Sufficient responsibility for system operation must be distributed to maximize the effectiveness of departmental operation. Personal computers give considerable freedom of operation, but it comes at a cost, particularly if there is any attempt to follow established standards and procedures. There are many cases where controlled connection to the central mainframe can be more cost-effective.

Some keys to cost-effectiveness with the alternatives are:

1. *Connection to the central mainframe.* If there is adequate central processor power, core memory, and available disks to handle the MSS application on-line, the process can be most cost-effective because the systems are in place and the terminals to be acquired are the simplest available. On the other hand, if a great deal of database access is required and there are a large number of analysts, a big central computer can be brought to its knees. Upgrading such computers to handle an increased load tends to be an expensive alternative.

2. *Departmental processor and PCs.* A powerful minicomputer frequently is the most cost-effective method of operation because it can easily handle the types of on-line inquiry made for MSS/DSS, and it is dedicated to only a few applications. It is not as economical on large sorts and file manipulation, but these seldom will be required. It runs with much less operational overhead because it has fewer controls and less complication.

Communications and Network Compatibility

To be effective for MSS, organizations must have information systems that are highly interconnected. As business strategies develop, their success frequently depends directly upon an organization's ability to share the data that has been generated internally and to communicate rapidly and efficiently with sources of information. In most cases these requirements favor some sort of connection to a central computer operation, either directly or through downloaded files on departmental processors. A communications system is usually in place, and the connection to it provides the necessary data access method.

If there is to be a great deal of information interchanged on a regular and on-demand basis, this would appear to favor direct connection to the central computer operation. It would be a direct tie-in to a sophisticated communications system that allows all the access to information that is required. There is one major problem to such an operation, however. It will be completely under central control, and the unique priorities of a local department may have little effect on the service that can be obtained. This may or may not be important. If the information to be obtained is organized primarily in files of a single application, access and response time generally can be satisfactory with a direct, on-line connection. However, it may be a different problem if access is needed to a number of files, particularly if they are scattered throughout the organization; several groups may be working together in one or more departments, and more data may be required from other groups than from the central files. In such cases, a local area network (LAN) may be most appropriate, with the computing done on the freestanding PCs connected to the LAN.

A LAN is limited geographically, but one of its major advantages is the ability of the user organization to exercise control over it. It has fewer constraints than other communications systems. Every device on the LAN is able to communicate with every other device, if it is so designed. It also has flexibility of structure, so it can be installed almost anywhere in a particular physical plant, and a variety of business applications can be integrated into it. If this approach appears to be desirable and feasible, then the interconnection of relatively freestanding micros may be the best alternative.

One of the most beneficial features of a LAN is resource sharing. It has the ability to enable all connected users to share resources such as storage devices, program loads, and data files. The cost of disks, printers, and connections to external communications can be split among all the users. Because it offers extensive savings through elimination of hardware duplication, a LAN enhances the users' opportunity to benefit from hardware that they might be hard-pressed to justify independently.

Many current LAN products are limited to mutually compatible devices, which usually means concentrating on a single vendor. This offsets the benefits of resource sharing. It also means that if a number of independent PC operations prefer to connect in this way, they must be completely compatible for the LAN operation. LAN may or may not be a solution for deciding on departmental or centralized computing, but it could be a very useful consideration. LAN technology is in its infancy, and it may be only a short time before all three levels of microcomputer management can be mixed and controlled at the same PC site.

Some communications and networking compatability considerations are:

1. *Connection to a central mainframe.* From the viewpoint of the user, communications available through a central mainframe can be the most simple to use and have the most functionality. The powerful communications systems that may be installed centrally can efficiently and cost-effectively handle all the networking that may be required.

2. *Departmental processor and PCs.* This approach may put another level of communications between the user and the network, but, more importantly, it basically is not designed for external communications. It is excellent for communications within the particular department, but usually is poor for networking.

Availability of Systems and Vendor Relationships

The two alternatives for MSS/DSS operation offer a wide difference in handling hardware and software systems and maintaining vendor relationships. The responsibilities to the end-users need to be put in perspective. There are many considerations that affect the economics and possible effectiveness of the vendors. Clearly, the larger the customer, the more readily systems will be available on demand and the more vendor support can be expected.

Some particular considerations are:

1. *Connection to the central mainframe.* The vendor of the central mainframe will be prepared to offer support in order to maintain the growth of the mainframe, and in hope of selling future upgrades to new models. In most cases, the terminals used for direct access and systems programs will be supplied by the same vendor, if only to prevent vendor "finger pointing" when systems problems with the MSS arise. This will usually mean a strong vendor relationship available to departmental users, which can help the rapid availability of systems and help experienced personnel debug any difficulties. It also means that vendor training courses may be available for the users, which makes training less of a burden to Information Services.

2. *Departmental processor and PCs.* Frequently, the mainframe and departmental processors are obtained from different vendors. After this break has been made, the terminals or PCs may be from a third vendor. These decisions are made on the functional capabilities and the price available. However, the effect these decisions have is to fragment the vendor relationship and support. This may not be considered a problem by the department involved. Because the depart-

ment has its own processor, it may consider itself a large enough customer to get all the vendor support needed. It may be satisfied with the software systems and application programs that are readily available, which may have come from a fourth vendor. If the support appears to be adequate, it may not be a factor in the selection decision. There is one warning, however. When two to four vendors are involved and there are problems with either the hardware or the software systems, it becomes difficult to pinpoint the problems with vendor help. The problems will always be "somewhere else." Therefore, if the mixed vendor route is taken, the organization must be prepared to have a strong enough internal staff to determine the cause of problems and recommend fixes.

One Station per User with All Functions

There is a wide variety of microcomputers and terminals on the market, and in selecting equipment there is always a danger that a department will choose computers that are incompatible with the other systems in the organization. PCs are acquired to perform specific, useful functions, but they may be difficult to install and operate. The best approach to their acquisition is to follow a systematic decision process that is integrated into the ongoing planning and management process of the organization. Careful definition of functional requirements is always one of the most critical early steps to take. Checklists and worksheets are useful at this point so that strengths and weaknesses can be compared on a tabular basis. It is important to include compatibility considerations in the checklists.

There are different problems with the different alternatives:

1. *Connection to the central mainframe.* A common situation is on-line terminals with minimal functions that are set up for specific applications. This may be entirely adequate for MSS in some cases. There can be expansion to other applications if similar operating procedures are used. All applications must be on the mainframe, however, and under the same controls and service levels. If local computing or connection to another network is desired, there are problems. It is not necessarily desirable to replace a dumb terminal with a PC. With a PC, the computing power may be enough to readily pierce the original security controls, and other problems arise.

2. *Departmental processor and PCs:* In most cases when departmental processors are installed, PCs are used as terminals or workstations. They offer sufficient functions to handle other types of applications or local computing. In addition, they are normally acquired as a group so that consistency and economy will exist. If further functions are required, the PCs can be expanded, also as a group. However, if too much memory and function are installed, they could also present a security problem.

There is no reason why one workstation could not be expanded to handle all the functions required. Each individual or small group should be able to operate with a single, multifunctional computer. The only compatibility problem is with programs or data files that are available. The only security problems are those that are defined locally. Such a workstation could be expanded indefinitely as more tasks are put on it. In the long run, however, it may be desirable to tie into an organizational network. In this case, it would be wise to have compatibility from the beginning.

SYSTEM DEVELOPMENT FOR MSS

In the old technology, system development was usually forced to follow the readily controlled standard system development life cycle (SDLC). Over the years, this proved most effective for management control of cost and delivery for most application systems. It frequently failed when installing management support systems (both EIS and DSS), however; when managers requested certain types of information for operational use, they loathed waiting through the whole SDLC for the programs to be designed, developed, and delivered. As soon as it became possible in the new technology (where applications are developed more rapidly with less control), a new approach became popular for all types of MSS.

The essence of the development side of new technology is being refined in the systematic approaches to *prototyping* for system development. Most decision support analysts did not necessarily understand that they were using a prototyping approach, but they proceeded in the same logical manner. The cycle is completing, and the two technologies are coming together. Consultant Richard A. Jokiel has given presentations in which he describes the transition from the old SDLC to the new types of project life cycle that are more appropriate for MSS/DSS.

Jokiel points out that the new approach is not radically different from the old SDLC. It simply replaces the most bothersome part of the SDLC—the definition or specification phase—for managers who want an MSS developed. The phase becomes an iterative process because many decision makers cannot define all their requirements in advance. They want to try different formats and calculations until they get what they feel is optimum. They want to experiment with the development phase, and they often gain valuable information along the way.

This approach to definition or specification, which has always fit management thinking, is called *application prototyping* (Figure 2–3). It recently has become feasible because of the increased availability of fine fourth-generation languages (4GLs), with which it is not a problem to experiment with the coding.

Application prototyping as the de facto approach to the development of EIS and DSS systems, and the general use of 4GLs for such work, is expanded on in the first section of Chapter Nine.

Systems have become more friendly with regard to the language in which they are implemented, in the type of processing we see going on, and in the area of

FIGURE 2–3
Prototype Life Cycle Model

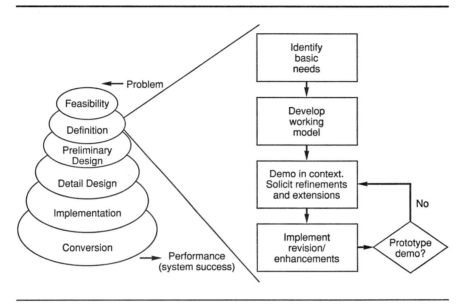

specifications (see Figure 2–4). Originally, when there was machine language (bit, bit, bit, bit, no bit, no bit, bit, bit, bit . . .), it was a marvel just to get it to execute; a big program was 50 lines of code. Then came the powerful tool called an assembler language, which was a way to put labels on things. The addresses did not have to be remembered, so the assembler language was a step forward. Specifications came about through Victorian novels. Systems analysts were paid by the pound or by the word. Then came the higher-order languages such as COBOL and FORTRAN, and, in Europe, ALGOL and PASCAL. High-order languages like PL-1 and structured analysis became the vogue.

The structured programming revolution began in the 1970s. People were dealing with written specifications, and their objectives were to find a technique for designing and proving algorithms and testing procedures to demonstrate those algorithms, for designs that would produce a high level of success in the software development process. It made sense and was developed to a refined level. The process of structured programming works.

Edward Yourdon and others then decided that a similar process could be applied to systems analysis and requirements definition, and they called it structured analysis. Completely predefining the system is frequently a problem. The users, in most cases, do not understand the problem as it relates to an I/T system.

FIGURE 2–4
Trends in Data Processing

FRIENDLIER/INTIMATE APPROACHES →

Machine language	Assembler language	High-order languages	Program generators

Batch processing	Transaction processing	Time sharing	Personal computing

No specifications	Victorian novel	Structured analysis	Prototyping

They have to discover it as the implementation unfolds. They have to discover the minor details that are associated with the problem at hand, and they often do this after the system is put into production. That is typical of MSS. Today, prototyping is the most friendly, user-oriented approach to developing MSS requirements definitions that produce much better results. The risk of incorrect specifications has to be reduced. If we have the wrong specs, it does not matter how good the programming techniques are: we are building the wrong system and solving the wrong problem. Structured analysis techniques that have been put in place have failed for MSS definition.

One of the reasons this has been a problem is shown in Figure 2–5. The cost of correcting problems in the software development process increases geometrically going from feasibility study to production. This is simply to say that the sooner the errors are found, the cheaper it is to fix them. Yet managers want low-cost systems fast for MSS.

So why prototype for MSS? To reduce the risk of incorrect specifications, and because the rigorous specifications approach often does not work. Most errors are traceable to requirements, and they become ever more costly to correct down the line, moving from feasibility to implementation. Strategy is needed, a technique for doing requirements definition that will result in a high probability for success, measured by user acceptance and workability at the time of production cutoff.

The standard life cycle starts off with feasibility, requirements definition, preliminary design, and detail design. There are little loops because errors are found, but they are tolerable. Next the cycle goes to implementation, and the

FIGURE 2-5
Cost-to-Correct Curve

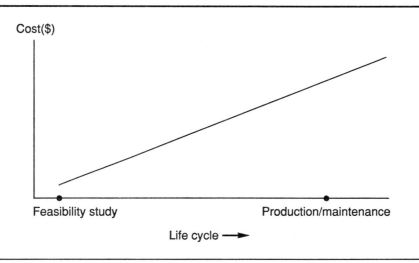

user says the MSS is wrong. Then another requirements definition has to be done. If the system is not defined correctly, those who implement it never have a chance.

The usefulness of prototyping for MSS is summarized in Figure 2-6. Life-cycle costs have to be minimized. The implementation schedule has to be minimized. The risk of failure has to be reduced. Prototyping has to be heuristic because it cannot be done any other way. There is going to be a learning and discovery process associated with it. Prespecification is difficult but not impossible. Iteration is necessary, desirable, and inevitable.

COMPARISON OF TRADITIONAL AND PROTOTYPING SDLC

Compare the requirements definition of the traditional and prototyping procedures in Figure 2-7. The traditional techniques, which accept the belief that prespecification is possible, that people do understand what they want for MSS, and that they are capable of communicating it, do not work for MSS. Paper is not an adequate representation of what an interactive system is going to be like. Paper does not communicate to the user in a clear, unambiguous manner what his or her on-line needs really are and how the system is going to interact.

FIGURE 2–6
Prototyping Definition Approach

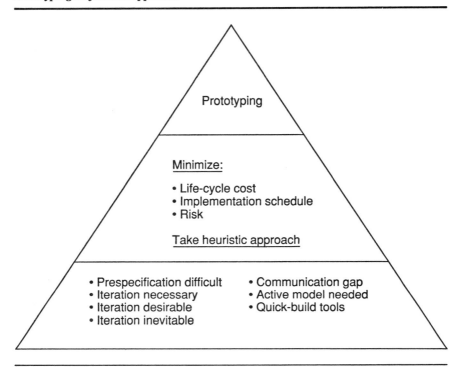

FIGURE 2–7
Requirements Definition: Traditional versus Prototyping

	Definition Strategy	
Assumption	*Traditional*	*Prototyping*
1. Final and complete prespecification possible.	X	
Prespecification extremely difficult.		X
2. Change to system is extremely expensive.	X	
Modern quick-build tools.		X
3. Good project communication.	X	
Inherent communication gap.		X
4. Static model is adequate.	X	
Animated model required.		X
5. Rigor tautology.	X	
Rigor once requirements are known.		X
6. Iteration is proof of definition failure.	X	
Iteration is necessary, desirable, inevitable.		X

In prototyping for MSS, the users become far more satisfied with the system, because whatever iteration is necessary is inevitable and desirable because it is a learning process.

Figure 2–8 demonstrates the type of life cycle most professionals want to implement for MSS. It goes through feasibility studies. It is not the type of life cycle in which the user meets with the prototyper, the prototyper produces the model overnight, the user reviews the model and criticizes it, the prototyper immediately fixes the model right in front of the user, and then the system is put into production and everyone lives happily ever after. That is not a realistic life cycle. This process is iterative and requires considerable communication.

When the prototype model of an MSS is finished, there is a great deal missing (Figure 2–9). There are no operational-run books. Data conversion procedures, backup/recovery, and database sizing have not been worked out. If this system is going to be put on-line around the country, the network issues have not even been looked at yet. Quality control techniques have not really been applied, certainly

FIGURE 2–8
MSS System Development Life Cycle

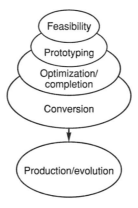

FIGURE 2–9
Missing Items at End of Prototyping

- Operational-run books
- Conversion procedures
- Backup/recovery
- Database sizing

- Network sizing
- Quality control
- Training procedures
- Full function

FIGURE 2–10
SDLC Comparison

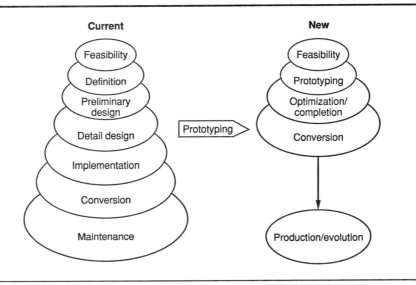

not to the code. The code was produced at warp speed. The training procedures have not been worked on. In many cases, all of the functions have not been implemented because they are well understood or trivial.

Figure 2–10 shows how prototyping fits into the early stages of the SDLC. The prototyping life cycle is a very attractive technique and offers tremendous benefits for the future. There is a feasibility study, and functional prototyping is done. Then the prototype will be optimized and completed. After this, data conversion is done to move data into the production system. Finally, there will be a functioning production system. This is a much more attractive life cycle than the traditional one, and it fits the requirements of MSS development because it has fewer steps.

MANAGEMENT FOR MSS DEVELOPMENT

Management for the development of the new MSS technology also has some major points of difference from management of centrally developed and centrally run applications. Again, there are critical capabilities that differ between the old and the new technologies in some important aspects. Some that should be considered are:

- Efficient and effective training.
- Practical consultation and support from a trained team.
- Control by each department of its own staff.
- Standards, security, and control for effective management.
- Communications with Information Services about plans and operations.
- Open marketing of ideas among all users.

Each of these areas of capability should be considered when planning the management of MSS development.

Efficient and Effective Training

The rapidly developing environment of MSS computing requires organizations to encourage workers at all levels to be knowledgeable, technically capable, and forward-looking. When more employees become proficient in computer use, the results will be better for the corporation, and it will be easier to agree upon reasonable controls. With the proliferation of personal computers, the tendency is for an organization to rely on its workers to keep themselves updated on computers individually by informal training, but this is a mistake. For any approach to MSS applications, training must be carefully planned, developed, and executed if the advantages are to be realized.

If the basic intent of the acquisition and installation of computing systems is to increase worker productivity, there will be little success unless the employees thoroughly understand methods, capabilities, and possibilities of the computing system. On a broad scale, this realistically can be accomplished only with an adequate training and development program. Usually there are different approaches to training and development for different approaches to computing, however. Some of the more obvious differences are:

1. *Connection to the central mainframe.* Training and development generally will be handled by the Information Services training group. There will be a need to understand features of the operating system, the particular language used, and the standards and controls that have been imposed. In addition to general introductory courses that need to be developed, systems and programming courses likely will be subsets of courses already given. Demands on end-users to learn the details of using the central computer will be greater than in other approaches because control is more sensitive. This is due to the fact that other programs can be affected by mistakes made by a user. Controls on system and information use are not just for personnel who have powerful PCs attached to the central computer. Employees working on dumb terminals need just as much information because they also have access to the central files, even though they cannot move between files as readily.

2. *Departmental processor and PCs.* Training and development for the use of departmental processors also may be the responsibility of the central group, but it is more likely to be handled within the department, or by an Information Center training group. The departmental system is less complex than the central processor, and there will be a smaller set of standards and procedures to use. After an introductory or concepts course, the training will be specific to the particular processor and system used, and the limited language set that it is likely to have. There should, of course, be instruction in security and controls, but that also will be quite specific because the controls will be more bounded. Because training for a departmental processor will be different from that given for the central computer, the central Information Services training group may not be familiar with it, and the type of training given will not lead to proficiency on the mainframe. It will be much more specialized. This specific training requirement must be factored into a decision to use a departmental processor.

Practical Consultation and Support

Another critical capability that must be considered for MSS work is the capacity to provide practical consultation and support. The need is to find the best fit for the organization's requirements.

Consultation and product support includes all aspects of making hardware and software realistically available and usable. Users need help in selecting products and learning about their most efficient use and their operation. The products are computers and other equipment, application software, outside computing services, and materials related to these items. The support includes selection, demonstration, supply, installation, control, and maintenance. It also may include technical assistance in problem analysis. (The considerations relative to software and hardware are outlined in a later chapter.) The problems of providing such practical consultation and support are important to the selection decision for MSS.

Alternative means of providing computing power offer different approaches to the way this critical consultation and support may be provided:

1. *Connection to the central mainframe.* First, support may become fragmented because many operating aspects connected to the mainframe fall under different groups in Information Services. The responsibilities may be handled by the computer center staff, the systems programmers, the communications group, the central training function, quality assurance, internal audit, and so on. Whenever a connection is made directly to a large computer, all the standards and procedures thereon should be followed, and specific groups should be prepared to police them.

Second, user proliferation and dispersal may become a major issue. Centralized organizations can maintain a span of control up to a point, but when the users are divided and dispersed throughout the corporation, control becomes difficult. The connection to the central computer is complex enough with a large, specialized support staff involved. It can become unwieldy if there are many different application systems that are frequently modified on PCs without adequate communications. Reasonable support can become impossible.

2. *Departmental processor and PCs.* Product consultation and support becomes much more specialized and centralized. There is a more limited span of interest by the users, fewer application systems are used, and the users want more specific answers. Consultants involved with a departmental processor can concentrate on a few systems and install local standards of use. There are no repetitive end-user analyses, vendor surveys, and discussions. Decisions are made according to departmental requirements, and local management can enforce those decisions in a simple way. In addition, the IC consultant can become more familiar with the limited set of systems being used and, therefore, can be more effective in the consulting role. With a departmental processor, it is simpler to have consultation and support provided.

Departmental Control of Staff

The managers of user departments may have strong feelings about departmental control of their staffs for MSS work, and the degree of cooperation they will give to a central consulting group. There are a number of issues they feel are important:

Information services response.   Managers may have had previous experience with long and costly system development cycles, and a lack of communication between programmers and analysts on the one hand and their own staffs on the other. This tends to make them favor a departmental processor, or even to give their own people a free hand on separate PCs.

Timely access to information.   Routine, periodic reporting of information seldom has been satisfactory for operational management. They desire access to information at any time they want it. Because they are operational managers, they need timely access to information, so the two key criteria are *availability* and *accessibility.*

Data availability and accessibility are sometimes lost on PCs because of inadequate records. Users need to know the name, source, and ownership of data files. They need to know the content and currency of information. They need samples of the data and documentation of it. In short, they need to know what data is available to decide if they want it. Such information is usually readily available for the central database, or for the data files on departmental computers. It is much less available for freestanding PCs. If there is too much departmental control of the use of computers by staff, there can be a considerable disadvantage in the ease of acquiring data.

Personnel productivity. There are many pressures to improve white-collar productivity. Productivity is hard to define in an acceptable manner, but managers may perceive it as the ability to get the computer power and data needed whenever they want it. This issue does not have an obvious resolution. Attachment to a central computer may give managers access to all the data that is needed, but it comes with restrictions on the mode of use. They can control a departmental computer, but the data refreshment times may be too far apart to get current data. They certainly have complete control of freestanding PCs, but they may not have the data availability they want.

Thus there is no simple answer to the personnel productivity issue. It depends completely upon the type of data access that gives the most advantages in specific situations.

Improvement of decision making. Computerized decision support systems (DSS) appear to fill the need, in many instances, to improve the overall quality of decision making. If a departmental staff has control of its own data-base and system, presumably it can pull in the specific information wanted, load the DSS file with any data wanted, and improve their decision making. It is not that simple, of course, because data is time-sensitive, and the right piece of data is often elusive. Direct connection to a central computer normally will make much larger quantities of data available. It will be the most recent data, and the large computer can handle powerful data search tools. Good extract data files on a departmental computer, on the other hand, may have sufficient data available and offer easy ways of manipulating it for a variety of analyses. The depart-mental manager has control of the type of data used, the volume of data, and the methods used to manipulate it. The decision-making analytical process becomes completely a departmental effort under control of the manager.

Some of the considerations about staff control under the alternatives are:

1. *Connection to the central mainframe.* With an on-line connection to a central computer, most departmental managers feel that they have lost some control of their staff, simply because others are prescribing rules and procedures and setting up controls and restrictions. For all practical purposes, there may be no real problem with these details of staff control, but many managers feel that they present obstacles.

2. *Departmental processor.* In reality, connection to a central computer and a departmental time-sharing processor can provide considerable departmental control, if the manager is familiar with the way the process works and applies the necessary controls.

Standards, Security, and Control

Maintenance of data integrity, audit control, and security should be of considerable concern with any system handling key organizational information and financial records. Management must be concerned with:

- The power to control data and databases.
- Controlled development of systems and the purchase of software.
- The control of read-only files.
- The security of information and the right to privacy.
- Policies, standards, and procedures that are approved.

Security and control can be managed best if there is standardization of operating systems, hardware, and software to promote compatibility; to simplify control, security, and audit; and to simplify data analysis. Only through such standardization can there be reasonable program and data interchange, effective data communication, and uniform data reporting.

Data standards are established most effectively through a central group, such as data administration. Hardware, software, and communications standards should be established by the appropriate groups in Information Services, which may include the Information Center. Standards normally should be published in a uniform format and maintained by a central group. The general considerations about standards, security, and controls are the following:

1. *Connection to the central mainframe.* If standards, security, and control are highly important, they can be managed most readily by a system that provides direct connection to a central computer. All inputs and inquiries can be checked by the system before there is any movement of data.

2. *Departmental processor and PCs.* If there are both central standards and departmental standards to manage, a departmental processor may be indicated; otherwise, it may be difficult to interpose the departmental standards on all the systems.

Communications with Information Services

There are many reasons why ready communications with Information Services staff groups could be one of the critical capabilities to consider for MSS work. They can be summed up in the fact that Information Services is normally an excellent source of data, methods, and information that will facilitate DSS/EIS computing. Every advantage should be taken of their experience and staff availability. Among the service advantages that I/S may offer are:

- Ways of increasing personnel productivity, through training courses, seminars, available literature, and hands-on testing of equipment.
- Library of available systems and programs, documentation, and access to sources of programs and subroutines.
- Knowledge of the central database and access methods to it.
- Experience in system development, project management and control, and estimation of application costs.
- Availability of operating systems and operations support systems that have been used for many applications and tested by others.
- Controlled and reliable data files that usually are handled on central computers with a high level of audit and security control, whatever the system.
- Experience in data processing experimentation, with several levels of hardware usage, system types, and system development approaches.
- Experience with many types of internal controls and audit trail methods.
- Understanding of security methods and procedures.
- Experience in disaster recovery planning.

There are analysts in Information Services who have moved through the learning curve on most types of system development and operation. They can provide consultation services, and although most probably work on larger systems, they are familiar with the problems facing a department in getting computer services.

The most important aspect of communication with information services, however, is in the area of computer and system production measurement and planning. If there is to be access to a central computer by direct connection or by downloaded databases, the effort required *must* be factored into the planning process of information services. Computer use can be heavy, particularly with direct access, and there is always an appreciable lead time needed to prepare the central computer to handle the load.

The effects on information services of the use of MSS generally can be stated as follows:

1. *Connection to the central mainframe.* Considerable increase is needed in central computer capabilities, including machine power, memory, storage devices, and security preparations. More staff is required for control and consultation. The approach, if successful, may lead to greatly increased demand for on-line and time-sharing services, with a continual demand for more computer power. Successful departmental analysts will want to extend from the particular application to which they have been given access and get on-line with other applications or with other parts of the database. This alternative for microcomputing puts Information Services firmly in control of all the computer power, but at a major cost in central hardware and software.

2. *Departmental processor and PCs.* This alternative has a relatively small effect on central hardware and software requirements, except for the extraction and downloading program, which would be run infrequently. It puts extra demands on the Database Administration and Data Control groups, however, because there must be continuous monitoring of the operation. Planning for future upgrades of the departmental processor will be the responsibility of the department concerned, but should be done in concert with Information Services.

Open Marketing of Ideas

The cost of DSS/EIS application development and the time required are usually great enough to require an effort at compatibility and the sharing of programs. In any organization, there should be an open market for sharing ideas, experiences, and code. This is one of the prime functions of an Information Center, although it can be handled by other groups in the Information Services department. Sharing ideas, tips, application program experience, and subroutines should not be left to informal methods. There should be a conscious, formal approach to the solicitation of information, writing it up, and distributing it to all who can use it. Some people will always want to make further adaptations and experiment with their own ideas, but the majority of users will be pleased to accept any proven experiences that could help them. There are slightly different approaches with the different computing alternatives:

1. *Connection to the central mainframe.* Most of the information about applications used has been documented by the development teams, and any further information is sent to the system development group. There are always possibilities of further tips and ideas for use of the applications, but these are likely to be minor. If an Information Center is involved, it will work mainly with system training and the availability of data.

2. *Departmental processor.* There is the likelihood of an Information Center located close to the operation with considerable exchange of programs and sharing of ideas. Because most users will be in the same department, any operating improvements or useful codes will be valuable and accepted. There usually will be a newsletter with space for new ideas, and periodic user meetings for direct exchange of information. Information Center consultants will pass on other ideas. The climate will be right for mutual exchange.

THE BENEFITS OF MANAGEMENT SUPPORT SYSTEMS

Organizations operate in a dynamic environment that requires them to constantly adjust. Thus various decisions are made to operate efficiently and effectively. No company or organization can function making only strategic decisions. In order to maximize an organization's accomplishment of its goals, it must be effective in making strategic, tactical, and operational decisions. It must be able to handle the routine efficiently while handling unstructured decisions effectively.

The role of an effective management support system is to deal with areas of inherent unstructuredness that are difficult for a classical transaction processing system to address effectively. The senior executive in charge of MIS needs to use MSS to enhance the organization's effectiveness through more efficient utilization of computer technology.

The benefits of effectively implemented MSS are to be found in improved performance of an organization. A survey among major users of MSS by John F. Rockart and Michael E. Treacy[2] indicated:

1. An increase in the number of alternatives examined.

2. Better understanding of the business.

3. Fast response to unanticipated situations.

4. Ability to carry out ad hoc analyses.

5. Improved communications.

6. Improved control.

7. More effective teamwork.

8. Time and cost savings.

9. More effective use of data resources.

This list describes the benefits an organization may achieve through implementation of the MSS capability. The remaining chapters will provide an understanding of types of DSS and EIS; how to organize an implementation; how to implement a DSS or an EIS; how to control DSS and EIS implementation, especially with the users; and a checklist, or baseline, to evaluate an organization's use of DSS and EIS.

---

[2]John F. Rockart and Michael E. Treacy, "Executive Information Support Systems," Center for Information Systems Research, MIT, April 1981.

Chapter Three

Organization and Information Delivery Issues

In this chapter, end-user computing is defined and described as an area in which executives and managers may make direct use of the wide variety of computer technologies available for individual use. EIS, DSS, and related MSS systems are typical functional niche applications that higher-level management may find helpful for direct participation. Some reasons for developing executive computing capabilities in the MSS area are discussed.

The Information Center may be an excellent facility to expedite the development of management support systems. Examples of the types of services offered by an Information Center and the functional service areas in which an Information Center might work for MSS are listed.

Some methods of delivering information to executives, or ways of facilitating information display for MSS work, are briefly reviewed. These include executive information-briefing rooms, terminal graphics, and hard-copy graphics production.

The MSS group must rely on at least three other Information Services groups: Operations, Communications, and Process Control for technology, systems, and data. In addition to the Information Center, some of the support services that may be grouped with MSS include the corporate library, office automation, corporate records, and consultation.

A group decision support system (GDSS) can assist in the process of reaching a decision through group interaction. It may be face-to-face, a large group, or a dispersed environment. The elements of a GDSS include a database, an application model, communications, and a facilitator. Aspects of GDSS technology are discussed, including those for messaging, conferencing, and computer graphics.

THE MOVEMENT TOWARD
END-USER COMPUTING

Information support systems for executives are not limited to terminals on their desks, the ability to readily prepare quality graphics, the tracking of Critical Success Factors (or other key factors), or an immediate staff that works with decision support systems. Executives are now in a position to draw on information immediately from any part of an organization by using microcomputers and communications. Hence, any technologies that can be used to draw conclusions or projections from data may be considered part of the management support system of the organization. This introduces a range of technological possibilities, many of which have been part of the accelerated use of computers to help arrive at corporate strategy decisions.

In the past, information from computers was available to executives only as lengthy output operational reports from data processing. Occasionally, executives asked for specific summary reports and projections to be calculated and appended to those reports. Such calculations were usually rigid and difficult to amend, however. Technical staff personnel, therefore, frequently made computer-oriented studies on special assignments for executives, and they still do. The idea of rapid inquiry into computer systems by a noncomputer professional, with responses oriented to specific, urgent inquiries of management, has been accepted and feasible only in recent years. The extended idea of senior managers actually making such inquiries themselves at computer terminals is now being considered and accepted.

A new approach has become available for management support under the general name of *end-user computing*. The development of information systems technology has reached a point where there are many possibilities for the true end-users and responsible executives to use all types of information services directly. This section discusses some aspects of this new thrust to end-user computing, even for senior executives, by defining it and giving insights from recognized leaders in the field of management of information services.

End-user computing (EUC) is the individual use or operating-group use of computer equipment, separate from an organization's computer centers, to manipulate data, perform analyses, establish local files, and generate reports for their particular purposes and direct utilization. An executive information system (EIS) is the highest level of end-user computing in an organization.

The *people* involved in EUC may be executives or managers, individuals or groups outside the I/S department, individuals performing staff work within I/S, or outside customers accessing specific capabilities of systems within the organization. Users may be managerial, professional, or clerical personnel.

The *mode* involved in EUC may be stand-alone computers, or computer terminals integrated with larger equipment. The computers may also be in local area networks, in distributed processing networks, in departmental networks of personal computers, or connected to time-sharing services.

The *technologies* involved in EUC may include personal computers and workstations, word processing and office computers, Information Centers, document storage and retrieval, graphics and micrographics, electronic mail and message systems, teleconferencing and videoconferencing, optical character recognition and other electronic readers, terminals and networks (including local area networks), and distributed data processing.

None of these technologies is independent, but they interconnect and interact in a variety of configurations. Different manufacturers add various functions to equipment and software to extend and overlap the capabilities listed.

EUC may be in the mainstream of an organization's operations, or it may be practiced in certain functional niche applications. Some of these functional niches are decision support systems (DSS), executive information systems (EIS), spreadsheet analysis and ad hoc reporting, professional and clerical workstations, computer-aided design, process control, information inquiry by staff or customer, and financial analysis and planning.

There are several good reasons for the development and support of executive computing capabilities:

• *To provide direct support to supply executive information.* Whether the executive personally uses the equipment, or it is handled by immediate staff, the access to computer output is provided directly.

• *To run the business better.* When properly managed, EUC can speed the flow of information in a business, supply more accurate data under good control, and provide new opportunities for directed action and responsiveness.

• *To increase the productivity of professionals.* Professionals are given ready access to data for manipulation, analysis, and a variety of readily used analytical programs. They are able to do minor programming as required.

• *To gain competitive advantage.* Technology facilitates the offering of new services to customers and allows rapid response to their inquiries and orders.

• *To provide marketing innovation.* New concepts tied to the use of small computer systems in customers' offices may effectively tie them into a supplier by offering additional and more rapid services, and lower cost.

• *To support management.* Ready analytical access to available data and the ability to perform changing analyses rapidly on new report forms gives managers and their staffs improved inquiry and reporting capabilities.

• *To increase the productivity of staff and workers.* Systems with immediate access to computer capabilities and current data can speed up the work of clerical personnel and factory workers by providing more accurate information.

There are two principal kinds of direct use of information files for executives with their own microcomputers. One is *status access,* and the other is *personal analysis.* Most executives who approach an EIS system will want only the status access capabilities at first. They will be content simply to make inquiries of the files. After familiarization, a few senior executives then will want to perform personal analyses on the data, although the majority will assign such activity to their immediate staff.

Status access. Most executives who accept a microcomputer will want a particular set of reports routinely available on their CRT. These reports may cover such numbers as the Critical Success Factors of sensitive operations, or Key External Factors. These executives may desire to have immediate access to regular operating reports, financial reports, or personnel reports.

For status access, a senior executive or staff member requires read-only access to specific data files that may contain information on Critical Success Factors or financial results. The information may be studied, but usually there is little interest in manipulating it. If a manager wants to have a number of calculations and transformations routinely done and reported in a certain way, this can be programmed and readily accommodated. Status access is commonly required because it is simple to handle, the results come rapidly, and the executive can pass any analysis on to staff members. Most market and external financial information is desired on a status access basis.

John F. Rockart has pointed out that the status access approach has been selected by some executives for two reasons. First, it provides an easy-to-learn, low-cost, low-risk means of allowing an executive to become comfortable with a terminal. Second, this approach has been adopted by some chief executives as a simple, low-cost signal to the rest of the organization for increased emphasis on quantitative analysis in the planning and control process.

Personal analysis. Some executives not only want to use their computer for status access, but also for analysis of data. They want to actively analyze the available information with either packages or simple programming. Such executives need to be familiar with the data elements in their database, and must learn the access language. They desire more function, and they must be trained and prepared to handle it.

The type of personal analysis used will differ greatly among managers. Some will use algebraic functions or perform simple statistical analyses. Others may work with time series analysis and extrapolation. Some may even work with simulation models that have been set up for them by their staff. Most will learn how to display data in different ways and how to call for graphic output. Graphical trends of variables are not only easy to comprehend, especially in color, but they also are useful to show to other managers and to talk about the results of the analysis. This type of executive develops an ability to review data, change it, manipulate it, and project it in many ways that are personally helpful.

Personal analysis is used only by executives who feel reasonably at ease with the medium, and by those who understand mathematical analysis. A computer is ultimately quantitative, and on-line, interactive manipulation of data can have meaning only if a manager's thinking is geared in that direction. In addition, a manager must be prepared to devote a considerable amount of time and energy to learning how to use a system, then to defining the data needed and the techniques required to access and manipulate it. The personal analysis mode can provide great benefits to organizations with technically minded managers, because they will learn the underlying relationships and movements of data, and will be able to analyze causes and effects from a technical point of view. Another interesting advantage is that they will obtain an accurate and detailed understanding of the many possibilities of data processing and may well institute new and effective directions for electronic data processing (EDP) efforts.

There are also two principal sources of help in defining the information to which senior managers may turn. Each source has its own style of analysis and its own empire to support. These sources are the corporate and personal staffs of the executive.

The *corporate functional staff groups* may be accounting, finance, marketing, or planning. They are set up for monitoring and analyzing their own activities, and they also like to follow what is happening in other groups. They will have large information databases and the ability to extract and analyze data from any part of their files. They will have a body of well-controlled, functional data, and will be able to produce any type of report from it that is desired by the executive. In particular, they can produce a controlled extract file of their data for the manager's own database and will be in position to explain the subtleties of the data movements. They usually will be able to consolidate and summarize the data at any level in the organization, and the reports will be completely consistent with all other reports circulated to the senior manager.

The *personal support staff* in the executive office may be general analysts or area specialists. Usually, their functions are information gathering, analysis, and interpretation. They normally handle unconnected requests for which a considered answer must be available rapidly. This group is more concerned with the meaning of data that is combined from various sources, and less concerned with data control and accuracy. When they receive extracts of data files, they will manipulate and massage them, adding other data from various sources, and will produce a report that may have different underlying data than the routine report from the functional staff. They perform an exceedingly useful function for the executive, providing analyzed answers to specific questions. They are the bane of information control in data files, however, because they intermix internal data with external data and controlled data with uncontrolled data.

Senior executives spend very little time handling documents, making inquiries, or doing analyses. They are not willing, therefore, to spend much time learning a system to get started, because they are always pressed for time. They want a tool that can handle questions immediately and with little effort. If it is easier to use an executive information system (EIS) than to ask subordinates, they will likely try it. They also may want an EIS if it will give them information for private analyses without problems or embarrassing questions. They need an intuitive interface that will provide responses in a reasonable way. They are looking for a desk appliance, more like a telephone than a computer workstation. Simple menu screens and clear data descriptions are required.

INFORMATION CENTER SUPPORT FOR MSS

The Information Center is both an organization and a facility designed to support managers and other end-users in handling some of their data processing tasks. It is an approach that expedites do-it-yourself computing power to a wide range of end-users, and it is normally under the control of Information Services management.

The objectives of an Information Center start with the goal of providing improved delivery of computer services to end-users. These services allow end-users to perform tasks previously performed by professional data processing people. The services are "enablers" to non-data-processing professionals in locating and using data, and in developing capabilities in data processing, word processing, and communications. They help end-users become directly involved in analysis, programming, and operations phases to satisfy some of their information needs.

The concerns of the Information Center, end-user computing, and the use of personal computers are intertwined inextricably. Because of this, there are overlapping organizational aspects of Information Centers with data processing, word processing, office automation, telecommunications, personal computers, and end-user support. This book focuses on Information Centers but also includes many other factors that normally are associated with a service function, such as staff relationships, controls, security, and affected organizations.

The widespread application of exploding new technologies and budgetary pressures to improve organizational productivity are causing a changing environment for Information Services. Users are pressing for a wider dissemination of computing tools, easier access to the more useful methods and training, and the capability of receiving rapid answers to specific questions. The microcomputer revolution has markedly increased the penetration of data processing in organizations. Management has an opportunity to mobilize this increased user awareness to meet business objectives.

Experience has shown that the skillful operation of an Information Center in an organization can strongly influence the manner in which microcomputer systems are used. The Information Center is an organizational concept with the goal of ensuring better delivery of Information Services support to end-users. Traditionally, this support has been provided through a highly structured approach.

Many users cannot wait for the formal cycle to solve their problems. Information Centers have proven to be an effective vehicle for bringing end-users and Information Services together in a way that enhances the delivery of information and support.

The Information Center's principal function is to enable personnel throughout the organization to do their computing quickly and easily. It helps users get direct but controlled access to on-line information. It usually offers walk-in services and deskside support, in addition to organized instruction. It is ideally organized for MSS work.

Information Centers vary widely among different organizations. They may be introduced as a way to speed clerical and analytical efforts, and to make basic information available outside of the traditional Information Services systems. An IC may develop into a separate group within Information Services that sets up access to extract databases and external data sources, and that aids management in the manipulation and analysis of data for decision support systems.

An Information Center is a viable concept for introducing management support systems of all types. It is a method for offering employees in the user community the skills and tools necessary to produce computer-generated reports themselves. It is a means of providing computing power to such end-users on their own terms, and to help them solve their own information problems. In essence, an Information Center is an in-house service group to train end-users, help them define their own requirements, and use the tools that are available. This is not a modest effort, although it may only take a small staff to perform the functions. There are different attitudes and concerns about Information Centers, as well as a variety of skills and demands in the management and end-user group. In each organization that establishes an Information Center, there must be a workable plan and a step-by-step approach. The most profitable and readily accomplished services must be selected for early implementation, and a great many other services must be implemented carefully as soon as they can be handled.

Before too much effort is put into planning, organizing, and developing an Information Center as part of the MSS effort, responsible individuals should review the possibilities and the list of services that may be provided in the future and select a few critical and useful services to enable the group to start up successfully. Because ideas regarding Information Centers are not universally the same, an approach that has a good possibility of local success should be selected and sold to management. Then the planning and organization can begin in detail.

The first question is, "What type of information services would be most useful to the managers in this organization?" The second question then will be, "Which of these services will be most profitable and most likely to have initial success?" There are two ways of looking at types of Information Center services: from the service-item point of view, and from a functional point of view. Some of the service items that managers will desire from an Information Center are:

- Financial analysis. Using spreadsheet and accounting programs to manage, budget, and analyze results. This may include profitability analyses, cost allocations, and management inquiry.
- Technical analysis. Using arithmetic, statistical programs, engineering applications, and special programs relative to the business.
- Reporting information. Developing clear spreadsheets and graphic aids for presentations.
- Inquiry, search, and retrieval. Examining files of information for trends or specific items.
- Planning and scheduling. Using statistical and spreadsheet programs to forecast information and allocate resources.
- Monitoring. Using systems to review results and actual numbers compared to plans by processing appropriate numbers in a systematic and simple manner.
- Writing. Using word processing systems and files of information to generate reports, letters, and other documents.
- Communications. Using systems to deliver messages, arrangements, and drafts of documents via data communications networks used on demand.
- Memory aids. Providing aids such as appointment calendars, "to do" lists, name files, etc. for rapid recall of information.
- Training packages. Offering various software packages to help users learn data processing or specific application programs and data handling methods.

All these service items are well-known to operating Information Centers, because they all are requested commonly. They usually are not simple to provide, however, because it is seldom just a matter of providing a package. The IC must set up, learn, and operate a package, and supply and control the data that will be needed to run it. To successfully operate an Information Center, therefore, functional services are more important than the specific service items. Thus planning should be directed to setting up an organization with procedures and priorities that will deliver the service items in the above list expeditiously and smoothly at the appropriate service level. Questions about the types of services that would be useful and most likely to succeed must be answered in a viable delivery mechanism. The key functional services to be provided are the managerial and organizational services that will get specific service items to the desks of end-users.

The following list contains the principal functional services that may be planned. Within this framework, specific requests, requirements, and priorities can be managed readily. Each service has a necessary part in the total delivery mechanism for end-user computing. Within each of these functional services, many specific service items need to be considered.

- End-user consulting. Includes contacting managers and other end-users, marketing the Information Center, planning its work, and negotiating the relationship with other departments.

- Product support for end-user computing. Includes all aspects of making hardware and its related software available for use.

- Technical assistance to the end-user. Comprises the necessary requirements analysis, and programming and communications support to provide smooth delivery of the systems and data.

- Training of end-users. Covers general knowledge and specific education, formal or informal classes, and group or individual instruction.

- Applications selection and development. Entails the technical expertise and organizational politics of gaining acceptance and some measure of standardization of the most profitable and useful programs.

- Management of data resources. Data handling and control problems that directly affect the end-user's work, but not the overall data and database management function of the organization.

- Information Center administrative services. Those services needed to keep the IC managed and controlled and to see that the end-users get what they want.

- Information Center operations. Includes set-up and display of equipment and software, and efficient delivery of the services provided.

- Monitoring and reviewing the Information Center. The management control function of seeing that what was planned is delivered and used in an efficient, effective, and controlled manner.

All of these services have distinct applicability to the planning, introduction, implementation, and operation of any type of management support system.

The Information Center idea has become technologically feasible in recent years, as hardware cost reductions have led to a proliferation of powerful microcomputer systems at users' desks, and other forms of distributed computing. There has been a greatly increased availability of user-friendly application packages, high-level languages, and decision-support tools. The Information Center pulls together users' analytical models with the store of controlled data in the computer center and the wealth of programs and methods that are commercially available. The Information Center may assist in the use of capabilities available on a central mainframe, distributed data processing systems, local area networks, communications facilities, personal computers, simple or specialized terminals, graphics equipment, corporate central data files, and external databases.

In addition, the Information Center may give instruction for and support MSS software, information retrieval tools, query and extraction tools, data reduction tools, report generators, graphics tools, modeling and simulation tools, planning and forecasting tools, statistical analysis tools, application generators, and fourth-generation languages.

The Information Center may also provide education, training, and support to end-users by all practical methods.

INFORMATION DISPLAY FOR EXECUTIVES

In addition to the massive transaction reports in an organization and summaries of them developed by the system or by staff personnel, there are three types of information delivery that are most effective:

1. Executive information briefing rooms.
2. Terminal graphics.
3. Hard-copy graphics production.

Executive Information Briefing Rooms

Top management requires meaningful and relevant reports, issued when the subject is of immediate interest, and spotlighting critical information; exception reporting that will alert them to financial and operating problems; and rapid documentation of any problem with supporting details.

Executive information briefing rooms are dynamic communications centers specifically designed for audiovisual presentations to disseminate currently pertinent information effectively to management for corporate decision making. They are one type of management support system.

An executive information briefing room that uses sophisticated equipment and has direct connections to mainframe data is an excellent way to keep management constantly and accurately briefed on the status of selected critical concerns, from cash flow and operating information (such as inventory control) to complicated growth plans projected for several years. Such briefing rooms (chart rooms, or "war" rooms) have been established successfully in large organizations, and they have proved to be an excellent way to transform micro-to-mainframe connections and computer output into meaningful visuals that are compatible with senior management's approach to discussions of summary results.

A briefing room is the epitome of good communication. It attracts and focuses attention. It is current and consistent. It is a complex but effective EIS. Computer terminals in executive offices have a worthwhile place for executives who are inclined to use them, but many executives feel more comfortable receiving an audiovisual briefing in their own board room or chart room. Audiovisual reporting cannot be overestimated. Studies have shown that most people remember 10 percent of what they read, 20 percent of what they hear, 30 percent of what they see, but *50 percent* of what they see *and* hear.

In communicating a message, it is the responsibility of the sender to get attention and retention. The transmission is in symbols, and the sender needs feedback from the receiver to be sure the message is received. Face-to-face communication thus is best, even of computer output. The presentation must be clear, effective, and efficient. These conditions can be obtained in a briefing room.

There are several considerations in establishing such a room.

Objectives.   The objectives of a modern executive information briefing room are:

- To display pertinent top management information in one central location, whether it is from internal or external computer files, or from related staff studies.

- To establish the best mode of communication of information that is current and consistent, and to attract and focus attention on the information.

- To foster management by objectives and to pinpoint problems in specific areas of responsibility, using reporting by exception in summarized data form.

- To formalize and discuss profit plans and budgets in an atmosphere where relevant information and alternative plans are available for all participants to see.

- To depict the current relationships of planned and actual use of people, money, and materials for evaluation of accomplishment and effect.

- To display performance information, factual norms, and current status for exposure and study, using graphical and statistical techniques.

Goals.   From the objectives listed above, a number of specific goals may be developed for planning and later comparison with results. Some of the areas in which goals may be stated are:

- To measure goal accomplishment in a current and consistent manner, using plan-versus-actual information from most recent computer data.

- To disseminate pertinent information in minimum time, such as certain reports to top management within a specified number of hours of their production.

- To display information in a related way, combining operational data with planning data and projections on computer-generated graphs.

- To compare information trends in an analytical way, using statistical and time series analysis techniques in consistent and routine forms.

- To attract and focus attention on reported exceptions, using new graphical techniques and appropriate color.
- To stimulate analysis and research, making analytical and graphics production techniques available to all staff members.

Use of statistical methods.   The briefing-room approach lends itself admirably to the consistent use of analytical, statistical, and time series analysis methods, because all the information must be summarized and put in an attractive presentation form. The measurement and control of plans and operations call for the use of statistics. It is necessary to identify and compare typical characteristics of masses of information. Whereas most senior managers cannot use the techniques on their own terminals, they find the approach helpful when the methodology is clearly explained and maintained consistently over time.

Data must be reliable, complete, and accurate, because the value of a briefing room lies in the accuracy of the statistical activity employed. Direct access to current mainframe data files is a necessity, and most briefing rooms should have a microcomputer and software programs to prepare the majority of the graphics that are shown. Also, the most sophisticated methods can be used to present trends, ratios, and indices in the clearest and simplest way.

Using micro-to-mainframe connections and graphics programs, statistics can be merchandised in an attractive way to sell the method of measuring accomplishments in relation to predetermined goals. The statistics must remain completely objective, however, meaning that the manipulation processes must be understood and remain the same over time.

Use of a computer in the briefing room.   Modern briefing rooms must have at least a microcomputer because of the speed and facility with which information can be manipulated and converted to presentation graphics. Senior management information is a perishable commodity, and the managers involved are interested only in the most recent figures. Also, approaches such as sophisticated multivariate trend analysis techniques cannot be calculated without a computer. There may be initial management resistance to changing current decision-making patterns, but once executives have become familiar with the step-by-step procedures used to prepare the information for decision, they will be able to rely on it.

A modern briefing room can have charts produced and calculations made at minimal cost because of the ready availability of microcomputers and the necessary analytical and graphical software. It soon becomes apparent that attractive graphs in full color can be produced almost instantaneously from the most recent data in the files.

In summary, components of a computerized briefing room are: a microcomputer with a large storage capacity; communication with the mainframe database; information selection and retrieval techniques; a range of statistical analysis and presentation software; large display screens; and hard-copy production capability for tables, charts, and graphs.

A briefing room certainly needs systems analysis help to set up the systems and programs. It then should be possible, however, to operate it with staff that understand the problems and needs of management and have been trained briefly in the use of the equipment and programs. It also requires operations people, one or two or more, who maintain and handle the equipment and the production facilities. The computer in the briefing room should never be more than a microcomputer or an intelligent terminal, because its principal use is to prepare output, rather than to do analysis. Any analyses that are performed on the data should have been developed previously and approved by senior staff.

Performance considerations. Executive information briefing rooms are high-visibility operations that need to be carefully planned and constantly supervised. One serious factual or presentation error in front of senior managers may be enough to destroy all confidence in its operation. Because it is a focal point for the delivery of executive information support, there should be no problem of staff or budget support. In essence, all presentations should be hand-held and hand-delivered by a knowledgeable staff person. There are a number of performance considerations that should be planned for in detail. These include:

- *Convenience of use* of the room and systems. They should be close to the executives' offices, and even in the board room itself if possible. The room should be usable at any time, and not just at planned or specified times for such things as routine planning reviews. Programs and visuals should be available for use and display on short notice.

- *Staff accessibility* to managers and their staffs for discussion of the methods used, data sources, and approaches.

- *Variety of display capabilities* in addition to the graphics and tables generated from the micro. It should be easy to also use 16 mm movies, 35 mm slides, records, tapes, recordings, and audiovisual mixes.

- *Hard-copy capabilities* for any reports or graphs that are displayed. A full-color printer of sufficient speed should be available to generate any reports requested during the meeting.

- *Verification of accuracy* of the information displayed. This may be from printouts of related computer reports, or on-line query access to certain mainframe files.

- *Adequate security* of information displayed and conversations in the room. The people operating the system must be cleared and instructed in security. The facilities must be locked with limited access. If the rear projection is into a chart room, no sound barriers are needed; but if the rear projection is into a board room, there should be complete sound insulation, with a double-glass screen, and a phone as the only communication between the board room and the projection area.

- *Simplified input requests* for the managers to ask for specific figures. The technical person in charge may have to know many systems details, but the senior managers should be able to ask for information with simple commands.

- *Flexibility of operations* with the capability of changing the mode of presentation, the information files being accessed, and the type of output being produced. There should be above-average speed in data acquisition and analysis.

- *Peak-period support* by extra technical staff and high priority on central computer access. If a senior management discussion or board meeting is underway, there should be nothing with higher priority.

- *Total system reliability* with routine maintenance, backup equipment, and absolutely minimum downtime. It must be integrated with the total computer operations, so that backup methods and equipment are immediately available.

Planning and installation of a briefing room.   Planning and installation of a briefing room should be handled with the same steps and controls as any other Information Services project. There must be approval of the idea, definition of functional requirements, general plans, detailed plans, installation, and a review of the operation.

Typical features of some executive information briefing rooms. The first major corporate briefing room in the United States was installed in the 1920s by the Du Pont Corporation in Wilmington, Delaware, principally to show details of corporate activity compared with plans for all divisions and major products. It consisted of large four-foot-by-eight-foot panels on overhead tracks. The panels were pulled out to be seen by managers in tiered seats. Colored figures and graphs were placed on the panels by hand.

For 50 years this type of room was copied. Many technical improvements have been made, and similar ones are still in use. Some of the improvements have included:

- Backlighted panels with edge-lighted plastic fronts for grease-pencil markings.

- Shadow boxes for charts of all sizes down to 8½ inches by 11 inches.

- Wall charts made of Mylar stretched over a foam core, so they can be carried around easily.

- Loose-leaf or multiplex units for additional wall space.

- Individual light controls on a number of display panels.
- Front-projection and rear-projection screens.
- Double-thickness rear-projection screens for security.
- Electronic consoles for requesting information.
- Computer consoles for calling up information on-line.

In recent years, advances have been made using computers on-line for delivery and display of information. Many of the old features are still in place in briefing rooms because they facilitate the comparison of present data with past data, and hard-copy charts can be perused at any time. Modern briefing rooms also have:

- CRT screen displays for specific inquiries.
- Large-screen CRT displays for presentation in the room.
- Microcomputer capabilities to define, extract, and display information.
- Extract databases of specific information to give immediate and rapid access to senior managers for any combination of data on any type of report or graph.
- Color graphics capability for display and rapid production of hard copy.
- High-speed printers for the distribution of specific reports on demand.

Many senior managers prefer the briefing room approach to the microcomputer in their office because they do not have to get involved in any technical problems; a professional staff displays the information; and access to the computer is handled in the center of a discussion group of other senior managers.

Terminal Graphics for Executives

A minority of executives will want to handle their own terminal graphics system. Those who want such a system will require one that has access to an appropriate database with few commands; powerful macro instructions for setting up graphs; flexibility for modifications and additions; good graphics quality; and the ability to create hard copy, possibly off-line.

Business graphics is a term frequently used for this area of computer output. It covers the type of graphics support needed by managers, rather than the complex plotting of statistics, CAD/CAM production, other engineering design, and geographic mapping. Business graphics generally can be grouped into two areas of interest:

1. *Communication graphics,* which are graphs and charts designed for presentation of information in meetings, scheduling and organization of activities, and graphics support for group decision making. Frequently,

executives who use terminal graphics have a number of profit-plan charts stored for display in small group discussions.

2. *Decision-making graphics,* which are simply an extension of communications graphics, using similar algorithms and formats with the capability of real-time modification to display variances, alternatives, and possibilities that arise in discussion meetings. The same types of graphics are used, but their use is more interactive as decisions are discussed.

The basic systems design of terminal graphics for executives has the same components as any other graphics system. These include a database of information to be used, interactive control, the ability to enter and manipulate data, a range of good-quality graphics functions, and extended features.

The *database of information* to be used by executives for terminal graphics is not necessarily put together in a single file, but the greater the simplicity of operation, the more likely it will be used regularly. The information may include internal and external sources. It is preferable for executive interaction on terminals to have all the information executives are likely to want assembled on a single extract database with relatively simple search and print commands. Obviously, this will not be a fixed database because executives are constantly changing their areas of detailed interest. There usually will be a few features of it that are relatively fixed.

For example, the database should contain plan-versus-actual data for most of the major projects or budgets in the organization. It also should include production and sales data of the major units of interest. The accessible database should be set up so that matrices of information related to subjects of immediate interest can be put into it rapidly by support analysts. There may be a certain amount of data conversion required from other data files, and establishment of a terminology for the data that is acceptable to the manager. This database should be thought of as a flexible file of data in specific areas of interest that can be accessed privately by the executive, even though constant support is needed in the file preparation.

Interactive control should be through a system of menus, fill-out forms, and function keys. The menus should lead through simple choices, such as the type of chart desired, and move to full-screen specification forms that allow the choice of graphic elements and data elements. The specifications should allow the manager to maintain an active "template" into which data can be added or manipulated with little effort relative to the output structure to be obtained. Normally, senior managers will not want to customize their charts, but will be content with specifications of plot size, color, size of type, typeface, line style, and other graphic elements for their particular template. They will want to produce a standard, expected chart at any time by pushing a single function key. They will then want to move back into the workings of the program to make changes in the data.

The *ability to enter and manipulate data,* other than the data in the internal database, is also a desirable feature for many executives. They are frequently in a planning mode and will want to examine a number of "what if" possibilities to determine the relative effects. They will want to build a table by aggregating data through simple functions, then observe the results on charts or data summaries. They will want to reorder, combine, or omit categories to get a more effective display that points up the area of immediate interest. Terminal data entry of long lists of data normally will not be attempted by executives, although they may request their immediate staff to do the job. They are more likely to want vectors of data from other sources entered into their database. This may include information from such external data sources as:

CompuServe, Executive Information Service.

Dialog Information Service, Lockheed.

Dow Jones News Retrieval.

NewsNet.

Nexis and Lexis, Mead Data Central.

The Source.

These are a sampling of the immense amount of information now available on-line. The information is up-to-date and frequently well cross-referenced for easy search. Some have an option of flagging items or values of interest. The information is retrieved rapidly and reasonably. Many executives will review such information only because of their interest in specific numbers. Some will want the capability to extract information from these external files and have it available for display in their own internal database where they can manipulate it. This capability will have to be handled individually by technical personnel.

Executives have a need for a *range of good-quality graphics functions.* They may want to look at straightforward bar charts and graphs, but they will soon want to be able to use a variety of chart types, layouts, and options with the attractive use of varied typography, fill and line patterns, scaling, grid lines, and color. They will be just as interested in selling the results of their analyses with attractive graphics functions as anyone else, particularly if those functions are available with little effort.

There are many *extended features* for graphics production being offered on the market. These may include the ability to place a number of graphs together with clean continuity, or an appropriate library management system to help the executive rapidly find and use a number of graphs at a later date.

The ability to move into the complex area of production of good terminal graphics, and to generate a subset of functions and commands readily used by a particular executive, requires a lot of planning and preparation by technical staff. The steps needed to plan and prepare for such use include:

- Discussing what is desired to be achieved with the executive and offering a number of alternatives that can be handled readily.
- Finding out what types of graphics will best fit executives' needs and having them available in a single package with a single set of simple commands.
- Discussing guidelines for good presentation graphics, such as scales, grids, data values, axis labels, and color combinations.
- Determining data availability and data accessibility.
- Stepping through the guidelines for specific extractions and specific charts.
- Making drafts of available charts.

Hard-Copy Graphics Production Methods

Executives will want three types of graphics production:

1. Terminal graphics (discussed previously).
2. Simple hard-copy graphics for review and discussion.
3. Presentation graphics for display at meetings.

First, executives usually will want to have an integrated graphics capability with the particular computer reporting on analysis systems they use. If it is to be simple data search and extract, or the more popular spreadsheet analyses and elementary statistical functions, there is a need for reducing the complex data relationships to clear visual images. Executives normally will do their analyses with tabular data at the CRT, and many will be inclined in that direction. When they have determined a relationship or a comparison that they want to discuss with others in a meeting, they may want to generate a graphic representation that has the approach they desire. The next problem is to produce that graph in hard copy. Simple graphs on local printers may be produced immediately. More complex graphs on sophisticated print equipment are usually produced off-line by technical staff.

Graphs may be wanted in the form of hard copy, slides, or overhead transparencies, or even blown up for display. Executives generally will use graphics programs that are integrated with their spreadsheet analyses or other systems. These allow them to review the possible results on the screen rapidly, and to observe the relationships in a picture as they proceed with their analyses. They will not want to be concerned with transferring output data to another set of graphics program modules. The types of graphics production handled directly by executives are usually variations of 8½-by-11-inch sheets in black and white or in color. Therefore, integrated programs are usually simply hard-copy printouts.

Stand-alone programs offer many more possibilities and are handled easily by support staff. The staff can take a graph that has been generated and create attractive presentation output. Such programs offer more graph styles and titling options to make the charts attractive, and they can handle more data than can integrated graphing products. Stand-alone programs can combine more data on a single page and produce different graph styles and titles on a page. They also offer more built-in configuration options for various plotters and printers.

The broad classes of hardware for graphics output include plotters, ink-jet printers, and dot-matrix printers. These are options in the immediate office area of the executive. (There are a number of other options, of course. If the data is sent to a central location for plotting and printing, laser printers and professional composition and printing services may be used.) Plotters are good for drawing on larger pieces of paper and for making overhead transparencies. Most plotters have continuous roll paper and come in a variety of widths so they can produce large wall charts, usually in color. Ink-jet printers are usually smaller and cheaper. They are good for transparencies and smaller paper sizes. They are not as fast as plotters, but they can double as text printers and can offer text and color graphics on the same page. Dot-matrix printers are even simpler and are usually connected to terminals for easy production of output reports at a slower rate, but very conveniently. They can also print text and graphics on the same page, although the quality is lower.

Whatever graphics production system is used, it is important that the available graphics software supports the selected graphics hardware. This seems obvious, but some combinations that are sold are difficult to use and not attractive to executives. It is easier to make a simple menu selection in the system used and have the graphics program immediately interface with the available data.

Integrated software that integrates a number of analytical and reporting programs together with the graphics output functions is clearly the type of system that most managers want to have. Present systems have limitations and are expensive, but rapid improvements are being made. Most have good word processing and spreadsheets, but marginal graphics capabilities. Others have excellent graphics, but are poor in data retrieval. Managers want to have the simple capability of using the same set of commands for word processing, graphics, database access, spreadsheets, and communications. As these capabilities become easier to learn and use, and as graphics capabilities are improved, integrated software will be ideal for senior executive to use in analysis, followed by graphics production.

ORGANIZING FOR MANAGEMENT SUPPORT SYSTEMS

Computerworld reported as early as November 1983 that DSS departments were becoming an MIS reality. It was pointed out that MIS has grown from finance, marketing, and management information systems departments. Some incorporate an Information Center or are planning to evolve in that way. The software tools used are very diverse. Whatever their structure, formal DSS departments have frequently become a highly visible adjunct to traditional MIS. Some are even reporting on a level equal to the MIS function.

In some companies the DSS department grew out of an increasing interest in operations research. In other companies there has been substantial growth in areas such as financial analysis, manpower planning, marketing, and program management. This has led to time-sharing networks, with DSS systems networked into corporate mainframes. Users generally work with DSS people to determine what MIS systematization is needed and then learn to do their own applications.

The MSS group's function—DSS, EIS, or Information Center—is to provide decision support services to the entire organization. It is more a methodology group than a repository of information, however. The MSS group instructs managers, implements systems, and coordinates management access to the various information resources. The MSS group must rely on at least three other Information Services groups: Operations, Telecommunications, and Process Control for technology, systems, and data.

Operations group.   Operational support includes the mainline EDP or MIS systems. They support the organization by capturing the base data, and providing necessary information to operate the organization. This group processes numbers, pays for people and supplies, keeps track of orders, monitors the manufacturing system, and keeps records of sales.

The way an organization decides to structure its operational support group will depend upon the function it supports. It may be along division lines in a multidivisional organization, or it could be along functional lines (sales, finance, etc.). There is no simple organizational chart that universally defines this group.

Telecommunications group.   The underlying system for all others is the telecommunications support system. The telecommunications system ties all the others together. The purpose is to improve the effectiveness of the organization through an architecture for communications, the most rapidly changing area in technology. This area requires concentrated effort and planning if an organization is to effectively reach its goal.

Process Control group.   Process Control is the area in an organization where technical computer systems interface in a process designed to eliminate manual operations. A technical process computer may or may not be an analog computer. In general, the process-oriented systems monitor and control a process or activity on a continuous basis using an automatic feedback system and, in turn, act on the feedback in a preprogrammed manner with or without human intervention. These systems supply a large amount of information useful to management. Examples of process support include:

- Automobile industry. Electronic robots and quality testing of electronic components.
- Construction. Computer conveyors that control the movement of material from one location to another.
- Transportation. Automated scale houses.
- Office buildings. Energy control systems that automatically turn energy-using choices on and off to relieve peak loading.

The MSS group may essentially be analysts or may supply a number of support services. Some of the functions that are sometimes grouped with MSS are listed in Figure 3–1.

Corporate Library. The Corporate Library can be a significant part of the DSS function. In the past, the library kept certain magazines and periodicals, maintained a law library, and stored a certain number of reference materials. It was useful as a support group for speech writing for the CEO, and sometimes reported to the public relations department. As part of a DSS group, the library moves quickly forward into managing information access to and from the external databases. There are now more than 5,000 metrically available databases on the market. Combining classical library techniques and methods with modern computer databases is a significant contribution that a DSS group can make to improving the decision-making environment in an organization.

Office Automation. Part of the process of decision making is effective communication of information from one person to another, regardless of location. The historical approach used by Office Automation was for this group to report either to Office Services (because Data Processing would take too long and would come up with an unusable product) or to Data Processing (because

FIGURE 3–1
Decision Support Services

Corporate Library
Office Automation
Corporate Records
Information Center
Consulting Practices

Office Services does not understand technology). Office Automation can be organized effectively as part of DSS because the function of DSS is to use computer technology to enhance the decision-making process. The DSS group should combine technological knowledge with practical and timely implementation.

Corporate Records. This function historically has been the responsibility of the corporate secretary. Unfortunately, the typical corporate-records function provides a secure place and storage system only for those records deemed legally significant. A more complete view of Corporate Records is to view it as a system of storage for all records throughout an organization. By applying a systematic methodology together with technological media such as computers, microfilm, and others, the organization's access to the internal database is greatly enhanced.

Information Center. The Information Center serves as a user-oriented aid to decision making. Using all of the computer capability, user-oriented languages, on-line terminology, graphics techniques, modeling, and other capabilities, this group can provide assistance throughout the organization. The IC typically would be the designer/developer of the executive information system.

Consultation. A very useful function of the DSS group can be to act as the internal management consultant to the organization. In many organizations, systems are designed and developed based upon which group in the MIS organization received the request. There are typically different methods or systems that could be implemented to solve a problem. Questions such as, "What computer?" "What mainframe, mini, or micro?" and "Which language?" need to be determined before a solution is implemented, not after. The DSS group can be designed as an internal consultant who can provide the answers to these questions on a timely basis.

This list of functions of a DSS group is not intended to be all-inclusive, but merely to illustrate the type of responsibilities that may be effective in a DSS group. The specific DSS group functions should be tailored to the needs of the overall organization.

IMPLEMENTING GROUP DECISION SUPPORT SYSTEMS

A group DSS should assist in the process of reaching a decision through group interaction. That is, it should facilitate the process by which groups of people reach conclusions and make decisions. Decision support systems designed for the individual enhance the decision maker's ability to obtain, examine, and analyze data preparatory to decision making. It can even lead the individual decision maker toward innovation. When used in a group setting, therefore, one would expect an improvement in the performance of the group similar to that of the individual. The potential for group DSS is even more substantial, however. Group DSS has the attribute of attacking the process of decision making by providing a clear focus for group discussion. It allows the group to communicate better, identify critical assumptions and objectives, organize discussion, and evaluate multiple options.

The Group Decision Environment[1]

To understand the role of group decision support systems (GDSS), examine the types of environments in which group decisions are made.

Face-to-face. This group is usually rather small and meets in a single physical location such as one participant's office. Meetings in an office normally consist of two to five people. When the group is larger, the meeting is more likely to be held in a conference room. Small groups meeting in an intimate and familiar location will use different media and support systems than larger groups. The types of GDSS will be more on the order of individual DSS models, external database inquiry, graphics, and spreadsheets.

Large groups/face-to-face. A large group in a face-to-face setting needs different kinds of support. In a typical meeting room, one might find a white board, chart, easels, and overhead or 35 mm projection as aids to the decision process. Extending beyond these rather simple aids one might find the use of computer-generated graphics or CRT projection capability. A large setting generally requires a single focal point, such as a moderator or facilitator. Use of individual DSS such as models or database inquiry usually must be prepared in advance. The decision is either somewhat structured or there is an advocate who is seeking ratification.

Dispersed environments. Frequently, participants in a group decision are geographically separate. For slow response the mail may be adequate. Normally, however, the telephone and digital telecommunications significantly facilitate decisions for small groups geographically dispersed. Advances have been made by means of audio and video conference calling, computer messaging and electronic mail, computer conferencing, electronic blackboards, and facsimile transmission. Each of these systems attempts to improve the decision process

---

[1] *EDP Analyzer,* January 1987.

of a geographically dispersed group by enhancing communications among the participants to reduce the negative impact of distance. They do not attempt to increase the analysis and decision process directly, however.

Types of Group Decision Processes

There has been considerable research into the group decision process. Geraldine DeSanctis and Brent Gallupe have described common types of group decision processes.[2]

In a face-to-face small group meeting there is usually an unstructured discussion. The chairperson of the meeting provides the structure, but it can be rather rambling. Often, such meetings are "fact-gathering" and may involve explorations for information, phone calls to others, inquiries, and so forth.

Nominal (desired) face-to-face.   This type of meeting is structured and involves a series of discrete steps. The problem is clearly stated and the group members generate alternatives. Solutions/alternatives are then presented to the group, and the alternatives are listed for the entire group to see. The process calls for each alternative to be discussed and rated, then leading candidates are chosen for more detailed discussion.

Delphi technique.   Group members are often, but not necessarily, geographically dispersed. The chairperson starts the process by clearly defining the problem. This information is sent to each participant, along with a questionnaire asking for potential solutions. Returned questionnaires are summarized and sent back to the participants with a new questionnaire. The process is repeated until a consensus is reached.

Brainstorming.   While alone in a group setting, participants generate ideas or identify problems. It is often counterproductive to evaluate the results of a "brainstorm" at the same time the brainstorming takes place.

Value analysis.   Using a group process to identify objectives and priorities together with a weighting scheme can be particularly effective in achieving group consensus. It allows the group to focus on assumptions and objectives, rather than interpersonal relations or personal agendas. Value analysis also provides a documented audit trail reflecting the process by which the decision was reached. This can be useful in the decision ratification process.

---

[2] Geraldine DeSanctis and Brent Gallupe, "Group Decision Support Systems: A New Frontier," *Data Base* 16, Winter 1985, pp. 3–10.

Design of a GDSS

The design of a GDSS should impact the process of arriving at a decision. Elements of a GDSS include:

- *Database.* Internal and external access to appropriate data sources on a timely basis, capable of display to group participants (CRT, use of Dow Jones, etc.).

- *Application model.* Capability of processing data and alternatives in a reasonable time period and communicating results to participants (spreadsheet, application software, etc.).

- *Communications.* The ability to achieve the best possible person-to-person interface and the best possible data-analysis-to-person interface (overhead projection, audio conferencing, etc.).

- *Facilitator.* The "people" component makes it necessary to have a group facilitator responsible for the overall group decision process.

Figure 3–2 shows the basic facilities that could be included in a group decision support system.

Facilitation. The facilitation of decision making in a group setting is the process of recording, summarizing, prioritizing, and selecting an alternative as a group. While much research has been done regarding the process, most of the technical support of group decision making has been either

FIGURE 3–2
GDSS Facilities

Data Handling	Data Sources	Communications
• Word processing	• Internal databases	• Telephone/audio conferencing
• Data processing	• External databases	• Video conferencing
• Spreadsheet	• Library (internal/ external)	• Electronic messaging
• Graphics	• Presentations	• Electronic mail
• Modeling	• Reading material	• Electronic blackboard
• Database management system		• Facsimile
		• Overhead projection
		• 35 mm slides
		• Chart boards
		• CRT
		• CRT projection

individual-based (data handling and data sources) or communications-based. There has been little work done that applies technology to the process of group decision making.

Group DSS Example

A large eastern chemical manufacturer was evaluating the construction of a $30 million manufacturing facility. For several months, each responsible group involved in the study developed and presented analyses and conclusions. Each of the presentations was convincing. However, the conclusions were contradictory, and the senior management committee was perplexed. It assigned a composite group to iron out the differences among the groups.

Despite the new committee, however, no agreement could be reached because each member represented a particular point of view. It was suggested that the group use a decision support model to assist them.

The committee members started with a relatively simple decision model. First, each of the underlying assumptions was examined and agreed upon by the committee. Differences in opinions were identified and were fairly easy to resolve. Within a week, the group had arrived at a consolidated recommendation. Several benefits were shown by this example:

1. The group was able to agree on a recommendation.
2. The individual members took ownership of the assumptions and conclusions, and thereby the decision.
3. The group members were able to eliminate the parochial views of their own constituencies (functional areas of responsibility), because those views became a part of the whole.
4. The basis of the decision was documented by a presentation for senior management review and ratification.

GDSS Technology

GDSS technology must include use of computer messaging and conferencing, computer graphics, and computer modeling.

Messaging and conferencing.   With today's technology, group decisions generally benefit by adding some video to an audio conferencing system. Full video conferencing is quite expensive, requires simultaneous attendance, and does not adequately capture group nuances.

Audio conferencing has improved substantially with "bridges" and call conveyors. Reasonably priced audio systems are available and common in boardrooms and conference rooms.

Another system that does not require simultaneous attendance is computer messaging and conferencing. Such systems also provide records of the messages. When complex issues are being addressed requiring multiple contacts, it can be damaging to the decision process to play "telephone tag." Further, it is a real advantage to be able to document questions, assumptions, answers, and other input as part of the process of communicating.

There is no question that effective uses of computer conferencing and messaging can enhance the group decision process, but it remains true that such elements as group nuances, inflections, and side comments are lost in this environment.

There has been some research into the social effects of computer-mediated communications used for group decision making. Sara Kiester discusses research done at Carnegie-Mellon University.[3] There are three types of effects when such new technology is introduced.

The first is the intended technological effects. Examples are greater productivity, reduced errors, and greater efficiency.

The second type is the transient effects. These involve organizational adjustments that may gradually disappear. An example is the loss of privacy due to the use of party lines at the introduction of the telephone.

The third type is unintended social impacts. These are permanent changes that are generally unintended. An example is the use of credit cards. The original intention was creation of credit. With the use of automatic tellers, credit cards have become a replacement for cash. The third area is where the Kiester group based their in-depth studies, and where they see some likely long-term social effects.

In face-to-face meetings, people are introduced and assigned a certain group status in the organization. However, computer-mediated communications, such as messaging and conferencing, do not provide the normal type of social-context information. What Kiester observed, which is also intuitive to users, is that communications tend to become "unregulated." Wording becomes more extreme and even impulsive. Users or participants tend to write in an uninhibited manner. In addition, hierarchical and departmental boundaries tend to break down. Because one user does not see the other in a normal social context, messages may be sent to all people on a distribution list, high and low in the organization, without adequate thought and care. Also, computer-aided mediated communication tends to provide people with more information than through conventional means. In the Carnegie-Mellon study, one long-time electronic mail user indicated that 60 percent of the messages of the average 23 messages per day would not have been received under conventional mail distribution systems. The

---

[3] Sara Kiester, "The Hidden Messages in Computer Networks," *Harvard Business Review,* January-February 1986, pp. 46–59.

result is twofold: (1) an increase in the number of people exposed to information; and (2) the possibility of information overload. The unintended result may be less knowledge in spite of increased information exchange. Therefore, structuring of information usage becomes increasingly important.

The Kiester research also explored the effects of computer communications on decision making. One experiment involved a group of managers making decisions about investments. The research compared decisions made in face-to-face meetings with those made using electronic mail. It found that members of the group using electronic mail were slightly less conservative in their investment decisions. That is, they were willing to accept a higher level of risk; yet the managers felt just as confident as when the decisions were made in face-to-face meetings.

Kiester also observed that it takes longer to reach a consensus using computer mediation; minority views are expressed to a greater extent; and less pressure is exerted to "go along" with the majority leadership.

The conclusion that should be drawn from this research is that computer-mediated or computer-aided recommendations in support of group decision making can result in improved decisions depending on such factors as the type of decision, ground rules, and structure. However, careful thought should be given to the kinds of decisions made using this methodology.

Computer graphics.   Significant progress has been made in computer graphics, and it is now possible, practical, and advisable to use computer graphics not only in analysis, but also in such areas as sales presentations and formal presentations within an organization.

There are two important elements in computer graphics for group decision support. First, high-quality graphics software is needed to create the graphics. Second, a good means of presenting the graphics is essential. The issue of quality graphics software is significant because it is essential to the analysis process that a variety of graphics capabilities be available, and to have the ability to analyze a situation and select the graph that best fits and presents the information. Dona Meilach has outlined a good view of presentation-graphics principles.[4]

There are a number of presentation techniques that can be used for group presentations of graphics techniques, including visual transparencies for overhead projectors using computer-driven pen plotters, 35 mm slides, and on-line projection systems.

---

[4]Dona Meilach, *Dynamics of Presentation Graphics* (Homewood, Ill.: Dow Jones-Irwin, 1986).

The technology for both black and white and color transparencies has advanced to a level that makes it practical for small to medium-sized companies as well as large organizations to implement. The use of on-line projections and 35 mm slides has become more economical, but they are not yet commonplace. According to the *EDP Analyzer,* January 1987, much progress has been made; graphics projections of acceptable quality were found in all price ranges, from under $1,000 up, at the 1986 National Computer Graphics Conference.

ESTABLISHING AN OPTIMUM BALANCE

The intent of this manual is to show how to establish an optimum balance of validity, efficiency, and effectiveness in the use of management support systems in an Information Services program. Individuals may find special advantages for their purposes in particular systems approaches. The organization, however, will always achieve greater value from its information resources when the systems and processes used are measured by these commonly accepted yardsticks.

Validity

- Is the information produced usable and timely enough to meet the operational decision requirements of management, as well as accurate enough to meet financial and statutory requirements?
- Are adequate controls maintained over computer processing and information use; controls that are commensurate with good operating principles?
- Does the use of the information output meet financial and legal requirements?
- Does the information produced meet the decision, operational, and technical needs of the organization?

Efficiency

- Do the methods and systems produce information at an optimum or competitive cost?
- Are necessary management and audit controls maintained over the use of the organization's information resources?
- Are reasonable procedures, techniques, and standards followed at all levels of the organization?
- Is there an adequate balance of personnel, hardware, and software so there are no system acquisitions grossly in excess of needs?

Effectiveness

- Are organizational resources being applied to the most profitable and useful applications of computer-based systems?
- Have proper priorities been given to MSS development and implementation, based on business needs and objectives?
- Do the installed systems continue to be used in accordance with management, cost, and profitability objectives that originally were established for them?
- Are significant opportunities being lost because of the lack of certain systems in the overall development and implementation plan and program?

The last point well may be the most important for many organizations. There *are* significant opportunities to be gained by implementing management support systems that will improve management decision making and control at different levels. These are opportunities that can be seized by understanding the many possibilities and applications of such systems. This fact should not give carte blanche to the development of any system that anyone thinks might be useful. When system requests are reviewed, the above list of management questions may be applied profitably to a proposed project to determine whether to proceed with it.

Chapter Four

Executive Information Systems

Executive information systems (EIS) are systems designed for use by the two top levels of management to help understand the significance of available information for monitoring and for status access. Executive information systems can be successful when they address specific management needs for information. If management explores them and uses them for insight, there can be a progression from simple reports to variance analysis to investigation and modeling. The organizational impact of EIS can be realignment of priorities, mainstream integration of Information Services, molding of executive expectations, and/or influencing data architecture design.

The components of an EIS are a database management system, inquiry and analysis functions, and graphical and report-writing functions. The presence of a business problem and accepted management sponsorship are needed for successful implementation. The stage theory of development is discussed. Some implementation problems are described, not the least of which is the corporate culture, or management style, of an organization.

The requirements for data and its acquisition are reviewed. Some approaches are the by-product approach, the null approach, the key indicators approach, and the total study approach. The Critical Success Factor (CSF) approach is favored, and the development of CSF tracking is described. The use of Key External Factors is noted.

Some data access challenges are discussed, particularly for foreign file interfaces. The advantages and features of micro-mainframe connections are listed. Human/machine interfaces and person-to-person interactions and their problems are discussed.

MEETING THE INDIVIDUAL
NEEDS OF EXECUTIVES

Executive information systems (EIS) and executive support systems (ESS) are terms used in the literature for MSS that are designed for the use of the two top levels of management. Their purpose is to make sense of information that has been extracted for management or is made available to them for search. They are used principally to monitor and to provide status access. Some managers prefer to look at a variety of information to improve their "feel" of the meaning of the information.

MIT's Center for Information Systems Research (CISR) defines EIS as a "terminal or micro-based workstation designed to provide access to personal, corporate and external databases." While this definition might encompass EIS, it is probably too nonspecific to add much to our understanding of this technology.

Computerworld offers a slightly more informative, if not more rigorous, definition of EIS: "EIS is an on-line, user-defined system that provides internal and external information, both data and text. They can extract, filter and compress data into useful information."

Unfortunately, neither attempt at defining EIS contributes much to an overall distinction between EIS and other forms of DSS computing. This is perhaps the reason why CISR has stated that the penetration of EIS into major U.S. corporations is approaching 50 percent. Without a rigorous definition of EIS, such statistics should be viewed with considerable caution.

How many corporations are actually using EIS today? Although no formal studies have been done, most would agree that when defining the user as an executive, EIS use falls below 5 percent. Among those, however, there is considerable enthusiasm. Robert Reuss, CEO of Central Corporation, said of his system:

> The financial statement information I now get through the computer enables me to run the company much better than before. It is more complete and timely, and I would rather get it this way than dig around in a file. When we want information we look to see how we can get it through the computer.

One of the fundamental problems typically found in addressing the subject of EIS is understanding an individual executive's needs. Most often implementors of these systems approach the executive's information requirements as an extension of their own experience. Such an orientation usually results in two polarized views of the executive:

1. The executive has no need for information, because the day is spent with people, not numbers. If any information is required, it always will come from the staff, not a computer.

2. The executive is a reviewer of information, never a generator. Status reports are the executive's mainstay. Therefore, any EIS should be designed around status reporting.

The first assumption usually leads one to dismiss the concept of EIS as ill-conceived and, therefore, not deserving of serious attention. The second leads to an increase in the number of reports submitted to the executive, prompting an increasing litany of laments from this misunderstood group. In the words of a midwestern manufacturing CEO, ''Why do I have to have dozens of reports a month, and yet very little of the real information I need to manage this company?''

It is true that executives are often decision ratifiers rather than decision makers. Most analysis and recommendations do not come from the executive, but from his or her staff. But this speaks less of absolute need for information than it does for the quality of information required.

The second (status reporting) assumption, while recognizing the executive's need for information, tends to take a very one-dimensional view of how executives learn and make decisions. Cognitive psychologists at Harvard University have been interviewing senior executives in the United States to better understand the executive manager's learning process. Though not complete, the study indicates that while a company's top management does not actively produce analysis, its role is significantly more than that of a ''rubber stamp.'' Its decision-making process is reflected in Figure 4–1.

During the 1960s, there was little information available to satisfy the needs of management. As a result, the major thrust was toward generating data. Low-level, high-volume transaction systems were created, and management began to receive the numbers it requested.

Then at the beginning of the 1970s, management began to rebel. It knew the answers it sought were there somewhere, but it lacked the time and commitment

FIGURE 4–1
Executive Decision-Making Process

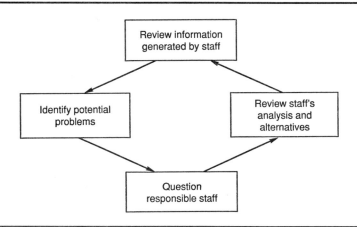

to find them. Aware of the problem, I/S began to shift some of the emphasis away from data production. What management needed, went the reasoning, was not data, but information. Information is nothing but data with perspective, and that could be produced through improved reporting.

The emphasis on reporting requirements, in turn, gave birth to a new generation of programming languages: fourth-generation languages. Armed with these tools, I/S began to deliver what executive management thought it wanted: reports. Estimates indicate that in 1985, data processing generated no less than 4.5 billion reports in the United States alone.

In the late 1980s, the need was not just for information (recall the manufacturing CEO's lament), but for *relevant* information. Indeed, it is this need for information relevant to the individual executive that is a major reason for EIS failure.

The executive management of a major defense contractor was frustrated by the inability of existing reporting systems to meet its needs. It requested I/S to "do something." The director of Information Systems created what he termed an EIS, using NOMAD2 as his implementation tool. Initially, his concept of "a few good reports" was met with enthusiasm. Soon, however, individual executives began to ask for modifications to the standard reports, each wanting a specific functional perspective. At first, the director could satisfy the requests, introducing menus with increasing size and complexity. Eventually, however, the sheer weight of the system was more than the hardware could support. Faced with the untenable choice of either nonrelevant information or huge commitments in resources, the executives began to use the EIS less and less, and it ultimately slipped into oblivion.

This is not to say that an EIS based upon the electronic delivery of standard status reports will always fail. There will continue to be executives who will find their needs sufficiently met through status reporting, so an EIS with this orientation will be viewed as successful. But as implied by the executive decision process (Figure 4–1), relevancy of information cannot always be determined before the fact. Indeed, in many cases, such relevancy is the product of discovery, which in turn is an outgrowth of exploration as in Figure 4–2.

THE ORGANIZATIONAL IMPACT OF EIS

Decision support systems among knowledge workers have had a subtle but pronounced effect on corporate data architecture as well as on organizational operations. The matrix effect, while significant, pales in comparison to the potential organizational impact of executive use of EIS, or specific DSS.

FIGURE 4-2
Creating Discovery through Exploration

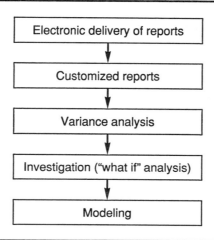

There are four major implications of introducing EIS into the organization:

1. Realignment of priorities. Priority alignment deals with the synchronization of priorities across an organization's hierarchy. In a study conducted some years ago, a CEO asked members of his staff what they felt were his priorities for them. The staff's activities for the past year were audited to see if reality agreed with their stated perceptions. Each staff member then performed the same function with his or her staff, and so on down through the corporation.

The conclusion of the study was that 55 percent of the organization's employees did not understand upper management's priorities, and that over 70 percent of staff had conducted the prior year's business without apparent consideration for those priorities. The report concluded that poor communication was the problem and recommended regular reviews to audit understanding and compliance.

While regular reviews might be a good short-term solution, they will probably fail in the long run because they lack the natural organizational inertia to continue. It is precisely in this regard that EIS can be such an invaluable aid.

When top-level management begins to use EIS regularly, the invariable consequence is that staff members ask Information Services for the same information (relative to their responsibilities). Knowing that the vice president is regularly tracking absenteeism, for example, will automatically and naturally sensitize the staff to that problem. No meetings, memos, or telephone calls need to take place.

Over time, quite by its own inertia, the successful implementation of EIS usually will bring about a realignment of priorities, and with it a far more synchronized organization.

2. I/S mainstream integration. Within many corporations Information Services is viewed and treated as merely a service department. This view is reinforced by the relative isolation of Information Services within the general business community.

If effective, an EIS can provide the springboard to integrate Information Services into the mainstream organization. While rarely credited for integration by itself, an EIS can provide Information Services visibility and an opportunity to display strategic vision. The rest, of course, is up to I/S personnel.

3. Molding of executive expectations. As discussed above, executives traditionally have been consumers of data, but rarely demanders of data. In effect, the I/S has been the Henry Ford of data processing, telling executives, "You can get cars in any color you want, as long as it is black."

For perhaps the first time, executives will feel a sense of control over the second most valuable resource in the company (people being the most valuable resource).

4. Influencing data architecture design. Many Information Services organizations like the idea of EIS, but balk at beginning. The prevailing attitude is, "It sounds good, but our data is a mess. Once we get the data in better shape, then we will look closer at it." This attitude will result in the perpetuation of the by-product approach to data. It must be remembered that executive use of DSS can determine just what data is required. How, then, can one expect to "get the data right" without direction from that use? And how can that direction be provided in the abstract, without actual hands-on use?

Executives can and should have an extraordinary impact on data flow in an organization, not just that which is provided directly from Information Services, but from all staff organizations as well.

It should be emphasized that the organizational effects that have been discussed are evolutionary, not revolutionary. They may take several years to fully occur, and most frequently, when they do happen, EIS will not be recognized as the catalyst.

In the same way, the impact of executive computing can be controlled by regulating the penetration of EIS into executive ranks. This may be important in terms of the overall organization, as well as the I/S organization's ability to support it.

COMPONENTS OF AN EXECUTIVE
INFORMATION SYSTEM

There are three major components of an executive information system. These components are:

1. Database management system.
2. Inquiry and analysis functions.
3. Graphical and report-writing functions.

In an overall decision support system in which an EIS is usually embedded, there are, from the technical point of view, a number of other separate components. They are those parts of the system necessary for it to operate but completely the concern of the technical staff of Information Services. They should be transparent to the users of the system. One of these hidden components is *multiple file management,* in which data is brought into the accessible file, possibly an extract database, from a variety of internal and external data sources. This includes the problems of data input control and security, and recovery and backup preparations. Another hidden component is *modeling support,* in which data from various sources is controlled and transformed into acceptable files for specific models. Individual analysts normally perform this function for their own models, but if a model is required by a senior manager, it would be expected to have tested algorithms and a standard data entry. A third hidden component is the *operating system commands,* which would be invoked automatically by simple commands entered by a manager at the microcomputer level.

1. The *database management system* observable by an executive organizes data in relevant and useful ways. It must provide ready access to the user and also be capable of collecting and storing data from many sources, such as transactional systems, operational databases, external data vendors, and data entered on-line by the executive or other staff members. It should be a straightforward procedure to enter new data or to change relationships between data groups. The data structure should be adaptable to changes in organizational structure and new reporting relationships. It would not be expected that the adaptations would be handled by the executive, but they should be handled readily by technical staff.

2. The *inquiry and analysis functions* are a variety of programmed subroutines and arithmetical and statistical packages that will be used for manipulating and analyzing the information organized in the database. All the routines should be organized so that the same data elements and lists of data will be accepted directly as input. There must be freedom to move data between subroutines without further manipulation so that the underlying relationships between various data elements may be studied. These elements may include financial, mar-

keting, external economic, and operational data. This sort of structuring is most readily handled in smaller extract databases. Senior managers are not likely to wait for extensive sorting and searching for the data they need. Much of it must be pre-analyzed and summarized after it has been deemed appropriate for the type of access desired. The inquiry and analysis functions then must be able to pass vectors of information freely among the routines that are available.

3. *Graphic and report-writing functions* need to be offered in a suitable variety to give executives the capability of viewing data from several angles. They also should be printed clearly with simple headings so that output results of any modeling or analysis can be communicated effectively.

An EIS thus is a special class of DSS in which a sufficient subset of possible functions is readily available. It need not be a comprehensive computer software system covering every conceivable type of analysis being used by staff. It must cover what senior managers feel will be used, however; and it must be flexible, with adaptable database management, powerful modeling capabilities with simple commands, and a full range of accessible mathematical and statistical techniques. It also must have user-friendly report writing, and the ability to produce presentation-quality graphics.

For rapid implementation of an EIS, most of these features must be found within the particular package selected. Such packages vary widely. Therefore, there must be a good idea of what goals and methods will be expected by the executives involved. Possibly it will be necessary to start up an experimental system, let the executives use it for a while, then determine what the system lacks. This will lead to a good set of functional requirements if the executives cooperate, or if senior staff will handle the analytical and testing phase. There must be active and ongoing support from potential top management users, although they may delegate the first steps of testing to their staff.

IMPLEMENTING AN EXECUTIVE INFORMATION SYSTEM

Implementation of an EIS system can be handled as a specific development project, with organizational, implementation, and operational phases. The development procedure is for a relatively unstructured service, however, rather than for a specific applications program. Frequently, senior management will not be able to specify what service they want until they have had an opportunity to try a few options. Essentially, a prototype system that provides useful numbers in a specific area needs to be developed and tested. If the results are acceptable, a more useful system can be put in place.

Eliot Levinson describes the stage theory created by Rand Corporation to develop and utilize technical innovations.[1] It considers that the utility of an innovative idea is discovered and invented as the idea is utilized. This is why prototyping can produce more useful systems with less effort. New technologies are seldom implemented as planned. To be successful, the technology of an EIS system must change and adapt as the managers using it discover the possibilities and refine the requirements. Levinson gives five key elements that impact the effectiveness of an EIS system. They are:

1. The presence of a business problem or vision used to define the purpose of the system.
2. Titular sponsorship by a senior executive and managerial sponsorship by his or her delegate.
3. The organization of management information systems (MIS) computing groups as effective support organizations that translate managerial needs into technical systems.
4. The existence of a well-defined, accessible database.
5. Effective management of resistance that occurs as the new systems change established procedures and reporting relationships.

These key elements will be of varying importance during the development and implementation of a system, but they all must be given serious consideration.

The tasks during the *organizational phase* are to define the business problem that will justify the system, to obtain sufficient support and technical capability to accomplish the objectives, to determine what types of information are available that the manager will require, and to state explicitly what is hoped to be accomplished.

The tasks during the *installation phase* are to define the technical aspects of the project, to obtain organizational support for the effort, to build initial databases and prepare access methods, to develop the required procedures, and to make adjustments to augment or decrease the scope of the system as the manager reaches an understanding of it.

The tasks during the *operational phase* are to aid the manager in using the system, and to make modifications and extensions to it as desired. Levinson points out that institutionalization of the system will occur as the system is used by successors to the original executive, as the system is diffused to other executives, and as the system effects changes in the work of subordinates. In some instances, the system will be discarded through lack of use or by direction.

---

[1]Eliot Levinson, "The Implementation of Executive Support Systems," CISR WP no. 119, Center for Information Systems Research, M.I.T. Sloan School of Management, October 1984.

A specific business problem should be identified, at least informally by a manager, if the EIS effort is to have adequate direction and defined objectives. The principal objective should be the solution of that business problem. There are three general reasons for implementing an EIS system:

1. To solve a specific business problem routinely.
2. To make executive decision making more efficient.
3. To signal to the organization that the executive feels that more use should be made of available computing technology.

The business problem that has been agreed upon will define the direction and extent of the development effort. Without identification of the problem at the early stages of implementation, the system will be perceived as a toy. There may be a serious cost control or investment problem that the top executive wishes to analyze frequently and in detail. If this is so, justification of the system is straightforward. In any event, clear statements should be made about the system's capabilities and benefits before the project proceeds.

Sponsorship of the development of the system should be stated clearly and understood by all who have a part to play in it. To be successful, it clearly should be the senior executive's system. The sponsor should sign off on the project before the development is started, and should be willing to create and fund the organization that will carry it out. The sponsor should be involved in the definition and development of the system, and should be prepared to use its outputs and to advertise its effectiveness if it proves reasonably successful. The initial sponsor also should be prepared to move the idea through the organization if it appears to be of value. The sponsor should be the end-user, at least initially, and thus should feel directly involved in the outcome of the effort.

Support of the data processing, or MIS, group is fundamentally necessary throughout the whole life cycle of the system. An EIS system is essentially a minor extract from large, maintained, controlled files. It can be handled smoothly and routinely, under tight security and control, or it can be a continual set of problems. Occasionally, MIS groups try to remain aloof from end-user computing functions. Since EIS systems are at a critically high level in the organization, however, they are an end-user function that must be given priority attention and support. Otherwise, there will be inefficient use of the computer and bothersome problems of data ownership. On the other hand, the systems can supply useful information to senior management and therefore will have a very high profile. Whatever the organizational relationships, EIS systems always should be given priority attention. If a proposed system does not appear to be technically feasible, this concern should surface at the earliest possible time.

There must be databases of useful information if there is to be a successful EIS system. Linear files and uncontrolled information raise too many obstacles to the successful use of a system by an executive. Any substantive business questions will require historical information, current operating information, and tested projection models available for use. Full database files are not a requirement, however. Controlled extract files that have been set up for ready search and access are usually superior for such functions because they have ready availability and reduced search time. This may require some sort of network access, which would ordinarily be simplified for executive use. EIS systems need a simple command language to be used successfully.

There will be problems of resistance to EIS systems at all levels in the organization. People will want to bypass, withhold information from, or actively oppose the system. This problem is discussed in the following section.

There are no hard and fast rules for the implementation process of executive computing. There are, however, some basic concepts to which one must be sensitive.

Opportune timing. In general, the best time to begin introducing EIS is during less-than-tranquil periods within the company. During smooth sailing, there is usually little interest on the part of executive management to change and to try new things. Quite the contrary, the prevailing attitude may be, "If it ain't broke, don't fix it."

A time when management is searching for solutions, however, might be excellent for introducing an EIS, particularly if it addresses any of the relevant issues grabbing the attention of executives.

Starting with a pilot project. If an EIS is launched from any executive "wish list" of Critical Success Factors, it rarely will be possible to implement those factors concurrently. Priorities will have to be set and followed.

Conventional wisdom dictates starting with a pilot approach, and starting small. This orientation is popularly used when implementing lower-level computer systems and is widely advocated by much of IBM's literature. The underlying philosophy of the pilot approach is to start small and fail small; however the inverse also applies (start small and succeed small). When dealing with long-term application development, a small success is perfectly acceptable. Executive computing, on the other hand, usually equates a small success with a trivial success. Such initial contact with EIS will merely confirm earlier suspicions. Convinced that the EIS approach does not offer any significant enhancement to the work day, the executive may remove it, the system, and EIS will be stillborn.

If practical considerations force a slow start, then begin with a large pilot project. Perhaps there is a pressing project under way that requires monitoring. Maybe the CEO reads an article in the *Harvard Business Review* and is suddenly vitally interested in inventory levels. When choosing a CSF to launch an executive DSS, one should never start small.

Selecting desired capabilities: What should an EIS do? While there are more differences than similarities among systems, the range of capabilities includes:

- Selective viewing of status reports and graphics.
- Automatic updating (refreshing), usually overnight.
- Organization and presentation of viewing options in a format meaningful to the individual executive.
- Customized, on-demand informal reporting and graphics.
- Variance analysis on predefined data.
- Access and delivery of public databases.
- Electronic distribution by the user of predefined and explorative information.
- Basic word processing for memo writing.
- Exploration of problems beyond strictly predefined boundaries.
- Ability to closely interface with any software familiar and/or necessary to the user.
- System and data security appropriate to the unusually sensitive nature of the EIS.
- The ability to master all capabilities with no more than a 30- or 60-minute instruction.

It should be mentioned that no existing EIS fits all these capabilities perfectly. As in any other evaluation of DSS software, one should test it to discover its weaknesses and then, if it is chosen, find technical and organizational methods of overcoming the software's shortfalls.

Gaining executive support.   Even the most sophisticated software will not remove Information Services from the burden (or opportunity) of supporting the EIS. Extreme care should be taken in selecting support personnel. The following guidelines should be helpful in working with this critical user group:

- Ensure that all personnel have a professional image. In short, they should not be people with whom the executive would feel uncomfortable.
- All support staff must be time-aware; that is, they should be sensitive to the value that both the company and the executive place on his or her time.
- Accessibility is important, since the frustration level of the executive typically is low.

- Anyone assigned to support executive computing should understand the needs of the individual executive. Few executives will want to continue reexplaining their particular requirements to each new staff member who appears. For this reason, it is advisable to assign support personnel to individuals, rather than pull from a pool of resource people.

The concept of extensive support is not contrary to the spirit of IBM's credo of helping end-users help themselves. Quite the contrary. Once implemented, EIS will enable executives to help themselves as they have never been able to before. This is simply the recognition that, given the importance of this particular user group, a little extra help is a wise investment.

A general review checklist for installing an EIS is given in Figure 4–3.

INFORMATION REQUIREMENTS AND DATA ACQUISITION

Critical to implementing an EIS is the identification of what information should be provided to the target executives. While most would acknowledge this issue as fundamental, few charged with EIS responsibility recognize the magnitude of this task.

Perhaps the single largest reason for failures at this point can be traced to the traditionally isolated service role of Information Services. I/S is typically far more comfortable responding to requests for data than initiating data flows. Fortunately, the proliferation of DSS over the past few years has helped bridge this consumer/provider gap. Unfortunately, lack of executive involvement in this trend has increasingly disenfranchised executives from this data-flow process. This trend has severely limited the ability of Information Services to understand and satisfy executives' need for information.

There are five basic approaches currently in use for assessing the information needs of an executive:

1. By-product approach.
2. Null approach.
3. Key indicator approach.
4. Total study approach.
5. Critical Success Factors approach.

The fifth method (Critical Success Factors), while by no means the most popular, is gaining increasing attention for use in establishing EIS.

FIGURE 4–3
Implementing Executive Information Systems

No.	Item	Yes	No	N/A	Comments
		Responses			
1.	Do executives use EIS for computer support?	___	___	___	
2.	Have executives been provided with a defined decision support process?	___	___	___	
3.	Do executives combine internal and external data for decision making?	___	___	___	
4.	Does the EIS support group understand the various methods of accessing executive data?				
	a. By product?	___	___	___	
	b. Null?	___	___	___	
	c. Key indicator?	___	___	___	
	d. Total?	___	___	___	
	e. Critical Success Factor?	___	___	___	
5.	Do you use Critical Success Factor analysis in defining EIS needs?	___	___	___	
6.	Are the Critical Success Factors defined by an interview process?	___	___	___	
7.	In designing an EIS delivery system, are the following considered?				
	a. Data access method.	___	___	___	
	b. Human/machine interface.	___	___	___	
	c. Use of graphics and color.	___	___	___	
	d. Response time.	___	___	___	
	e. Type of entry system.	___	___	___	
8.	Have the following been explored for the EIS?				
	a. Selective viewing of status reports and graphics.	___	___	___	
	b. Automatic updating.	___	___	___	
	c. Organization and presentation of options in an individualized format.	___	___	___	
	d. Customized, on-demand informal reporting and graphics.	___	___	___	
	e. Variance analysis.	___	___	___	
	f. Access and delivery of public database.	___	___	___	
	g. Electronic distribution of information.	___	___	___	
	h. Basic word processing.	___	___	___	
	i. "What-if" analysis.	___	___	___	
	j. Exploration of problems beyond predefined boundaries.	___	___	___	
	k. Ease of use by the executive.	___	___	___	
	l. Security and disaster recovery.	___	___	___	
	m. Ease of learning.	___	___	___	

By-Product Approach

The by-product approach is the most common method through which information is targeted for management consumption. The foundation of the by-product approach is a large investment in production systems. The information generated by these systems is provided to the lowest level of knowledge worker, who then extracts and summarizes from this vast body of data. This organizational level then passes its interpretation up to the next level, which in turn interprets, extracts, and summarizes the content, ultimately continuing the upward flow.

This bottom-up approach to shaping the data flow is effective in that the information finally received by the executive is quite usable, having been refined from its raw state. There are several aspects of the by-product process, however, that render it incapable of satisfying many critical managerial needs.

Wrong data.   To some extent, virtually every corporation employs the by-product approach. But ask typical executives how well they think the existing system satisfies their need for information. Most often, success is merely coincidental, because the effectiveness of this approach is largely dependent on the ability of analysts and lower-level managers to correctly anticipate the needs and workstyles of top management.

Bland data.   Because information is being delivered in production-line fashion, what ultimately arrives on the executive's desk is the lowest-common-denominator version of the corporation's critical data. Because the data is rarely personalized for individual needs, the executive is required to sift through dozens of reports to find the meaning behind the numbers. Ironically, because the information lacks targeting, the reward for this effort all too frequently is answers to questions the executive is not asking.

Old data.   Every level of interpretation, every stage in the process of summarization, takes time. Manually, delivery of information can be slowed to a point where it is stale beyond usefulness. The judicious use of DSS can, as has been demonstrated, accelerate the delivery process. In this way, DSS can be used to limit the aging effect of the filtration process. The structured use of DSS, however, tends to enforce a production orientation to information delivery, which in turn limits the ability to target the data flow to the individual executive's needs.

In a very real sense, the by-product approach is a de facto admission on the part of the organization that says, "I really do not know what information is required, so I will provide whatever I think the executive might want, and let him or her choose." The by-product method of information definition often lacks the ability to deliver the right information to the right person in the right form at the right time.

Null Approach

This approach takes a more direct view of the executive's information requirements. The null view states that the executive is a ''gut feel'' person, an intuitive type who bases decision making not on the external availability of information, but on a sixth sense. In other words, the executive does not really rely on data to function, so why go to the trouble and expense of defining and delivering information that will not be used?

While few would be so explicit, most would admit that high-level management spends less time with data and certainly relies less on its existence than most knowledge workers in the organization.

The Harvard research project cited earlier observed that, unlike analysts, most executives are not information gatherers. That is, when faced with the need to make a decision, analysts will generally gather all the relevant information first, even if this means delaying the decision. Because decisions at this level are less time-critical, this orientation is practical. Perhaps also contributing to this approach is the number of levels of review to which most decisions are exposed.

However, there is a time-sensitivity to most executive decisions. Rather than delay a decision until all the information is gathered, the executive will act based on strategic timing. Increasing the information float results in a corresponding increase in the risk associated with a time-sensitive decision.

Unlike the null approach, which assumes an unwillingness on the part of the executive to *use* information, the Harvard study describes an unwillingness to *wait for* information. Perhaps this is one reason the executive is thought of as being intuitive. In the face of irrelevant or missing data, the senior manager has very little else upon which to rely.

Key Indicator Approach

This method is a well-intentioned effort to avoid the problems associated with the by-product approach. Existing information delivery systems provide too much data, and too little relevant information, and they provide it too late. To solve this problem, proponents of the key indicator approach try to define that data which represents the pinnacle of the data flow, and then automate its delivery. The major thrust of the key indicator approach is to concentrate on delivering only that data determined to be most critical to the corporation. This orientation is a step in the right direction and, in fact, represents recognition of the limitations of a bottom-up flow of data. Its primary weakness, however, is in the definition of critical data, or the key indicators.

Key corporate indicators typically are defined at the top of the organization. While such indicators as stock price, corporate cash flow, and profitability may be of critical interest to a CEO, a vice president of manufacturing would find them of little use in day-to-day decision making. The same, of course, could be said of most of the CEO's staff.

The key indicator approach is right to want to limit and target information. Its failure is in the rigid manner in which the selected data flow is defined.

Total Study Approach

This approach is the antithesis of the key indicator method, in that it seeks to involve *all* executives in the data definition process. Under this methodology, a consensus of indicators is sought, and then data is targeted around that consensus. A full systems analysis is required.

The total study orientation is right in trying to involve all executives, since only through involvement will they accept ownership of the data, and only through ownership will an EIS work.

The problem with the total study approach to data definition, besides the painful process of consensus management, is that it unfailingly results in a lowest-common-denominator definition of critical data. Individual perspectives regarding functional, divisional, and application needs cannot be accommodated. It is precisely these different perspectives, however, that transform EIS from mechanistic mediocrity to a powerful and focused executive aid.

Critical Success Factors Approach

Establishing Critical Success Factors (CSFs) is a method by which the EIS implementor can define what is critical, not only to the corporation, but to the individual executive. Because the information being delivered is customized, it has a much better chance of being useful. Because it is targeted, rather than bottom-up, it has a much better chance of being used. While CSFs imply a recognition of factors vital to an organization's success, they are more appropriately tuned to the executive's success. This avoids the lack of proper targeting that is often at the root of much of the EIS failure.

Because the primary value of CSFs is in targeting information to an individual's needs, it is fundamental that the delivered information be clearly relevant. This basic premise mandates that each executive define his or her information needs. It is critical that no intermediary be employed. Neither I/S nor a staff assistant can fill this function. Even if clairvoyant, no assistant can instill the sense of ownership of data that is required to form a successful EIS.

While a needs assessment is perhaps the most pivotal part of establishing CSFs, most executives are unprepared to express their information requirements. Sometimes this results from decades of being molded by the by-product supply of data. Frequently, at least in part, many executives have had such preconceived notions regarding the unavailability of data as to inhibit their ability to even create a wish list of information. For whatever reason, a common first step in CSF definition is the interview process.

Conducting the interview.   The executive interview naturally should be scheduled in advance, and the participant should be informed in advance as to the purpose of the meeting, its duration, and expected outcome. It is best to keep the interviews short (one or two hours). For this reason, the interview is frequently broken into two segments: the first meeting identifies objectives and goals, and the second identifies measurements for the CSFs.

As mentioned earlier, the identification of Critical Success Factors is not an intuitive process. The interview must be creative and extractive in both form and content. While the interviewer should certainly not overlook the obvious (what factors are most important in conducting your business?), the use of open-ended questions is usually far more effective.

- Imagine you have been on vacation in Bermuda for one month, far from contact with your office. It is Monday morning; you have just returned to your desk. What are the first things on which you will want to be briefed?

- If you could have ten minutes of access to your competitor's information, what would you like to see?

- If your competitor had access to your information, what would you least like him to see?

Each question is designed to help the executive reach beyond data that traditionally has been available and to extend into the data that has the most critical impact on his or her business.

The second part of the interview is designed to help transform the wish list into a practical data flow. This requires assignment of measures by which CSFs can be tracked and explored. Like the assignment of CSFs, developing measures requires imagination and flexibility.

In general, there are two types of CSF measures, "hard" and "soft." *Hard measures* relate to those factors for which specific, concrete definitions can be obtained. In the purest sense, stock price can be considered a hard measure, since there is only one, uncontestable value.

Soft measures, conversely, are poorly defined. A good example of a CSF for which only soft measures exist is employee morale. Few companies can access a database on the first of the month and find that morale for the preceding quarter was "8.4." Yet this indeed might be a legitimate CSF for any number of executives.

Having defined the CSF, it is the interviewer's responsibility to help arrive at reasonable measures for morale. One might, for instance, pick a composite index for employee morale consisting of such incidental measures as the number of sick days, turnover, inventory shrinkage by theft, and items in the suggestion box.

Naturally, not all measures are purely hard or soft, but rather various degrees of "firm." Revenue, for example, may appear hard at first glance. But many companies have existed and continue to exist with multiple definitions for revenue. If this sounds questionable, ask Accounting, Finance, and Sales for last month's revenue numbers. It is not unusual for considerable disparities to develop, reflecting the multiple ways one can define revenue (intercompany transfer pricing, intracompany transfer pricing, eliminations, foreign exchange gain/loss). Any multiple definitions of CSFs must be negotiated away prior to establishing a data flow based on the definition. Obviously, achieving agreement on such politically charged topics is rarely a trivial matter.

Who should conduct the CSF interviews? Not surprisingly, there is considerable disagreement on this issue. While the use of corporate staff ensures that interviewers have familiarity with the business, they may lack internal credibility and interview experience, and, in addition, may bring to the interview preconceived notions that may inhibit its usefulness.

The use of outside consultants is quite common, despite their lack of familiarity with the company's business. Although a good consultant will compensate with a thorough study of the subject corporation, the source of the interviewer will no doubt continue to be subject to individual preference.

Selecting the indicators.   Following are some general rules to follow when selecting CSF indicators:

- Although some commonality among indicators is to be expected, considerable diversity will and should exist.
- When selecting the indicators, probably the most important consideration is that they be assignable for accountability. What possible value is there in insight that cannot be followed by action?
- To assist in assigning accountability, all variables should tie to lower-level indicators applicable for mid-management.
- All indicators must be documented as to their definition, the data sources, and the requisite frequency with which the data should be refreshed.

The importance of emphasizing the current information needs of the executive must be recognized, rather than merely static status reporting. Critical active projects, for example, very well might be found on many executive CSF lists.

Finally, and perhaps most fundamentally, the identification of CSFs must not be restricted to that data which is most easily supplied. To do this is to pay lip service to CSFs, yet continue to practice the by-product approach. It is imperative that the interview process be conducted without "practical" constraints, as it is all too easy to pull back from the creative challenge of finding soft measurements by employing such rationalizations.

Benefits of CSFs. In addition to the visibility afforded I/S, the use of Critical Success Factors yields considerable benefits to the executive and the organization:

- CSFs aid in shaping executive focus on those factors critical for success.
- The process of interviews and implementation helps develop good measures heretofore nonexistent.
- The information flow process is oriented toward the strategic value of information.
- By supporting migration and the exploration process, the executive is assisted in his or her primary function; that is, the identification of problems, their assignment, and the evaluation of alternatives.

TRACKING CRITICAL SUCCESS FACTORS

Many executives have become familiar with the concept of Critical Success Factors (CSF) or Key Success Factors (KSF) through numerous articles in management literature. The analysis of these factors and other types of plan-versus-actual comparison will normally be a major application on EIS systems. After CSFs have been determined, if only tentatively, it is worth setting up data files so that they can be readily extracted and displayed. It is not a coincidence that John Rockart, of the Center for Information Systems Research at MIT, proposed the use of CSFs as well as the development of executive information systems. They are related approaches to providing management and control information to senior executives.

Developing a set of CSFs at the time of planning a large project, which may be followed by an EIS system, has become a popular way of extracting top management's key concerns in discussions with them; drawing attention to the central business advantages of the proposed activity; giving uniform direction to the planners and systems development personnel working on the project and those working on the EIS system; and stating general goals that can be examined and tested by senior management without the effort of obtaining exact, specific figures.

Critical Success Factors are particularly appropriate for EIS because the areas they are searching may be technically ill-defined and changing. The chance that executives will accept specific results is great, however, if there is a general measure of the work, which they can extract, that points to accomplishment of a goal. In operational systems, success is measured by bringing up equipment or operating facilities. If this can be summarized in a simple number that designates time, cost, or degree of completion, it will be attractive to have it available on the executive's terminal. In financial systems, success is measured by the accomplishment of business objectives for which certain factors are critical to be attained. These can be made available routinely in the extract database.

Financial or time-completion CSFs are usually expressed as plan-versus-actual. This is readily understood by management, and it is straightforward to also supply them with variance analysis and critical variance flagging. When such information is available at the touch of a few keys, it becomes extremely useful for executives to have an EIS system close to their offices.

The original idea of CSFs was to limit the number of factors that would be considered critical. After discussions with top management and analysis, the few most critical factors would be put forward and held up as a goal for subsequent operation and control to achieve. Occasionally, some users have listed most of the principal goals of the systems or operations as CSFs. This greatly waters down their impact, as executives do not want to have long reports drawn out on their micros. They simply want appropriate key factors noted and compared to the plan.

CSFs can come only from or be agreed to by top management. If the result is not a prime concern of the leader who is using the EIS, then it is not critical.

CSFs must be stated specifically as objectives that are attainable and can be measured and reported on the screen. There is no way that general optimality or a feeling of increased productivity can be represented for computer recall. The executive will get that feeling from routine discussions. The EIS must clearly draw out bottom-line effects or percentage improvements.

The development of Critical Success Factors that can be readily analyzed and displayed is a very appropriate element of an EIS. It takes analysis and programming to make such figures readily available, but they fit well with the type of information that executives will expect to be made available.

KEY EXTERNAL FACTORS

Key External Factors (KEF) are essential management data elements that may be requested by executives, but which may be difficult to capture and display. Such factors bear heavily on the outcome of business issues, strategies, and objectives. The problem is to determine the nature and existence of these factors, as well as their relative importance, before strategies can be formulated to capture and transform them to be ready for display in an EIS. In addition, external factors are prone to change, as senior managers will constantly find new movements in the market that will affect the organization. Thus there must be a capability of bringing numerous external factors into the system in a form that is retrievable and comparable to the internal factors in the files.

All Key External Factors are not amenable to inclusion in an executive information system. Many can be identified and handled only by an in-depth strategic analysis. The majority will be handled directly as a result of the experience and understanding of the senior manager, apart from data systems. There are a number, however, that can be digitized and included for display on the manager's microcomputer screen. These may be government statistics or financial data available on external databases, which may be accessed by technical personnel and transferred to the senior manager's database. There also may be client and market information that can be gathered by staff and entered into the system. Another class of external information is consolidated market data sold on tapes, and the manager may want to use an available computer or terminal to access the external file directly, at any time.

For extensive financial analysis of competitive data, one common source is Standard and Poor's Compustat tapes, which provide data on many business variables for the past 10 years. In a large number of industries, relative operating data is available from industry associations or other published sources. There is also a great deal of relatively "soft" data available from market research surveys and salespersonnel's opinions.

Thus, a great deal of data in standard computer formats is on the market, and it may be purchased routinely and transformed into files of Key External Factors for the perusal of senior managers. The biggest problem always will be to determine which of the data should be routinely captured and which is only of interest in answering specific questions. The first type should be entered regularly into the EIS. The second type should be researched by staff whenever there is a need. A number of packaged systems can extract, filter, and compress a broad range of external information, but the value of maintaining specific information routinely on an accessible file must be examined.

DATA ACCESS CHALLENGES

The CSF interview process usually takes place without regard for the practical limitations of data availability. Once the CSFs are identified, however, I/S is faced with the very real challenge of materialization of the desired information. Fortunately, there are some options available.

Data architecture for EIS. As a result of the break from bottom-up by-product orientation, EIS will, as a rule, draw data from a variety of diverse, often hostile, sources (see Figure 4–4). As with other forms of DSS, this situation is usually addressed by using a form of staging database. Unlike the

FIGURE 4–4
Data Access for CSF

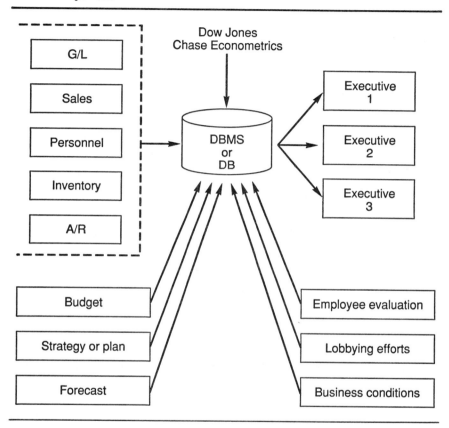

situation with knowledge-worker and user computing, however, the data sources transcend the application databases and begin drawing from very atypical sites.

While it is certainly possible to service the needs of an EIS with a staging database targeted for all end-users, there are several issues that suggest a more segregated database approach:

- *Security.* Given the level of user served, security is of paramount importance. If vigorously enforced, however, security can be accommodated through traditional channels.

- *Timeliness.* Much has been made of the incredible impatience of the corporate executive. Unfortunately, this is one stereotype that appears to fit.

Anchoring an EIS to a staging database may introduce a multitude of variables, any one of which can reduce control over response time. The response-time issue can be critical, depending upon the tolerance of the organization's executives, the ability of the I/S department to commit support, and the amount of time spent on the mainframe versus the micro.

- *Simplicity.* As previously stated, the staging database requires tremendous planning and effort. It is not unusual for such an effort to take several years before it is functional. Using the same database for both categories of users might well result in significant delays in implementing EIS.

If none of the above issues pose particular problems for an organization, one well might plan on combining both the knowledge-worker and executive DSS delivery systems under one database.

Data access technologies. Employing such technologies as foreign file interfaces (FFI) and direct access trunk lines (DATL) affords the best opportunities to overcome most of the problems inherent in data access. There are some concerns, however, when applied to EIS:

- Many FFI systems cannot aggregate. This results in relying on the EIS system to perform the aggregation. Since most modeling and relational (and relational-like) software is relatively resource intensive, this can cause very real problems, depending, of course, on the volume of data to be aggregated.

- Many FFI systems are resource intensive themselves. If the FFI can aggregate, one capability can offset the efficiency limitation. If the system lacks aggregation, this consideration becomes a much higher priority.

- Many FFI systems are nonintelligent, meaning they do not handle dynamic changes in the source files. The implication is that the integrity of the entire system may be put in jeopardy.

The importance of hostile-data access cannot be overemphasized. EIS must be designed around the executive's need for support of the decision process. Lack of attention to data access realities invariably leads to an EIS that is little more than electronic delivery of by-product information.

MICRO-TO-MAINFRAME CONNECTIONS

Executive information systems are usually developed as some type of micro-to-mainframe connection. They are often set up on a specialized, intermediate database that has been specifically designed for senior management inquiries. Such a database should be carefully maintained, of course, and under the constant supervision of a technical person who is able to keep it up-to-date and readily accessible. The advantages of linking a senior management micro to a mainframe or an intermediate computer include:

- Cost-effective capability for on-demand data analysis and report generation.
- Ability to extract selected data from an arranged database, download it, and have it available for manipulation and inquiry.
- Rapid response to a manager's needs for information.
- Creation of documents at the manager's microcomputer, with no need to go elsewhere for printing or graphing.
- Ability to have changing and flexible requirements for data analysis, if the manager has the capability of defining them.
- Use of the regularly updated, large data storage capacity of the central computer as an available archive of information on request.

Micro-to-mainframe connections can help support better decision making on a more timely basis. Accurate, recent data can be made available to managers promptly, together with sufficient data-manipulation capability to perform the desired functions. The data needed can be delivered with optimal support in minimal time.

There are a number of considerations that should be addressed in order to ensure that the necessary data that is retrievable via EIS systems. Some of these considerations are:

- *User-oriented.* The data must be transformed to the necessary formats with no effort by the user. It must be extractable by simple definitions of data type and range.
- *Integrated system.* There must be a single system and a single set of relatively simply commands to extract and manipulate data. All types of data requests and calculation commands must be integrated.
- *Interactive system.* Response must come rapidly, with high priority, when the executive is using the micro. The system must be completely interactive to typed inquiries and commands.
- *Flexible system.* Senior managers frequently change the types of information they want and the types of calculations they want to perform. There must be sufficient technical support to assure that the system can be flexible and responsive to the user.

There are many micro-to-mainframe software packages that may be considered for Executive Information Systems. The one that is selected should be relatively simple, since its use by executives will be irregular. It also should be a system that is in constant use in the organization, so that the best version is running in good order.

For more extensive inquiries by senior managers, there usually will be staff available who can express the inquiries in the necessary language or other reporting system, and who can discuss with I/S personnel how to gain access to the desired information. Executive information support is highly visible to senior people, but they see just the tip of the iceberg. It is not possible without the large structures of operational databases, complex data location and retrieval capability, and, usually, routine preparation of reasonably large intermediate databases that can be accessed easily. Some management inquiries are consistent over a long period, as they follow changes in the business. Other inquiries are relative to any problem that may arise in the organization. These latter inquiries are more difficult to support and usually can be handled only by technical staff lower in the "iceberg."

Most uses of decision support systems are the result of developing a data handling and analysis model over time, based on the interactions that are likely to be investigated. Frequently, further investigation is called for, and the analyst must go beyond specific data-and-time-series items that are immediately available in the model. Additional data is needed to grasp the problem, and the model must be expanded. This is particularly true of executive information support. There are ad hoc inquiries that are difficult to handle by the use of traditional programming methods in assembling the model rules. This requirement usually is met by the use of a nonprocedural, or fourth-generation, language whereby the user describes everything known in a reasonable order, and the program does the work of sorting out the underlying logic that is required. Thus, a DSS for executive support goes far beyond simple modeling, status reporting, or specific analyses. Forecasts are requested, trends are noted, interrelationships are discovered, and unexpected cause-effect relationships may be determined, not necessarily by the senior manager, but more likely by the analyst preparing the model. Strategic inquiries usually lead into unanalyzed areas.

In addition, inquiries by managers usually are not defined as a complete problem from the point of view of an analysis, or a financial model. They are central to the current thinking of the senior manager, but they are seldom structured in a logical way. Thus, for information support for executives, there must be capability of multidimensional searches in the mainframe files.

Chapter Five

Decision Support Systems (DSS)

Decision support systems (DSS) are computer-based information systems developed to improve the decision-making process in an organization. They are useful in addressing complex problems that involve large amounts of data and money and that may have a significant impact on the organization.

Comshare President Richard L. Crandall's integrated view of a DSS is summarized, with new features and their benefits. These features provide state-of-the-art decision support for productivity-minded companies. The benefits may be summarized as the ability to make better decisions by obtaining timely performance data and carrying out investigations without knowing the entire problem up front.

A DSS can provide support in identifying problem objectives, developing and examining alternatives, and choosing an optimum solution. There are many different levels of support that a DSS may provide, including simple access to facts in the files; understanding and recognition of patterns; making a variety of computations, comparisons, and projections; and developing complex models for management study.

The use of DSS involves understanding, using, validating, and accepting assumptions. It is a model-making process with great simplification.

The equipment, software, and human building blocks of DSS are outlined. Typical uses of DSS are noted, and a checklist is provided.

WHEN TO USE DECISION SUPPORT SYSTEMS

Decision support systems (DSS) are computer-based information systems developed to improve the decision-making process in an organization. Although there are many definitions of DSS, they are commonly accepted as the use of computer technology to support the decision-making process of an organization rather than to replace managerial judgment; and to improve the effectiveness rather than the efficiency of the organization.

P. G. W. Keen and N. S. Scott Morton have pointed out that the impact of DSS is on decisions where there is sufficient structure for computer and analytical aids to be of value, but where managerial judgment is essential. The payoff of a DSS is in extending the range and capability of managers' decision processes to help them improve their effectiveness. Keen and Morton explain that the relevance for managers is the creation of a supportive tool under their own control, which does not attempt to automate the decision process, predefine objectives, or impose solutions. Their definition of a DSS is:

> . . . a coherent system of computer-based technology (hardware, software, and supporting documentation) used by managers to aid their decision-making and semistructured decision tasks.[1]

It is important to understand the definition of DSS. While the words carry an intrinsic meaning, it is often necessary for managers in the I/S function to explain the elements of DSS to other managers and executives of an organization. A clear distinction must be made between the completely structured applications of MIS and the semistructured environment of DSS. There must also be a distinction between the functional analysis performed by DSS—which may use statistical analysis, management science, and operations research models—and the more complex, defined modeling of statistics, management science (MS), or operations research (OR). There are no sharp distinctions that always hold, but the advent of low-cost computer technology, personal computers, and simpler programming languages has made the use of DSS by staff analysts attractive. They can move from simple file extracts to complex analyses in a semistructured manner, and there are many ways to making effective, coherent calculations rapidly.

Decision support systems are useful in addressing problems that may have any or all of the following attributes:

- They are complex and require analysis.
- They involve large amounts of data.
- They involve large expenditures of money.
- They can have significant impact on an organization.

These criteria are useful but subjective. DSS may be used any time that an analysis is needed and the computer systems are available for use. In a particular situation, only two or three of these criteria may hold true. For example, a company's problem may involve finding a competitive edge in marketing its

---

[1]P. G. W. Keen and N. S. Scott Morton, *Decision Support Systems: A Management Approach* (Reading, Mass.: Addison-Wesley Publishing Company, 1978).

product. Although complex, and having significant organizational impact, such a problem may have very little data available, and the solution may result in a rearrangement of existing resources rather than new expenditures. DSS may be of help in the analysis, however.

AN INTEGRATED VIEW OF DSS

Richard L. Crandall of Comshare has had considerable experience in developing and supporting DSS systems with features desired by corporations. He recognizes the everchanging nature of the DSS that may be requested, and the need to constantly upgrade DSS capabilities that are offered to managers who have found advantages in such systems. Crandall defines decision support systems as an evolutionary development integrating previously disparate management tools. His analysis of the changes in management expectations for a DSS and currently available features and their benefits follows.

A good DSS is easier to put to use than to define in detail. Attempts to define a DSS either get very technical (in terms such as an integrated combination of relational data management, multidimensional modeling, time-series forecasting, etc.) or very conceptual (a system providing pertinent information on demand, based on incomplete and estimated data with only partial problem descriptions and widely dispersed information sources).

Perhaps the best way to define a DSS is by describing the circumstances under which one is needed. A typical user benefiting from a DSS is a manager or business analyst (in finance, marketing, general management, production planning, administration, corporate planning, etc.). In the 1960s, computers were put to work on accounting applications — rigidly formatted, strictly defined, repetitively run, and based on precise and complete data. Any information that became available for decision support was purely accidental, incidental, and usually too late.

Then came the 1970s and time-sharing. Interactive information handling systems, such as data management and financial planning languages, were created to provide rapid solutions to specific information analysis problems. At last, a manager or business analyst has some hope of getting answers to questions such as:

1. How can data be obtained on sales and expenses for all divisions under plan and whose profits have dropped to a loss?
2. Where is performance weakest? Strongest? (*management reporting applications*)

3. How am I doing in relation to plan? (*budgeting systems*)
4. What will happen if conditions change? (*"what if" modeling*)
5. How does the future look based on past trends? (*time-series forecasting*)
6. What do my expenses need to be if I want EPS to reach $1? (*goal-seeking*)
7. What would this acquisition do to earnings, taking economics of scale into account? (*pro forma consolidations with allocations*)
8. How do these trends look as compared with each other? (*color graphics*)

Each of these questions can be answered by some particular package — a data management system is typically adept at questions 1 and 2; a financial planning system would solve questions 3, 4, 6, and 7; a time-series forecasting package would address question 5; and a color computer-graphics system would address question 8.

At the outset of the 1980s, Comshare had an isolated assortment of packages to solve any of the above decision support problems. But there was no package that could do it all. The result was inconsistent terminology from one package to another; little or no data linkage (for multiple-application systems); low emphasis on a diversity of commonly available, high-quality output; and total incompatibility of internal data structures, thus defeating any attempt at a corporate database.

Still, these systems flourished because they brought desperately needed problem solving and exception reporting to the non-accountant. However, the more these data management and financial planning systems were used, the more the need arose for less structured systems.

Decisions must be made before the whole story is known. Performance problems must be detected before history is written. The difficult part of a manager's job is to develop an instinct about where to look for problems or for clues as to what information is essential to a good decision.

Decision support systems differ from traditional computer-based approaches to problem solving in that they are used to help solve unstructured problems using incomplete data typical of the decision maker's real world. Unlike the traditional techniques of operations research and computer simulation, decision support systems rely on the decision maker's insights and judgment at all stages of problem solving — problem formulation, choosing relevant data to work with, picking the approach to be used in general solutions, and evaluating the solutions presented to the decision maker.

Perhaps the most significant aspect of DSS is that they go beyond just problem solving; they can be of tremendous help to a manager in *identifying* problems. As the old adage goes, once a problem is correctly identified, it is nearly solved.

Current-generation financial systems rely on the user to program a completed model of some operation and then elicit specific reports from data that had been selected with the solution in mind. These systems do solve specific problems, but they do not allow a broader investigation of allied data.

For instance, a manager wishing to look at profit deviations may build a model of a profit and loss statement with rules or interrelationships all specified up front. Then data specific to the model is input and some "what if" questions may be asked. However, if that same manager saw some unexpected impact in the results, he or she would be limited to the model at hand in any investigation.

With a DSS, the same model can be developed, but when further investigation is called for, the manager has the power to look at record or time-series data items that go far beyond the specific data that was in the model. If the investigation shows that additional data is needed to get a handle on the problem, in a DSS it would be available instantly and the model could be expanded.

This ad hoc approach is the bane of traditional "programming" methodology of assembling model rules. The implied requirement is nonprocedural language whereby the user describes everything he or she knows in whatever order it is thought of, and the computer does the work of sorting out the underlying logic of the model.

This is but one example of how DSS goes far beyond simple modeling, status reporting, or specific analyses. Forecasts can be developed, trends spotted, interrelationships discovered, and unexpected cause/effect relationships determined.

Furthermore, in a DSS, a complete problem definition is not required. The user may understand only parts of the problem and, once described to the DSS, partial modeling and analysis is possible. These results may give clues to more of the problem, whereby more of the model can be built. This interactive process again may take the user far away from his or her initial understanding of what data is needed to solve the problem at hand.

In technical terms, a DSS goes beyond financial modeling by embedding data-management facilities that give a multidimensional perspective on all available data whether or not those data were initially thought pertinent to the model.

Applications appropriate for a decision support system are difficult to define, which is exactly why they are candidates for a DSS. The very fact that a proposed system cannot seem to be expressed on a company's computer proposal forms may be the evidence for DSS use. Rather than cost savings, which is the traditional way of justifying an application, decision support systems are more concerned with cost avoidance.

The most likely acquirers of DSS are *strategic* decision makers. They are the people who must deal with unstructured situations in marketing, planning, finance, and overall management control.

Another way of describing a DSS is to portray a table of comparative features and benefits, as shown in Figure 5–1.

FIGURE 5–1
Decision Support Systems

Features	Benefits
Relational data management software.	Investigate and extract large quantities of data from different internal and external sources and formats.
Multidimensional business planning software.	Top-down and bottom-up budgeting, consolidating results along many perspectives, allocating costs, applying currency translations, asking "what if" questions of either simple row-and-column or more complex record-oriented data.
Time-series analysis software.	Forecasting based on past trends; simplified time-dependent analyses.
Nonprocedural, English language structure.	Communication with the computer in a manner similar to the natural thought processes of the user.
Color graphics and laser printing hardware and software.	Presentation-quality portrayal of results in tabular or graphic form on paper, slides, or transparencies.
Worldwide telecommunications.	Collect raw data from diverse sources, report results to geographically dispersed users.
Centralized time-sharing and compatible remote personal computers.	Large consolidations and maintenance of master databases on large interactive systems, personalized modeling and reporting on micros local to user.
Locally available problem-solving expertise.	Quick response to user training and problem-solving needs for maximum productivity; recovery from turnover or other staff mobility.
Summary: State-of-the-art decision support for productivity-minded companies.	*Summary:* The ability to make better decisions by obtaining timely performance data, and performing investigations without knowing the entire problem up front.

LEVEL OF SUPPORT PROVIDED BY A DECISION SUPPORT SYSTEM

There are wide areas for the application of DSS, but some specific areas of capability and certain problem sizes cannot be handled. Typically, a DSS addresses a reasonably large problem that requires extensive manipulation of data and extensive computations. Furthermore, there are usually time restraints for the overall analysis and resolution of the problem. It is seldom feasible to organize a study team to work on such a problem for six months. A principal function of a DSS is to provide approximate answers in a timely fashion. A DSS is, therefore, most useful in three major areas of decision making. These are:

1. Identifying the objectives of a problem.
2. Developing, examining, and comparing alternative solutions.
3. Choosing the optimum solution from approximate data.

This always means that DSS development is not begun seriously until the necessary assumptions have been identified, tested, and agreed upon. The more time spent in this phase of DSS analysis, the more straightforward will be the task of creating systems and comparing alternatives.

The level of support provided by a DSS can range from simple access to available data, to detailed analytical models. Following are possible DSS levels of support in increasing order of complexity.

Access to facts by information retrieval. This level of support usually is supplied by a database management system that allows on-line inquiries for specific items. The data can be from a variety of sources, both internal and external to the organization. For example, company sales, financial, and production information could be combined with economic data from an outside service to provide a useful database. Since the accuracy of data stored in the database will directly impact decisions, it is important that the data be verified. A further consideration is data consistency. By using a common database, the same values will be used for data items that are part of several decisions by different analysts, thus assuring consistency.

At this most basic level of support, such DSS serves as a memory aid and expander. Two examples of this use for DSS are:

1. In a one-of-a-kind job shop, an inventory system with data retrieval capabilities allows shop-floor foremen to locate and, if necessary, re-allocate parts to meet production commitments.
2. FOCUS (For On-line Computer Users) is a popular product that allows users to request information and perform simple manipulations of data to generate specialized reports quickly from existing databases.

Pattern recognition. This function of DSS involves using a computer to group information and discover patterns that may exist. The data in a company's database may be combined with external databases and small models. For large databases, it is possible to specify "viewpoints" or aggregates and subsets of the data on an ad hoc basis. Graphical output is particularly helpful in these systems. Two examples of pattern recognition are:

1. A large plant of an aerospace manufacturer has 125 major contracts that involve a variety of weapons systems, research projects, and maintenance projects. With a DSS package called System W, it is possible for the general manager to group information by weapons system, client, and firm, versus by potential business, type of project, etc.

2. A police department plots locations of crimes by type to determine where special details (e.g., robbery, vice) could be used most effectively.

Simple computations, comparisons, and projections. In this use of DSS, operations are performed on the data to allow managers to assess the implications of the assumptions made. An example is the use of spreadsheets for budgetary or simple financial analysis. Comparisons may involve variance calculations between planned and actual statistics. Projections may include trend analysis based on simple linear regression. An example is Lotus 1-2-3 used to compare market penetration versus projections.

Complex models for management study. In this most complex use of DSS, a manager is provided with computer models and can test their solutions. A variety of modeling techniques are available to support decisions, including simulation models, tactical models, analytical decision models, operational models, and financial models. The manager can interrogate the model and investigate the implications of changes in assumptions about the external environment or future internal operations. Two examples of models are:

1. Full managerial models written in a fourth-generation language such as IFPS or EXPRESS that allow extensive "what if" analyses.

2. Decision aids such as Expert Choice that allow managers to compare alternatives when many of the factors (e.g., preferences, prestige) are not quantifiable.

THE ROLE OF ASSUMPTIONS IN DSS

In creating a model that represents the elements of a business decision, many assumptions are made about the present situation and the future. These assumptions include what the important variables are, which present and past data are applicable to these variables, how the variables are related to each other, and what the effects of time are (e.g., discounted rate of return).

Peter Keen, president of Infotech, has pointed out that decisional assumptions include the decision maker's beliefs, hopes, dreams for the future, fears about the future, habits of thought, and opinions on how the world works. The role of the DSS is to help the decision maker recognize and review these assumptions. The sequence of steps in this process is:

1. *Externalizing* the assumption by identifying it as such.
2. *Understanding* the assumption and what it means.
3. *Challenging* the reasonableness of the assumption.
4. *Exploring* the assumption and its effects.
5. *Communicating* the assumption to others involved in the decision process.
6. *Believing* the assumption is well-founded.
7. *Owning* the assumption and claiming it as yours.

The decision maker has to identify the assumptions, consider the legitimacy of these assumptions, and consciously accept or reject them. Once this is done the actual decision is, in most cases, relatively straightforward. For example:

A capital budgeting decision is to be made by a company's executive committee. The Information Systems department wants to replace its IBM 3081 with an IBM 3090. In preparing for this decision, the important variables include (1) the current and anticipated workload on the existing system, (2) the performance anticipated for the 3090, (3) the salvage value of the 3081, and (4) the cash flows for rent versus lease versus buy, based on assumed rates of taxation.

Note that with the exception of the current load, almost all the parameters involve estimates about future conditions. Many assumptions, such as anticipated workloads, are based on extrapolations of past growth suitably modified by notions of the future. A financial model that creates pro forma balance sheets ties these assumptions together and allows the decision maker to make judgments. The assumptions are critically time-dependent in terms of the workload growth and the cost of money.

BUILDING BLOCKS FOR A DSS

From a decision maker's point of view, a DSS consists of a process in which the degree of uncertainty may be reduced by clarifying issues and exploring alternatives in a logical manner. The DSS architect will view it as a process and a set of tools. The type of computer system used to accomplish this goal is really secondary. Typical of the architecture are a terminal connected on-line to a time-shared mainframe and a personal computer that allows interaction with the mainframe through communications.

The associated software provides English-like queries for data retrieval and for asking "what if" and goal-seeking questions of models. Results can be displayed graphically or as text on a screen and also obtained on paper. The interaction between decision maker and DSS is made as easy as possible, a process often referred to as "user-friendly." User-friendly approaches try to minimize typing by providing menus or pointing devices, or requiring only single keystrokes for complex commands.

The same characteristics apply to a microcomputer-based DSS. The main difference is that a manager must either work with a smaller database and a smaller model than in a mainframe system because of the storage limitations of the microcomputer, or spend time and effort to download data as needed from the mainframe. When using this approach, precautions must be taken to ensure that downloaded data are updated to remain current. A microcomputer also can be used to create the model and run test cases, after which the model is uploaded to the mainframe and production runs are made that involve the use of the corporate database.

Figure 5–2 lists the various building blocks used in designing a DSS. Although this is not an exhaustive list, it does indicate that the tools are available to create a DSS tailored specifically to an individual. A DSS can be assembled from those building blocks that are most suitable to the decisions being made.

FIGURE 5–2

Building Block	Relevance to Manager
Equipment	
On-line time-sharing system	• Getting answers quickly • Access to extensive databases • Use of sophisticated models
Personal workstation	• Personal databases • Privacy of inquiries • Communication connection to a variety of mainframes
Graphics	• Understanding complex data • Matching personal cognitive style
Mouse, touch screens, icons	• Devices for reducing typing
Telecommunications networks	• Sending messages and data as well as crunching numbers • Access to decentralized units
Software	
DSS generators	• Software packages that create models with "what if" goal-seeking and risk-analysis capabilities
Query languages	• Ease of communications with computer
Databases	• Extend range of information available for decision making • Improve access to existing files • Allow answers to complex questions
Models	• Allow ad hoc inquiries

TYPICAL USES OF DECISION SUPPORT SYSTEMS

Decision support systems have been used in a large number of industries and for a variety of purposes. Following are some typical applications:

- *Financial planning.* In this application, cash flows, returns, budgets, and similar information are produced. Most DSS computer packages were originally developed for use in financial planning.

- *Market models.* Analyses are provided of advertising effectiveness, marketing strategy, product planning, and price decisions.

- *Distribution and location models.* These models support branch location, work force staffing, and transportation decisions.

- *Portfolio management systems.* These applications were originally designed to assist investment decision makers in institutions (e.g., bank trust departments, pension funds) select a portfolio mix.

- *Geodata systems analysis.* These are graphic systems to show map and maplike information for city planning and for such tasks as designing police beats, setting school district boundaries, and allocating sales territories.

REVIEW OF DSS ACTIVITIES

A general checklist review of the DSS activities in an organization is given in Figure 5–3.

FIGURE 5–3
Review of DSS Activities

No.	Item	Responses			
		Yes	No	N/A	Comments
1.	Do you have a decision support system department?	____	____	____	
2.	Does the DSS group have a published mission and goal?	____	____	____	
3.	Does the served organization concern itself with effectiveness issues?	____	____	____	
4.	Is there an Information Center in the organization?	____	____	____	

FIGURE 5–3 *(continued)*

No.	Item	Yes	No	N/A	Comments
5.	Does the Information Center work with the DSS group?	——	——	——	
6.	Does the DSS group have a support staff?	——	——	——	
7.	Does the DSS group support the decision-making process of managers?	——	——	——	
8.	Does the DSS group tend to improve the effectiveness of the organization?	——	——	——	
9.	Does the DSS group think of itself:				
	a. as an "operations research" group?	——	——	——	
	b. for work directly with users?	——	——	——	
10.	Does the DSS group focus on unstructured decision making in its efforts?	——	——	——	
11.	Does the DSS group focus on tactical and strategic decisions?	——	——	——	
12.	Is the emphasis of DSS to increase the number of alternatives considered?	——	——	——	
13.	Has the DSS work helped improve management's understanding of the business?	——	——	——	
14.	Is the DSS group prepared for fast response to unanticipated situations?	——	——	——	
15.	Does the DSS group have the ability to carry out ad hoc analyses?	——	——	——	
16.	Does the DSS group support improved communications among decision makers by improving the focus on critical factors?	——	——	——	
17.	Does the DSS group help promote more effective teamwork within the organization through use of improved decision-making tools?	——	——	——	
18.	Have the DSS that have been programmed resulted in time and cost savings throughout the organization?	——	——	——	
19.	Have DSS been used to assist in identifying objectives?	——	——	——	
20.	Have DSS been used to assist management in creating alternatives?	——	——	——	
21.	Have DSS been used to assist management in choosing a solution method?	——	——	——	
22.	Has the DSS group helped improve management's access to facts for information retrieval?	——	——	——	

FIGURE 5–3 *(concluded)*

No.	Item	Yes	No	N/A	Comments
23.	Has the DSS group assisted the decision makers in recognizing information patterns?	____	____	____	
24.	Have the DSS models improved decision making by identifying and exposing assumptions by:				
	a. externalizing the assumption by identifying it?	____	____	____	
	b. understanding what the assumption means?	____	____	____	
	c. challenging the reasonableness of the assumption?	____	____	____	
	d. exploring the assumption and its effects?	____	____	____	
	e. communicating the assumption to others involved in the decision process?	____	____	____	
	f. believing the assumption is well-founded?	____	____	____	
	g. making the decision maker the owner of the assumption?	____	____	____	
25.	Is DSS generally viewed as a process combined with a set of tools?	____	____	____	
26.	Have you considered incorporating the following functions or departments into the DSS organization?				
	a. Corporate library.	____	____	____	
	b. Office automation.	____	____	____	
	c. Corporate records.	____	____	____	
	d. Information Center.	____	____	____	
	e. Consulting practices.	____	____	____	
27.	Does your Information Center accomplish the following for the end-user?				
	a. Exposure to new and existing products.	____	____	____	
	b. Training on products and hardware.	____	____	____	
	c. Advice on the purchase of computing resources.	____	____	____	
	d. Consulting help on design.	____	____	____	
	e. Assistance with applications development.	____	____	____	

Chapter Six

Data Management Issues

There is a need to understand how information is handled in decision support systems and executive information systems, and to establish necessary controls over its use. Methods will differ depending upon whether the work is done by individuals, departmental groups on linked computers, or varied groups with access through communications systems. As the volume of data requests increases, there is not only a problem for the operations groups, but perhaps also for the users who receive considerable redundant data.

The data management alternatives of local data management, on-line extract files, and on-line active databases are discussed. The general approach of DSS and EIS is to move from the traditional application perspective to data files to a subject perspective. The data requirements for each are compared.

The new responsibilities and roles in data management are noted. There must be basic understanding of the rules of data sharing and ownership. The concept of internal and external files needs to be understood. DSS and EIS users require three types of information about data resources: what data is available, where the data is located, and how to get the data. Information Services needs input on the volume, stability, and currency of information, and the frequency of use required. A checklist is provided to review data access requirements. The problems of database administration relative to DSS and EIS are reviewed briefly.

Management of data security is discussed, and checklists are provided for software and database security and records management. Critical points often not considered in the DSS context are noted.

Few managers consider the fact that their computer work is subject to disastrous loss. Therefore, the principles of disaster preparedness and recovery are outlined briefly.

DATA MANAGEMENT FOR DSS AND EIS

Modern personal computers are widespread, and they are more powerful than the central computers of only a few years ago. They can manipulate large quantities of information, which can be taken quickly out of the mainstream of the con-

128

trolled and audited information in an organization. It should be of considerable concern to management that the information being manipulated may be critical to the well-being of the organization, and also may be classified as sensitive, or even vital or secret. There is a need for management to clearly understand the problems involved, the way the organization's information is being handled on DSS, and the methods that may be used to facilitate and control data use. The necessary data controls must be established at the same time that employees are encouraged to use personal computers and the available data for their support systems.

Any individual work in problem analysis and the generation of program plans and reports can be demonstrably aided by the use of personal computers. Newer integrated applications have greatly reduced the time necessary to transfer data from one problem approach to another. A concern is that these same integrated applications also transfer files of data rapidly from one computer location to another, and it soon becomes difficult to know how accurate and sensitive the data is, and to what extent it is mixed with external data.

Groups that are working together on analyses, planning, or a project are now interconnecting their personal computers and sharing information in pieces or in large blocks. They even may be linked in a local area network (LAN) and have immediate and frequent computer-to-computer transfer of data. They may enjoy shared resources such as high-speed printers, communications lines, and data-bases, as well as disks. There may be a mixture of person-to-person communications and unrequested use of information on disks that are available within the group. Also, there may be a common minicomputer the group uses with a database that is not as strictly controlled as the central database. The problems of control of data use and accuracy are evident.

At a broader level, whole departments may have access to minicomputers, or even mainframes, through relatively straightforward communications systems tying into their personal computers. Groups that have different purposes and concerns may be using information that is critical to other groups. Reports going to higher management may come from several different corporate sources, each of whom added to the available data and manipulated it to suit its analytical purposes. It is obvious that central management of data on scattered personal computers can become almost impossible. Often, all that is done is to control the central database as well as possible, allow access to certain data files as access is needed and approved, and issue general policies and guidelines that encourage the reasonable use and control of the corporate data.

The problem of data management is accentuated when there are communications systems that allow all approved members of a corporation to access data files for their particular purposes, whether they are related to the original purposes of the data gathering or not. Clearly, interpretations of policies, guidelines, and procedures will vary greatly. Data will be used for analyses for which it was not designed or intended. Complex networks will allow micros to be tied into minicomputers and mainframes beyond the routine observation of the "owner" of the original data. Extensive controls on data files and data entities become imperative.

Controls are most readily placed on data when it is used within a single application. There are many banking, inventory, manufacturing, and other applications that are large and complex yet have very strong controls imposed on all the sensitive data. Those who use their DSS and EIS to access that data must pass through several levels of control. Such controls work very well until the desired data has been extracted and put on a file in the personal computer. There the user will have considerable freedom to handle it in any way desired.

The problem is clear. The best solution is to encourage or direct the use of accepted data management approaches whenever corporate data is to be used for DSS and EIS. There is no reason that controlled files and databases cannot be required on microcomputers. Many excellent packages are available. Microcomputers are powerful, and the approaches used on them for data control and security can mirror the approaches used on the central computer. If management insists that sensitive data be used only on controlled databases that will maintain data integrity and leave data trails, it is possible to require adherence to necessary rules. Data can be managed on personal computers with the tools available today. It is critical that it be so managed.

DATA MANAGEMENT ALTERNATIVES

The *principles* of data management for DSS and EIS are identical to those for larger computer systems, but the size limitations of microcomputers make the *practice* of data management a minor subset of the records management systems in big computer centers. One of the realities of microcomputing is that the sizes of the files are smaller, the instruction set is more limited, and there are fewer peripherals available. Certainly, access to large databases can be provided for the small systems, but control of those large databases remains with the mainframe computers. There are also practical limitations with micros in areas such as the size of the names and the fields used, the number of fields, the size of records, and the practical number of records that can be handled.

Figure 6–1, lists the possibilities that may be considered. Many users will prefer the alternative of local data management, under their own control, for stand-alone applications. They may not be amenable to direction, but there are many solutions, controls, and standards that should be suggested to them. All the principles and solutions described here are directly applicable to local data management and aid their operation.

FIGURE 6-1
Data Management Alternatives

Local data management

• Information gathered by the local user for stand-alone applications.
• Under control of individual users.
• Solutions, controls, and standards can be suggested.
• Local user responsible for control, security, and disaster recovery.
• Usually few applications for each database.
• Usually simple data structures.

On-line extract files

• Information extracted from the central files for individual use.
• Under control of a support group or the local user.
• Agreed data files extracted from the central computer files.
• File extraction at specified intervals, not continuously on-line.
• Central computer files updated and maintained centrally.
• Controls more rigid in extract phase than in usage.
• Relies on corporate data dictionary.

On-line active database

• Used against active production files.
• May be either static or dynamic applications.
• Applications are open-ended, and new reports may be generated.
• Data files may be continually expanding during use.
• Possible updates of data elements during use.
• Multiple users with multiple applications.
• Controlled by corportate data dictionary

Except for straightforward technical calculations that require files organized in a simple way, most data should be organized in a database for the broad requirements of management, control, updating, and sharing. Users must be given help in setting up standard database files that will provide them with the level of capability that they need. There is a wide range of database systems to choose from. The level of sophistication chosen will depend upon the requirements of the problem, the amount of data sharing that will be expected, and whether there will be a connection between the personal computers and the mainframe database. "Local data management" does not mean that there will be no connection with other computers; it simply means that a group separate from Information

Services will plan and organize its data files; "own" the data that is on those files; and be responsible for the control, updating, and security of the particular files of data.

The proven approaches to data access requirements, data management software, and the use and selection of database management systems are equally appropriate for data files that are maintained locally, shared with others, or downloaded from the large central computer. Modern microcomputers are powerful data processing equipment, and management principles that have been learned on central computers should be applied to the management of data files on the personal computer.

The use of on-line extract files or replicated production data is popular for data management since it makes data available from the large data files on the central computer, yet usage and security can be controlled. With well-managed file extraction, there is little problem of contaminating the data in the central files. A specific support group can manage such an operation and supply agreed data files that are extracted at intervals from the main-line systems in the central data files. Controls can be rigid in the extract phase, though usually they are rather lax in the usage phase. Multiple users generally have free access to the extract files, but there is never uploading of data without rigid controls.

The use of on-line active databases by managers and analysts obviously is necessary in some systems and will be the future direction of many other systems. When adequate controls have been installed, there can be multiple users with multiple applications. The applications can be open-ended with continuous revision and expansion. On-line active databases can be critical to an organization, however, and problems of management and data control need careful analysis, with users having read-only access to most files. Frequently the problem with this approach is possible degradation of performance on the central computer when many personal computers have access to the files.

Combinations of the approaches listed in Figure 6–1 are used. The three approaches represent different management problems, however, and are best considered separately.

In looking at alternatives for data management, there must be a realistic understanding of how much data flow can be supported and controlled. With larger computer systems, the data files and computer power can be increased considerably, with the major limitation being cost, compared to the value that will be received from the system. Microcomputer systems have more limitations, however, if they are still to be manageable by the users. Personal microcomputers under separate control place severe limits on the available capabilities for data management. As soon as the users get beyond a few simple files, the effort required for planning, design, and system development will begin to match that for larger systems.

PROBLEMS WITH THE VOLUME
OF DATA REQUESTS

Almost all corporate decision making requires data. Occasionally, end-users possess all the data necessary to address the application. More often, however, the data exists outside the control of the end-users. Whether external to the company or "owned" by the department down the hall, it is the responsibility of the Information Systems group to establish a method of satisfying data requirements.

The data access problem is not unique to decision support systems. For years, every major corporate I/S department has either created applications or provided sporadic access to selected data for unique computing requirements. The traditional approach generally provides data to approved users via selective batch extractions from the production-source database. On a user-by-user basis, this method is reasonably effective because it satisfies the goal of providing users with a set of defined data.

As the volume of requests increases and the type of data needed for decisions grows, the traditional process becomes increasingly inadequate. For example, I/S involvement becomes more difficult. What was once the exception becomes a standard request. Like developing DSS applications, obtaining data for decision support is an explorative process. In finance analysis, for example, only about 5 percent of the numbers reviewed actually add to a final solution. This trial-and-error approach only leads to increased frustration and confrontation between users and I/S.

Also, redundant data is a particular problem when dealing with end-user computing. Under the traditional approach, the redundancy overwhelms the user with its volume. Users are rarely given direct access to the production database, for several excellent reasons:

• While production data is timely, this is not always an advantage to the user. On-line systems need to be as up-to-date as possible, but many applications need consistent, understood data more than timely data. For example, due to eliminations, transfer pricing, and end-of-quarter adjustments, any numbers other than those that have been "sterilized and blessed" would be of little use. In fact, for many applications they could prove dangerous.

• Direct access might violate standards set by the internal auditors. This is particularly a problem with end-user access, given end-users' lack of rigorous adherence to security practices.

• If demand for access gets too vigorous, central machine performance may be degraded. On critical production machines and applications, this can cause serious problems.

• General control diminishes because of a lack of proper database administration. Extracted files from the production system are only data files, not databases. Security may be limited to password protection. Lacking a dictionary, access cannot be traced.

• Storage and machine efficiency suffer as volume increases. Typically, because users cannot prespecify their data needs precisely, and because those needs can be volatile, I/S provides them with a large range of data. This, they believe, will limit the number of requests that must be serviced. As a result, at any time a user can potentially "own" two or three times the amount of data actually required. In addition, although the user may need only summarized data, the extraction is often from detailed transaction records, and therefore of a much larger volume than actually required.

DATA REQUIREMENTS FOR A SUBJECT PERSPECTIVE

Data management alternatives for DSS and EIS that can satisfy a *subject perspective* for managers must be selected. The general approach of production computer systems is an application perspective. Production system design is oriented toward single applications, not the perspectives required by users (Figure 6–2). To satisfy a single request for specific subject data might require extraction from two, three, or even four source production files. The I/S staff and hardware must bear this burden.

Despite these problems, the production files extraction method has survived for a number of years and should be considered a part of the DSS solution. Now, however, there are data requirements to be met for DSS. These are:

• Multiple data access paths. Data sources for decision support computing can be quite diverse. External sources, on-line databases, different production files, and other end-users and end-user systems can contain data relevant to DSS needs.

• Adequate flexibility to support the frequency-of-change characteristic of DSS applications. If the system structure is sufficient enough to reflect a change only after significant effort, it can be a barrier to computing.

• Proper database controls necessary to ensure reasonable integrity of the data. Since most DSS data is targeted for internal use only, this is less a public reporting requirement than a recognition of the strategic importance that corporate data plays in the organization.

• Ability to support multiple views of corporate data.

• Ease of use by a data administrator or sophisticated user. If the system could retain its ease of use for novices as well, that certainly would be desirable. But as a critical minimum, a system is needed that can support a proficient user.

• Sufficient efficiency to encourage use.

FIGURE 6–2
Satisfying a Subject Perspective with a Production System

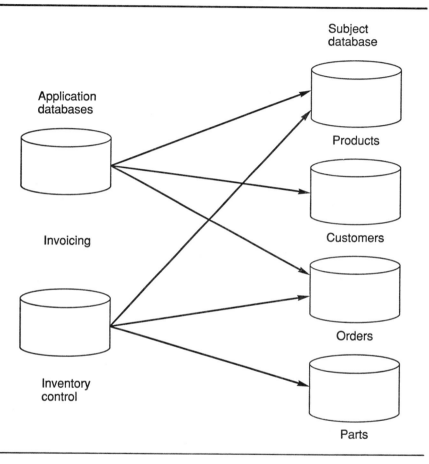

Figure 6–3, shows a concept called a *staging database*. It supports redundancy of targeted decision support data. It is not a question of 100 percent versus no redundancy, because almost every company with an I/S function currently embraces some redundancy in its informal end-user network. The real question is planned versus unplanned redundancy. Many organizations find that a thorough inventory of extract files and their derivatives results in close to a one-for-one relationship between planned and unplanned access. The major question, then, becomes the decision support benefits of a staging database versus the cost in

FIGURE 6–3
Staging Database Architecture

Application
databases

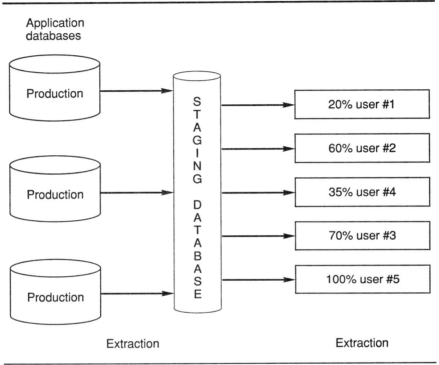

Extraction   Extraction

money and time to establish such a system. Most objective surveys will indicate they are not only cost-effective, but, over time, unavoidable.

Many organizations use a staging database on a medium-sized departmental computer, thus offering control over what is downloaded, and ready access to the database without affecting central computer production.

A staging database is not a panacea. Because the data is specifically targeted for decision support computing, it must be designed carefully so it will not unconsciously disfranchise groups of users. Further, since there will be a degree of redundancy, every effort must be made to keep data duplication at a minimum. The juggling act required to meet user needs as well as good machine habits requires a significant amount of planning before implementation.

The task of properly planning and executing a staging database is certainly not a trivial one. Recently, this responsibility has fallen on the shoulders of the database administrator. This position has been charged with the job of understanding and satisfying the long-term data and processing requirements of the business professional.

RESPONSIBILITIES FOR DATA MANAGEMENT

Most applications developed for DSS and EIS will be designed for access to at least some of the data in the central files. Users may prepare some of their own data files, and they may access external data sources for particular analyses, but much of their data requirements will be served by data that has been assembled by and is considered to be "owned" by others. A number of areas of management responsibility must be faced, including data availability, consistency, accuracy, and control. In addition, someone must take ultimate responsibility for security and control. Microcomputer users will be looking at particular files of data from their own points of view, and will change and select it to suit their own analyses. Important data can be destroyed or misused if the responsibilities of each person are not made clear.

Figure 6–4, outlines how microcomputer users and Information Center, Data Administration, and Systems Development may interact. It summarizes the relationships between the roles. If the users are developing their own data files independently and will have no interaction with the central files, then all these responsibilities will rest with them. On the other hand, as soon as they send data to and from the central files, the responsibility must be shared.

The basic understandings that must be reached are in the areas of data ownership and sharing of data. These agreements, and access to central data by end-users, are frequently facilitated by the Information Center acting as an intermediary, guaranteeing that sufficient controls will be applied. All the microcomputer users who are developing applications will create their own local databases for their own purposes and will control them as they see fit. Problems may arise when this data is intermixed with other controlled data in reports to management, and on files that third parties can access. If an extract database or staging database is set up for several users for their own applications, it must be understood how it is controlled.

Data ownership should be defined clearly before modification of the extract database and sharing of data are added. Responsibility for the source of particular data and the maintenance of its integrity should be understood. One possibility is to define external files and internal files in reference to the users themselves who frequently mix data from many sources. *Internal files* then would be those files within the users' working group that would remain completely their responsibility to control and maintain. *External files* would be other corporate

FIGURE 6-4
Responsibilities and Roles in Data Management

Management of:	Manager or Other End-User	Information Center	Data Administration	Systems Development
Data availability	Describe data requirements. Document requests for specific information.	Support user requests. Determine if possible to fill.	Study data availability and control. Try to meet requests.	Prepare requested access programs and controls.
Data consistency	Indicate if any data has been modified unilaterally.	Encourage consistency of data sources and usage.	Maintain normal controls on all extract files.	Compare files if requested.
Data accuracy and correctness	Maintain adequate controls on use of data.	Teach problems of data accuracy and control.	Maintain normal controls.	Compare files if requested.
Use of data dictionary	Follow accepted data element names and descriptions.	Teach use of data dictionary.	Maintain data dictionary.	Develop the data dictionary.
User's own data	Maintain files and keep records of use.	Teach control of personal data files.	Give information on existing data file practices.	Be aware of possible data sources.
Internal data	Maintain consistency of data in reports.	Make data available through extract databases.	Produce extract databases with controlled data.	Prepare programs for extract databases.
External data	Indicate whenever it is mixed with internal data.	Help make public databases accessible.	Publish standards on data usage.	Control mixing of internal and external data.
Data storage requirements	Plan routinely for own requirements.	Consolidate plans for user's data storage requirements.	Plan for central data storage requirements.	Estimate data storage requirements.
Data modification	Indicate if internal data has been modified.	Instruct in data control.	Maintain controlled internal data files.	Compare files if requested.

and publicly available information that users require in their inquiry and analytical work. To a user, then, an external file would be: (1) data derived from corporate operational activities, (2) data that is the product of application program systems, (3) publicly available data that relates to corporate activities, (4) data available from the central data files, and (5) data available from application programs in Information Services. By these criteria, external files then would be files of data for which the user is not responsible and is not authorized to change in organization or content. Usage is restricted to read-only access.

Despite this definition, two practical problems arise with external files:

1. If there is insufficient security control on them, users may browse through them and change data either inadvertently or intentionally.

2. Users may copy and alter them, then pass on the altered copy to management, claiming that it is correct.

External files are never the private property of the manager or other user, even when they have been copied into that user's work space and combined with other internal files. They should be offered in a computer-processable media, using standard file organization and data representation, and available on a read-only basis. They may be files that are copied or extracted from corporate or other databases and made available to the end-users for their analyses. These facets of data ownership should be established and stated clearly. People may break through security controls, but the data ownership must be understood thoroughly by the management responsible for controlling and maintaining each external file. Technical people may have to be called in at times to verify data accuracy and to demonstrate the correct files.

Presentation graphics produce one of the more difficult aspects of data control. When data is expressed in a graph, which is an analog rather than a digital format, it is difficult to compare it closely with audited, controlled files of data. Yet presentation graphics are a popular way of presenting information. If there is a problem, the only solution to this dilemma is to revert to a comparison of digital information.

Use of public databases is popular with many managers and analysts, who mix the public data with data from controlled corporate files. There is nothing wrong with this unless some of the data from the public databases is read back into the central files without adequate flagging.

DATA ACCESS REQUIREMENTS

Users of DSS and EIS require three types of information about data resources. These are:

What data is available. Users need to know the name, source, and ownership of data files. They need to know the content and currency of the information. They need samples of the data and documentation about it. In short, they need to know if they want the available data.

Where the data is located. Users must know where the data files are and how they can be made available, with or without the help of the technical staff. In large files, they need to know where the data they require is located. They also need to know where the data is located physically in named files and logically with access codes.

How to get the data. Users need to know the file organization (e.g., SAM, ISAM, VSAM, DL/1, etc.) and whether it is in conformance with the interactive product they are using. They need to know if the data representation is in conformance with standards. They need to know on what machine-readable media it resides.

Conversely, Information Services requires four types of information about data resources from the personal computer user. These are:

Volume of information required. The user should describe, possibly with analytical help, the number of data records that must be accessed, and the number of data fields within those records that are to be processed. Users may want a few fields of data extracted from a large number of records, or all of the fields from a few records. This information is needed only for specific requests. If the requests are relatively standard, on maintained extract databases, the information need not be developed.

Stability of the information required. Some users will want the same data items routinely. Their requests will be stable, or static, and will be handled normally by the system. Other users, particularly in analytical areas, will want different types of data each time they communicate with the database. Their dynamic needs will pose different problems to the file structure and access program.

Timeliness of information. Some analysts will want historical information that has long been on the data files and has been well controlled and reported. Other analysts will want the most current data available; last month's or even yesterday's data will be of little use to them. They require pertinent, real-time information for their studies. Such access may be difficult to provide, although it may be possible to obtain frequent data extracts to be made available to them.

Frequency of use. Some users will want to interface routinely and regularly with the data files. Their ongoing analyses may be for planning or decision support systems and will be the center of the user's activities. Other analysts will work routinely at their problems with their own data and only occasionally will want access to an external data file.

All of these variations of data access requirements must be factored into plans for data access. There are usually several approaches that must be taken to satisfy users, but there may be a large percentage of them who fit a similar pattern of data usage and requirements, and the extract database and data access methods can be set up to handle the majority of users readily. Other users then could be supported with specific help.

Central to planning, therefore, should be preparation of data files for EIS and DSS users that satisfies the bulk of their stated requirements. These normally will be extract copies of master files that are:

- In a format compatible with the software products most generally used.
- Updated routinely, with a periodicity sufficient for most users.
- Controlled to prevent unauthorized access to specific, sensitive information.
- Made available with a response time acceptable to most of the users.

Data extract requirements need to be analyzed and reviewed frequently to have the most efficient extract operation possible on the large databases. There may be a considerable expenditure of resources to prepare the extract files. It is the responsibility of the Information Services staff to determine routinely whether all the extract is still required, and whether the extraction runs have been reviewed to minimize the number of necessary passes through the files. It may be possible, for example, to produce cumulative calculations and summaries at the same time as the data is being extracted. This could save significant reprocessing time. It also may be possible to introduce some audit control figures into the extract file during the extract process to introduce a partial audit trail to the end-user work.

Figure 6–5, is a checklist of a number of the more important points that must be considered in planning or reviewing access to databases by end-users.

Some considerations in the control of data access are summarized briefly in Figure 6–6. When data is made available to users, its use will be defined completely by local management and, centrally, there will be little or no control possible. If the work that is coming on-line is to be production use, it must be reviewed by the Data Administration group. There will be necessary authorizations and controls to install. The frequency of the normal update of the extract file probably will not be sufficient for the use. If the work that is coming on-line is analytical and nonproduction work, however, the Information Center, or another group, should be able to support the request, produce files of information

FIGURE 6–5
Data Access Requirements

No.	Item	Yes	No	N/A	Comments
			Responses		

Microcomputer user requirements

1. Are subsets and summarizations of data available to reduce user search time?

2. Does the user have "immediate" access to data of interest, based on the level and priority of the user?

3. Can users add to and change data in their own files with sufficient controls in place?

4. Does the user who "owns" the data in a file have control over changes and updates to that file?

5. Do data files with access by more than one user have sufficient controls to maintain the desired level of stability of the data?

6. Are reports of data that are prepared by users identified as to the source of the data?

Application system requirements

7. Is the data in an application system constantly updated to the current level of available data for the users?

8. In transactional applications, will different users get consistent responses within the updating time frame?

9. Is the integrity of data maintained in any operational system to which users have access?

10. Are all uses of and changes to data controlled in an auditable manner?

Database management requirements

11. Are data files handled without duplication or redundancy, except for extract databases?

12. Is there centralized control in Information Services over all data resources?

13. Is data storage managed efficiently relative to the types of uses required by users?

FIGURE 6–5 *(concluded)*

No.	Item	Yes	No	N/A	Comments
14.	Is data considered as a corporate resource, in the sense that:				
	a. there is corporate ownership of all data?	___	___	___	
	b. costs of data handling by users are analyzed and reported?	___	___	___	
	c. uniform control methods are applied over all uses of specific data?	___	___	___	
	d. the value of the data has been discussed with senior management?	___	___	___	
	Data copying requirements				
15.	Are copies exact duplications of selected database contents?	___	___	___	
16.	Are copies efficiently summarized into the subsets required by the users?	___	___	___	
17.	Does central Data Administration retain control over all extracted and copied databases?	___	___	___	
	Access to external files				
18.	Are the files on the installed equipment directly usable?	___	___	___	
19.	Is ownership of the data in the files clearly understood?				
	a. Are they public information files?	___	___	___	
	b. Are they files sold by a specific vendor?	___	___	___	
	c. Are they confidential material from an external source?	___	___	___	
	d. Is control over the data, and reporting of its use, required?	___	___	___	
20.	Are files maintained and updated with sufficient frequency for the intended uses?	___	___	___	
21.	Do files have standard and accessible organization methods?	___	___	___	
22.	Do the microcomputer users understand the implications of the file data ownership?	___	___	___	

FIGURE 6–6
Considerations in the Use of Databases by End-Users

Subject	Production Use	Nonproduction Use
Access to file	Requires frequent updates	Routine update of extract file sufficient
Input to file	Authorized and controlled	None for end-user Used only after transfer to private file
Updating of file	Under control only	Private file only
Control of work	Central	Local
Direct use of data	With sufficient controls	For management analyses and reports only
Spin-offs of data	Information for further use	Recognized as based on analysis private file

to be used, and train the users in the installation of their own controls for their private files.

DATABASE ADMINISTRATION

If the users of DSS and EIS systems are handling their own data, working on their own problems, and producing reports for their own management, it is not necessary that their data structures be controlled centrally. In many large organizations there are senior groups that are self-sufficient in their data management and require no imposed standards and controls. Many users of personal computers, however, need to use data from the operational application systems that are run on the central computer. Whether these analysts use printed outputs, extract files, or connections to the central files, the programs that they work with are simply extensions of the larger operational programs that already are tightly controlled by Information Services. The problem is that they will be producing reports that supposedly are based on the centrally controlled database, yet they may alter some of the data or use data structures that are incompatible with other programs. This can result in lack of control and some misunderstanding by management. Another problem is that the operational database structure may be changed, or new data definitions may be imposed, creating problems with extractions and local processing. The only solution to the difficulties that inevitably will arise in such circumstances is to demand that all users of data from the central files follow the procedures and standards established by the central database administration group.

FIGURE 6–7
Problems with Database Administration

- Lack of organizational cooperation
- Lack of agreement on data definitions
- Database administrator is a technician
- Magnitude of the task is underestimated
- Design of stable data structures not well understood
- Computerized tools not used to administer the data models
- Data model design confused with implementation

The fundamental difficulty is that while Information Services personnel are familiar with the need to follow the dictates of the database administration group, most end-users do not understand why such cooperation is necessary. Figure 6–7 summarizes the main reasons why the concept is a difficult one to implement among end-users outside of the Information Services department.

First, there is frequently a lack of organizational cooperation. Outside departments do not always understand the need to keep all uses of the same data controlled for accuracy and consistency. They have no technical understanding of how rapidly the reliability of a database can be destroyed by the uncontrolled use of it.

Another problem is the lack of agreement on data definitions. While the central staff usually requires refined definitions that are quite specific, many end-users deal with subsets of the overall problem and feel that their more simplistic data definitions are adequate. To make communication more difficult, the database administrator often is a specialized technician because of the complexities of managing the database. Such a person is much more oriented to the systems and programming staff in Information Services than to end-users.

A problem for I/S is that the magnitude of the task of data administration usually is underestimated. Work on data definitions and administration for a few applications is complex enough, but when end-users start bringing in many program and system variations and completely new views of the data, analysis becomes exceedingly difficult. A number of analysts, dealing with a variety of end-users, must determine cooperatively how the data is to be defined, recorded, and controlled.

The design of stable data structures is not well understood. One application may be handled with a fixed sequence of records whose length is agreed upon in order to simplify records management. Another application may need the same data, but with attributes that are added or deleted in a record. This may be very difficult to do without rewriting the entire file, unless it has been well-organized at the start. All data structures, particularly sequential files, affect the information processing capabilities of a system. The more types of uses of data that are required, the more complex the database system must be to handle the data readily. Database systems vary from the relatively simple handling of connected files to sophisticated commands for multiple functions. From the user's point of view, the more complex systems are much easier to use than simple systems.

There are many advantages to the current movement toward relational databases, but these are frequently overshadowed by the difficulties of the necessary modeling of data before implementation can be done. Quite often users do not wish to wait for data requirements to be analyzed, data to be modeled, and necessary files to be set up. They cannot see the long-term advantages of the effort. These advantages come about from the standardization that is possible with a higher-level language, increased ease of communication between applications, and much simpler programming after the initial work has been done. Since data independence is the main objective of a database, the relational model is superior for use. Unfortunately, it requires a good deal of analysis. In fact, at present, the current use of relational databases frequently may be less efficient in getting a system started and running for a few applications. Relational tabular views of data and the third normal design, required for relational databases, are going to become the standard and will increase productivity, however. What must be faced is that there will be a difficult transition period. Computerized tools must be used whenever possible, and costly standardization must be insisted upon, in order to gain great advantages in productivity at a later date. In the meantime, work on data model design must proceed, even though it does not implement programs in itself. Implementation is simpler after sufficient design work, but the transition period may be lengthy.

DATA SECURITY CONSIDERATIONS

Management of the security of data used for DSS and EIS is complex. In central computers, there can be sufficient control over the data input, output, and storage to force the use of security procedures, particularly for sensitive data. In the use of personal computers, it is virtually impossible to enforce similar procedures in all uses of the data. Policies, guidelines, and procedures may be promulgated by Information Services, or from a higher level, but enforcement will depend upon the interest of local management. It remains up to the owner, and not necessarily the user, of the systems and data to decide what has to be protected and what does not, and to what degree it has to be protected.

The problem of information integrity and security in personal computers also includes the rapid loss of data by removal of floppy disks from the premises or the use of data in uncontrolled communications networks. It is certainly not cost-effective to install $30,000 worth of physical security, however, to protect a $4,000 microcomputer that does not contain highly sensitive or valuable data. Thus security considerations must be analyzed for each small group of personal computer users and the information it handles. In some cases, high security will be indicated. In other cases, minimal security will be adequate. Clearly, a commonsense approach to security needs will be the best approach.

Adequate security usually can be realized through proper employment of security administration, risk analysis, disaster planning, and security awareness training of the people involved. Reasonable physical security, hardware and software security, communications security, and good auditing techniques can be integrated into a sound security plan, which can provide a level of protection to meet the needs of a business.

Information security is the protection of data against either accidental or intentional destruction, modification, or disclosure. Security methods are needed to maintain the accuracy and integrity of the computerized information used in the operation of a business. A good security program is achieved by the consent of the personal computer users and their managers. All groups must be involved to have an effective program.

The management of data security in personal computers must start with the security of software. Security software packages or routines for microcomputers are currently very limited and usually provide only access control via menu security or password schemes. These packages or routines frequently are provided by the manufacturer of the hardware or the vendor of the operating system. Security in the stand-alone, desktop environment simply does not have the high priority that security in the network or micro-to-mainframe environment has. Also, microcomputer system overhead, in terms of storage and system resources, may not be able to support any significant software security packages or routines while other applications are being processed.

Figure 6–8 is a checklist for reviewing the basic concerns in software security for DSS and EIS. It should be scanned for applicability before it is used.

Microcomputer-based data files.   Little has been done in the area of securing the software and data stored on the stand-alone, desktop microcomputer. The hierarchical database security structures that include authorization, departmentalization, and compartmentalization schemes that are used in the mini and mainframe database environments are essentially nonexistent in the microcomputer environment. Often, managers simply lock their offices at night, which works well until the janitors unlock them. The reason is primarily one of economics. As indicated previously, it is difficult to justify the cost of the software and the system overhead required to run database security software. Also, most micros are limited in the number of programs that can be run at the same time, unless multitasking/multiprogramming is featured. Companies that need to enhance database security beyond the password stage have written their own custom software or have modified software application packages.

FIGURE 6-8
Software Security

No.	Item	Yes	No	N/A	Comments
			Reponses		
1.	Is the software protected legally by:				
	a. copyright?	___	___	___	
	b. patent?	___	___	___	
	c. trade secret?	___	___	___	
	d. employee contract?	___	___	___	
2.	Has a company identification and protection statement been embedded in each source program?	___	___	___	
3.	Are protection hardware/software devices being used to protect the company's proprietary software?	___	___	___	
4.	Have the following controls been placed on sensitive programs, including new programs and program changes?				
	a. Control list of sensitive programs.	___	___	___	
	1. Program name/description.	___	___	___	
	2. Programmer responsible for program.	___	___	___	
	b. Separation of programmer duties.	___	___	___	
	c. Appropriate storage of sensitive programs and related documentation.	___	___	___	
	d. Documentation check-in/check-out logs.	___	___	___	
	e. Restrictions against program patching.	___	___	___	
	f. Management review of all changes and requests for changes.	___	___	___	
	g. Audits of program changes.	___	___	___	
	h. Review and approval of program test results.	___	___	___	
	i. History log of programs and program changes.	___	___	___	
	j. Documentation.	___	___	___	
5.	Are controls established so the wrong version of a program will not be processed?	___	___	___	
6.	Is backup operating-system software available that is identical to the:				
	a. operating system version?	___	___	___	
	b. operating system release?	___	___	___	
7.	If the backup operating system is not identical, is it compatible with the present operating system?	___	___	___	

FIGURE 6–8 *(concluded)*

No.	Item	Yes	No	N/A	Comments
8.	Has there been a test of running the operating system software on the backup computer?	___	___	___	
9.	Have the application programs that are vital to the company's operation been defined and listed?	___	___	___	
10.	Are these programs copied at regular intervals?	___	___	___	
11.	Is a copy of the source code maintained?	___	___	___	
12.	Is a copy of the object code maintained?	___	___	___	
13.	Is a set of test data (including the desired test results) maintained for each application system for testing at the backup location?	___	___	___	
14.	Are application programs written so as not to depend on any one particular piece of hardware?	___	___	___	
15.	Is adequate security provided for on-site and off-site software storage?	___	___	___	
16.	Are relevant storage cabinets and safes resistant to:				
	a. burglary?	___	___	___	
	b. fire?	___	___	___	
	c. smoke?	___	___	___	
	d. water?	___	___	___	
17.	If vendor-supplied software is used, is there a clause in the contract that extends the terms of the license to permit use of the software on backup equipment?	___	___	___	
18.	Is someone assigned specific responsibility for software backup, security, and control?	___	___	___	
19.	Are surprise inventories taken of the software maintained at the backup location?	___	___	___	
20.	Have copies been made for storage at the backup site of:				
	a. utility programs (sorts, merges, file, reorganizations, file recreates, etc.)?	___	___	___	
	b. new operating system updates that have not yet been applied?	___	___	___	
21.	Have "waiting periods" been established for routine program operations in which, after a certain length of time and no matter for what reason, certain action is necessary? (A list of approximate run times should be maintained to aid in scheduling as well as a check to determine if a program may be in a loop.)	___	___	___	

One way to control micro-based data is to assign responsibility for it to a specific individual. Such a person would be known as the "owner" of the data and would have complete responsibility for its control, security, and backup.

Access control and encryption. Some firms offer microcomputer database security packages, which may even include DES (Data Encryption Standard)-level encryption features for transmission of data as well as for file storage. Other firms offer a mainframe type of data protection feature that uses a hierarchical password structure and an advanced "private-key" encryption technique. With these controls, users may be restricted to file access in one of four levels.

Records management. Each organization needs to identify what information is critical to its survival. This includes not only administrative, accounting, and financial records, but also proprietary and trade secret information. In order to determine what information is vital, ask the question, "Can my company/department, etc., adequately function if the microcomputer-based information becomes unavailable for use?" Senior managers should be asked if their files have become critical.

The National Fire Protection Association (NFPA) has defined four classes of records as follows:

1. *Vital records (Class I).* Essential to operation, irreplaceable, or needed immediately after a disaster. Cannot be quickly reproduced. Examples: master files, programs, company records.

2. *Important records (Class II).* Essential to operation. Can be reproduced without critical delay. Examples: data files, input/output files.

3. *Useful records (Class III).* Inconvenient if lost, but loss would not prevent prompt restoration of operations after a disaster. Examples: historical files and data.

4. *Nonessential records (Class IV).* Not necessary to replace if lost.

Magnetic media storage. Adequate, environmentally controlled, secure storage for magnetic media is essential in micro-based operations. Diskettes and cassettes have suffered many indignations at the hands of micro users who were in too much of a hurry to get the job done, or who used their diskettes as substitute coasters for their coffee cups so they would not damage their desks. A diskette may be the product of hundreds of hours of work and may contain your company's total accounting records. Even when working with cassettes/diskettes, use the proper desktop storage devices. Magnetic media storage considerations include:

- Dust-free environment.
- Fire-rated, smoke- and water-resistant storage cabinets.
- Lockable storage cabinets if necessary.
- Controlled access.
- Off-site backup: extra copies of software, data files.
- On-site backup: extra copies of software, data files.
- Primary copies handled and stored correctly while in use.
- Sensitive information: files kept separate and controlled.
- Working files kept separate from scratch/work files.
- Proper labeling: external and internal.
- Periodic inventory of media taken and control logs maintained.
- Environmental controls: safe temperature and humidity levels.
- Media stored away from window ledges, magnetic devices, etc.

Magnetic media erasure devices. One means of ensuring that diskettes or cassettes containing no-longer-needed sensitive data do not end up in an unauthorized person's possession is to erase the data using special devices designed for that purpose. Magnetic erasure devices are available for diskette, disk, and cassette.

Backup. The term *backup* refers to the creation of a copy of a file or documentation for recovery purposes; and to equipment or procedures that are available for use in the event of failure or overloading of normally used equipment or procedures. In general, it is recommended that three copies or "generations" of a database file be kept: the son, father, and grandfather generations.
Backup considerations include:

- Database size. The size of the database will determine the time it takes to "dump," or copy, that database.
- Backup schedule. The scheduling of backup depends on database size (volume), criticality of the data (vital or nonvital), and processing time constraints. Every organization needs to establish a backup plan for each of its files. While daily backups will be required for some files, others may need to be copied only once a week or month.
- Differential backup. Differential dumps involve copying only the records that have changed since the last run.
- Dual updating. This involves updating two identical files by means of the transaction being processed.

- Audit logs/journals. As a database record is updated, the originating transaction record and the database "before" and "after" records are recorded in a log file.
- Some database files never need to be copied because it would be easier to recreate the file.

Magnetic media recovery. Loss of data on magnetic media caused by such occurrences as equipment malfunction, software problems or errors, operator error, erasure, or overwrite potentially can be recovered. Sophisticated software packages that have been developed facilitate the retrieval, restoration, and/or rebuilding of lost or corrupted data. These packages typically provide the following features: disk file recovery; restoration of a file after it has been killed; and recovery of data after the file's directory has been damaged.

Figure 6–9, is a checklist that can be used for reviewing these security considerations.

DISASTER PREPAREDNESS AND RECOVERY

The purpose of disaster recovery planning is to prepare in advance to ensure the continuity of business information if EDP capability is lost. Thus disaster recovery planning is a management rather than a technical issue. It deals with the realities of people, organizational relationships, and special interests. Disaster recovery actions are highly prioritized, and many normal operations are neglected. Management must take the lead and continually assess the technical considerations involved. Few managers consider the fact that their computer work is not only valuable, but also subject to disastrous loss.

Disaster recovery planning and arrangements for contingency backup operation are just as important for DSS and EIS as they are for larger systems.

Management must realize that EDP professionals agree there are no entirely secure computers. Many computer operations have fine methods for security in place, and management can be assured that the best possible actions have been taken, but there are always people, electronics, and natural disasters that can disrupt operations suddenly. Management must realistically look at legal obligations, cash flow maintenance, customer services, competitive advantages, production and distribution decisions, logistics and operations control, purchasing functions and vendor relationships, ongoing project control, branch or agency communications, personnel and union relations, and shareholder and public relations.

Management should assess the importance of personal computer system operations to these facets of its business, then decide on the type of effort that should be put into the backup of the computer function. Management also needs

FIGURE 6–9
Database Security and Records Management

No.	Item	Yes	No	N/A	Comments
				Responses	
1.	Has the value of data processing records been classified into the NFPA classes of vital, important, useful, and nonessential? Have the following records been classified?				
	a. Input records.	___	___	___	
	b. Source documents.	___	___	___	
	c. Control documents.	___	___	___	
	d. Magnetic tape/disk file records.	___	___	___	
	e. Programs.	___	___	___	
	f. Output data.	___	___	___	
2.	Is there understanding of and compliance with record-retention regulations for:				
	a. Internal Revenue Service (IRS)?	___	___	___	
	b. insurance?	___	___	___	
	c. legal considerations?	___	___	___	
	d. customer/product history information?	___	___	___	
3.	Have your records/files been evaluated for all possible types of threats and vulnerabilities?				
	a. Data entry errors.	___	___	___	
	b. Data transmission errors.	___	___	___	
	c. Mechanical malfunctions.	___	___	___	
	d. Program errors.	___	___	___	
	e. Updating of wrong files.	___	___	___	
	f. Computer operator errors.	___	___	___	
	g. Lost files.	___	___	___	
	h. Defective magnetic media.	___	___	___	
	i. Theft of records.	___	___	___	
	j. Criminal activity.	___	___	___	
	k. Loss by natural disaster.	___	___	___	
4.	Are duplicate copies of all vital records maintained?	___	___	___	
5.	Is a list of critical files maintained?	___	___	___	
6.	Is reconstruction capability maintained for paper and magnetic files? (possibly in the three-generation, son-father-grandfather approach)	___	___	___	
7.	Are daily file dumps and transaction files maintained for construction purposes?	___	___	___	

FIGURE 6–9   *(continued)*

No.	Item	Yes	No	N/A	Comments
8.	When magnetic files are copied for off-site storage, are the copies checked for:				
	a. readability?	___	___	___	
	b. accuracy?	___	___	___	
9.	Are on-site and off-site magnetic media storage cabinets:				
	a. fire resistant?	___	___	___	
	b. smoke resistant?	___	___	___	
	c. water resistant?	___	___	___	
	d. movable so that they may be relocated quickly in the event of disaster?	___	___	___	
	e. secure?	___	___	___	
	f. fitted with casters for easy evacuation?	___	___	___	
	Note: Make sure storage cabinets fit through doorways.				
10.	Are critical records microfilmed as an additional means of providing backup?	___	___	___	
11.	Is there a procedure for evacuating critical files in case of emergency?	___	___	___	
12.	Is a paper shredder or an incinerator used for the disposal of:				
	a. computer and typewriter carbon paper?	___	___	___	
	b. old classified documents?	___	___	___	
	c. program listings and test data?	___	___	___	
	d. old reports?	___	___	___	
	e. worn-out magnetic diskettes?	___	___	___	
	f. microfilm?	___	___	___	
13.	Is access to information on the micro's database strictly controlled?	___	___	___	
14.	Are detailed transaction records kept for a safe period of time? (If a micro user is low on diskettes/cassettes, needed files are sometimes accidentally erased.)	___	___	___	
15.	Are there ways of ensuring that the correct version of the database file is being used?	___	___	___	
16.	Are outdated files controlled so they are not processed accidentally?	___	___	___	
17.	Does the software provide for internal label checking?	___	___	___	
18.	Is the magnetic cassette/diskette erasure (degaussing) device stored in a secure place?	___	___	___	

FIGURE 6–9 *(concluded)*

No.	Item	Yes	No	N/A	Comments
19.	Have these magnetic media storage controls been considered?				
	a. Dust-free environment.	___	___	___	
	b. Fire-rated, smoke- and water-resistant cabinets.	___	___	___	
	c. Lockable cabinets if necessary.	___	___	___	
	d. Controlled access.	___	___	___	
	e. Off-site backup: extra copies of software, data files.	___	___	___	
	f. On-site backup: extra copies of software, data files.	___	___	___	
	g. Primary copies handled and stored correctly while in use.	___	___	___	
	h. Sensitive information files kept separate and controlled.	___	___	___	
	i. Working files kept separate from scratch files.	___	___	___	
	j. Proper labeling.	___	___	___	
	k. Periodic inventory of stored media and audit for compliance with procedures?	___	___	___	
	l. Environmental controls: safe temperature and humidity levels.	___	___	___	
	m. Media stored away from window ledges, magnetic devices.	___	___	___	

to consider how the microcomputer disaster recovery plan will interface with existing organizational policies and procedures. There already may be a disaster planning guide for the overall business. In this case, the EDP guide should fit into it. Most organizations have plans in place for at least some of the following:

Fire protection equipment installation and maintenance.

Emergency fire alarm procedures.

Fire monitor or instructor training.

Guard duties, training, and procedures.

Relationships with external emergency alarm services.

Relationships with local fire and police departments.

Bomb threat procedures.

Strike or mob threat procedures.

Storm emergency information and restoration plans.

Emergency control centers.

These are all supportive of EDP recovery, and management must see that the microcomputer plans fit with them.

Priority Concerns of Management

For most organizations, the principal area of concern in disaster recovery operations is the safety and well-being of personnel. This concern should remain paramount. The principal *business* concern is the maintenance of accounting records and customer services. Losses from interruption of business must be kept as low as possible, and the required cash flow maintained. Legal and reporting requirements also must be maintained.

The purpose of a disaster recovery plan is to minimize the costs resulting from loss of or damages to the resources or capabilities of the microcomputers and related services. The plan's success depends on recognition of the potential consequences of undesirable events. There are many resources related to microcomputer system operations, and some particular subset of these is required to support each function that is provided to others in the organization. These resources include people, programs, data, hardware, communications equipment and systems, electric power, the physical facility and access to it, and even items such as paper forms.

All resources are not equally important, nor are they equally susceptible to harm. Safeguards and elements of a contingency plan therefore should be selected with an informed awareness of which system functions are supported by each resource element, and of the susceptibility of each element to harm. The cost-effective protection of a microcomputer system operation is thus dependent on the importance to the organization of each of the component parts of the computer functions; the general probability of something undesirable happening to each of the components; the likely results and ramifications of various types of disasters; and preparations made to minimize the chances of disasters, and the costs if they do occur.

Any part of a disaster recovery plan is overhead cost until it becomes necessary to activate it. Thus it is necessary to consider the importance of the resources and services, and to justify all the parts of security and disaster recovery measures by estimating the losses that could occur through lack of these precautions. The combination of initial expenditures and insurance coverage must be balanced against the necessity of the services and the probability of the need for the recovery procedures. However, there are some actions that are mandatory. They must be taken regardless of the cost.

Three levels of security and disaster recovery measures should be considered in balancing cost against need. These are *mandatory, necessary,* and *desirable* measures. There is no absolute scale, and these measures will vary as conditions change. Management must review what is mandatory and necessary for its organization, support those efforts first, and then perform a justification analysis of desirable measures.

Mandatory measures. Mandatory security and disaster recovery measures are those related to fire control, alarm systems, evacuation procedures, and other emergency precautions necessary to protect the lives and well-being of people in the area involved. Mandatory measures also include those needed to protect the books of account of the organization, and to hold its officers free from legal negligence. The protection must include the assets of the organization as much as possible. The cost of these mandatory measures must be included in the cost of doing business. The items also must be reviewed periodically as to routine operation and adequacy. They should be reviewed with organization counsel.

Necessary measures. Necessary security and disaster recovery measures include all reasonable precautions taken to prevent serious disruption of the operation of the organization. This will include selected areas of manufacturing and distribution, engineering and planning, sales and marketing, and employee relations. The necessity of the measures must be determined by senior management, which also should review its understanding of the need periodically. Since the necessary measures will be included in the base operating cost of the organization, each selected measure must be reviewed as to both degree and speed of emergency backup required.

Desirable measures. Desirable security and disaster recovery measures include reasonable precautions taken to prevent real inconvenience or disruption to any area of the organization, and to keep the business under smooth control. The cost of some precautions related to personnel is small, but planned action is important to maintain operational efficiency and morale. The cost of other measures, such as arrangements for alternative sites for systems and programming personnel and their terminals, may be large. Estimates and plans must be made, however, to allow reasonable and cost-effective management decisions once the extent of a disaster is understood. Many of the microcomputers in an organization will fall into the "desirable measures" category and will not be given priority in disaster recovery planning.

Note: The mandatory measures should be implemented as soon as possible. The necessary measures should be implemented in time-phased, prioritized order, with a definite plan approved by senior management. The desirable measures should be implemented as circumstances allow. Overhead cost is balanced against perceived need and desirability.

Practical Levels of Disaster Recovery Measures

A disaster recovery plan should be specific to an organization and tailored to its needs. An off-the-shelf plan is of no use whatsoever at the time of a security event, when individuals need to know exactly what their roles are and the steps they must take. The presence of a plan on paper does not in itself provide a disaster recovery capability. All people in an organization who may be involved in a recovery activity also should be involved in the plan's preparation, training, and testing.

The best approach to disaster planning for microcomputer systems is for a small team to gather under the direction of a supervisor and make a short-term, high-impact plan to get something in place that will handle the most pressing needs and have high visibility. The steps it should take are:

1. Assemble all readily available operations and systems documentation, including vendor material.

2. Assemble reports of any audits or security studies of related computer functions.

3. Create lists of the operating application systems as a first estimation of the order of priority.

4. Consult with senior management to get its opinions as to the mandatory and necessary applications in an agreed order of priority.

5. Determine the minimum configuration on which these mandatory and necessary systems can run and arrange for tests on backup microcomputers.

6. Determine if these critical systems can be backed up and run off-site in an emergency, and in the time required.

Chapter Seven

System Modeling Issues

Computer modeling is the development and use of a computer program to simulate a business situation. Most spreadsheets are models. Management considerations in modeling are reviewed. The types of computer models may be categorized as ad hoc, production, and structured resolution.

Model development begins with defining the environment and the purpose for the model. Decisions must be made on the uncontrollable variables, the controllable variables, and the dependent variables to use in the model. Viewpoint modeling is the addition of dimensions or perspectives beyond simply stating the values of the variables over time. The presentation can reflect a marketing viewpoint, a final viewpoint, or a specific operational viewpoint, for example.

An approach is presented to aid in the estimation of model development time. The steps for developing a model are discussed. The acquisition of data for the model, the creation of study reports, debugging, and documenting are all briefly outlined.

Some of the investigative capabilities of models are described: "what if" analysis, goal-seeking (backward iteration), step-function "what if" (sensitivity analysis), and risk analysis. The important design considerations of causality and multidimensionality are noted.

THE USE OF COMPUTER MODELING

Computer modeling is the development and use of a computer program to simulate a business situation. It involves the use of either a mainframe computer or a microcomputer, and usually a fourth-generation language or package program for simulating relationships, testing variables, and analyzing a business situation in a symbolic representation of the problem. Multiyear plans, future production schedules, budgets, and proposed distribution schedules are all models of one sort or another. Most spreadsheet applications are models.

This chapter deals with the types of computer modeling that will be experienced in most decision support systems (DSS) or executive information systems

(EIS). It will touch on the large and complex area of management science and operations research (MS/OR) applications. The steps and management principles are the same in all these areas. The differences lie in the complexity of the mathematics and the programming involved. In DSS work, the time horizons are frequently short, and the effort is carried out on a microcomputer. In MS/OR applications, the time horizons are necessarily long, multivariable and multi-level statistical and algorithmic equations are employed, and a much finer structure of system behavior is described. In brief, DSS computer modeling usually makes many more assumptions and is satisfied with understanding the probable behavior of the business system. MS/OR computer modeling makes assumptions at a lower level of detail and attempts to elucidate basic forces and business behavior according to the variables. They are simply two ends of a continuum of modeling.

There is usually a five-step approach to computer modeling:

1. *Defining the environment.* Setting the objectives and direction of the model.
2. *Developing the model.* Determining the variables, the viewpoint to be taken, and the logic of the system, and putting them all together.
3. *Debugging the model.* Finding both system-detected and fundamental errors in logic.
4. *Documenting the model.* Making it usable for others.
5. *Investigation.* Using the model on real problems.

Computer modeling is a simulation that involves data, relationships, and analysis. Although it can vary in scope from simple spreadsheet applications to large, complex, national econometric applications, the bulk of DSS and EIS models do not go beyond micro-sized applications until an analytical staff is involved. The computer is an efficient tool for performing complex calculations that involve large volumes of data. Because of the computer's inherent accuracy, extensive calculations can be performed predictably and consistently. Also, the computer is an excellent tool for executing the many repetitive and routine series of calculations that are required in any model.

In modeling applications, the computer is not only efficient, but is an extremely effective tool as well. When used in an investigative mode, a computer model can provide enormous insight into the dynamics and limitations of the business environment. Variables can be implicated and tested, and their ranges can be examined.

As with other tools, the use of computer modeling is an investment in time and effort. This cost should be compared with the expected benefits of modeling a particular application. Sometimes, model builders become overzealous in using models, losing sight of the fact that the process of modeling is not an end in itself. Modeling is appropriate when:

1. The expected development time is significantly less than its manual computational equivalent.

2. Repetitive use of the model increases the benefits beyond initial development-time efficiencies.

3. Quick turn-around time for a series of solutions becomes the overriding consideration (as in negotiation models).

4. The model includes functional calculations normally too complex to be handled manually.

Each modeling application should be independently evaluated as to the suitability of either micro or mainframe usage.

The *microcomputer* is ideally suited for small models. It is also useful for data entry, validation, development, and editing of large models. Although the size of the model developed is now controlled by the technological limitations of micros, continuing advances will increasingly blur the distinction between micro and mainframe applications.

Mainframe computing should be used for models of significant size. Additionally, it is the ideal place for centralized, professionally managed data to reside. Since models also serve as a means of communicating concepts and shared applications, the mainframe has some advantages.

Ideally, the choice should not be micro or mainframe, but rather micro *and* mainframe, using distributed computing. Distributed modeling joins the micro with the mainframe through communication links, enabling the user to pass both data and models from the mainframe to the micro and back again through the use of identical syntax. A distributed environment takes advantage of the strengths of both forms of computing.

TYPES OF COMPUTER MODELS

Models are developed in response to a need. This need (and the models developed) can fall into three categories:

Ad hoc models. This is also known as "putting out fires." These models are developed for a specific application and typically are prepared on a very tight time schedule. Ad hoc models are usually small and do not require much documentation. It is not surprising, therefore, that these systems have been called "throwaway" models. Examples of this type of model include an evaluation of an issuance of stock, or the simulated impact of a potential strike.

Production models. Unlike ad hoc models, these systems are used regularly and typically require more time for development. They usually are of considerable size and often are well-documented. Many production models are computerized equivalents of existing manual systems, being more results-oriented than investigative. Examples of production models include monthly consolidations, performance reporting, and forecast models.

Structured resolution models. These models often include both ad hoc and production characteristics. The primary purpose of the structured resolution model is to simulate and understand major challenges to the business environment. Thus it is distinguished by its intended use. Although the most common example of a structured resolution model is in planning or budgeting, negotiation models, acquisition models, statistical models, and linear programming models are also good examples.

The model builder first should assess the environment to determine which of the three types of models is required, as this influences the amount of development effort required.

INITIATING MODEL DEVELOPMENT

The first step in developing a computer model is to define the *environment* and the *purpose* for developing the model. The purpose of a model can be defined as the *problem that the model is intended to solve*. For example, a production model, although necessarily concerned with product mix and line-speed requirements, might be concerned more specifically with a problem of minimizing inventory. A budget model, in addition to traditional objectives, might lend particular emphasis to measuring and tracking the profitability of a new product introduction. Each functional area in every company has its own individual problems and goals for which the model is developed. Indeed, it is these problems and goals that give the model its character and usefulness.

Establishing the true purpose of a model may prove difficult. Although often misleading and insufficient, existing reports and documents on a problem often provide a suitable starting point. Collection of documents always should be followed up with interviews and discussions with those involved in the targeted area.

It is not unusual to discover multiple users for a proposed model during this early phase of development. The purpose in the exploration phase is to collect uses for the model rather than to evaluate or prioritize. During this investigative process, requirements of indirect users may be discovered. An indirect user is one who desires the output from the model. An example of an indirect user is the treasurer who requires information from a distribution model in order to feed it into a production plan, generating an inventory level against which an accounts payable forecast can be projected.

Once the applications for the model have been identified, an early evaluation of the scope and priorities of each application begins. The purpose is not to fine-tune priorities, but rather to weed out those applications that are clearly of low priority or disproportionate complexity. This will establish the scope of the model. Finally, a judgment can be made regarding the appropriate hardware and software needed.

A *profile* needs to be developed for the proposed model. What issues will be dealt with in the model? What kinds of decisions will be supported through its use? Answering these questions helps develop the model profile, forming the basis for further development. With this goal in mind, the most common procedure is to begin at the end. That is, start with the reports. Because a model is characterized by its objectives, and these objectives are realized in the reports, proper design of the reports (formal or informal) is critical to model development.

Decisions about model structure are made partly by following established procedures, partly by studying past data, and partly by intuition. The better the grasp of known facts and relationships, the more effective the intuitive aspects will be.

Variables are the line items necessary in the model building process for decision making. They can be subdivided into three types:

1. *Uncontrollable variables.* Factors outside the control of management, such as market demand, inflation, currency values, etc. Uncontrollable variables are treated by the model as input data.

2. *Controllable variables.* Parameters of running a business that decisions can change, such as pricing, staffing levels, and advertising expenditures. These usually also are treated as input data.

3. *Dependent variables.* These variables arise from computations (rules and relationships) of uncontrollable and controllable variables. For example, profit, return on investment, cash flow. Although usually common calculations, these too can be viewpoint-specific.

The dependent variables are often figures, such as profit contribution or earnings per share, that are used for setting objectives. Therefore, the success of future decisions is measured as comparisons between desired and actual dependent-variable values as future time periods are reached.

Often a decision is assisted by collecting and sifting various data from past events and then modeling their relationships to investigate alternate possible outcomes. Procedures include:

- Forecasting future uncontrollable variables based on past data and intuition.

- Modeling past relationships to assume future relationships. Future values of dependent variables have a relationship to future values of controllable and uncontrollable variables. The relationships generally are stated as mathematical rules observed in the past and expected in the future; for example: profit = (price × unit sales) − (expenses × inflation factor). The assemblage of such rules is a model of the problem under investigation.

- Varying decisions on controllable variables to investigate alternative outcomes of dependent variables. This is the investigative process often called "what if" modeling. It tests the fluctuations in outcome as compared with desired objectives.

VIEWPOINT MODELING

Models consist of three basic components: the *data structure, calculation rules* (variables), and *report specifications*. The data structure could be a simple two-dimensional spreadsheet consisting of time periods and variables, as shown in Figure 7–1.

Frequently, management desires to view its business from other perspectives, such as by location, as shown in Figure 7–2.

Each "city" box in Figure 7–2 is a two-dimensional spreadsheet, with P & L line items (also called variables) and time periods. The "all locations" box is of similar format in which the sum of each corresponding data item from the individual cities is contained.

Adding dimensions beyond time for the variables contributes meaning and substance to the model. This process is called *viewpoint modeling*. Viewpoint

FIGURE 7–1
Two-Dimensional Spreadsheet

	National Motors Corporation		
	1991	*1992*	*1993*
Sales			
Expense			
Profit			

modeling allows one to operate the model from several perspectives. Ideally, each additional perspective provides greater insight as to the dynamics of the environment. Examples of viewpoints include product, location, channel of distribution, version of data (budget or actual), and customer type. To the extent that each user's objective can be treated as a viewpoint, the model does not necessarily change. In this way, a regional director, a product manager, and a division executive all can use the same model, yet customize the modeling requirements.

Figure 7–3 indicates three different viewpoints: location, distribution channel, and product. The implications of viewpoints on model design depend primarily on the modeling language used.

Spreadsheet languages typically deal with viewpoints either by creating separate models for each viewpoint (Figure 7–4 and Figure 7–5), or by treating viewpoints as variables— for example, NY retail cars revenue = (NY retail cars sold) × (NY retail cars price). Such methods, however, tend to be duplicative and rigid in data handling, rule construction, and reporting.

FIGURE 7–2
Hierarchy for Consolidation

	All Locations	
New York	Chicago	Los Angeles

FIGURE 7–3
Sample Report — Summary of Sales

	Summary of Sales		
	New York	*Chicago*	*Los Angeles*
Wholesale			
Cars			
Trucks			
TOTAL			
Retail			
Cars			
Trucks			
TOTAL			

FIGURE 7–4
Location Hierarchy

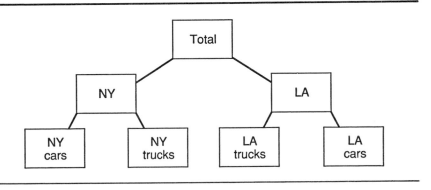

FIGURE 7–5
Product Hierarchy

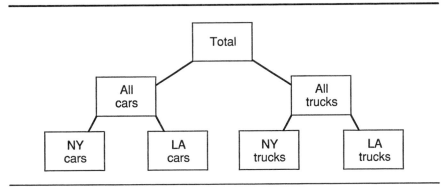

Languages that simulate multidimensionality typically accomplish viewpoint modeling through *data file manipulation*. They partially circumvent the "separate model/separate data" problem by permitting complete structures of multiple hierarchies of the same data. An example of products and cities is shown in Figure 7–6.

While it is true that there then is only one copy of the base-level spreadsheet, thereby eliminating the data inconsistency problem, file manipulation puts its own unique design requirements on such systems. A true multidimensional language provides the easiest means of incorporating viewpoints, since it eliminates the need for file manipulation entirely.

FIGURE 7–6
Multiple Hierarchies

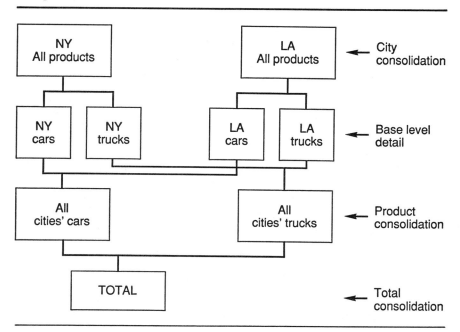

MODEL DEVELOPMENT TIME

The problem of estimating development time in modeling is universal to both novice and experienced modelers alike. Uniqueness of model and application puts practical limits on the accuracy of any guide.

Few things slow down the modeling process as much as having to redesign the model. The most common reason for redesigning is that the initial design of a model is incapable of generating or handling the required information. This problem is typically of two types: (1) poor concept of purpose, or not fully understanding the type and quality of information required; and (2) too few reasonable assumptions, in which the lack of understanding of the modeled system causes too much detail to be handled.

Another significant cause of timing problems in modeling is the handling of too much information. Such difficulties arise from a philosophy of "when in doubt, include." The problem of too much data usually is characterized by:

- Lack of selectivity. Poorly planned models often develop into dinosaurs. A properly developed model profile targets the model to the user, thereby increasing the selectivity of the data and variables included.

- Lowest common denominator (LCD). When used improperly, the LCD principle can cause a model to be overly complex and detailed. The LCD principle is not merely to break down the variable to its lowest level. Rather, the concept requires breaking the variables down to the lowest level necessary to accomplish the goal. For example, a long-range strategic plan might require a consideration of distribution costs, but most certainly would not benefit from such detail as projected costs of shipping by rail to Idaho.

- Poor use of viewpoints. A viewpoint in a model is simply an alternative means of looking at that part of the business. Typically, viewpoints can include product, sales location, distribution channel, customer type, production location, and division.

Viewpoint modeling, or multidimensional modeling, has become increasingly popular because real-world, non-spreadsheet view of the business entity. Unfortunately, most modeling languages simulate multidimensionality by incorporating viewpoints. Each calculation rule is associated with the attributes desired. For example, a model with four products (A, B, C, D) containing the rule

$$\text{Revenue} = \text{Units} \times \text{Price}$$

introduces the viewpoint product by replacing that one rule with

Product A Revenue = Product A Units × Product A Price
Product B Revenue = Product B Units × Product B Price
Product C Revenue = Product C Units × Product C Price
Product D Revenue = Product D Units × Product D Price.

Effective use of a truly multidimensional language can significantly reduce the size of a model and the time required for its construction. This eliminates the duplicative requirement of making many rules (and reports) viewpoint-specific.

Figure 7–7 is intended to help the modeler estimate the time to allow for model and report construction. Even if not used, the weighting structure provides valuable insight into the significance of each of the modeling factors. The schedule assumes that the user has developed the model profile, selected relevant viewpoints, and selected and categorized variables. The last step is critical in determining both the size of the model and the source of data.

Following are brief definitions of the critical modeling factors in the schedule:

- *Data availability.* Ideally, all data are known and controlled by the modeler. Realistically, data collection can take as long as the modeling process itself.

- *Knowledge of business.* Although lack of knowledge of the business is usually not a significant obstacle, few modelers will possess sufficient

FIGURE 7–7
Estimating Model Development Time

Environmental factors: Rate each environmental factor from 1 to 5, with 1 being optimum. then multiply each rating by the given factor weight and add the totals to get the total weighted ratings.

	Rating 1–5		Factor Weight		Total
Business factors					
Data availability	_____	×	6	=	_____
Knowledge of business	_____	×	2	=	_____
Complexity of rules	_____	×	4	=	_____
Complexity of business system	_____	×	2	=	_____
Personal factors					
Modeling experience	_____	×	3	=	_____
Software experience	_____	×	2	=	_____
Continuous time spent	_____	×	1	=	_____
Software factors					
Degree of nonprocedurality	_____	×	6	=	_____
Flexibility of report writer	_____	×	6	=	_____
Total weighted ratings					_____

Multidimensionality (MD factor): Choose the appropriate MD factor, according to the number of dimensions in the model and the software's degree of multidimensionality.

	Software MD Factor		
Number of Model Dimensions	*True*	*Simulated*	*Other*
2	1.0	1.0	1.0
3	1.5	2.6	3.0
4	2.0	4.6	6.5
5	2.5	9.0	12.0
6	3.0	18.0	22.0

MD factor: _____

Number of model variables: _____

Calculate estimated time (hours):

$$\frac{\text{Total weighted ratings} \times \text{MD factor} \times \text{no. of model variables}}{300} + 2 = \text{no. of hours}$$

Example: Assume the total weighted ratings is 70, the number of variables is 200, and the model requires simple consolidation (3 dimensions) using true multi-dimensional software (MD factor = 1.5):

$$\frac{70 \times 1.5 \times 200}{300} + 2 = 72 \text{ hours, estimated model development time}$$

understanding of the business being simulated to not require contributions from others.

- *Complexity of rules.* Some business calculations require complex algorithms and sophisticated financial functions. As calculation rules increase in complexity, the time required to write, debug, and document those rules also increases.

- *Complexity of business system.* A complex business may consist of 20 sales locations, each selling 30 products; 3 production locations, each producing 15 products; different distribution channels; and multiple customer types. Even with relatively simple rules, such complex structures can tax all but the most sophisticated software languages.

- *Size of model.* Generally, the larger the model, the more time required for construction, debugging, and documentation.

- *Modeling experience.* This is a measure of how comfortable the modeler is in all phases of model construction.

- *Software experience.* Regardless of modeling experience, software illiteracy can grind the modeling development time to a snail's pace.

- *Continuous time spent.* Much modeling is accomplished as a purely part-time endeavor. In the absence of continuous development, momentum is lost while successive start-up time is increased.

- *Software ease of use.* Included in this category are such factors as non-procedurality, multidimensionality, useful financial functions, English syntax, and sophistication of report writers. To the extent that each of these factors is present, model development time can be reduced significantly.

Implicit in the conversion factor used by the time estimate schedule is the 80/20 rule. This axiom states that 80 percent of the model development will be done in 20 percent of the time, and 20 percent of the model development will require 80 percent of the time. For most modeling applications, this rule is universal to all users.

DEVELOPING THE MODEL

The steps for developing a model are:

1. Draft or get copies of all required reports. Determine the types of investigative questions that will be asked.

2. List all viewpoints and viewpoint members to be included in the model.

3. Construct an informal schematic of those viewpoints to determine data structure.

4. Construct an outline of the logic and develop the logic rules.

5. Using the outline, break the model into several relatively independent modular concepts.
6. If using a procedural language, determine the sequence of calculations.
7. Program the logic for the computer.

In constructing the schematic of the model structure, it is advisable to begin at the top of the structure. This will help you better understand how data will be consolidated and allocations accomplished.

Outlining helps provide a mental discipline to the modeling effort. Generally, logic, which is first outlined, tends to provide better documentation and require less debugging time; and it is easier to change and lends itself more to a modular development approach.

In larger models, modular development can be a particularly significant aid. Smaller models are easier to write and debug, thus decreasing development time. Equally important, however, is that modular development tends to promote several small successes, as opposed to prolonged periods with no visible achievement. This can go a long way toward keeping enthusiasm high in an environment of protracted, part-time model development. It is often advisable to create a prototype of the full-scale model. This will aid in testing the data structure and complex rules.

Sequencing the calculation rules tells the computer the correct order in which to process the model. This requirement results directly from the inflexibility of procedural programming languages. It must be emphasized that this step is redundant with a nonprocedural language.

Once the model is organized, the next step is to enter the calculation rules. In constructing the logic that drives the model, remember the caveat "it is better to be approximately right than exactly wrong." Many modelers, infatuated with the computer's capability for accuracy, tend to overbuild the model with a confusing array of complex rules as they strive for accuracy. It is vital to remember that all models have their own tolerance for accuracy, which seldom benefits from overindulgence.

Following is a set of practical considerations to incorporate when writing logic rules:

Lowest common denominator (LCD). Make sure that rules relate to the lowest level of variables necessary to satisfy the requirements for the model. For example, in a pricing model, it would be inadvisable to have financial calculations driven by average product pricing if the intent is to examine the impact of product mix on a company's pricing policies. In addition, all critical variable interrelationships should be identified. That is, distribution costs may impact not only cost of sales, but pricing, inventory, and receivables. A modeler should ensure that these interrelationships are reflected in the design of the logic.

Modeling for investment.   It is not unusual for modelers to discover upon completing a model that users may want to investigate business factors for which no provision was made. While reports help provide an architecture for the model, the investigative demands of a problem must play a role in a model's structure.

Outline as narrative.   The outline is an explanation of the modeler's intention at each logical juncture. As such, it is an excellent narrative, providing comments to accompany the logic.

Writing to be read.   For ease of documentation and debugging, the modeler should always indent related successive rules for easy reading. Furthermore, all operations should be separated by spaces.

KISS.   The KISS principle (Keep It Short and Simple) is particularly applicable in modeling. Several small, simple rules are much better than one large, complex rule. Besides significantly reducing the chance of error, small, simple rules are easier to document, debug, and understand.

Variable names.   Within the restrictions of the individual software, the modeler always should strive to make the variable names as understandable as possible.

Analytical rules.   Analytical rules aid in the analysis of model relationships. For example, gross profit percent and other contribution ratios help measure and analyze performance. Always leave analytical rules for the last part of the logic. This is for three reasons:

1. Since analytical rules have a separate purpose from development logic, separation does not interfere with the flow of the logic.
2. Some languages allow analytical relationships to be specified in the report. Imbedding analysis into logic restricts the modeler from using this highly flexible feature.
3. Once developed, the part of the model logic that typically changes the most is the analytical logic; therefore, segregation is less likely to interrupt the model itself.

DATA FOR THE MODEL

The importance of data to the modeling process is underestimated all too often. There are primarily two types of data: historical and forecast. Historical data typically is used for one of three applications:

- *Forecasting.* Using statistical techniques for developing future data values based on historical relationships.
- *Analysis.* Examining history for quantitative relationships, usually in the hope of using historical relationships to project future performance.
- *Variance.* Quantitatively comparing past performance to current and/or projected performance.

Forecast data is data that is input directly into future periods of the model as distinguished from data results calculated by the model for forecast periods. Typical examples of forecast data related to uncontrollable variables would be interest rates, raw material prices, and wage rates. Controllable-variable data values, such as budgeted expense items, also will be input directly into the model for forecast periods.

Historical data is data usually found in the ledger or some other corporate database. Forecast data often may be found in the organization's budget or accessed from third-party data services such as Dow Jones or Citibank. Transferring data from one of these sources can be accomplished in several ways:

Manual input. While this method is quite common, it suffers from significant drawbacks. Input often requires considerable time and effort, so the productivity cost is high. Because "to err is human," we can expect the manual process to be error-prone. Also, manual input becomes a bottleneck between data availability and model execution, so timeliness suffers.

Manual input can be accomplished by any or all of four methods, depending on the language used:

1. Use full-screen editing to enter data into an empty "spreadsheet."
2. Allow the computer to prompt for all required data values.
3. Enter the data as part of the model logic.
4. Establish user-created files of data required (data files).

Of all manual methods listed, the inclusion of data as part of model logic is least desirable, since any change in data would require editing the logic rules. If the model subsequently "bombs," a search may be forced for inadvertent changes in logic, as well as errors in data input. The other manual methods should be evaluated based on individual preference, application, and the operating characteristics of the software.

Foreign file interface (FFI). These systems typically extract data from a computerized file (source file) and create selected two-dimensional data files (object files). The user can accomplish this either interactively or, more typically, in batch mode (automatically) by instructing the computer about the location of the desired data. Once established, object files can be called into the model.

These systems offer the obvious advantage of increased productivity and accuracy, since the data are "untouched" by human hands. Because FFI systems often require significant instructions, however, they usually are limited to large and/or repetitive data requirements.

Direct access. Under this process, the model directly accesses a source file without the need to establish a temporary object file. While this system offers all the advantages of FFI, possible technological and/or security issues specific to an operating system may need to be addressed.

Remember that one of the few problems modelers do not face is lack of data. In fact, most models suffer from the opposite problem of being overburdened with irrelevant data. The modeler should incorporate only minimum data to meet the model's requirements.

When entering data, it is always a sound policy to proof for accuracy prior to running the model with calculation logic. It is far more difficult to evaluate/debug the logic of the model if the accuracy of the data cannot be relied upon constantly.

STUDY REPORTS

There are two common types of reports: tabular and graphic. Both types also can be classified as "quick and dirty" reports, which are for the user's own consumption; and formal reports, which are primarily vehicles for communication.

The purpose of formal report-writing is communication. Reports should be designed to maximize communication by first asking the question "What information needs to be conveyed?" This selection process is much easier in graphics, which, due to their simplified structure, force the modeler to communicate only a few critical relationships. Tabular reports, unfortunately, can be as numerically verbose as the size of the paper allows. Reports should be designed selectively. The format should maximize communication of that information deemed important.

The most common report format is characterized by time periods across the top and variables down the side as shown in Figure 7–8. Viewpoint reporting (Figure 7–9) can be an enormously powerful communication tool, especially in light of recent developments in multidimensional software. It allows easy focus on the information to be conveyed in a format that is most useful to a particular audience.

The level of report detail should vary inversely with the executive level to which the report is to be submitted. A vice president rarely will wish to see the level of detail that is common to a department manager. Such a level of detail rarely aids communication and, in fact, often proves to be a significant obstacle.

FIGURE 7–8
Spreadsheet Reporting

	1Q	*2Q*	*3Q*	*4Q*	*Total*
Sales					
Cost					
Gross profit					
Overhead					
Net profit					
Profit as % of sales					

FIGURE 7–9
Viewpoint Reporting

	NY		*LA*		*NY B/(W) LA*	
	Cars	*Trucks*	*Cars*	*Trucks*	*Cars*	*Trucks*
Sales						
1Q						
2Q						
3Q						
4Q						
Total year						
Profit as % of sales						
1Q						
2Q						
3Q						
4Q						
Total year						

DEBUGGING AND DOCUMENTING THE MODEL

Once the model is written, the process of debugging begins. Following are some guidelines to help this process.

Logic that works versus logic that is right. By far, the easiest errors to find are those that "bomb" when run by the computer. In almost all cases, such system-detected errors are highlighted by their location and by their cause as well. Begin by pursuing the error messages generated throughout the system. System-detected errors are most frequently of three types: typographical errors; incorrect syntax; and procedural errors (when using procedural languages). Remember that although the logic may work, it should not be assumed that it is necessarily right. Problems of incorrect logic are much more difficult to discover.

Back to the report.   Once the model runs, the next task in debugging is to see that it runs accurately. In checking for accuracy, one should be selective in the data chosen to audit. The report is an excellent source in selecting auditable variables.

Testing.   The primary method of testing for accuracy is by comparing calculated results against other data. There are three primary methods of accomplishing this task:

1. *History.* By designing a test run of the model with historical data, calculated and known results can be compared.
2. *Parallel runs.* In designing a model to replace manual systems, a common technique is the parallel run. Parallel runs are dress rehearsals for the model, and the manual systems become mirrors.
3. *Test data.* One can also calculate the model manually, using test data and known results. It is recommended that such tests initially be limited to critical variables and uniquely calculated time periods.

Documentation.   Documentation is the lifeline of a model. In its absence, models tend to become "black boxes," resisting change and promoting suspicion and nonuse. When properly prepared, documentation serves several functions. It serves as a refresher for the model builder upon subsequent changes to the model. It provides the Information Center with reference material through which it may catalog the model for subsequent use by others. It provides all users with the necessary information to revise and adapt the model for their respective applications. Finally, it provides a critical communication link between the model developer and the respective user communities.

Depending upon the size and scope of the model, the documentation package can be quite extensive. The documentation package potentially should include:

- Purpose of the model and its limitations.
- History of the project.
- Those lower cost/benefit and priority applications that were dropped along with corresponding rationale.

- Critical assumptions implicit in the model.
- Data required and sources of the data.
- A system-wide explanation (how models are organized).
- Logic explanation.
- A test run of the model with reports.
- Key variables for monitoring, and respective tolerance levels.

While laudable, inclusion of all of the above documentation items is not always required (depending on the model type). For example, ad hoc models typically need very little documentation. At a critical minimum, all models should include both the system and the logic explanations.

While some modeling systems are said to be self-documenting, it is usually in the context of logic documentation where this is intended. Self-documentation is usually nothing more than the fortunate by-product of program rules stated in English syntax. This type of logic documentation is rarely sufficient, which explains the provision for comments in most modeling systems. It is advisable that such user-applied documentation be provided concurrently with rule development. Too many models go undocumented due to stale memories and conflicting post-development priorities.

The initial debugging and documentation must be followed by routine monitoring of the model as it is used. Since most models are designed to simulate and/or forecast an aspect of the business environment, a model's performance against these objectives should be monitored periodically. As the business changes, such monitoring helps keep the model current and accurate.

While the most common method of monitoring model performance is comparison-to-actual, some models, by their nature, do not lend themselves to such analysis. Product pricing models, for example, are intended to simulate the financial impact of various pricing alternatives. Since it is quite possible that none of the proposed alternatives were implemented, there may be no consistent actual data against which to evaluate. In these situations, it is common to simulate actual data by recreating the actual scenario as closely as possible.

It would be neither practical nor desirable to attempt to monitor all model variables. As in other phases of the modeling process, the report should provide assistance in choosing key variables to monitor. In addition, all variables monitored should be higher-level, derived variables, such as dependent figures of merit.

Finally, the monitoring process should include the audience for whom the model was prepared. Does it continue to satisfy the audience's requirements? This nontechnical but important aspect of monitoring is often neglected, even when the audience is the modeler.

MODEL INVESTIGATION

A primary benefit of computer modeling lies in the ability to alter and test the dynamics of the simulated business. The following is an explanation of common investigative capabilities of models, as well as their use and limitations.

"What if" analysis.   This type of analysis allows one to make temporary changes in the model and is by far the most common investigative technique used in modeling. "What if" modeling is analogous to making several "cuts" or "passes" at the problem. Temporary changes can be made either to uncontrollable variables ("What if the prime rate increases two points?") or to controllable variables ("What if the price of my product increases 10 percent?").

Goal seeking (backward iteration).   Goal seeking is the process of determining how to achieve a desired goal by changing a specified variable. Although not as popular as "what if" analysis, goal seeking can be very useful, especially in cash management models ("What must my inventory level be to maintain a minimum cash balance?"). Through goal seeking, one also can arrive at a starting point for "what if" questions, as it avoids concentrating on variables that cannot assist in reaching goals reasonably.

Step-function "what if."   Sometimes called *sensitivity analysis,* this investigative process allows the user to put the model through a series of incremental or decremental changes and see the results at each step, ("What if oil prices changed from + 15 percent to − 10 percent in increments of 5 percent?"). In addition to providing the user with a better concept of the model's dynamics, this technique is extremely useful in negotiations. For example, through a sensitivity analysis, one can arrive at a rule of thumb for measuring the impact of changes to critical variables. ("For every wage increase of one dollar, my total labor expense increases by $800,000.")

Risk analysis.   The most common technique used for risk analysis is Monte Carlo simulation. This involves associating selected variables with probability distribution ranges when single-point estimates are unavailable or inappropriate. Each range describes the operating characteristics of each variable. This technique can result in such statements as, "There is a 15 percent probability that costs will be more than three dollars, and 85 percent probability that they will be less." Although useful, this technique has had limited usage, primarily due to the difficulty of obtaining meaningful distribution ranges. Furthermore, even when appropriate, management is often skeptical about probabilistic "derived" values, disregarding them to fall back on an "upside downside" approach.

There are two important design considerations when using investigative techniques:

1. *Causality.* Make sure that all critical variables have causal links. For example, it is not unusual to link inventory levels with cash balances. Similarly, inventory turnover ratios are derived from inventory levels. Yet, unless the turnover ratio is linked to cash, the user cannot ask the meaningful question, "How will my cash balance be affected by decreasing the ratio to ten?"

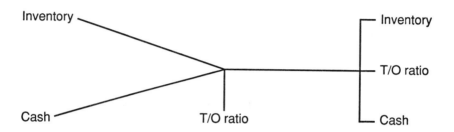

Causality design issues can be aided through such modeling features as "what uses" or "what effects." These features allow the user to see all causal links for any designated variable, thus allowing effective investigative development.

2. *Multidimensionality.* Most languages with otherwise excellent investigative capabilities lose their functionality across other levels of hierarchy or other dimensions. As a result, the user might be precluded from asking, "What should the profitability of the eastern division be to increase corporate profits to $3 million?" Or, "How would a proposed change in product mix impact the agricultural division?"

In the face of such limitations, one can construct the model only so that all dimensions are within one set of logic rather than separate segments. In effect, this reduces the multidimensional problem down to two dimensions. Unfortunately, while this solves the immediate issue, it leaves unresolved a host of other design/reporting issues covered previously in this guide. Therefore, for two-dimensional and simulated multidimensional languages, the model builder usually should limit use of investigative techniques to consolidated two-dimensional models.

Chapter Eight

Special and Future Management Issues

A number of special and future management issues relative to MSS are reviewed in this chapter. Computer resource management is particularly important. Three levels are available: connection to a central mainframe with central control, connection to a departmental processor with departmental control, and stand-alone personal computers. General considerations for the alternatives are noted.

Data management trends are blurring traditional boundaries, and, as micro-computing efforts expand, there are emerging horizontal and vertical interfaces. The obvious direction for MSS is toward relational database systems.

Data ownership and data sharing are discussed because the informal sharing of data is no longer adequate. Information must be viewed as a corporate resource. Critical attention must be paid to the subject of data ownership and control. This includes functional control, custody of data, and control of the information generated.

Creative ways of improving the quality of management information must be examined. Some aspects of quality assurance are discussed as a positive influence in gaining more data accuracy and standardization. Standards and procedures, and test management are good possibilities for use with MSS.

There are a number of security and disaster requirements that should not be overlooked. Some proven and useful operational policies are provided for MSS use.

COMPUTER RESOURCE MANAGEMENT

The areas of concern for those involved with decision support systems have greatly widened in recent years. The emphasis is no longer on single, stand-alone microcomputers and a few packaged programs; it has expanded to include networked systems, libraries of programs, and more complex data retrieval systems. The maturing of the Information Center concept has opened up new possibilities for management review and analysis.

There are now commonly three levels of computer resource management available. Each of these levels offers different concepts and controls in establishing management support systems. These three alternatives to the management of decision support systems are (1) connection to a central mainframe with central control, (2) connection to a departmental processor with departmental control, and (3) stand-alone personal computers with departmental control.

None of these alternatives precludes the others being used at the same time. They are each very much equipment-dependent and operating-system-dependent, however, and must be planned carefully with considerable allocated funds. They are alternatives with specific requirements and specific capabilities. In many corporations, two or three of the levels are in place simultaneously. Each organization should look for the particular mix of these alternatives to satisfy its own needs in an optimal way.

The Information Center should have a part to play with each of the alternatives. The problems involved should be clearly understood, however, so that the IC is properly staffed, offers the appropriate types of support, and issues guidelines that fit various situations. A single IC can handle more than one alternative approach, but the offerings will differ, and the attitude of the IC staff will have to be adaptable.

Connection to the Central Mainframe

An important aspect of microcomputing connected to the central mainframe for MSS is that it is under central control, which is essential to establish equitable functions and priorities. Many organizations already had large applications designed for on-line inquiry and use. If they could be expanded, then a useful centralized computing operation could be set up, and strong control could be maintained centrally. A major advantage of this type of operation is that it could be set up and maintained readily by an existing systems staff. Many organizations have gone this way. Others, such as financial institutions, felt that the security exposure was simply too great. There would be too much at stake to allow multiple access to central files with insufficient control available. Therefore, as time progressed, the concept of direct connection to the central mainframe was viewed as useful for only engineering and operational information systems.

The majority of Information Centers are in IBM environments because the great majority of corporate computers are IBM processors. Basic IBM system products are frequently combined with other system products and unique designs. This means that they will access data in files with IBM organization, on mainframes with IBM architecture. Even if minicomputers of other manufacturers are used to handle time-sharing of downloaded data, or if systems programs are purchased from other vendors, the basic data access will be from IBM files, and IBM system products will always be considered for use.

For data access in IBM environments, there are many combinations of file and data specifications, end-user programs, and interactive programs. At present, a variety of operating systems and intersystem communications are available. The data access approach that is selected must center on the end-user products desired, the data requirements, and the operating environments. Other considerations that need to be addressed include type of service demanded by the users, type of data that will be required, methods of extracting the information from the files, necessary reformatting of data for the products being used, and concurrent servicing of multiple users.

The combinations and strategies available for data access from IBM equipment are numerous and can be selected to satisfy individual requirements. There are two general approaches to data access that will strongly influence the selection of systems: periodic and dynamic. *Periodic access,* or a batch processing system, is handled on a scheduled basis with planned end-user needs. There are generally scheduled data updates of an extract file, which, in turn, are made available to users. The data is usually historical, which means it is from any file previous to the current cycle of the application. The applications are usually those that are run routinely, with all the data available in fixed formats. Any data that is used thus will be stable over the period that is being analyzed since it will not be further updated until the next cycle. Such an approach is suitable for analyses that have high-volume data usage, since any reasonable amount of data can be extracted from a historical file with good control. It is also suited for analyses that use many different data elements. On the operational central file, a variety of data elements may be difficult to locate and extract rapidly, but on an extracted file, they all can be pulled off and arranged in a usable sequence. Periodic access creates a nonoperational file, so it does not interfere with current operations.

Dynamic access, or an interactive processing system on an operational file, is essentially time-sharing. It offers direct access to central computer files at the existing level of updating. End-users are given data updates on demand, with current data from operational applications, including applications that are being updated in real time. In such systems, the data usually will be variable during the period being studied, and the results that are obtained may not balance exactly with any particular periodic report. Thus the data is considered to be "unstable." Dynamic access usually is characterized by low-volume data usage, because the period of access does not give time for large-volume data extractions. The end-user also has light usage of the data that is extracted because ad hoc analyses often are being made under a time constraint.

The data files available on central computers are relatively large compared with personal computers. The problem is to reduce the volume and complexity of the available data. The extraction process must change the physical structure of the data and restructure it logically so that it corresponds better to the needs of the end-users. Large, hierarchical data files are difficult for ad hoc searches. Usually a relational view of the data, or a flat file view of a relatively small amount of data, may be most appropriate to the user's requirements. Utilities are obviously available from IBM and other companies for handling the extraction, and for loading the restructured data into the files that are accessible to the end-user's computer or to an auxiliary processor. It is generally the responsibility of the Information Center to arrange for such extractions and to set up standards, procedures, and controls of the extracted and copied files. The IC staff must inform users as to the structure of the data they can expect, its timeliness, and its validity and controls.

If end-user work space is on the central computer files, it will be controlled by the Data Administration group in Information Services. Whenever users have direct connection to the central mainframe, they must come under all the operational methods and controls that have been established for the security and integrity of the files.

In the case of periodic updating, or batch processing systems from the central computer center's viewpoint, data access is handled by the computer operators in a batch processing mode on a scheduled basis. There are a number of file reformatting service programs through which file copies, subsets, and extracts may be prepared for use by end-users at specific times that have been agreed upon. If necessary, IC staff also should be prepared with such a system to program and initiate special extracts to meet the needs of users, based on the priority of their requirements. They could use the same extract services at different times than those scheduled.

Departmental Processor

Many organizations concerned about a lack of system and data control if they allow on-line access to their operational files have opted for a *departmental, distributive-system* concept. From the central Information Services viewpoint, this approach can be much easier to manage because each departmental processor is under the control of departmental management, which can cover the reduced span of users and apply procedures relevant to their areas. Such tasks as standardization of personal computers are accomplished much more readily in a single department. A departmental operation also is managed more easily because local knowledge of the system applications permits managers to determine if they will be cost-effective to implement.

It should be made clear to all departments, however, that their systems must be compatible with the central computer system, which may be IBM's SNA or a similar environment. It is foolish to permit stand-alone environments for departmental computers, because sooner or later they will have a need for corporate information. Typically, for example, engineering groups do not see why they cannot install their own processor with capabilities specifically useful to the engineers, then be left alone. The reason they should not is simple. As their work develops, they also will want access to corporate data. This may be for budget analysis, for costing their designs, or for transfer of information to other departments.

Technicians must have access to the business side of the organization, and vice versa. Therefore, any departmental processor that is incompatible with the systems on the central computer could lead to later troubles and expense. There are so many ways to achieve compatibility between the central and departmental computers that there is no excuse to neglect this function of data interchange.

The great attraction of the departmental processor is local management and control. The costs, operation, and priorities fall under managers who are responsible for the success of a particular group. They feel that they are not unduly loaded with overhead, as they easily can be from a central processor. They have a say in their own strategies, long-term and short-term. In the long term, however, they should be expected to freely interchange information at all levels, regardless of what projects individuals are working on, and whether they are using only the departmental system or the mainframe directly. In the short term, they are expected to set their own goals realistically and to raise the data processing awareness of executives and managers in their areas. There should be corporate insistence on sharing of information and openness about learned experiences.

This means that although there is local management and control, there must be involvement of all departments that are learning from computers with other departments in the organization. This can be done in a number of ways. The most formal is to establish a steering committee made up of equivalent managers from all departments who will discuss progress, standards, and plans. An intermediate approach is to have the Information Center staff talk to the departments regularly and relay interesting information to others. An informal approach is to have a users group or distribute a newsletter about achievements and problems solved.

A steering committee is probably the best approach to establish some coordination among departmental processing groups, because managers will be pressed by their peers to cooperate and produce. It is also possible to educate a particular group at its own level, and to make personnel aware of the imaginative uses of technology through site visits, presentations from vendors, and demonstrations. A steering group helps give order to the growth of the departmental systems concept. It can recommend the best approach to implementing departmental systems. It can get divisional involvement with the people responsible for the technology. It can secure commitment and a reduction in organizational resistance by showing that everyone is in the same boat. And it can give each departmental or divisional manager confidence that he or she is proceeding at the expected pace.

Stand-Alone Personal Computers

The third alternative for managing microcomputers for MSS is to foster the acquisition and use of stand-alone personal computers. These units could be attached to a communications network that provides access to a mainframe or to local departmental computers, but usually they are not. Most of their use is strictly stand-alone for analysis and word processing. Every organization will have many microcomputers in this mode, particularly smaller businesses. PCs are now cheap enough to replace most desk calculators and typewriters, and the bulk of the work done on such stand-alone equipment will be on-demand, irregular applications, and smaller, routine analyses. This all will be departmental or small-group work, so it clearly will come under departmental control. The cost of such units normally will fall under the departmental manager's discretion.

There are several problems with this widespread, innocuous use of microcomputers. Some departments will grow to a considerable size with many computers, the support for many types may become difficult, and sooner or later most departments will want to acquire corporate information from the larger computers. Despite these problems, there always will be a relatively large number of stand-alone computers compared to the organization's networked computers. The only solution is to be aware of the situation, try for some standardization of hardware and software, and understand the normal problems that will arise.

The growth in power of stand-alone computers can be considerable. Peripherals and large amounts of memory can be attached to them so that they can handle large and complex problems with substantial data files. Larger departmental computers have a habit of growing even further, and it is not uncommon for an internal impasse to be reached, so that external consultants are called in at management's request to force integration with the central computer. What started as a few personal computers successfully develops into a minor data processing shop.

A more difficult problem is that stand-alones often are selected without planning by managers, strictly on the basis of some interesting features or price. The fact that they are not compatible with the other corporate computers is not considered until troubles develop and hardware repair or software support is needed. Information Centers cannot be staffed to support more than a few varieties of personal computers. When there is a proliferation of vendors, the organization has very little clout with any particular vendor. Reasonable support is feasible only if there are limitations on the types of computers that can be acquired.

The problem with interchange of information is particularly common with office systems and engineering groups. Difficulties arise when their information has to be shared with other departments or with corporate, when files of information are required from the central computer, or when little attention is paid to data security. As groups become sophisticated in their computer use, they want to send messages back and forth between members in their own division. They also want to share applications. They can be justifiably upset if they have not been told previously that there is a compatibility problem and that the standards and procedures that were developed were not primarily to gain control, but were designed to make future computing easier.

Even when rules are in place, there always will be many freestanding personal computers in an organization because they are simply too easy to acquire; and there always will be a proliferation of vendors. The most sensible argument for standardization is that both present and future support can be provided realistically only if there is some cooperation. It is virtually impossible to "manage" stand-alone personal computers centrally, but cooperation can be made most attractive. Greatly reduced costs for hardware and software can be provided when there is some standardization. The most telling argument, however, is that systems the departments can grow with should be required. Most PCs look so small that little thought is given to their future expansion, but managers should understand that they will be used heavily and soon will "run out of gas," and that future steps must be considered. People putting smaller programs on PCs do not dream of the time when they will be faced with major conversion efforts unless it is explained to them by those who have had such experience. The prospect of major retraining of staff usually is not pointed out initially. These problems must be noted without attempting to try to stem the flood of PCs that will arrive.

Stand-alone PCs are not managed just by means of standards, directives, and attempted control through the purchasing function. Many are priced too reasonably for a rules approach to be effective. The best way to manage freestanding microcomputers is through training courses that emphasize the advantages of compatibility for present operation and future growth. If managers are given education in these principles, sufficient management control soon will be exercised. Widespread microcomputers can be managed most effectively by the "carrot" process, offering substantial advantages in price, support, and information availability.

General Considerations for the Alternatives

Some general management considerations for alternative modes of computing are given in Figure 8–1. Note that the questions are directed to in-house analytical and management support applications, and not to large on-line production systems. There are completely different considerations if an extensive production system is being developed with on-line access. In such a case, the central computer and network would be designed and acquired specifically to handle many users. For example, question 11 suggests that if only one to five users access any given data file, then a system connected to a central computer network is favored.

FIGURE 8–1

Departmental and Centralized Computing: General Considerations

No.	Item	Yes	No	N/A	Comments
			Responses		
	Considerations favoring a departmental processor				
1.	Do 10 or more managers need to access the same data files?	____	____	____	
2.	Is a wide variety of application software needed?	____	____	____	
3.	Do managers require information or documents as a shared resource?	____	____	____	
4.	Are terminal and network management capabilities needed within the department?	____	____	____	
5.	Will the number of users, the number of applications, or the size of the database probably be expanded?	____	____	____	
6.	Is integrated office automation software being planned for the department?	____	____	____	
7.	Can central files be downloaded routinely, as required?	____	____	____	
8.	Will there be a need for problem determination and resolution that is unique to the department?	____	____	____	
9.	Is frequent peer-to-peer communication being planned within the department?	____	____	____	
10.	Does the department as a group require access to other external networks?	____	____	____	
	Considerations favoring a central computer network				
11.	Do only one to five users access any given data file?	____	____	____	
12.	Will the group of users for any file remain small?	____	____	____	
13.	Do users require on-line access to rapidly changing data in an operational system?	____	____	____	
14.	Are full-capacity personal computers or workstations required?	____	____	____	
15.	Are many different types of personal computers and workstations required?	____	____	____	
16.	Is general access to a large, active central database required?	____	____	____	

FIGURE 8–1 *(continued)*

No.	Item	Yes	No	N/A	Comments
17.	Are complex mainframe software and communications packages required?	—	—	—	
18.	Is database security and control critically important?	—	—	—	
19.	Is controlled access to the central computer in the company network required?	—	—	—	
20.	Has an established local area network proven satisfactory, or is an extensive LAN being planned?	—	—	—	
21.	Are the required software packages available for the system?	—	—	—	
22.	Are usable 4-GL development tools available?	—	—	—	

Requirements for the computer being considered

No.	Item	Yes	No	N/A	Comments
23.	Are other desired productivity tools available?	—	—	—	
24.	Is the database capability sufficient?	—	—	—	
25.	Are there adequate database support and inquiry packages?	—	—	—	
26.	Is the network management control sufficient?	—	—	—	
27.	Are there strong security and recovery capabilities?	—	—	—	
28.	Does the system interface with the required IBM networks?	—	—	—	
29.	Does it interface with the client-server environment?	—	—	—	
30.	Can the proposed departmental staff support the operation?	—	—	—	
31.	Will planning and funding for departmental training be required?	—	—	—	
32.	Does the system have sufficient library facilities and document distribution?	—	—	—	
33.	Are there easy upgrade paths and conversions available or planned for the system?	—	—	—	
34.	Is the software licensing favorable for the plan?	—	—	—	

Considerations favoring stand-alone personal computers

No.	Item	Yes	No	N/A	Comments
35.	Are there small groups of analysts with highly specialized program requirements?	—	—	—	

FIGURE 8–1 *(concluded)*

No.	Item	Yes	No	N/A	Comments
36.	Do their applications not require access to central data files?	___	___	___	
37.	Are they using self-developed or purchased programs?	___	___	___	
38.	Are their programs continually being modified?	___	___	___	
39.	Is their main data use from external files or time-sharing files?	___	___	___	
40.	Is there a strong need for confidentiality?	___	___	___	
41.	Are specialized graphics or printing equipment attached?	___	___	___	
42.	Is computer portability frequently required?	___	___	___	
43.	Is specialized equipment being tested?	___	___	___	
44.	Is the location not connected to the network?	___	___	___	
45.	Does the department want to operate independently?	___	___	___	

There are at least two reasons for this. First, if there are very few users, it is unlikely that a departmental computer can be justified. Second, if files in a large central computer are being accessed for analytical purposes, the number of terminals must be kept low or production jobs will be degraded in operation. Similar considerations apply to the other questions.

Keep in mind that this checklist is merely a screening vehicle for determining the feasibility and desirability of the alternatives.

DATA MANAGEMENT TRENDS AND RELATIONAL DATABASE SYSTEMS[1]

There are three forces in the industry that have posed tremendous challenges to both the users and vendors of software products. These forces are the demand for information, the increasing literacy in and acceptance of computing, and the need for integration. They have created a dynamic and expanding environment and marketplace.

---

[1]This section is extracted from a presentation given by Leonard P. Bergstrom, Real Decisions Corporation, Darien, Conn.

The demand for information is part of an information revolution that is going on, and it very much affects our lives. We know that access to timely, reliable, and accurate information is a critical success factor for continued success as a business. At the same time, it is difficult to keep up because there are better options in hardware and software, and very active communications. It is hard to stay on top of things. It is a major opportunity area for people in the service business and for people trying to supply services to large in-house groups.

At the same time, there is increasing computer literacy. This is particularly evident with the younger generation, but it is also true for many managers.

There also has been much more of an acceptance of automation. Management productivity has become an important type of consideration for people. MIS, in general, has moved up in the hierarchy, and it has expanded and let people move on to horizontal careers. The reason for this is that if we are delivering information services to a major corporation, we really have to know what makes the corporation tick and what is important for it.

Finally, there is a need for integration. Most organizations are using a large variety of hardware and operating systems and software packages. That is why people are putting tremendous pressure on trying to integrate all the diverse systems they have purchased over the years into some type of cohesive strategy.

It is important to note that information has become a critical success factor. There are three types of information that people need to address. The first type is external data. These are publicly available databases, such as financial, econometric, and demographic databases, that historically have been the problems of remote computer-service vendors such as DRI, CompuServe, and ADP. The second is private information that is controlled by the user and needs to be identified and shared. Then there is corporate information, which historically has been controlled by Data Processing. One view that can be taken of this is that a window is needed to the "corporate data warehouse." We cannot let this information be locked away in COBOL programs. We need to get it and distribute it to key managers in the corporations.

Why do you want information? (See Figure 8–2.) Obviously, information gives knowledge and power and is the leverage of the corporate information

FIGURE 8–2
Information: Why Do You Want It?

Leverage a corporate resource
Gain a competitive edge in the Information Age
Respond to increasing complexity
Deal with performance squeeze

---

resource. The most successful user of information has the most leverage. It gives you a competitive edge in this Information Age.

Information, of course, is the reason for an Information Center's existence. One of the problems in many of the early Information Centers in corporations is that not enough information was available. That is one reason they got off to a slow start and had a lot of failure.

In the modern corporate environment, managing a business has become more complex. There is more international competition, and there are more people getting into different businesses, even domestically. So there is a performance squeeze. Obviously, there is a great need for better-informed management.

Many groups are managing with executive information systems (EIS). Observations on these types of systems that are being installed are, first, that outside comparisons are very important in executive information systems. It is not enough just to deliver internal data. People need to look at their competitors, their peer groups, and see how they compare. It is also important to be able to provide historical information or a pattern over time.

The second thing is that the information underlying these EIS systems is more important than the software and tools used to access it. Start out with an individual database geared to the users. They tend to learn more quickly and expand from it much more rapidly. This leads to the theory that less is more in information databases. Many of the EIS systems coming out now present too much information. They are not updated with new information, so they really cannot work very well with it. If possible, have the databases driven by the users themselves. That has become more important.

People must cope with the forces in the industry. There has been a blurring of traditional boundaries. On a minor scale, we see a lot of vendors who had traditional DSS products moving into more data management activities. On a major scale, people who are traditional providers of corporate software are moving down into the realm of the departmental and personal types of users. It is an attempt to be more of a total solution with one vendor.

This is especially true in the data management area (Figure 8–3). Vendors are expanding their product lines from corporate systems to departmental to personal computers, all with interconnections.

FIGURE 8–3
Data Management Trends

Corporate/departmental/personal
A relational emphasis
Emerging horizontal and vertical interfaces
Expansion of micro efforts

Obviously, there is now a relational emphasis. Of all the structures, relational technology is easiest to understand and work with. The problem we see is that now all vendors have "relational" capabilities. Into these old products that were more hierarchically based, they put a MATCH and a JOIN, and they say, "Now we are a relational system." Be sure to scrutinize those type of claims as to what is truly relational and what is not.

There are many emerging horizontal and vertical interfaces, especially with structured query language (SQL). Everybody in the industry is connecting to SQL in some way. There are more vertical interfaces among some of the 4-GL vendors, and it is possible now to reach up and get the corporate data that is in a DB2 or an IMS database. Some of the horizontal interfaces are used by the people in Information Centers. A typical combination of software is called FITS, where they have FOCUS, ISPS, Telegraf, and SAS. Each is there to do different kinds of activities. There has been a tremendous explosion of the micro efforts. They lag behind some of the earlier financial products efforts, but now, with the increasing power of microcomputers, there are some significant developments. The development of micro software is now driving mainframe developments.

There are good reasons for the increased emphasis in the database and data management area. Figure 8–4 shows some of the statistics from the Real Decisions Corporation program. When people are using software, close to 60 percent of the usage is in the data management area. Many times it goes up to well over 90 percent. Other areas include graphics, statistics, and financial modeling. Note that some of the data management products now have these other types of capabilities within them. Data management is the most widely used software resource. Cullinet handled corporate data for years with IDMS product. Its new release was IDMS/R with new relational capabilities. It came down to addressing user needs. Then it came up with an information database idea, which should be a repository for people. It connects that with its Golden Gate product. There is a "paper strategy" to deliver systems in all three types of areas: corporate, departmental, and personal. ADR has a similar approach with its DATACOM, its DB Dictionary system, IDEAL, Data Query, and some personal products.

The traditional departmental vendors have approached this a little differently. Information Builders has made a complete personal-computer-type version for FOCUS, so that it has almost all of the capabilities of the mainframe version. In addition, it has expanded its departmental type of reaches with versions for the VAX and WANG. It continues to try to get those tightly knit hooks into the IMS, DB2, or even IDMS types of databases that are used for the corporate data.

One vendor that has done something different is Martin Marietta Data Systems with its RAMIS program. It is rewriting its core database so it can handle the larger, more production-oriented transaction systems. This is an example of a traditional, departmental, fourth-generation language vendor trying to move up into the corporate information area.

FIGURE 8–4
System Usage Breakdown

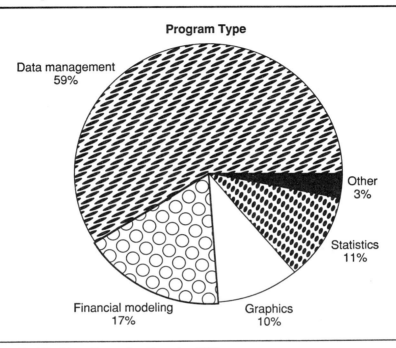

Source: Real Decisions Corporation, December 1985.

The Characteristics of Systems

It would be helpful if there was one vendor, one solution. However, differences between providing solutions in a corporate environment, as opposed to the personal-decision-support level, mean that vendors have a problem trying to do both (see Figure 8–5). MIS and DP are accustomed to being in control. They have very large systems and large volume. They are well-defined, scheduled systems, and they are transaction-oriented with a rigid structure. In an Information Center or decision-support environment there are user-controlled systems, selective information, and a lot of ad hoc work. Users need access to extracts and summaries, and they have to deal with a very flexible structure. These things are in direct conflict with what the vendors are trying to do in these software arenas.

On the data processing side, people always have processed a solution for a direct-cost benefit. On the decision-support side, you evolve the solution. It has much more added value. On the data processing side, you want to optimize your hardware. On the decision-support side, you want to optimize your management.

FIGURE 8–5
Characteristics of Systems

Category	MIS/DP	DSS/IC
Processing	Control, volume	Ad hoc, selective
Data	Process solutions	Evaluate solutions
Usage	Experts	Generalists
Evaluation	Logical, cost benefit	Associative, added value

On the data processing side you deal with experts with very logical types of orientation for systems, whereas on the decision-support side you get more generalists who use more associative means of thinking.

The Data Warehouse

The "data warehouse" concept (Figure 8–6) is the key to the solution. A data warehouse is a facility that provides users with access to all of the data they need or are allowed to see at that point in time, and in a manner that facilitates the productive use of the data and its transformation into information. With the computer phenomena that are out there, such as Information Centers, personal computers, and the 4-GLs, we can see that the users and, increasingly, management are expecting more and more to be able to access corporate data.

As for the principal elements and prerequisites for success, we see basically three or four different factors. One is speed. Obviously, the typical corporate data resource involves incredible amounts of data. Multiple 3380s are very common. People want to get to the information they need, then use it within a reasonable amount of time in an interactive environment. It is very important to look at speed.

The second factor is ease of use. Are there products that really are easy to learn, easy to remember, that get things done easier, and that are also functionally rich enough?

The third factor is descriptive information about the data. The origin, nature, and timeliness of data, and the date it was updated are essential. The major prerequisite for success of a corporate data warehouse solution is a strong, centralized data administration function and, by extension, a well-maintained and active data dictionary.

There are three central components of the data warehouse. They are the *data engine, data extractor,* and *delivery tools.* The data engine in the corporate data warehouse is usually the DBMS system. There are some circumstances that

FIGURE 8–6
Data Warehouse

Definition
Principal elements
Prerequisites for success
Central components
• Data engine
• Extractor
• Delivery tools
Requirements/attributes

---

argue against using this, however. Data Processing may be reluctant to allow users direct access to data, for obvious reasons. Much of the data in the DBMS is very application-oriented, structured specifically for certain types of processing. It becomes very difficult for people to get at this data and use it in a general fashion. Also, the data may not even reside in the DBMS you have. In many cases, there is a lot of data existing in sequential or VSAM files. Finally, the DBMS might not be the proper choice. It might lack the appropriate data within it: the formats, organization, and ease-of-use flexible tools that are needed.

The ideal attributes of this data engine are its ability to actively monitor and control data, its usage and validity, and its structure to accurately represent data in the way the corporation wants to use it. You must be able to flexibly change it as business strategies and needs change. You also need to store aggregates in some large volumes of data. Finally, you must be able to deliver that data, by the use of the data extractor, to different areas, wherever it is needed.

There are two types of data extractors. One is a type of a universal interface mechanism that is provided by the data engine itself. It promotes some standardization of how to extract and, hopefully, some efficiency of usage. The second type of extractor is a third-party interface, and you pay in terms of system overhead.

The delivery tools are the area of the end-user. Users come in all shapes and sizes. It could be someone who is a systems programmer, an applications specialist, or a manager. For the latter, we find a lot of ''user-seductive'' software. This is where he can push buttons and things pop up. When you are looking at a system, you must find one that is extensible. It should not intimidate the manager-user, but it should carry on to where people are application specialists, so they will not be frustrated with a lack of functionality in the product. This is a very difficult challenge. A lot of the menu-driven, push-the-button, fill-in-the-blank types of products have severe limitations when you get to more sophisticated applications.

Relational Database Systems

The obvious direction for management support systems is toward relational database systems. They provide all of the advantages of the data warehouse, and their use is readily understandable by management. The CODASYL databases and other "navigational" databases have proven very difficult to use as well as to maintain. Only database experts can truly use them effectively, yet the future direction is obviously manager-user access to databases.

Relational database systems have all data as two-dimensional tables, or flat files. There are no separate constructs. Tables are simple and are understood universally. Both data entities and data relationships are described using the same simple construct. There are no other constructs. There are only six relational algebra operations. Three are for update:

STORE: add a new RECORD.

ERASE: delete an existing RECORD.

MODIFY: change a value of a FIELD in an existing RECORD.

Three are for retrieval:

SELECT: works on a horizontal sheet and extracts all RECORDS from a RELATION that satisfies some condition.

PROJECT: works on a vertical subset and extracts only specified FIELDS from a RELATION and eliminates duplicates.

JOIN: a logical, dynamic RELATIONSHIP that combines two RELATIONS (usually based on identical values in common FIELDS) by concentrating ALL FIELDS from the first RELATION with ALL FIELDS from the second RELATION.

In relational algebra, each OPERATOR takes one or two RELATIONS as its OPERANDS and produces a new RELATION as its RESULT. The relational operators are

SELECT, PROJECT, JOIN, and **PRODUCT.**

In set processing, the algebra treats entire RELATIONS (tables) as OPERANDS. The set operators are

UNION, INTERSECTION, and **DIFFERENCE.**

This is clearly a rather simple statement of relational systems, but it indicates the ease of understanding and learning. Relational DBMS is like a *compiler*. It translates "high-level" data management language (DML) statements into "low-level" navigational code. Performance is determined by how well the compiler optimizes the query requests. Data navigation is performed automatically by the DBMS. In other DBMS types, the navigation is performed by programmers or trained users developing handcrafted application code.

While other database structures require an intimate knowledge of indexes, pointers, inverted lists, pointer arrays, chains, hash totals, and so forth, a relational system can access data irrespective of its physical structure. The relational DBMS approach is relatively simple. This makes it usable by managers, as well as productive and extensible.

One of the keys of relational DBMS is that the system is forgiving. This appeals to the occasional user. You do not have to do the work all at once; logic and physical design can be worked on separately. You also do not have to get it 100 percent right to get good results. The system changes as the requirements change. Relational systems provide shorter development times, lower development costs, and a higher ROI for the work. The earlier that files are moved to relational, the less it will cost in the long run in terms of people productivity, development costs and schedules, and maintenance costs and schedules.

To a user, most software is difficult, because it does not follow your thinking process and is unforgiving of changes and mistakes. To a user of relational systems, the external schema are query tables, view tables, and snapshot tables. All are readily understood. Users do not need to know the details within the system. To the systems programmer working with relational systems, there are also the conceptual schema, or base tables, and the physical schema, or data files and index files. These take a great deal of work to set up and manage.

It should be obvious that there is no easy way to suddenly shift many corporate files from hierarchical and sequential to relational to capture these clear advantages. The problem is vast and expensive in most organizations and can be approached only with considerable planning. It should be equally obvious, however, that new applications and files should be set up as relational whenever possible. The current systems are efficient and effective. It is obvious that the only direction to take is to give better support to management whenever it is feasible to do so. All the new systems coming out are relational, and they are becoming steadily more efficient. They are already the most effective systems for handling management support.

DATA OWNERSHIP AND DATA SHARING

All management support systems require data, usually from a variety of sources. In the past, there has been informal sharing of data files, but too often data has been altered and used improperly or injudiciously. There is a growing awareness that information should be viewed as a corporate resource, similar to financial resources, physical assets, and human resources. If this is true, then the subject of data ownership and control becomes critical. Direct attention must be paid to the problems of functional control of data, including the related concerns of data ownership, legal responsibility, custody of data, and control of the information generated. Attention also must be given to the administration of corporate data as it moves away from central control to a variety of decision support or management support systems.

There is a great need for compatible systems and equipment for both efficiency and the practical use of the large bodies of data that have been accumulated. As micros proliferate, this problem concerns those who worry about the integrity, security, and privacy of the data that they "own" or for which they are responsible. Thus, on one hand, there has risen a demand for centralization and control of data resources. On the other hand, many users of information view the data as their own property and want to retain control of it. These two opposing views can be made compatible if data ownership is carefully structured and defined.

It has been realized for a long time that information is not free. Information flows, and files are valuable and costly assets that must be managed and protected. It has been obvious that Information Services groups work under budgets and financial controls and generally must report on their planning and costs in considerable detail. It has been less obvious that the value of the data and information products is clearly understood. Also, adequate controls may not be in place on the use of data outside the immediate owner groups that created the information and initially used it as planned. It is clear now that the owners of data must be concerned about both its cost and value. If they are to retain control of it, they must be ready to budget for its acquisition and indicate its level of importance and value to the organization.

The federal government and many corporations have adopted the position that information resources management (IRM) includes the overall management of data processing, systems development, communications, office automation, and other related efforts under a single, senior focal point. The great advantage of this approach is that the most efficiently structured organization can be obtained, and the utility of the information presumably can be maximized. It implies central ownership of data, shared data, and coordinated efforts in data handling. It implies a high reporting level and a cooperative structure for all information services. It has been accepted widely as the most effective method of information management in many federal government departments and in numerous other organizations. This approach assumes that all the data is owned by the organization as a whole, and that central standards and procedures will be applied uniformly to data acquisition, control, and use.

Some organizations, on the other hand, have decided that information or data by itself should be given special management attention, and they have developed the concept of a chief information officer who may or may not be a data processing professional. This approach has arisen because of senior management concern over the ownership and control of information end products, which are of considerable value to an organization. It entails the development and implementation of policies, standards, and guidelines regarding the organization's data in any type of files, magnetic or hard copy. It addresses ownership of the data directly. It analyzes the costs and criticality of data gathering, retention, manipulation, and reporting. It usually is directed by an individual outside of the Information Services group, as it is more similar to a controller's function. It is a staff function, rather than operational. This type of approach tends not to assume that data is centrally owned, but looks at each data file related to an application as part of the particular area of the business that is primarily responsible for its generation, control, and use. This approach to data ownership is not centered on EDP thinking, but favors giving data authority to operational management. Of course it is complicated by intergroup use of the same data.

One way of stating the difference between these two approaches to the management of information as a resource is to distinguish between functional and operational control of data. ("Data" used here is indistinguishable from "information" because the concern is with its ownership and control from its source, when it is clearly data, through its modification and extensions, when it may still be data, to its final use, when it is considered to be information.) Functional control is control of the uses to which information is put, or the functions of the information. Operational control is control of the planning and operating actions required in the generation and initial distribution of information.

The subject of functional control of information as a corporate resource (the chief information officer approach) includes related concerns of data ownership such as legal responsibility, custody of data, and control of access to and distribution of the information generated by the computers. This includes the use of information in employee relations, external analyses, and government relations. Most corporations have strict controls over press releases and the sharing of operating data. Similar controls may be imposed on all levels of information generated by the computers, depending upon the ownership of the data and its criticality to the organization.

The problems of operational control of information (the centralized IRM approach), on the other hand, usually include all the data capture and handling processes, including computing and communications. The concerns here cover the accuracy and validity of the data, production efficiency, and effective use of the information. Less attention is paid to data ownership, because it all is considered to be centrally owned. The controls imposed have been studied widely and are usually well understood. Responsibility for them is assumed by the various departments in the I/S organization. These operational controls will include processing controls, internal controls, security arrangements, and disaster recovery preparations. Such operational controls are usually highly structured and integrated. The areas left unstructured are usually ownership of the data and senior management's responsibilities in a functional sense relative to the produced and distributed information.

If data or information is to be considered a corporate resource, it is a different kind than the other resources in the corporation. It can be modified and expanded at will, yet most often is held in controlled sets on a carrying medium. It has little value out of context, yet it may be of critical value when seen in a recognized structure. It has a status that usually is undefined, yet its necessity is concrete. If managers grapple with the importance, substance, and ownership of the information used in their own organization, however, realistic methods can evolve for managing, controlling it, and assigning responsibility for it, and for putting it to the most profitable use. As soon as the ownership of data or information is understood, and as soon as managers realize that they are responsible for that particular resource, each operating entity will approach the management and control problem from its own viewpoint. This may not produce a clean result from the viewpoint of Information Services, but it probably will yield the most value from the information on file.

Because of the efficiency, accuracy, speed, and control of data processing methods, corporations are becoming more and more dependent on their information systems in normal business operations. To compound this dependency, the information generated includes the books of account, which must be protected to hold the corporation's officers free from legal negligence. Other information also is mixed in the flow—it is just as critical operationally, and it is perceived as being owned by different departments. It therefore is mandatory that measures be taken to assure management oversight of this information in all its aspects. Data ownership implies management responsibility for decisions relative to its handling.

When the matter of operational control of all information resources, including ownership of data, is considered, the questions facing senior management include organizational structures, lines of reporting, and intergroup cooperation. When functional control of the information resource is considered, the questions facing senior management are:

How will critical information be defined?

How will ownership of the data be defined?

How should the data's use and manipulation be controlled?

Should the position of chief information officer be established?

Where is it appropriate for this position to report?

How can information be controlled functionally, distinct from operationally, so that its owner can be assured of its validity?

The ownership and control of information is a critical issue today as a result of the proliferation of microcomputers and operation of management support systems. Users can obtain data from many sources, and too often they dilute its accuracy and value by manipulating it in their own private ways, and by combining it with uncontrolled data from various sources. Results are displayed attractively with spreadsheets and graphics, even though they may be based on inaccurate information. People with access to files may take data owned by someone else and alter it. The problems involved are complex, and most of the solutions are of a technical nature. There is a great need, however, to define and control the ownership and accepted use of much of the available data.

Concerns about Ownership of Data

Because of the great variety of data, applications, use of information, and controls, there is no monolithic solution regarding the ownership of data and the actions that should be taken. The best approach to the subject is to survey the extent of it, then review some of the solutions to problems that arise. Information Services professionals need to consider all aspects, then relate them to their own situations.

Definition of data and information.   There is a need to define data and information as broadly as possible, since personal computers reach across organizational lines. Specific management responsibilities can be assigned, depending upon the sensitivity of the data and the demand for its usage.

There frequently is insufficient understanding of and distinction between the controlled, detailed information in data files and the summarized information that is generated by different computers and returned to the same data files. A management report is usually summary information, and the data systems and processes supplying it may not be consistent or at the same level of updating. There also may be internal and external data on the same report. Clear definitions are needed as to the structure and ownership of specific data and its intended usage and control. Such definitions are normally maintained under a database management system.

Ownership of data and information.   Information Services usually has custody of data, but ownership normally resides with the operational user management that has acquired the data in its business actions. It should have the function of administration of the data from an ownership viewpoint. "Data Administration," however, is currently the designation of the technical job in the systems and operations areas for the operational management of the data. This includes handling the computer problems of data files, databases, and data communication. Frequently, the user groups do not handle all the aspects of the functional control of the data they own, including administration of information control and distribution, confirmation of data dictionary rules and data standards, management of data by their own controller, and final determination of data entities and relationships.

For ownership of data to be accepted, the responsibilities for its management and control must be accepted also. If these responsibilities have been given, by default, to Information Services, then the data ownership has been passed also.

Use and sharing of information. All corporate data is interrelated in some area, and there always will be a need to share it. Access to all data may be required by various groups that have a need to know. Although access is given to certain data, the information must be protected and not modified, ensuring its accuracy and control. Other data may be modified at will for use in analyses, forecasts, and studies at the discretion of a second user group.

All data that is neither private nor critical should be made available for sharing in an organization. The information requirements of different groups and the distribution of information throughout the corporation thus require analysis and management direction. Some units may be justifiably reluctant to have other units tapping into their databases, but they can supply usable files of data for others to study. This has the double advantage of keeping a measure of security and of making a clear statement about who owns the data.

In some cases, units may allow the free use of their data within the corporation, but require control of the data for external use. This is a difficult security problem, because analysts with free use of data tend to handle it on floppy disks, which are removed from the premises easily. Once again, if free use of owned data is allowed, it is best to pass it to the user in the form of a controlled extract file.

Once data has been made available for sharing, there are technological obstacles in distinguishing between various levels of data security and in maintaining data consistency across all of the reports that will be generated using it. Shared data becomes modified rapidly and frequently is used erroneously or in the wrong context. This is a very real problem.

As microcomputers become widespread, it is impossible to administer all corporate data through a single corporate umbrella. The problem is too complex, and one point of control cannot respond adequately to demands. Those who assert their ownership of data must be ready to administer it. It is impossible for central data administration groups to properly manage the functional use of data. They are completely occupied with the technical problems of operational control in the computer system. They can administer the output from their systems, but once the data has left, they cannot administer its functional use.

Points of functional control of information. In most companies, Information Services handles the operational control of data, and the controller's group picks up aspects of the functional control of information that are in practice. This has been an outcome of their management of internal accounting controls, their responsibilities for external reporting to the SEC, and their concerns about the legal responsibilities of management in holding corporate information secure. Corporate policies may establish additional requirements, such as the group responsible for the release of information for any purpose other than legal and operational requirements. Thus, if users have shown no interest in functional control of data, the responsibility has been handled by the controller, at least partially. It even may be written into corporate policy.

Because of his or her routine handling of information, it seems reasonable in many firms for the corporate controller to also be the corporate data administrator. This is partly because the chart of accounts is frequently at the heart of data administration. The controller's position could be defined just as easily, however, as the apex of the operational control of data, while the functional control of corporate information is distributed elsewhere.

A rather small staff, reporting to senior management other than the controller, generally offers the best possibility for generating the necessary policies, procedures, and analyses for the distributed functional control of information. The procedures should have different emphases than that of operational control.

Any approach to the management of information as a resource and to the classification of data ownership is unlikely to have a successful start and follow-through unless a number of the senior managers agree upon its necessity and application. Policies about information ownership should not be established by staff members unless there has been a critical review by senior management of their intent and application.

Policies regarding data ownership. There are a number of critical policies that are helpful regarding data and information management and ownership. These may be instituted differently by various groups in the organization, but they should be brought to a focal point to assure that they offer adequate coverage of information control. Some of these corporate policies should cover:

- Distribution of information within the corporation.
- The degree of information sharing to be expected.
- Disclosure of information externally.
- Systems and information planning responsibilities.
- Application of security rules to users of shared data.
- Contingency plans for disaster recovery of data files.
- Code of ethics for employees of the corporation.
- Legal considerations regarding responsibility for information.
- Considerations of employee privacy and rights.

Costs of information. The cost of information is normally a sensitive issue because of the general desire to maintain and increase operating budgets.

Analysis of the costs of information must be related to ownership of the information, and the analysis must be mandated. It usually is difficult to find appropriate cost factors to apply, so the effort frequently is confined to data processing operations, where the overall costs are fairly well known. Many costs are buried in operational departments in data input, use of personal computers, word processing, telecommunications, output handling, contracted outside services, and so on.

An approach that is often satisfactory is to establish a chargeout or chargeback system. The major effort then falls on the computer processing area, but the results are sometimes illuminating. They may cause user management to modify its requests for information or to introduce stricter controls on its own people.

Some organizations develop their information costs explicitly, then introduce information as a line item in their budgets. This has the direct effect of focusing attention on the chargeback numbers, even though they are known to have been developed arbitrarily. The results become a measure of the importance of information to each operational unit. If it has paid substantially for the information, it usually will want to exercise its ownership of it.

In some systems, such as customer information, it is clear that the data gathered is of great value, although it is difficult to assign a monetary figure. A cost analysis can help the functional manager compare the operational costs with the perceived value of the information. This can be helpful in assessing the value of the information owned and controlled by the group, and the need to control it more closely.

Control of information in microcomputers. As microcomputers have proliferated in the hands of users, they have brought in a huge appetite for data. This also has resulted in a concern about ownership and control of information. Data must have the same meaning and value for all users to avoid confusion in reports. As information, it must be treated under appropriate control, so there must be guidelines and procedures established. To satisfy the data need, under control, an information management group could compile indexes showing where information resides, and the procedures for its distribution and security. This would not only define ownership and help control the use of information, it also would increase the productivity of the professional workers. They would have uniform, simplified rules for access to and use of data.

It is difficult to have uniform oversight of the subsequent use, modification, and interrelationships of information that is produced, printed, and distributed by users with microcomputers. This is an important problem that has not been satisfactorily resolved. These powerful little computers can analyze, restructure, and modify data for particular uses with no concern about whether the information correctly cross-checks with other reports. Senior management receiving computer-generated reports may have no idea as to whether the data is the same in all the reports, or whether the data it owns has been misused.

Corporate and Noncorporate Data

Many management microcomputer users will use data from a variety of sources in their work. This data may come from analytical work in their own department (possibly corporate data); informal data sharing arrangements with other groups; downloaded data from the central computer (clearly corporate data); public-access data banks; or purchased files of data.

A problem may arise when data from various sources is intermixed and there is an insufficient audit trail, and analytical reports are produced that purport to contain acceptable information. The final mix of data may be quite different from that used in other reports generated by the central computer. Because the average microcomputer user will mix this data from a variety of sources, not only will its validity be in question, but ownership of the intermingled data will be obscured. In fact, the user actually may lay claim to ownership of the assemblage of data, although certain elements may have been developed and controlled by others. To retain the advantages of any degree of data ownership and control, therefore, it is necessary to define the source of the data, as above, and apply appropriate standards to its usage.

Corporate data may be defined as:

- Data that affects the financial position of the company and is part of the permanent records of the company.

- Data that is mandatory to be maintained by company officers to execute their custodial responsibilities, such as the books of account.

- Data on which routine or periodic management decisions are made.

The basic nature and importance of corporate data dictate that it be safeguarded with the proper controls to maintain its security and integrity. Only with the agreed controls in place should users be allowed to share this data resource and use it to help make operational decisions. Microcomputer users may have access to such data for making analyses. Many organizations have a policy, however, that such data may not be developed from applications on the micros because of their usual lack of adequate controls.

Noncorporate data may be defined as:

- Data that is developed from analytical work without adequate internal controls.

- Transient or short-lived data used in studies.

- Data obtained from public sources.

Microcomputers are used to process noncorporate data in many applications. Usually the only rule is that the economics of such work be favorable and approved by local management. Noncorporate data can be most valuable for specific analyses, but it should never be intermixed with corporate data in the central files. Such data may be used by several people in the same department or shared with other departments. It may be circulated through the company's communications network, interleaved with but separate from the corporate data.

Corporate and noncorporate data are always kept separate in the central computer, though they usually are mixed together in microcomputers. The documentation of corporate data is usually complete. It is always useful to document noncorporate data, to retain backup information in the event of a problem, and to report the information to Information Services, which, in turn, should have a facility to inventory it and arrange to share it with potential users. Although ownership of noncorporate data is frequently mixed, some records may be kept on it for tracking problems. The ownership of corporate data is always clear.

Access to Corporate Data

The utilization of corporate data files by users of microcomputers normally will be supported through the Information Center or other designated I/S group. There must be a way to expedite approval and delivery of specific data files to which access has been granted. It is usually not necessary for the actual owner of the data in the files to oversee transfer of the information, as procedures will have been set up to allow approved access. The normal approach is to review the ownership and approval of use of the data and then download the appropriate files under rigid controls. The files may be downloaded directly to the requesting microcomputer, or to an intermediate minicomputer where they will be available for several persons in a department. Data is made available only in designated formats.

Figure 8–7 is a typical policy covering the transfer of data from the central computer to approved users.

Because disk storage on microcomputers is minimal compared to mainframe systems, the primary mode of operation is usually file summarization and extract, handled by the central department. Certain files are established normally for end-user access, and they become the primary source of data that is extracted for the micro systems. These data files will be created through standard production processes and, therefore, will be mirror images of the production files. This will allow similar inquiry and report-writing programs to be used on both the micro and mainframe computers, with an expectation of similar results. The end-users will have standard programs to sample and summarize the central files.

The problems of data ownership and control thus will be settled in advance for a number of production files. The procedures for user identification and use of the owned data will be published and followed. The actual owner will have given blanket permission. If a request is made for other corporate data files to be made available, however, special permission must be obtained from the owner of the

FIGURE 8–7
Policy: Access to Corporate Data

Microcomputer users will be allowed access to corporate data under stringent controls if they are properly authorized and identified. Both the individual requesting access and the microcomputer that is being operated must first be identified through passwords, IDs, or other means for each session. Access to the specific items of data requested by a microcomputer user must have been authorized for that user by the owner of the data or the owner's representative. The mainframe computer programs used to gain access to corporate data on behalf of the microcomputer users will be fully under the control of the corporate data processing organization, which is responsible for the data's integrity and security.

Microcomputer users are allowed to create and modify corporate data maintained on the mainframe only when their microcomputers are operating as terminals of the mainframe computer, using the same programs and controls as for traditional on-line terminals. Such emulation will be done using only company-supported microcomputers and software.

The downloading of data, or the transfers of data in bulk, from the mainframe to the microcomputers, or to departmental minicomputers, will be done by mainframe programs. These programs will have full controls, with appropriate capability for selection, summarization, and reformatting. Such data will normally be directed to minicomputer hard disks or to the diskette units within the microcomputer. They may be manipulated thereafter by the user. Downloading programs from the mainframe to company-supported microcomputers will be written and maintained by the Information Services department.

When company-supported microcomputers are used as stand-alone word processing devices, they may send or receive text from other devices, including other microcomputers, by using the corporate network of mainframe computers as intermediaries. Special mainframe and microcomputer programs, with full controls, will be written and maintained by Information Services for this purpose.

---

data. This usually will be carried out by following a standard procedure under control of Data Processing.

A list of the corporate data files for which the owners have given approval to use normally will be kept by the Information Center and made available to end-users. The list will contain file definitions for each file and the normal creation cycle of the files, and will be published by the Information Center. This list should assist users in verifying that they are working with current data and let them know when the production cycle will make fresh data available.

Some corporations use an alternative to the downloading of data, which requires high-speed telephone communications. They create diskette files in the computer room as output from generalized report generators that are similar to the programs used on the microcomputers; and the diskettes are delivered to the microcomputer users.

Public Data and Private Data

The terms public data and private data occasionally are used to identify two types of data for which ownership is usually not a problem. They both may be classified as noncorporate data. The problems of data ownership usually center on corporate data or data kept in divisional or group files. Other types of data may be readily available, with few restrictions on their use.

Public data is data that is published openly or is available from the government or from proprietary databases. Once it has been acquired, there is usually little restriction on its use within the corporation. Published data has no restrictions of ownership unless it is claimed specifically. Frequently, however, such data is entered into a microcomputer, then intermixed with corporate data. This obviously is permissible for an individual study, but it can be a difficult type of data degradation to handle if it is circulated in an organization. The record of ownership of some of the data is destroyed, and people may use it for inappropriate reasons without knowing that it is mixed with information that is owned and restricted.

Data that is available from the government is used frequently for statistical comparisons, time-series analysis, and forecasts. Its normal use is stand-alone, or in tables and graphs that are labeled clearly as to their source. It is the basis of most sales, population, and economic trend forecasting. It usually is not intermixed with internal data; thus there is little chance of pollution of the controlled and owned data.

Establishment of databases of proprietary information, or of public information organized in useful ways in proprietary access programs, has become a popular service bureau offering. Frequently, these databases are simply reorganizations of data available from government sources, but they are handled in ways that make them simpler to use. They may combine a variety of time-sharing services with simplified access programs to large databases of information that are updated frequently. The companies that sell them offer training in their use, as well as analytical programs that are helpful to apply. Once such information has been sold to an organization, there are usually very few restrictions on its internal use. Ownership of the data has been transferred by the sales agreement. The same problem exists as with other public data files, however. If they are mixed during analysis with controlled and owned internal data, it may be difficult to separate the data later and to know which data should be handled with restrictions.

Thus public data may be defined as any data obtained outside the corporation that can be used internally with no restrictions, unless some are in the sales contract. There is certainly no problem of ownership of public data within a corporation.

Private data is not the opposite of public data. Private data may be defined as the data developed by an individual user or group of users for private analytical purposes. Note that this is not data related to the privacy of individuals. Such data would be called "confidential." Private data is merely that data generated in an uncontrolled or separately controlled area that will not be intermingled with the corporate data files in normal operation. Usually, Information Services personnel will have no concern about the control or security of private data. Those problems must be handled completely by the owners of that data. The Information Center may give them training and support in developing their own security and control methods, but there will be no interconnection with the central files.

Again, like public data, private data is sometimes intermingled with corporate data. To make matters worse, this occurs most frequently in special analytical reports that are prepared for senior management. Since printouts from a micro are frequently indistinguishable from printouts from the central data processing operation, there can be confusion over differing results reported from different sources in the corporation. There is no simple answer to this problem of data confusion, except to make clear which are the controlled reports that are the official records of the organization.

A certain amount of private data on micro systems may be the personal property of individuals—financial or travel records, for example. If this private data is maintained on floppy disks, which are removed by the individual, there is little problem with it except for wasted company time. If the data is maintained on hard disks or is left lying around the office, there can be problems if others pick it up. This practice is difficult to control.

Data Validation and Data Integrity

Data validation is the process of obtaining accurate and acceptable data, while *data integrity* is the condition of the data that is the result of initial validation and subsequent control. When ownership of data is considered, the condition of the data may be raw input, validated data files, or information on reports. In each step of the process, there are many opportunities to correct the data, modify it, or dilute it with other data. Thus, those producing and owning raw data may not always be able to claim their ownership of information that has come from a number of modification and data addition processes. The analysis may be complex, or it may be simple. If the subject of data ownership is important down to individual data elements, then each application and data file will need to be studied to determine how much owned data may have been intermixed with other data.

A significant portion of the operation of mainframe application programs is devoted to the validation of input data. Programs include checks at all steps in the input process, and appropriate controls and error messages are generated to ensure that the checks are in place and are being observed. The checks are carried through to the generation of output, and the maintenance of control totals is incorporated in all programs.

In a stand-alone microcomputer environment, the user accepts unique responsibilities when developing programs and capturing data. In a typical data processing environment, Information Services ensures both the integrity of the data and the correctness of the programs being run, which are the operations performed on the data. Both of these are important activities designed to guarantee that the information being used to make business decisions is accurate, timely, and significant. Microcomputer users also must see that the data they capture meet these criteria. It is important that users be able to demonstrate the accuracy, timeliness, and significance of their data should the need arise. There is little point in establishing ownership of data that is not of some value.

Thus the user has a responsibility to ensure that the programs being used, which can be purchased or self-developed, are correct and provide the information results that are anticipated. If this is not done, there may not be an integral body of data worth considering as to ownership. The owner can be assured of the correctness of a program by testing it, using data that will provide a known result if the program is operating as expected. Usually the Information Center staff can help users determine the best method of testing a program and the accuracy of its data handling.

Responsibility for data validation broadens in a situation where data for a reporting process is obtained by the user from production data files. When using production data for reporting, the user also must ensure that the interpretation of the meaning of the data elements used in the reporting process correctly reflects the meaning of the data elements in the production file. It is very simple in statistical reporting, for example, to greatly change the apparent results by using only a subset of the available data.

Thus, data validation normally will be carried out by Data Processing for all production files and by individual users for their own files on the microcomputers. Data ownership may be claimed for raw input data, for validated data files, for output of programs on the central computer, or for output of programs on the micros. The further through the calculating process the data is moved, the more likely it is to be intermixed with data owned by others.

Data ownership can be tracked readily only if it is validated initially and controls are maintained on its transformations, modifications, and additions. Such controls will maintain the integrity of the data throughout the uses to which it is put. Data that is claimed as owned in the original files will be identifiable, and ownership can be assigned in subsequent files. Claims for data integrity are valid only up to the point where controls were last applied, when there has been a reasonable check on the program that has processed the data, and where there is some way of tracking and determining ownership. Validation is necessary throughout all the processes of data use to ensure data integrity.

Data integrity has three different, but related, aspects:

1. *The completeness or wholeness of the available data.* All the data that is pertinent and related is available in the file. There has not been an unreported data selection process.
2. *The unity of the available data.* The data in the file is interrelated in a way that is expected and is not polluted with extraneous information. Ownership of the data is clear.
3. *The correctness of the available data.* The data in the file can be considered reliably as validated and correct to the best understanding of those who handled it. It has passed all the tests that were designed for it.

Data integrity means that you have all the data, only the data that is expected, and tested data in the file to be used. If files are downloaded from central computers under reasonable control, it can be assumed that there is data integrity. If those files have been accessible to and modifiable by end-users, then there is no way that data integrity can be assumed unless stringent controls have been applied. Data ownership can be assigned reliably only if data integrity is maintained.

Data integrity is an attractive term in management discussions. It has a substantial ring to it. It is present in well-controlled systems on central computers. It seldom can be assured in microcomputer applications, however, unless a complete set of controls has been established. Thus if data ownership is a serious consideration, then data integrity must be assured.

Data Sharing

Data sharing is a fundamental necessity in the successful use of management support systems. It would be undesirable and impossible for all users to enter all the data they need into their own systems. It is imperative that, if corporate analyses are made on data, the source of the data is in existing files in most cases. Thus data sharing is very common in corporations. At the same time, it is at the core of most problems of identifying ownership of data. The assumption is that shared data will be further manipulated in some way. The result that comes out in the end may bear little relationship to the original data that was claimed as owned.

Whenever possible, data already existing on another system should be used by file transfer in order to reduce possible inconsistencies and inaccuracies associated with reentry or transcription. By downloading data extracted from an existing mainframe database directly into a microcomputer by means of a communications interface, the amount of data validation required by the microcomputer program can be reduced. At the same time, if identification of data ownership is important, a record can be maintained through the transcription.

Intrasystem data sharing. There is a concern about maintaining the integrity and identity of data when it is shared among a number of different programs within the same microcomputer system or in a tightly linked group of systems. This is the sharing of data resources among functions of a single multifunctional system. The key concern is the degree of compatibility among the various functions provided by the system. Ownership identity can be transferred readily only between compatible systems.

The ability to expand functionality is one of the most important characteristics of microcomputer systems. Expanded functionality can be achieved by both software and hardware methods. The most readily achievable method of expanding functionality is via software, yet this approach may have the most impact on data ownership records. Expansion can be accomplished simply by obtaining software packages that provide the desired functions. Problems typically arise when the software is developed as independent, stand-alone packages that are not designed to operate together and do not have similar file structures. The key problems are inability to share data directly among the various programs and lack of a common user interface among the various programs.

There is a growing trend among commercial vendors supplying software for administrative and management applications to integrate multiple functions within a single program or family of programs. These vendors combine commonly used functions into an integrated package having a consistent user interface and the same data file. The programs then have the capability to use the output of any one function as input to any other function. Typical functions in these programs include spreadsheet processing, word processing, business graphics, database management, and communications, which may be terminal emulation.

A single integrated program, as a rule, allows for easier switching from function to function than does a family of compatible programs. On the other hand, the family of compatible programs usually provides a more extensive set of features than is found in the single integrated program. Both approaches allow ready maintenance of data integrity and, hence, records of data ownership.

Intersystem data sharing. There is a greater concern about maintaining the integrity and identity of data when it is shared among a group of systems serving a multiuser environment. In this case, the key concern is the degree of compatibility among the various systems. Data transfer may require substantial file changes that will affect the ownership record.

In most organizations, the microcomputer systems are connected in some way to the central computing facility, either through an intermediate computer or accessible data files. Some organizations also interconnect their microcomputer systems. In scientific and engineering applications, the interface is usually primarily to provide access to a high-speed computational capability. For applications in software development, this interface is important for testing and integrating elements of a larger system under development. For administrative and management applications, the interface provides access to a shared corporate database.

In situations where there is a need for data and resource sharing among microcomputer systems or between microcomputer systems and a central computing facility, a few relatively simple alternatives are available other than an expensive, tightly controlled, but technically complex network. Each has its own data integrity problems. These alternatives are:

- Interchanging diskettes by using format conversion software.
- Transferring files via a direct communications link.
- Using shared resource systems.

Manually exchanging diskettes by using format conversion utilities can be an effective method for data sharing. Incompatibilities, which cannot be resolved by software utilities, can occur because of differences in diskette drive design and the physical characteristic of the diskettes. Software utilities can solve incompatibilities based on the soft-sectoring of the diskettes or the logical structure of the files. Any file conversion, however, entails the possibility of some loss of the record of data ownership, since the data may be restructured in ways that do not show the initial relationships.

A second approach to data resource sharing is the electronic transmission of files via direct cable connection between input/output ports on the systems. There are commercial and public-domain products that support this method of file transfer. The limiting factor in this approach is that the systems involved must be located relatively close to each other, typically within 50 feet. A variant to this approach that overcomes the distance limitation involves the use of modems and telecommunication lines to establish the data path for file transfers. In this setup, the records remain substantially in the original format.

Most organizations have terminal access to their central computing facility using direct wire or telephone. Data sharing between microcomputers and the central computer is accomplished by using the central computer as the communications link. In this arrangement, data from the sending microcomputer is placed on the mainframe. The receiving microcomputer accesses the mainframe to obtain the data. There are three advantages to this approach. First, the mainframe is presumably always up and ready to be accessed. Thus the sending microcomputer system may transmit at any time and need not depend on the receiving microcomputer being switched on. Second, two microcomputers can exchange data even if they are unable to exchange physical media. Third, the software control in the central computer can force data integrity and ownership controls, if desired.

Shared resource systems are multiuser systems in which one or more of the system components are shared among the users. In these systems, users must give up some measure of control over their individual operating environments and accept the central control, and degradation is likely to occur in performance due to the need to schedule access to shared resources.

A *network* is a collection of computer systems interconnected by communications facilities to allow multiuser access to shared resources. The network approach to data resource sharing should be considered only after careful analysis of the requirements, including data control. The advantages of the network approach are:

- It gives high performance and reliable access to shared data and resources.
- Users can have the benefits of a multiuser environment without surrendering autonomy of their individual operations.
- All those involved in the network can be directed or encouraged to use the same controls over their data and to log its transmission.

Establishing, operating, and maintaining a network is a highly technical activity, and usually those in charge are more concerned about the operational aspects of the hardware than controls on the data. Networks tend to complicate the tracking of data ownership. Data files that are transmitted usually do not remain intact in their new location and frequently are intermixed completely with other files.

Many decentralized organizations have data exchange between different user locations. Such exchange is encouraged because it reduces document turnaround time, reduces duplications and errors, and promotes responsiveness. Most Information Services organizations are concerned merely with line capacities and technical problems, however. They establish authorized types of communication, modems, and terminals or computers, and they leave the data integrity problems up to the users of the data.

Standards of Data Usage

Data can be shared or downloaded from a corporate system to a microcomputer with the beneficial results to the end-user of local response time and local availability. There are times, however, when this convenience can backfire for other users of the corporate system.

For example, one group may alter the discounted cash flow (DCF) calculations, done to support central budgeting, in order to parallel its own unique requirements and formulas. A microcomputer user working with one of the more common spreadsheet packages may not calculate net present value or internal rate of return in the same manner. This is not crucial unless the microcomputer user's output data is used in later calculations by another group or if the blanket assumption is made that figures from the two systems (mainframe and micro) are safely comparable.

Another problem similar to this has been termed "report integrity," which simply means having reports in which the source data has satisfactory integrity and, therefore, the results can be trusted. It should be possible to distinguish an authorized company document, such as those that are the result of highly controlled mainframe programs, from documents produced locally using word processing and graphics software and possibly some uncontrolled data.

It is not uncommon to find data owned by someone else mixed with uncontrolled data to produce reports for senior management. This has been called "visioning." It describes what is done to some executives who are swayed by reports that look as if they came from central data processing and contain controlled data, when, in reality, they were assembled quickly on microcomputers with a mixture of data and software to help prove a point. Such reports appear to contain controlled and checked data and look as if the data would be owned by the unit in question. They tend to attract more attention than either the voluminous output from the central computer or in-depth studies produced on typewriters along with hand-drawn graphs.

It is obvious that, while data can be shared readily and easily between mainframes and microcomputers, it does not necessarily follow that all data should be shared when ownership and integrity are important. It is critical to have corporate standards of data usage and sharing.

Figure 8–8 is a representative set of standards that should be considered when data is shared in an organization. Figure 8–9 is an illustration of the types of methods and procedures that can be put in place to monitor and review compliance with the standards.

FIGURE 8–8
Policy: Standards of Data Usage

Information Services, through the Information Center, shall prepare a Data Standards Manual for all users to ensure that standardized methods of data use, access, security, and privacy are maintained. The standards will include:

1. Department and individual user identification.
2. File-naming conventions.
3. Data dictionary interface.
4. Accounting and billing requirements.
5. Ownership of data files.
6. Access to data not owned by the user.
7. References to corporate policies that define audit requirements and fiscal-system integrity procedures.
8. Data security and privacy procedures.
9. Retention periods for data.
10. File backup and recovery procedures.
11. Methods of space and file allocation in the central files.
12. Documentation requirements.
13. Program and data file maintenance procedures.

FIGURE 8–9
Policy: Review of Data Usage

To ensure compliance with standards, and to verify that data is being handled according to corporate standards and that efficient processing is taking place, user applications will be occasionally monitored and assistance will be provided by the Information Center if a potential for operational improvement is observed.

Data files or processes that deal with corporate financial data or other critical data are subject to review by the Internal Audit Department and must meet all requirements of the Corporate Accounting Control Manual. This includes, but is not limited to:

1. System documentation.
2. Revision and maintenance-change control.
3. Maintenance of data ownership records.
4. Transaction audit control.
5. Data integrity and accuracy procedures.
6. Procedures for maintaining the security and privacy of data.
7. Data backup and recovery procedures.
8. Conformance to corporate standards.

Information Center staff will offer assistance to users in interpreting all data usage control and in understanding the responsibilities inherent to all parties in data ownership.

EFFECTIVE USE OF QUALITY ASSURANCE

Accurate and timely information is a vital corporate commodity. With the current complexity of end-user computing, there is a need for an effective quality assurance program to assure the reliability of information products. Quality assurance (QA) is the bringing together of various control disciplines to enable data processing production and service at the best economic level for full user satisfaction. Creative ways of improving the quality of management information must be examined.

Quality assurance is part of the continuing evolution of information delivery methods and is a positive influence in aiding the acceptance of data accuracy. A program of education, standardization, and use of new techniques is required. Everyone should be involved to some degree.

A material part of this effort concerns itself with a formal quality assurance program, which deserves to be an element in any corporation's strategies. Such a program is not a luxury item. An effective program will help ensure the best economics as well as the most favorable use of human and other resources. Doing things over or working with less-than-desirable products are not satisfactory alternatives. Establishing and running a formal program is an effective way to reduce human errors and nonhuman faults. It is as appropriate to information products as it is to products that are manufactured on an assembly line.

Quality assurance is now recognized as an accepted function in Information Services management. The present understanding of quality assurance and realization of its profitability did not suddenly become manifest, however. It developed with experience and the increasing complexity of supplying required information services. The need has long been apparent and has been met in a variety of ways by traditional audit and control procedures. What, then, are the present-day relationships and distinctions among the four information areas that may overlap in their functions: quality assurance, quality control, audit, and security control?

> *Quality assurance* is a staff function in Information Services that analyzes, develops, and implements control and review systems in all areas of information analysis and production. This staff usually does not perform the full quality review work itself, but develops methodologies and oversees them. It should raise corporate consciousness of quality information products.

> *Quality control* is usually a line function in Information Services, particularly in the production areas, that is responsible for routine accomplishment of all prescribed quality tests and analyses and reporting of results.

> *Audit* is a staff function. It is responsible for reviewing adherence to procedures, compliance with rules, and integrity of the operations completely independently of the other Information Services groups. A prime concern is the quality of information products, but it seldom is applied to management support systems.

> *Security control* is usually a staff function in Information Services. Its main purpose is to control and protect the assets of the organization, and, in doing so, it may become involved with various aspects of the quality of the information products. It should be of direct concern to MSS users.

These four groups frequently have the same end in mind and may overlap in their areas of concern. Figure 8–10 summarizes a number of the differences and similarities among them. They operate in distinct functional areas despite the fact that they frequently have common goals and examine the same information areas.

In general, quality control and security control staffs are "doers" in their specific areas. Quality assurance staffs are planners and overseers, while audit staffs are reviewers. The QA staff should be the one that works with management on MSS.

There is no single, succinct definition general enough to present a full picture of quality assurance as it is being practiced. The essence of QA work for MSS, however, includes:

FIGURE 8–10

Relationships and Distinctions in Quality Management

Area	Quality Assurance	Quality Control	Audit	Security Control
Overall purpose	Raise consciousness of quality and expedite quality control	Examine quality of information production in specific areas	Examine adherence to procedures, compliance with rules, and integrity of operations	Control and protect the assets of the organization
Overall view	Pragmatic	Specific	Analytic	Control
Quality objectives	Determine measurable objectives	Work with specific objectives	Review established objectives	Security and control objectives
Organizational need	To gain uniform attention to quality	To control operation in particular areas	To meet legal requirements and be assured of financial control	To protect assets adequately
Interest in causes of problems	Fundamental	Peripheral	Fundamental	Security problems only
Interception of the information path	At end of each development phase and in operations	At specific production points	At areas suspected of possibly causing problems	Security risk areas
Quality standards and procedures	Develop and provide direction	Use established standards and procedures	Review	Install for protection against loss
Quality control methodology	Develop and provide direction	Use	Recommend	Use for protection against loss
Audit controls	Recommend	Report on operation	Authenticate and recommend	Analyze in risk areas

Structured development and coding standards	Develop standards and train in use	Use	Review and recommend	Review in risk areas
Use of test and analysis tools	Recommend and cooperate in use	Use as assigned	Use independently when deemed useful	Occasional use for analysis
Amount of information reviewed	Large samples in suspect areas	Sufficient statistical samples in assigned areas	Sufficient statistical samples in assigned areas	Outline data, with samples in suspect areas
Statistics on production	Gather in suspected problem areas	Gather at specific control points	Request and analyze	Review aberrations
Period of checking	Before-the-fact	Immediately after-the-fact	Traditionally after-the-fact	During the actual operation
Level of personnel	Experienced systems personnel	Junior systems and clerical personnel	Accountants and trained system personnel	Trained specialists
Technical view of personnel	General technical level	Detailed technical level	Financial with sufficient technical training	General technical level
Training	Provide	Receive	Recommend	Provide

- Efforts targeted at ensuring that information products meet the level of quality expected by management and also meet a prescribed level of service.
- An effective system to integrate quality development, quality maintenance, and quality improvement efforts of various groups in an organization to ensure that information supplied is at the optimum economic level for full user satisfaction.
- A planned and systematic pattern of all the actions necessary to provide adequate confidence that data and services conform to established technical requirements and achieve satisfactory performance.

Quality assurance is part of the continuing evolution of information delivery methods and should be considered for the positive influence it will have in helping information-handling functions within the company develop from an art to a discipline.

Today's business executives and line managers have increased demands for the benefits of the various information technologies in their decision systems and require greater functionality and capability year after year. Impacting trends include growth in the number and variety of applications being supported, growth in the importance of computer systems to the managers involved, growth in technological complexity, growth of computer sophistication in the management community, and a trend to end-user-developed systems and end-user-operated software and hardware.

More people are becoming involved with more hardware and more software to accomplish more business functions. More end-users are expressing the urge to be masters of their own information resources and are doing their own data processing as opportunities present themselves. Within this context, it appears improbable that a corporation can cope with the issues and intricacies of achieving the right balance of quality on an informal basis. Managers need assistance in dealing with the quality of systems that cross organizational lines, use multiple technologies, and run at multiple locations.

There is also a hard-dollar motivation. Doing a job right the first time, and doing it well, consumes less resources over the life cycle of a system. Therefore, certain aspects of quality assurance yield a favorable return on investment that is directly traceable to their implementation.

The Quality Assurance Program

A viable quality assurance program emphasizes quality as a strategy to produce better products in a more timely and economical manner. It is critical to recognize that a successful QA program normally focuses on a few key measurable areas at the outset to gain credibility and provide useful figures for management decisions. The use of measuring, modeling, and metrics is important. Many organizations publish measurable information monthly to compare results from data processing centers or user development groups. The efficiency and effectiveness of various DSS and EIS are of great interest to their users. Other important tasks of a quality assurance program are to:

- Provide education and training on techniques and methods that inject into and verify the quality of the MSS system throughout its life cycle.
- Provide guidelines, standards, and policies that clearly outline the level of quality desired.
- Investigate new techniques that are applicable to the MSS environment, and include them in the program.
- Provide mechanisms to check, review, and report on the actual state of quality being achieved.
- Provide a consulting service on quality to all interested managers.

The emphasis should be on involving everybody to some degree, publishing parameters to work within, opening lines of communication, heightening awareness of quality concerns, execution of quality control procedures, verification of controls and validity, and follow-up of findings from audits and quality reviews.

Use of Self-Assessment Checklist

The quality assurance self-assessment checklist may be used to identify areas where quality improvement can provide a quick payback to an organization. This checklist may be used by a manager considering the advantages of establishing a quality assurance checklist function or by a QA group that wishes to identify areas that can provide profitable results rapidly.

The checklist is designed so that a "no" answer indicates a potential area for improvement and possible rapid payback. It does not provide the detailed steps and methods necessary to conduct a careful review of the area under investigation. The situations with a "no" answer therefore should be investigated by a QA analyst to determine what the real possibilities may be. Certain areas, of course, will not be applicable to MSS work. These can be indicated in the N/A column. Other comments also may be inserted to assist in further investigations.

It is important to note that in the MSS area, quick payback for the effort is not as important as providing management the assurance that its MSS efforts are as valid and realistic as is possible.

The quality assurance self-assessment checklist is not meant to be definitive or cover the subjects exhaustively. It is simply provided for management to quickly determine if a quality assurance function is helpful or necessary. It may be used by QA personnel to aid in looking for quick payback areas.

FIGURE 8–11

Quality Assurance Management Considerations

No.	Item	Yes	No	N/A	Comments
			Responses		
1.	Are training courses or consultation provided to aid the manager in defining problems and to help communication between the manager and the analyst in solving problems?	____	____	____	
2.	Is the manager requested to allot sufficient time to interact with data processing personnel on the subject of QA?	____	____	____	
3.	Has responsibility been assigned to develop procedures and methods for systems maintenance for the MSS system?	____	____	____	
4.	Are staff members asked to plan the time necessary to assist in developmental areas?	____	____	____	
5.	Have the roles of the data processing support units been adequately defined and publicized?	____	____	____	
6.	Have procedures been established to assure that users understand the proper definition of requirements?	____	____	____	
7.	Does your organization have an established working relationship among all related data processing areas in order to eliminate misunderstandings?	____	____	____	
8.	Is there a post-installation audit/review function made available to managers?	____	____	____	
9.	Is there a precontract vendor evaluation function?	____	____	____	
10.	Is vendor performance measured?	____	____	____	
11.	Are procedures established to monitor the performance of programs to determine when they should be rewritten or replaced?	____	____	____	

Figure 8–11 touches on some QA organizational and functional considerations.

There are a number of traditional functions that can be handled by a QA group, but the two that can most effectively impact MSS work are the *standards and procedures* function and the *test management* function.

Standards and Procedures Function

Established standards and procedures can be of great help to managers in MSS work. The standards and procedures function is responsible for the publication of administrative and technical guidelines, standards and procedures (collectively known as practices), and any other educational material such as display graphics, reference cards, manuals, or other materials that may be required to support I/S development or MSS areas.

Mission statement.   To assist management, administration, cost centers, and operating and project groups in creating and publishing timely, useful, clear, and concise written and graphic communications; to provide editorial assistance to authors of practices and manuals; and to facilitate delivery and maintenance of published material.

Activities.   Advise I/S on user department standards and guidelines; advise users on Information Services standards and guidelines; consult with originators on planned publications; determine compliance with testing standards; design specific publications for originating areas; develop and improve standards for all Information Services areas, including MSS; develop publication plans and schedule; manage the publication process, including coordination of text graphics, outside consulting and services, and interfacing with forms control and purchasing; provide writing guidance and editing expertise; and provide writers to create practices needed for implementing new technologies.

Test Management Function

Managers usually need help in understanding and implementing test management, which consists of analysis of software and hardware test requirements, monitoring, certification of test results, and evaluation of test reports. The test management group would develop and establish a standard testing program. The goal of implementing the program is to gain increased efficiency and management visibility in software acquisition and maintenance, leading to higher quality software products at a lower total life-cycle cost, and assuring efficiency when operating systems. This should provide management with additional assurance that the systems are performing up to requirements.

Mission statement.   To develop and establish a standard testing program with I/S. The goal of implementing the program is to gain increased efficiency and management visibility into the software development, acquisition, and maintenance process, leading to high-quality software products at a lower total life-cycle cost.

Activities. Analyze software requirements to determine testability; determine that the testing plan is adequate and that the testing procedures are efficient; monitor tests and certify that test results are actual findings of the tests; provide input for test sections in the design package (i.e., conversion plan, test plan, installation plan); review test plans and procedures; review test requirements and criteria for adequacy, feasibility, and satisfaction of requirements; and recommend tools and techniques that will increase confidence in software products.

SECURITY AND DISASTER RECOVERY REQUIREMENTS

Because of the complexity of control of user-developed programs and data, it is recommended that a set of operational policies that include ownership of data be established. Ownership of data will not have any meaning unless adequate security safeguards are applied to the operations, systems, and data files.

The problems of data and software backup in the event of a disaster or other physical loss is a critical subject to be investigated.

Legal considerations in the use and distribution of data by company users include problems of privacy legislation, user-developed software, purchased software and data files, employees working away from the premises, and vendor contracts.

Operational Policies

Managers use and develop programs that are intended both for single, analytical studies and for ongoing use. They or their staffs frequently assemble corporate data, mix it with other data, generate reports, then use the outputs from the first reports to do subsequent analysis. If they are not aware of the problems of data ownership and security, they may mix a great deal of data of varied lineage and produce reports that are not truly correct. This may distort or misinterpret the data that is owned by others. Because microcomputers are ubiquitous and because large amounts of data can be moved easily on floppy disks far beyond the reach of those who should control it, there are not simple or universal ways to maintain data integrity and records of data ownership. The least that Information Services should do, however, possibly through the Information Center, is to establish a set of operational policies regarding user responsibilities for data. These must be approved and promulgated at a high level, distributed widely, and clearly covered in training classes.

Policies regarding data ownership will never stand alone, but must be completely interwoven with the policies covering microcomputer operation, security, backup, privacy, legal considerations, and so on. It is all part of the same fabric, and data ownership is simply one thread that runs through the whole and is dependent upon all other policies for support.

Of course, there are various levels of MSS programs, and data ownership is not an important consideration in a great many instances. There must be awareness, however, about when data ownership is important. While developing programs for ongoing use, managers should be required to follow the corporate standards for microcomputer programming and data handling, when such standards or procedures have been established. Clearly, managers cannot be expected to adhere to standards that are not pertinent to one-time or temporary programs, yet even then adherence to the spirit of the standards should be encouraged.

When microcomputers are used in ongoing production applications, conformance to the tested and proven corporate standards and procedures definitely should be expected. If the corporation's many years of experience in data processing are disregarded, the result could be clearly harmful and possibly cause significant loss.

Operational policies that outline user responsibilities, including those regarding data ownership, should be accepted at all levels of the corporation. It would even be useful to have the various managers review their programs and use of data periodically, possibly every quarter, and turn in their program listings and data control actions to a central repository, such as a corporate microcomputer inventory. Regularly bringing program and data documentation up to date would have the effect of reminding all the users of their responsibilities regarding data control and data ownership.

Figure 8–12 is a representative set of standards that covers the principal operational policies. Managers must be aware of and take action on all of these responsibilities if there is to be proper maintenance of the rights and obligations of data ownership.

Security of Data

There is no way in which the ownership of data will have any meaning unless adequate security safeguards are applied to all operations, systems, and data files. Managers must become familiar with the normal security precautions that are taken relative to data processing and be aided in deciding which procedures and methods are applicable to their work. The subject of security is a broad one that has been described at length in other documents, and no attempt will be made here to cover many of its aspects. It is sufficient to point out that most professional data processing personnel understand the ramifications of security, and those who work with users should be ready to interpret the time-proven security rules to them. The Information Center, in particular, must be prepared to give aid and instruction to managers.

FIGURE 8-12
Policy: User Responsibilities for Data Protection

Because microcomputers and downloaded data are directly in the hands of authorized users, it is imperative that those users maintain a high level of responsibility in adhering to corporate standards of control.

Users shall protect data in microcomputer files from disclosure to or modification by unauthorized individuals. Magnetic storage devices containing sensitive data should be securely locked when not in use.

Users shall recognize the particular ownership of any critical data and shall take steps to maintain the integrity and ownership records of that data.

Users shall protect data and programs from accidental erasure or other loss. Proper use of equipment and proper procedures for data backup are essential. It is strongly urged that critical data and programs be copied and stored off-site for emergency backup.

Users shall provide adequate documentation of both the data and program for continuity of the application when the current developer and user are not present.

Users who develop programs and data files shall see that a second user is trained and that the program and data are documented with adequate user manuals.

User-developed programs should be logical, structured, and well-explained, and should adhere to corporate standards of data control.

User documentation should be protected to survive a physical disaster.

Users shall ensure that microcomputers and software purchased by the company are restricted to company use.

Users shall ensure that data files generated within the company shall be restricted to company use.

There can be no meaningful agreement on and no recording of data ownership unless all affected data files are held reasonably securely and control is passed automatically from one holder of the data to the next. If any data is to be considered as owned by any particular group, then controls must be applied to that data to give it security. Without such controls, any records of data ownership will be lost rapidly and irretrievably.

Some of the broad aspects of data security were included in Figure 8-12. In Figure 8-13, a number of rules are laid out that have been used in actual practice in some corporations. This figure offers a shopping list of policies that may be applicable in specific situations.

Each of the extract microcomputer files created from corporate data files will have special security situations, some of which will concern data ownership. By nature, these files are highly transportable and provide good summary "snapshots" of financial and corporate operations. These files could be of interest and value to competitors, particularly those that contain customer-oriented information. In addition, the privacy of employees and customers could poten-

FIGURE 8–13
Policy: Security Measures Required for Data Ownership

Users with appropriate security clearance will be able to access only copies of company production data stored on the mainframe computer for which access has been approved and arranged.

Downloaded information is to be kept on diskettes that are locked up when not in use or on a hard disk that has a security package that restricts access.

The hard-copy reports resulting from the use of secure information should be locked up when not in use.

All microcomputers and their peripherals will be identified by a reference number by using a security tag or engraving. Microcomputers handling protected information will also have software ID codes and passwords that are assigned by the Information Services security officer.

The only microcomputers that may be removed from the premises are the recommended portable microcomputers available from the Information Center. In particular, hard disks and physical storage devices other than floppy disks will remain on the premises. It is impractical to restrict the movement of floppy disks, so users who have such disks containing secure information will be held personally responsible to exercise reasonable precautions regarding those disks.

Department managers should make all their employees who use corporate data files aware of their responsibility to secure that information from misuse. The misuse of corporate data will be viewed as a serious infraction of corporate policy and may result in termination and possible legal action.

All computer programs and data developed by employees using company-owned computer equipment are company property. Individuals leaving the company must return all copies of their programs, data, and documentation to the company.

---

tially be violated if information about them was made available outside the organization.

Data and Software Backup

One facet of security, frequently overlooked, is data and software backup in the event of a disaster or other physical loss. Users who handle information important enough to require a record of its ownership should be instructed by the Information Center in the methods and procedures that are available to handle routine backup and storage of the information. The user's files may not be critical to the corporation, but they will always represent a certain amount of effort by the user in developing them and, therefore, are worth protecting from loss by disaster. A brief corporate policy should be developed and published for all to use. Data and software backup is not difficult when handled routinely, and it has considerable payoff if a contingency arises.

FIGURE 8–14
Policy: Data and Software Backup

The corporate standards and procedures for backup and disaster recovery shall be applicable to any microcomputer system that handles critical or valuable data, or contains necessary records of data ownership.

All critical data and programs shall have extra copies stored in a secure, remote location. The storage shall be handled routinely at agreed periods.

Users shall provide for continuity of an application when the current developer and user are not present. There shall be preparation and maintenance of good user manuals and other documentation. Normally, a second user will be trained in the requirements and controls of the system. If there are special considerations about data ownership, these will be documented and passed to other users.

Figure 8–14 gives some idea of the level of the policy that may be promulgated.

Some people believe that any program that is so vital that it must be backed up using the sophisticated backup technology of the central computer operation probably does not belong on a micro. If it is critical to the operation of the company, then the program should be evaluated for migration to the central system. On the other hand, one must be careful not to assume that a program and data worth backing up must meet certain standards of criticality to the company as a whole. It may be of great importance to only the particular user group, and it may represent considerable development effort by the group. Almost any program on a microcomputer that has cost an appreciable amount to develop is worth backing up. Also, if that program contains variations of data that are considered to be owned by others, then a permanent record should be kept of how that data was handled and what form it has taken.

Most data and software backup on microcomputers is handled on floppy disks, which are readily taken to another location and locked, or by transmission from a hard disk to central computer operations, where it is handled readily in the normal backup stream. True hard-file backup technology is relatively new, and only a few stand-alone systems are available that allow backup to removable tapes. The alternative of transmission to the central system may not always be available. Thus each system must be reviewed on its own merits.

Legal Considerations

There may be legal considerations in the use and distribution of data and purchased software by company users. These will need to be considered by each organization and clarified by its own legal staff. Some of the considerations center on privacy issues, while others center on data ownership by third parties. Areas that should be reviewed include the following:

- Privacy legislation imposes restrictions on processing some data about personnel on microcomputers unless adequate controls are in effect. Tighter controls are required on data that is stored and processed in computers than for data that is handled manually.

- When users develop software and data files on company equipment and on company time, steps must be taken to ensure that it is protected from unauthorized copying and distribution outside the company.

- When company software or data banks are purchased, the license agreements with the vendor usually expressly forbid its copying and use on more than specifically designated microcomputers. In this case, the data is owned by a third party. These restrictions frequently are ignored, either deliberately or through ignorance. If such an abuse surfaces, it is quite possible that the company could become the target of litigation by the vendor, particularly to seek publicity and discourage further abuse.

- Most purchased computer software and data have copyright protection, but many users treat the copyrights with the same laxity that allows photocopying of copyrighted material generally. Copyrighted material is seldom treated as carefully as patented items. Education is needed in this area to keep the company free from suit.

- Ownership of software or data files developed by employees at home or during off-company hours can be a complex issue. Legal opinion is needed as to potential conflicts of interest. If data clearly owned by the company is involved, the rules should be made explicit to employees.

- Frequently employees work away from the premises on portable microcomputers. A policy may be required as to whether particular types of programs and data should be handled in this way.

- If support and training are provided by a vendor for a particular software package, the course material should be reviewed to determine whether the information given about program and data ownership is consistent with company policy.

- When external vendors are working with employees on programs and data files, the security of critical data and ownership of the files used in instruction or testing should be reviewed and discussed with the vendor.

- When specific license terms have been agreed upon for programs and data, all users should be given the necessary information to abide by the terms.

Chapter Nine

Special and Future Technology Issues

A number of special and future technology issues relative to MSS are reviewed in this chapter. Application prototyping and fourth-generation languages (4-GLs) are particularly important because they allow the rapid application development that is required. Prototyping has been made readily available through the use of 4-GLs. General management considerations for both areas are discussed.

Artificial intelligence and expert systems are used increasingly because their patterns of problem solution are amenable to management decisions. Complex decisions can now be reduced to usable programs. Some definitions are given, and the artificial intelligence process is reviewed.

Business graphics generally are used in MSS for the presentation of information. An introduction to graphics is given, and a useful checklist on the features of graphics systems is supplied.

Microcomputer networking is becoming necessary for effective MSS work. Three types of networking are outlined: micro-to-mainframe links, departmental computers, and microcomputer peer networks. Integration objectives and management considerations are given.

Document image processing that is oriented to optical disks is a newly available technology that will play a key role in future MSS support. It provides the capability of storing and rapidly producing documents in the same form as they actually appear in hard copy. A number of integration and design issues are noted.

Teleconferencing and corporate videotex have special value for management and group decision support. The ability to regularly interchange documents electronically has great significance for executive information systems. The use of teleconferencing is explained, and management considerations are discussed.

One of the immediately useful technological advances to aid management support systems is the use of CD ROM (compact disk read-only memory). It promises to greatly simplify the management of archival materials. Some examples and offerings are listed.

230

APPLICATION PROTOTYPING AND FOURTH-GENERATION LANGUAGES

Application prototyping is the use of mocked-up CRT screens, output reports, and procedures to exhibit the possible results of an application to a manager or other user and to refine specifications through discussion and interaction. It is system development that is rapid and in context. If a management support system being developed has any complexity beyond the structure of the package used, prototyping is clearly the best way to proceed with the manager.

Prototyping has been made commonly available through the use of high-level fourth-generation languages. They offer the tools that make prototyping feasible.

DEFINITION OF APPLICATION PROTOTYPING

Application prototyping is the development of application systems of new design by first creating functional models of parts of the application in order to test and verify the specifications and assumptions. It uses small models of the desired system to communicate between the participants in the project and to review the requirements with demonstrations. Then the full application system design is developed in an iterative manner and enlarged systematically as particular features are agreed upon.

Application prototyping also is called requirements definition prototyping because it is a strategy for obtaining, observing, and refining the requirements by producing a series of increasingly complex models that converge to the final, required design. The process assumes that users generally do not know all their requirements and how to communicate their requirements to systems analysts, and that users' needs are changing continually.

Application prototyping is similar to the modeling and prototyping that has long been part of the design process for complex engineering projects. In that process, engineering theory and physics are applied first to build scale models, which then are tested under stress and in wind tunnels. A full-scale model, or prototype, then is created and subjected to a number of realistic tests, after which the final design is modified and agreed upon and put into production. In application prototyping, the scale models are usually screens and reports. The users look at them and can determine readily whether the content and presentation are what they desire. The full-scale prototype usually consists of the core programs in the application, without all the exceptions and refinements, and without all the system interconnections that will be made later. A usable, intermediate product is generated that can be tested to see if it fulfills all the functional specifications that have been established, as well as the wants and needs of the users that may not have been established yet.

Application prototyping is sometimes called rapid prototyping because interesting and observable models are produced in days rather than months. It is also called modeling, evolutionary development, or successive refinement, because these terms describe the process of prototyping. Sometimes it is called simulation, but that term has a somewhat different meaning. Simulation means developing mathematical equations that are like the process, so that factors affecting it may be investigated. On the other hand, prototyping is the mathematical production of the process itself, in a step-by-step fashion.

Another term that is misused for prototyping is heuristic development, which has a similar but particular use in developing artificial intelligence programs, where heuristics are the rules of thumb—the empirical rules—that are tested to see if they lead to likely solutions. Heuristic development is the use of exploratory problem-solving techniques that involve self-evaluation, or feedback, to improve the system performance. Certainly, that is very similar to prototyping and even may be said to be a kind of prototyping. However, it generally is centered on the algorithm involved, whereas prototyping usually is centered on the structure of the application and the form of the screens and reports produced.

The essence of application prototyping is that it is rapid and in context. Large-scale systems that may have hundreds of screens and dozens of record types in the database get bogged down in development by attempts to iron out all of the details before any attempt is made to show the user the probable product. In the many months that it takes to coordinate installation of such large systems, the details of the products that the user wants will change markedly, and the actual users themselves may change. The slowness of development means that the final product is not likely to be in the form desired by the user at that time. With application prototyping, however, there is rapid production of forms for the final products, and of the calculations for getting those numbers. The user sees the final result while the discussions about the application are still remembered and appropriate. Similarly, the initial screens the user is asked to look at are in the form they will be expected to have upon completion of the project. Questions of specifications and conceptual feelings about the form of the screens are completely in context with the whole application system.

Just as there is no single term agreed upon for application prototyping, there is no single version of how it should be done. Generally accepted approaches will be described in this chapter. In practice, application prototyping will vary from producing business models with spreadsheet generators and then tying them together, to developing fully integrated systems in a step-by-step fashion.

Application prototyping is a relatively new approach to system development. Elements of it have been tried for a number of years, but few articles were written about it until 1982. The reason is obvious; it is difficult to do rapid prototyping in COBOL. Too many elements have to be predefined, and too much coding is involved in most third-generation languages. The new fourth-generation languages are most useful for prototyping, however, particularly when much of the data required already resides in a database. Application prototyping has become generally useful since rapid software tools have become available and since users have felt comfortable sitting in front of CRT screens.

At this point, not only has prototyping been proven as an excellent approach to generate specifications and to bring systems on-line quickly, but it also has become recognized as a design process that can be handled systematically and under control for even the most sensitive applications.

Prototyping Compared with Prespecification

In the standard system development life cycle (SDLC) model generally used as the basis for planning application development work and estimating the resources that will be required, the phases are well-defined and separated. Figure 9–1 shows a typical SDLC in comparison to prototyping.

The original planning and initiation should not be omitted simply because someone gets a bright idea and can implement it rapidly with prototyping. Prototyping requires substantial resources, and its use needs to be planned the same as with any other resource. Software must originate in management's

FIGURE 9–1
SDLC Comparison

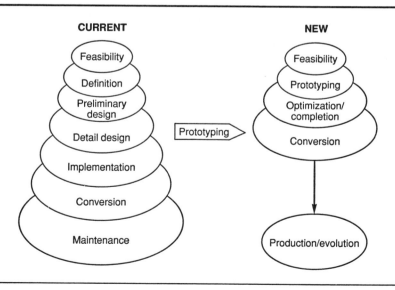

concepts and plans for an organization in order to become acceptable to it. Systems whose time has not arrived can never be implemented and operated successfully. Software should be developed to satisfy real needs. The first step, therefore, is to identify the needs of the users. The second step is to conceive methods to satisfy those needs and fit them into the plans of the organization. To be successful, any prototyping effort must be responsive to the strategic needs of the organization.

Feasibility analysis should never be overlooked. Preliminary estimates should be made of the costs of operating the proposed system and then compared to the estimated benefits to be received. In many cases, the justification of systems is obvious to operational management. It simply wants the systems at the lowest possible cost and as rapidly as possible. It accepts the responsibility for cost justification. Agreement on operational feasibility and cost justification, however, should never be overlooked or bypassed. Prototyped systems may be less expensive to develop than other systems, and they may be obtained rapidly, but they may be more costly in the long run in terms of personnel and machine time, and they must be developed under financial control.

The program definition phase is the point where prototyping varies from prespecification. The steps that are to be taken and their timing suddenly and dramatically change. In the older approach, the user's functional requirements are closely defined and coordinated in great detail with system requirements and the interactions between programs in the system. Lengthy analysis is undertaken, and paper models are produced that describe the programs in terms intelligible only to professional systems people. Specialists make analyses without discussion with the users, because their principal concern is getting the system efficiently installed on the computer and meshed with the anticipated internal data flow.

In the prototyping approach, no attempt is made to define all the system details and interactions at this time. The focus is on satisfying the user's requirements first and making sure that the user signs off on the system while there is still interest in it. The prototyping process of program definition encompasses these tasks:

- Identify only the basic needs of the user using the key elements of the output.
- Develop a working prototype model centered on the screens the user will see.
- Demonstrate the model until the user is familiar with it.
- Solicit refinements and extensions and implement them immediately.
- Demonstrate the refined prototype and discuss it again.
- Develop a preliminary design, incorporating all the information received.
- Proceed with the detail design, further programming, and implementation.

FIGURE 9–2

Requirements Definition by Prototyping

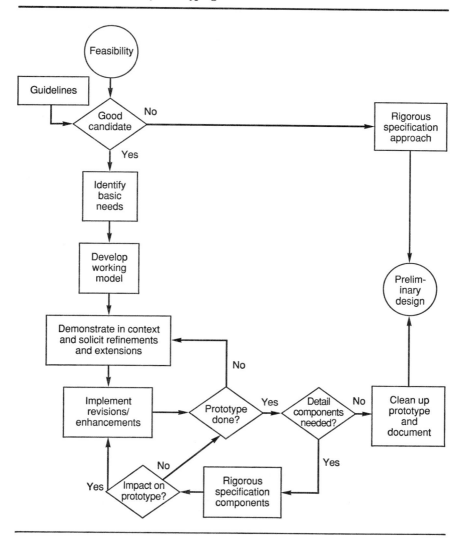

Figure 9–2 illustrates the prototyping steps from the point of feasibility and management guidelines to the point of cleaning up and documenting a useful prototype. This new prototype development life cycle is very attractive and offers tremendous benefits for the future. It has fewer steps. It does not need the

usual alpha test, where the users frequently say their requirements have not been met. It takes less time and saves money.

Figure 9–2 shows that once the proposed system is accepted as a good prototyping candidate, it is evaluated carefully, segment by segment, to determine which segments are appropriate for prototyping and which are not. For the appropriate segments, the prototyper meets with the user and identifies basic needs. Then a working model is developed and demonstrated in context to the users. After the demonstration, refinements and corrections are made. This process is recycled until it is determined that further refinements are trivial. If there are simple changes to be made, such as page dating or numbering, these are noted for later inclusion. They are not really functional requirements, but are nice to have.

There is some point at which it is agreed the prototype is finished and the analyst steps out of the prototyping loop. Now it is time to document all that has been accomplished and produce a full requirements definition statement. This should be done carefully, checking to see whether anything in the requirements impacts what has been agreed upon in the prototyping effort.

Note that when the prototype model is completed, there is still a great deal missing from the system. There are subsequent steps to prototyping. Some of the elements of the system that must be completed are:

- Database analysis and sizing.
- Network analysis and sizing.
- Many operational functions of the system.
- System conversion procedures.
- System backup and recovery planning.
- Operational run books.
- Quality control analysis applied to the code.
- Training plans and procedures.

The code produced in the prototyping has been obtained very fast and can be relied upon for producing the desired results; however, there is other code to write. Some users have estimated that prototyping saves from 15 to 25 percent of the total billed cost of initial system development. Added to that is increased user satisfaction, so that the large costs of post-implementation modifications and additions frequently are eliminated. In total, the savings are great.

Note that the prototyping approach does not reduce the amount of time on program definition. In fact, it may increase that time because the user is encouraged to reconsider all details as they are reviewed in the context of the final products. The prototyping approach, however, reduces the considerable time normally spent on coordinating the general system design and producing the detail system design. Not only can many months be cut from the process in the middle stages, when the systems analysts frequently work in their own technical vacuum, but the final result is preverified as being what the user wants. When system development projects take from nine months to more than a year to complete, they almost invariably come up with output products that are not exactly what the users want or require; time has gone by, conditions have altered, the users have changed. The classic SDLC process nearly always finished with out-of-date results and a long list of modifications to be made before it could be implemented.

Prototyping is a way of assuring that the end products are up to date, wanted by the user, and prechecked by the user. In fact, the user stays in the design cycle of the system until a usable output screen, or a large set of screens and reports, has been produced, examined, and discussed. In many cases, the prototype models may be immediately usable for study and analysis work and simple operations. There is nearly always a substantial amount of further coding and testing required, of course, to fit the operating application system into a coordinated system with other programs that can operate in a production mode.

Prototyping has proven its usefulness over pre-specification in many types of applications for several reasons. First, it is difficult to prespecify all requirements. Most managers simply do not know what they want in computer system terms. They can state their objectives and the type of application system they want, but most cannot make an objective definition of all their functional requirements. It is necessary for them to see the sort of results they can obtain and learn how to ask for the items they want. The standard SDLC demanded complete definition of all details. Managers would answer analysts' questions, but they did not know how to include variations and items that they assumed would be present. In the prototype life cycle, the users give enough requirements to get the process started, then point to the screens and ask for numbers that they feel should have turned up naturally.

There is a natural communications gap between systems analysts and managers. Systems analysts think in terms of data structures, manipulation processes, and definitions. Users think in terms of what they like to see on paper and how they will correlate the numbers in their minds. Verbal English is a poor specification language, but users may not comprehend the structures of computer languages. Translation is difficult. A picture is better. Thus prototyping has an advantage because it shows the user the actual screen pictures that may be produced. The manager and the system analyst can use a prototype to communicate with objects that are before them on the screen.

Tools are now available that make prototyping feasible. Five years ago, prototyping of large applications was simply not feasible. Small systems could be put together rapidly with FORTRAN or BASIC, but they would bog down on further development. Large systems written in COBOL or PL/1 required all details to be predefined before a coherent structure could be produced, and weeks or months of programming were a prerequisite to obtaining a few example screens. Software tools are now available that make prototyping a reasonable approach to system definition and development. They may be expensive to run on the computer, but the reduction in development time more than offsets such costs. Some of the tools that have made prototyping practical include:

- *Relational database management systems* that provide ready access to information in a variety of files and aid data modeling and program development.
- *Integrated data dictionaries* that coordinate, control, and supply most of the data definitions that are required.
- *Nonprocedural query languages* that allow rapid extraction and assembly of all the data that may be necessary.
- *Nonprocedural report writers* that give easy access to the data dictionary and the DBMS and simple tabular display of information that is extracted.
- *Interactive screen-generation programs* that can paint a variety of reporting structures on a screen while providing input editing.
- *Application-generation programs* with simple procedural languages that have many functions and automatic default handling for developing the procedural portions of applications.
- *Automatic documentation* of the resulting programs through a data dictionary reporting function.
- *Interactive workstations* that sometimes are called "prototypers' workbenches" when they are provided with the necessary peripheral equipment and software.

Managers work best with an interactive system model. The old adage that a picture is worth a thousand words has proven true again in system development. When systems analysts approach a manager with pen and paper and talk computer language, there is no way that the manager will understand or feel comfortable with the final result. When the analyst and the manager talk together as they look at a screen, there is direct communication. Specifications can be modified dynamically, and the results can be observed and understood. The various screens in the application can be studied and modified again and again, until all parties concerned are satisfied that what they are looking at is what they want. There is a further advantage. Not only will the manager be satisfied that the desired specifications have been interpreted correctly, but there also will be no surprises when the system is finally operational, and there will be no reason to complain that the system needs further modification.

Extensive iteration is necessary and desirable. Iteration is not wanted in traditional system development. Considerable time is taken to define specifications at the beginning and in trying to document the manager's requirements so that the final product, when produced, will be operable as it stands. This always has been a stumbling block to users. They see no reason why many changes should not be made in a system, particularly if many months have elapsed between its definition and its completion. It is far more profitable to allow many iterations in the process of specification, development, and review of system programs. Without iteration, the users must be content with their preconceived ideas of the system. With many iterations, they can find out what the possibilities really are and can look at a number of iterations that may offer increased function, clarity, and operability.

A disciplined development process is always imperative. An excellent feature of the traditional system development process is the discipline of stepped accomplishment and confirmation, with good planning, a way to estimate subprojects, and the ability to follow the management of each phase of the project. Management could always know where the process stood, even if it did not know how much longer it would take. This feature of imposing a rigorous discipline over the steps taken and reporting on their accomplishment can and must be maintained with a shift to prototyping. In the first phases of building the prototypes and developing the final specifications, there naturally must be some leeway as analysts and users learn the process and discover how to interact to best advantage. Even here, there should be planning and discipline applied to the recycling phase. Modifications should be made systematically in groups. However, in the subsequent phases of detail system design, programming, coordination, and implementation, the same rigorous SDLC approach that has long been used should be applied.

The principal source of system errors has always been in the requirements specification. Studies have shown that the errors appearing in a system when it should be ready for production can be traced to inadequate requirements definition. According to some studies, this part of the system development life cycle usually accounts for 60 to 80 percent of the final errors. Interpretation errors, communication problems, and technical errors are minor compared to definition problems, and they are readily handled by consistent management review during the progress of the development. Traditionally, definition errors remained in place throughout the lengthy development, however, then had to be faced when the deadline had passed and the costs of further delay had greatly increased. At the point of hoped-for implementation, the user turned out to be completely dissatisfied with the product. This disastrous result has occurred many times in large systems. Prototyping is an approach that can greatly reduce this tremendous risk of incorrect specifications that can account for up to 80 percent of the final system errors. The detailed and rigorous prespecification approach has not worked well in the past. Prototyping appears to offer a viable solution to the problem.

Delivery of Business Application Models

Prototyping may be used profitably in any type of application system development where the problems of system specification and agreement on output design are central to producing an acceptable product. In general, these are business application models. Engineering and technical analysts have long used approaches similar to prototyping, in that they have built up systems equation by equation, report by report, until they have developed a satisfactory application. Business application models present a different problem. They usually must draw on large, controlled files of information and produce reports that are under the same level of control. Acceptance of business application models depends on two different factors. First, there must be assurance that the data files were searched correctly, and that the data produced truly applies to the particular analysis being presented and is maintained under control. Second, information must be presented in the form that is wanted, including the amount, types, and display of data.

For many years, business application models were slow to produce results, because there was considerable time taken deciding on all details of the prespecification and COBOL coding of the extraction from the files was laborious. It simply takes great effort to be assured that COBOL sorts and searches are being handled correctly. This process has been greatly speeded by the use of high-level fourth-generation languages, yet the problem still remains as to whether the output is as truly usable as the recipient envisioned it to be.

Prototyping solves the problem of determining the best way to present data in a form that is desired. Non-EDP business people were never very comfortable trying to prespecify requirements in unfamiliar terms, but they soon became comfortable stepping through specifications in the form of simple screen displays. Within hours, initial models are developed and shown to the user in a way that facilitates communication. There is no pressure to finalize the specifications; there is simply an interactive process that will lead to finalization more quickly than any other way of communicating. Most users quickly become familiar with the terminals—after all, CRTs look exactly like television screens. Shortly they become familiar with what is displayed on the terminals, because they can see what column and row headings they want and have them prepared in moments.

Users soon learn that "what you see is what you get" and start interacting with it. They become enthusiastic when they realize that their rapidly changing business requirements can be matched by equally rapidly changing displays.

Many business application requirements do need a large traditional system development effort. Many financial reporting applications, for example, are already rigidly predefined, and the reports to be received from them are known specifically. A large part of the development effort must be directed toward establishing the complex control system that is absolutely necessary and does not lend itself to prototyping.

Many of the outputs from traditional business applications, however, and nearly all the analytical operational management systems are admirably suited to prototyping. With these applications, the essence to be captured is the usability of the screens and reports, rather than the legality of them. First, managers want information fast. This now can be handled with 4-GLs. Second, managers want the information on their own terms. They can express those terms simply by pointing at the screen in the course of prototype development.

One problem is the tendency to abandon prespecifications completely. This is a dangerous direction. System specifications have their place and may be the only reasonable means of communication with the technical support staff in the data center. There are many parts of a complex application that naturally will be prespecified. In fact, prototyping is most successful when it fits into the traditional SDLC and only replaces those steps where it can show dramatic improvement.

Approaches to Prototyping

There is no single best approach to the introduction of prototyping. It can be used in a variety of ways and should be tried where it appears to be best suited. There are several general approaches to prototyping that can be "mixed and matched" to get optimum results. This has been called the use of *hybrid strategies*. Some approaches that can be identified are:

Sample screens. System outputs are created as sample screens, and the user decides what the best results of the program should be. Sample layouts with possible hard copies are generated and discussed. The agreed screens then become the system specifications. There are several levels of such sample screens. The simplest is screens with literals. Screen generators are used to paint screens quickly, to make them look like what the users will receive. They are easy to discuss. Models are shown and changed. The only issue is screen content and appearance, which can be a crucial element in some systems. Sample screens can be expanded to have some editing and flow. They can be brought up in a way that the user can enter data and receive error messages, instructions, and some output, which gives a more interactive feeling to the sample screen and lets the user see what will happen in the finished system.

Functional models. The next step in prototyping is to create simple working models of parts of the application so the user can make additions, changes, and deletions. These models allow some realistic interaction with the system, and they can then be built up to simulate the functionality of the proposed system, step-by-step. They will not contain all the final features, so they will be thrown away after the system has been designed and programmed. The functional model is simply a realistic demonstration of the system that draws on a selected data file. Even if it does not evolve into the final system, it is an excellent communications tool that may be justified.

Evolutionary systems. If the whole system can remain with the same fourth-generation language, the functional model can be adapted step by step until it becomes the final application program. A number of fourth-generation tools are required for this approach, including file handlers and the ability to interconnect systems. The advantage is that the first steps are not lost, and the user can continue to follow the development as more and more complexity is added to the system.

Purchased applications. Prototyping can be used to develop the requirements for an application before an attempt is made to purchase a large package. Or you can consult with a vendor to try to develop a package as the first version of a prototype system. In either case, you work with a subset of the requirements, while the vendor supplies the definition of a large part of the requirements. Using the vendor's package, the prototyper and the user can test variations and develop the final specifications. In this way, a package may be modified quickly to conform to the requirements of the organization.

Fourth-Generation Languages in Prototyping

Prototyping has been used occasionally for many years, but it has become popular and readily used by many groups only since fourth-generation languages (4-GLs) have become efficient and available. Fourth-generation languages are programming and systems development tools that are nonprocedural and claim to increase the productivity of application development. No rigid definition has been accepted for 4-GLs, but the features available in such language tools are exactly the features that expedite the development of prototypes. A fourth-generation language generally has simple terminology and structure without a great variety of grammatical forms. Most of these languages will sacrifice operational efficiency on the computer for a considerable increase in programming efficiency by the user.

Fourth-generation languages have proven their effectiveness in many areas of application development that are concerned with complex data files and varied output reports. These are the kinds of problems where prototyping makes the most sense. Third-generation languages, such as FORTRAN, BASIC, and COBOL, can be used for prototyping whenever the data files being used are simply structured; application is principally algorithmic, or a set of procedures; calculations are recursive, and computer efficiency is most important; and outputs are simple lists.

In general, third-generation languages are most effective for prototyping many engineering and scientific applications, and for data reduction problems. COBOL can be useful for some business applications if the analysts and programmers involved are very familiar with it and if all the data files being used are structured for COBOL. Most other applications, however, will have considerable complexity in extracting data from files and programming screens and reports, so the 4-GLs will be much more effective to use. The term "transparent to the environment" is used to indicate that users of fourth-generation languages need to know very little about data storage structures, interfaces with memory units, and conversions from one data form to another. Users of 4-GLs are able to work at a "high level" and issue commands that call for complexity of manipulation with very little effort.

Figure 9–3 lists a number of functions that may be found in such languages. The list is not necessarily complete, and all languages will not have all these

FIGURE 9–3
Features of Fourth-Generation Languages

---

* Nonprocedural language.
  Specifies what is needed for the program or screen, not how it is to be obtained.
* Simple language subsets.
  Rapidly learned and used, and easy to make substantive changes.
* Capable of application expansion.
  Little or no recording of file use to handle growth in capability, which is exactly what is needed as a prototype system grows.
* Independent of the hardware environment.
  Dependent only on the operating system, which means that prototypes can be built on a micro and transferred to a larger system.
* Powerful software facilities.
  Interfaces, output aids, and programmer assistance to speed the prototyping process.
* Multiple database and file interface.
  Prototyper is not concerned with data handling, but can gather data from any source available to the operating system.
* Programmer workbench capabilities.
  Such tools as command facilities and text editing are available at the prototyper's workbench.
* Logical user views.
  Prototyper accesses data in a relational manner.
* Integrated data dictionary and directory.
  A fundamental necessity for prototyping effectiveness.
* Data integrity and security.
  The command structure supplies the necessary data integrity and security without the need to program it.

---

functions, but they are exactly the tools needed for rapid prototyping. These are the types of features that aid application development productivity, giving speed to the prototyping iterations. The key to these languages is that data and procedure specification is in general terms only. There is a linking and storage of high-level commands that is not visible to the programmer. They offer considerable flexibility over the rigid programming structures of the third generation, and the degree of speed that is needed in changing commands for fine-tuning prototypes.

Fourth-generation languages are usable by people with little programming experience as well as by programming professionals. This is an important feature, because only some system analysts adapt well to prototyping, so the prototyping analytical capability need not be frustrated by the use of a complex language. The 4-GLs have the great advantage of speed of system development, a necessity for handling prototyping iterations. It is clear that these interpretive aids are offered at the expense of computer operating efficiency. They function best for projects where response time need not be in fractional seconds. This is a reasonable trade-off for prototyping, because the final result of rapidly developing the language will more than offset some operational inefficiency. Fourth-generation languages excel in application development ease and speed, which is exactly the prime requirement for effective prototyping.

Note that *heuristic development*, which is used with fifth-generation languages (5-GLs) for artificial intelligence systems, is somewhat related to prototyping. These 5-GLs may be used to develop applications that are extremely difficult to define, but they are generally not a further improvement in speed of application development. They are, rather, an improvement in information handling that expedites the massive data searches required for artificial intelligence programs and other applications that use relational searches of very large storage files. This may be the type of system to be prototyped. Generally, however, prototyping is applied to systems with many inputs, outputs, and user interactions, and the fourth-generation languages are most effective.

In summary, fourth-generation languages are useful for prototype application development because they offer:

- Fast system implementation.
- Ease of creating initial prototypes, then extending the system.
- Handling of most available file types.
- Ease of expansion of size and functions.
- Ease of maintenance.
- Ease of documentation.
- Transparency to the systems environment.

Calling a product a fourth-generation language simply states that it is purported to be a high-productivity tool. It also means that it is nonprocedural, but this can be deceptive because many of these languages have procedural subsets. It does mean, however, that it is a likely candidate for use for prototype application development. The majority of prototyping today is being done with these 4-GL products.

ARTIFICIAL INTELLIGENCE AND EXPERT SYSTEMS

Senior managers are being introduced frequently to artificial intelligence and expert systems as possible ways of helping them solve certain problems. It is similar to the way that prototyping is being used to get away from the rigid development patterns of the standard system development life cycle. The old SDLC simply does not fit with the thinking process of most managers. They want to see early results, and they want to be able to change their minds as the development process proceeds. Prototyping and 4-GLs provide a solution to that problem.

Similarly, most managers do not think in rigid algorithms or fixed patterns of problem solution. As a problem is being solved, they want to pursue different avenues of thought for different solution volumes, with changes for varying situations. Such thought processes can be programmed, but only with great numbers of lines of code and with far more time than the manager is willing to allow for the programming. The methods of artificial intelligence more nearly match management thought processes and are now available.

At lower levels of management, complex decisions can now be reduced to programs that change the solution route depending upon the immediate findings at any solution step. These are the expert systems, which emulate the decisions that an expert would use to provide the calculation path in the computer.

The use of artificial intelligence methods, and specifically expert systems, shows great promise for management support systems at many levels. More complex programs can be used at higher levels. Controlled expert systems can be used to aid decision support at lower management levels. The approach has been proven many times.

Artificial intelligence (AI) is the use of computers to learn new facts, make decisions, and deal with new situations in a way that would be considered intelligent behavior if humans made the decisions or performed the tasks. The computers are programmed to search for and apply knowledge (or a group of facts) and to manipulate the information relative to the environment that exists at the time.

Artificial intelligence is a way to program computers so that useful answers may be obtained without knowing in advance the exact calculation steps that are to be followed. The computer searches databases in ways that are not predetermined and produces results that appear to be good, but may not be the best. AI greatly expands the areas of knowledge (or facts and conditions) that computers can deal with and opens up a new world of computer capabilities. Theoretically, it is an approach to making electronic computers think and act like humans. In reality, only the first useful steps in that direction have been taken, but more complex steps will follow rapidly. We are at the dawn of a new era in the use of computers, in which they truly will become "thinking machines," as many people characterized them in the early years when they were simply high-speed calculators.

The majority of practical AI systems and programs on the market today are expert systems. When AI is discussed in the literature, it frequently is limited to some aspect of expert systems. Most consultants who style themselves as "knowledge engineers" are experienced principally in the development of expert systems. The field of "knowledge representation" attempts to represent the knowledge or applicable facts in the most efficient way for their use in expert systems.

An expert system has, involves, or displays specific skill or knowledge that was derived from experience or training. It allows the use of the stored information to enable anyone to make appropriate decisions based on an existing set of facts. In every area of any business, there is a routine need for problem solving based on voluminous, but incomplete, uncertain, and even contradictory, information. This type of information can be captured in the computer as data and can be called knowledge, which is simply a group of facts or conditions about something. The problem is how to use this data/knowledge to make appropriate decisions. Up until now, conventional data processing has simply printed out large amounts of information based on the assumption that the questions being asked will always be the same. These computer printouts are of great use for routine, fixed applications, such as payroll, but are of little use when decisions are demanded based on a current set of unexpected conditions. The design and use of expert systems can help solve such problems. They present a powerful new way to assist decision making from the production line to the boardroom.

Expert systems can be described as programs that help the computer make decisions in a way similar to an expert in a specific domain (subject area) of interest. It has been shown that there is a wide range of practical applications that can be computerized, from medical diagnosis to diesel engine repair, from space shuttle operational decisions to quality control on a production line. The critical subsets of decisions made by experts are analyzed, defined, programmed, and put into a logical sequence for application. These AI systems do not make wide-ranging, random searches through a large body of facts. Instead, they are given a series of specific selection points based on IF-THEN-ELSE logic (meaning IF this condition exists, THEN accept this fact, ELSE step to another decision point). All searches are made up of defined "trees" of decisions, and the sequence to be followed is prescribed by the decisions that are made following the "branches" of the trees.

Intelligence is considered to be the capacity for reasoning and understanding and for reaching truth from reviewing facts that are stored in memory. It is the ability to learn, understand, and/or deal with new situations. While conventional programs follow fixed patterns of steps, AI programs modify themselves according to the results of the calculations and the types of data encountered. This is why they are called intelligent. They are designed to use a built-in reasoning capability. The idea of calling computers intelligent should not be anthropomorphized. Many researchers study natural intelligence through computer analogies and programs. Commercial users of computers, however, simply are searching for new, effective computational approaches and new ways of searching great masses of data. This use of expert systems is one of the most successful ways of endowing computers with intelligence under the control of people who need to make decisions.

The Use of Expert Systems

An expert system is a computer program that stores a large number of facts, assumptions, and miscellaneous pieces of information; expedites a search to be made of stored knowledge; and expedites decisions that will correspond to decisions that likely would be made by a human expert in that subject.

Expert systems can help make routine operating decisions that normally require an experienced individual to handle. Each expert system is used only in its own specific area or domain of decision making and can handle only those decisions for which it has sufficient information, including facts and decision rules, stored in its knowledge base or database. When current data is entered into it, an expert system frequently can supply a decision that is a close equivalent to the decision that would be supplied by a human expert looking at the same data. An expert system, however, seldom is used to make routine operational decisions that are immediately carried out, in the same manner as a process control program or an accounting program. An expert system is more likely to be used as an intelligent assistant to a human who needs to make a decision, but who does not have the experience of an expert. An expert system simply gives a "best guess" to the human, who can then use the answer from the system with reasonable confidence, add more current data and request another answer, or reject the answer from the expert system and make another decision.

An expert system is thus an aid to thinking and decision making that has certain advantages. It is able to accurately retrieve a great many facts and rules. It provides a less-experienced individual with the decision rules of a person who is experienced and expert in a particular field. It is portable and can be installed at any number of locations.

Edward Feigenbaum of Stanford University defined an expert system as follows:

> An expert system is an intelligent computer program that uses knowledge and inference procedures to solve problems that are difficult enough to require significant human expertise for their solution. The knowledge necessary to perform at such a level, plus the inference procedures used, can be thought of as a model of the expertise of the best practitioners of the field.

The knowledge of an expert system consists of facts and heuristics. The facts constitute a body of information that is widely shared, publicly available, and generally agreed upon by experts in the field. The heuristics are mostly private, little-discussed rules of good judgment (rules of plausible reasoning and rules of good guessing) that characterize expert-level decision making in the field. The performance level of an expert system is primarily a function of the size and quality of the knowledge base that it possesses.

An expert system has, involves, or displays special skill or knowledge of a particular subject that derives from training or experience. The store of knowledge (which is a group of facts or conditions about something) in the expert system usually will be accumulated systematically over time by many specialists of diverse experience. In this way, the expert system continually becomes more useful, and it may attain a level of problem-solving ability that exceeds the abilities of any one of the experts who contributed to it.

The three key components of an expert system are:

1. A knowledge base of fact, solution methods, and solution rules that are attested to by the human experts in a particular field.

2. A program control structure, or inference procedure, that searches the knowledge base for the solution to a problem in a systematic manner related to that of the human expert.

3. A working memory, called a global database, that keeps track of the problem status, the input data for the particular problem, and the trail of relevant work that has been done thus far.

An expert system can be thought of as an attempt to "clone" a human expert. Some part of a routine human activity is systematically broken down into its component parts, and the information is put into computer memory. The system is supplied with a search and reasoning process that resembles the way the human makes decisions about the subject. The result is a computer program that can make in-depth use of the stored knowledge about a subject area, reason logically to reach decisions or formulate plans, be "trained" with a set of rules or sample cases, generalize from incomplete knowledge, give an explanation of the decisions reached, and respond to questions about its knowledge base.

What is the value of an expert system? It is more stable and consistent than a human, because human beings frequently are slow and inconsistent, get emotional or tired, and may retire, quit, or die at any time. It is more flexible than the familiar data processing methods because the expert knowledge is completely separated from the program procedures and is maintainable, transportable, consistent, and stored in readily retrievable form.

Traditional data processing programs operate in a single mode; that is, they are given specified input data and produce predefined results in an expected report format. Expert system programs may operate in any of the following three distinct modes:

1. They may produce answers to problems as other EDP programs do, except that the form of the answers may be unexpected.

2. Their store of knowledge and their rule base may be increased or modified by human experts without touching the computer program itself.

3. Their knowledge base may be searched independently by a human using a wide variety of assumptions and approaches.

The first expert systems built, and many since then, were put together by interviewing a recognized human expert and attempting to capture that person's knowledge and decision techniques. The field has expanded since then, however, and many systems are being built that contain knowledge that can aid in complex decision-making situations, but which was not derived straight from human specialists in the area. These became known as *knowledge systems,* and now the two terms for such systems are interchangeable.

Expert-System Definitions

A number of definitions follow, but it must be realized that all are not strictly defined and accepted. The field is new, the competition for sales and attention is great, and no one has a copyright on the terms. Hence many of the words are defined to mean whatever the user wishes them to mean. A good example is calling an on-line spelling checker in a typewriter an example of artificial intelligence. The checker compares the spelling of a word that has just been typed in with the spelling of similar words in a dictionary and indicates those words that differ from the approved list. This useful tool is an exceedingly elementary artificial intelligence application, but it has every right to use the name because it aids in an unstructured decision. The following definitions, therefore, are useful guides rather than approved statements.

Artificial intelligence. The use of computers to carry out tasks that would be defined as intelligent behavior if the tasks were performed by humans.

Domain. A specific knowledge base for a given subject. It is the set of elements to which a logical variable is limited.

Expert. A person who has special skill or knowledge in a particular subject that has been derived from training or experience.

Expert system. An AI computer program that uses expert knowledge to solve problems by relating the facts, assumptions, and inference procedures in a knowledge base through heuristic methods suggested by human experts.

Heuristic. Providing direction in the solution of a problem along the paths most likely to lead to the desired goal. It is the expert's rule of thumb. It covers exploratory problem-solving techniques that use self-evaluation, or feedback, to improve performance.

Intelligent assistant. An AI expert system that aids a person in the performance of a task; a computer program that aids the thinking process of an individual.

Knowledge. A collection of facts or conditions about something.

Knowledge base. A database containing facts, inferences, and procedures corresponding to the types of information needed for the solutions of particular problems.

Knowledge engineering. Systems analysis of a knowledge base and of the problems that are to be solved to determine the best list structures and organization of the knowledge base and the best modes of search.

Knowledge representation. The formal way of representing facts and rules about a subject or a special area of interest in a knowledge base.

Knowledge systems. Computer systems that embody knowledge, which may consist of facts that are inexact, heuristic, or subjective, in addition to exact or controlled facts.

A human expert in the particular domain of interest usually collaborates with professional knowledge engineers to help develop the knowledge base and then the expert system. The knowledge engineer is a specialized systems analyst who interrogates the expert about the facts that are needed for any particular decision, the points of decision, and the rules of thumb that have proven to be necessary for obtaining the answer to a particular problem.

The knowledge engineer begins by trying to replicate the behavior of a specific expert in a narrowly defined problem. First, a set of facts and rules of thumb that the expert uses are determined. Second, the inference strategy that the expert normally uses to find the solution is brought out. Third, a system is developed that uses similar knowledge and inference strategies to simulate the expert's behavior. Finally, information from other experts and from actual use of the system is used to continually restructure the approach to obtaining decisions, because once an expert system has been developed, it is never left in that particular form. It is always improved continuously by adding new knowledge, even if the knowledge is only partially known or is oblique to the usual solution and new decision rules that have proven to be helpful to fine-tune the results.

Example of an Expert Systems Application[1]

Expert systems are being used now in many organizations at lower levels of decision support. They are particularly useful when decisions must be made based on general characteristics and varied background information. One popular type of expert system, for example, is used in making loans at financial institutions. It is always necessary to assess some environment quality in loan decisions (this includes customer quality and transaction quality) before an action is recommended. A good decision thus can be made if there is sufficient input on the following questions:

Is there a good lending environment?

Is this the kind of customer to make a deal with?

Is the transaction itself very good?

Based on those questions (the answers will vary greatly), the bank can make a decision as to whether to make a deal. There are several benefits to such a management support application:

- *Reduced operating costs.* If such a decision can be made quickly, involve fewer people, and increase revenues, then more business, and perhaps better business, can be done. Once an expert system is installed and a large number of units are being used, the return is realized with the cost reduction benefits.

- *Clarification knowledge.* When a systems analyst works with an expert on such systems, the expertise is enhanced as a result of going through the process.

- *Training.* In the process of learning the system and its rules, the knowledge engineer really learns the application. In the process of using the system, the professional making the decisions is trained in detail in the application. Average performance is improved measurably.

The best approach in developing such systems is to first develop "demonstration prototype" systems. These have around 50 to 300 rules, opposed to the thousands of rules in useful systems. The objective is to perform some small but real task and give the experts and the managers an appreciation for what the technology can do. These systems can be distributed throughout the organization to give potential users an appreciation for what can be done on a hands-on basis.

A decision will rely on the program's action down to a detailed heuristic level. In setting up such environments, there are program structure rules and a hierar-

---

[1]Adapted from a talk given by Peter Strell, vice president and manager of Systems Planning, First National Bank of Chicago.

chy; for example, of trader quality and transaction quality. Each of the premises contributes to the conclusion of good, fair, or poor. Clearly, if the trader quality is bad, the trader environment is bad, and the transaction quality is bad, then the decision would be negative. In most cases a decision is not obvious, and there are many rules that come up with a variety of conclusions. In order to assess trader quality, for example, it is necessary to know something about the trader's financial status and reputation. There will also be judgmental responses that are not visible to the user of the system; for example, relating to the goods that are being traded. These premises and conclusions are internal to the process, and the user does not see his or her action except at the detailed heuristic level.

What does it take to make a good trader financial status? If the trader's income statement, balance sheet, or cash flow is good, and if the trader's bank relationship is good, the trader's financial status is good. Then another premise, the trader's bank relationship, should be looked at and determined that it is good. Why do we need to conclude that? This can be the interesting part, the detailed heuristics. Up until this point, all of the answers have been judgmental. The terms good, fair, and poor are all judgmental words. The heuristics are no longer judgmental. If the trader's bank is a major money center bank, it can be looked up. There is a list of banks that are classified as to whether they are prime banks, regional banks, or whatever. If the line of credit at this bank is in excess of $1 million, it can be found from the list. That is a fact. Is the relationship duration over a year? Is the trader a key customer? These are facts that can be looked up also. If these facts are as they are stated, then the trader's bank relationship is good.

This is a brief outline of an example, starting at the top to determine whether or not a deal should be made, all the way down into the trader's bank relationship. By the time it gets down to this level, there are a few hundred rules with this amount of detail. At this point, the structure of the program is laid out, an agreement is made with the expert that these are the right concepts to talk about, and this is the right order in which the concepts should be addressed. There is a calibration that, if these inputs are as they are expressed, then the output should be as it has been concluded. This is an example of what a system is like. This problem can be keyed in with a text editor, put behind the inference engine used, and run.

In this process, first identify the application, select the experts, select the tools, research the application, and prime the experts.

We have a checklist of about 80 concepts that we are looking for in identifying an application. Once we have found them, we find an expert. Our process is to get the best expert, put together a system with that person, and then bring that result up through the organization. We will show it to the expert's boss. If the expert's boss likes it, typically he or she likes the process but not the rules. That is how we bootstrap our way up to the top experts. The tool that we use is Teknowledge M.I. All we have to do is program the logic, the content, and the rules that we solve. We have to figure out which concepts are important and how they relate to each other. That is the knowledge engineering activity.

The first thing that should be done in the knowledge engineering activity is to identify the objects. When talking to experts, ask what it is they are interested in, what is important to them, what are the main things they care about. The list of things that an expert cares about are what we call the objects. In the trading case, the objects were the environment the trader cares about. The banker cares about the customer and about the transaction.

The next step is to identify what attributes are associated with those objects. For example, you might say you care about the financial status and the reputation as the attributes of the trader or customer. Once you have gone through and tagged all of the objects with all of the attributes that the expert cares about, then you identify what *values* might be associated with those attributes. A line of credit, for example, is an attribute of a bank relationship that can take on a monetary value. It can be zero dollars or more. What kinds of value can the trader's bank have? It can be a regional bank, it can be a primary bank, it can be a major money lender bank. These are the possible values that the attributes for the objects can take on.

Go through that process and identify the objects. Identify their attributes and their values. At this point, start grouping these together. Figure out what it is that you want to conclude with this process and then identify the "if-then" relationships.

In the process, do not come up with the rules first. Come up with the building blocks first. Build a vocabulary, and then when you have an understanding with the knowledge engineer and the expert on what it is you are talking about, start grouping this vocabulary into rules. As you write the rules, the structure will begin to emerge. At that point, where the problem solution structure has been worked out, you actually can get a working expert system. When the system is working to the satisfaction of the expert, then you are asking the right questions. You are asking them in the right order and getting approximately the right answers. After that process takes place, it is possible to start assigning weights to the various object-attribute values. You can start assigning certainty factors. Finally, it can be programmed. Programming means that you key your object-attribute value "if-then" structures with a text editor, type that up, place it behind your inference engine, and run with it.

Testing these systems is different from testing third-generation systems because you do not know if the expert is doing the right thing. There is no real proof that what you are doing is correct. What you can do, however, is validate that the system does what the expert does, in the same way that the expert does it, and that the process is somewhat natural.

The development time is not very long for demonstration prototype systems. To engineer the model, to front-end it, takes about ten hours of the expert's time. Try to have five two-hour sessions. At the end of these sessions, you will have a system that contains somewhere between 50 and 200 rules. Then the expert is no longer needed. You can do a rough polish of the program and work out the wording of the questions and the answers. Then they can be shown to the expert. When you have gotten some agreement that the program is working right, you can install it, which means that you turn the floppy diskette over to the system operators and walk them through it. Tell them how to start up, how to save their output, and that sort of information. This should take about five hours of work, and then they can be left alone. The next step is to install full systems where the expert system is actually integrated with a major database. For a fairly small amount of input you can get a good demonstration system. A good strategy is to do a lot of small systems rather than a few large ones.

ADVANCED USE OF GRAPHICS

Business Graphics

Business graphics, engineering graphics, and statistical and scientific graphics all deal with data analysis, computation, and presentation of information. Control graphics deal with much more complex mathematical relationships and simulations and tend to be used in continuous, monitoring modes. Image generation is used in engineering design. Planned objects are visualized for design studies, and the effects of changing parameters are noted. It is a complex process that is constantly changing and is not a routine, operational function. Image processing usually covers a completely different area, that of entertainment, advertising, and art. These are not mutually exclusive modes of graphics, but are rather defined areas in a range of overlapping graphics applications.

Graphics for business, engineering, statistics, and science generally have the following attributes in common:

- They are developed from organizational data files or databases.
- They make use of operational or process data in the organization.
- They soon settle into the use of standard graphs, charts, symbols, formats, and presentation methods.
- Their functional requirements can be described accurately (or almost accurately) by technical personnel before they are acquired.
- Their routine output generally can be defined and measured.
- Their development and operating costs are reasonably independent and can be measured and compared to plans on an ongoing basis.

Business graphics cover a wide range of uses, but generally are graphics related to analyses, presentations, and reports produced by managers or business staff at any level. The data for most business graphics is obtained from internal computer files relating to financial, marketing, personnel, and operational areas of the business. Data from external data files frequently is used for comparisons. The preponderance of business graphics derive from spreadsheet data and planning analysis. In practice, therefore, they come from the popular microcomputer spreadsheet analysis programs or similar packages.

Figure 9–4 classifies a variety of business graphic uses to aid in consideration, analysis, and management.

Analysis and decision support graphics are the planning, forecasting, and analysis uses handled by lower-level managers and their analysts. Appearance and readability of the curves are not as important as their capabilities for manipulation, comparison, modification, and extrapolation. These graphics are designed for studying conditions and relationships represented by available operational data. They may be data plots and graphs for specific analyses. They may be outputs from spreadsheet analyses and related graphics. They may be financial or operational analysis and forecast lines. They tend to be presented predominantly in terms of dollars or units of production.

Presentation graphics are the "cleaned-up" results and summaries from analysis and decision support work. They tend to have minimal information to

FIGURE 9–4
Classes of Business Graphics

Analysis and Decision Support Graphics
Data plots and graphs
Spreadsheets and related graphics
Analysis and forecast lines

Presentation Graphics
Plots and diagrams
Color graphs and charts
Illustrations

Report Graphics
Summary presentation of analyses and forecasts
Normalized presentation graphics
Mixture of text and graphics

Control Graphics
Project and resource organizers
Organization chart systems
Variance and diagnostic displays

Entrepreneurial graphics
Visualized designs
Advertising art and animation
Attractive displays of information

---

emphasize particular points that are to be made. They have the same curves as decision support graphics, but with cleaner formats and bolder lines for clarity and ease of reading. They are designed for viewing on a screen with discussion by a group or for transfer to slides or other projection media. Presentation graphics may be simple plots, diagrams, graphs, and charts. They may be black and white, tinted, or in color to encourage viewing and enhance ideas. They may have specialized printing fonts or illustrations to make them more attractive and easily read.

Report graphics are designed for publication. They are selected summaries of data for illustration in reports, usually summary presentations of analyses and forecasts. They usually require consistency over a set of charts, so they are normalized presentation graphics—that is, all figures and data are brought to the same formats and scales. Report graphics may be more complex to produce because they are printed as a mixture of text and graphics, with the text in several fonts. Primary consideration is given to how they will be placed and appear on an 8½-by-11-inch page.

Control graphics are fixed-format summary charts routinely produced as operational reports in order to show management responsible for a project how the effort is progressing. One example is project and resource organizers such as Gantt charts and PERT charts. There may be bar charts, bubble charts, or a mixture of charts and tabulated data. Organization chart systems are control graphics because they show how lines of authority are assigned and the distribution of control reports. Other types of control graphics are variance and diagnostic displays that give a visualization of problem areas or the relative sizes of variances. These may relate to operation of the business as a whole, or operation of areas such as computers or telecommunications, or processing errors in specific functions.

Entrepreneurial graphics are the business uses of graphics for sales, persuasion, or informational presentations. They tie together art, design, and factual information to create a message attractive to the viewer. Occasionally design graphics are used internally in an organization to give more zest to a presentation. This usually happens only in marketing, however, and generally is viewed as a misuse of effort in financial and operational discussions. Such an attitude is unfortunate, because visualized designs can aid in the transmission and retention of information. Advertising art, animation, and attractive displays of information help sell products, services, and concepts. They center on creativity rather than analysis.

End-user business graphics thus span a wide range, and it is important to keep this in mind when trying to sell the concept of graphics to a variety of people. One approach does not fill all requirements. A systems analysis should be made to assess possibilities for the use of business graphics in any particular situation. Some of the key questions that should be answered before any equipment acquisitions are planned are listed in Figure 9–5. The answers to these questions

FIGURE 9–5

Considerations for End-user Business Graphics

No.	Item	Yes	No	N/A	Comments
		Reponses			
1.	Are charts and graphs used in management reports and presentations?	____	____	____	
2.	Are the graphs to be produced by professionals?	____	____	____	
3.	Can end-users profitably use equipment that can directly produce graphics?	____	____	____	
4.	Can Information Services offer substantially more-sophisticated graphics capability?	____	____	____	
5.	Have average costs been determined for:				
	a. microcomputer-generated graphics?	____	____	____	
	b. mainframe-generated graphics?	____	____	____	
	c. graphics from specialized office-automation tools?	____	____	____	
	d. hand-generated graphics?	____	____	____	
6.	Is there a reasonable way to make graphics data available to end-users from:				
	a. mainframe databases?	____	____	____	
	b. extract databases?	____	____	____	
	c. databases downloaded to microcomputers?	____	____	____	
	d. databases developed on microcomputers?	____	____	____	
	e. external databases?	____	____	____	
7.	Should Information Services supply support to graphics end-users for:				
	a. selection and purchase of equipment?	____	____	____	
	b. application planning?	____	____	____	
	c. formal training and demonstrations?	____	____	____	
	d. informal training and support?	____	____	____	
	e. operational troubleshooting?	____	____	____	
8.	Should Information Services charge for support given to end-users?	____	____	____	

can be most helpful in defining the functional requirements of business graphics. They should be answered in consultation with the technical staff in Information Services who supply data capabilities, and with the concerned managers who know what data they want to graph. This is a planning checklist to see what areas need more study and consultation.

Business graphics produce output to be used for management reports and presentations. This output may be used on CRT screens, plotted on paper, or transferred to slides or overhead foils. The graphics usually will be created directly by the person who is doing the analysis and making the presentation.

Business graphics are a heavy user of computer power. They are rapidly becoming one of the largest end-user computing applications. Graphics adapters on microcomputers, equipment for plotting, and graphics-reproduction facilities are becoming substantial budget items.

As the use of business graphics increases, the demand also increases for production graphics. Production graphics are the facilities and services that take end-user graphics output and produce multiple copies of presentable prints, slides, or foils. As graphics prove to be effective, managers want to use this tool as part of their normal reporting and presentation procedures. Production graphics equipment is generally more complex and expensive than the output equipment it replaces. It usually requires trained technical personnel to handle it. It is best concentrated in a service department of Information Services.

Studies have shown that many managers are not convinced of the value of graphics output, and they are more attuned to looking at tabular data to make decisions. Certainly, graphics will never bring about the rejection of summarized tables of data for senior management decision making. But because management is being faced today with huge volumes of tabulated computer output, any methods that draw attention to critical points and trends and variances are most welcome. In presentations, business graphics can be used to get the point across much more readily than lists of numbers. They are of value whenever complex, voluminous data needs to be focused.

Another advantage of business graphics is that end-users who are not oriented to computers find the output is very user-friendly. They feel comfortable with such output summarizations, particularly when they can use very high-level instruction commands. They are able to observe the effects of parameter changes readily and make comparisons between plan and actual.

A third advantage of computer-driven business graphics is that they are superior to graphics that have been produced laboriously by hand in the past. Most business reports and presentations have always had some graphics. The new business graphics are easier to read, more accurate, faster to produce, and cheaper than those done by hand.

Presentation Graphics

Presentation graphics are an important subset of business graphics with considerations that are unique to their use. Most business graphics are analytical studies, but the culmination of the analytical effort is when selected graphs are summarized, cleaned up, and made into presentation form. At this point, the accurate technical detail is combined with considerations of form, art, and sales, and output is produced to hold people's attention.

Several different delivery media for presentation graphics are listed in Figure 9–6. These distinctions should be understood clearly, because different modes of delivery require different types of equipment and programs. The best selections for some approaches are not the best for others. The original functional requirements should be used to distinguish among claims for different media.

Static video graphics are similar to the traditional tray of slides that can be sorted quickly and used on demand for a presentation. Summary graphics are prepared, edited, indexed, and stored in computer memory, either in a local microcomputer or central mainframe. These can be called out rapidly in the desired sequence on demand. They also can be converted to slides, transparencies, and opaque documents for direct use in presentations, or for handouts and reports. These are camera-based or screen-based graphics.

Dynamic video graphics are used by analysts and technical personnel to study situations and variations, plan activities, and prepare for presentations. These graphics usually are handled by an individual or a small group at a keyboard in front of a CRT screen. They may be projected on larger screens for group discussion. Dynamic video graphics require not only the variable graphics in a computer memory, but also all programs that are needed for structuring the graphics, and lists of the input and output data that have been developed. The graphics production equations are retained and are available for restructuring the charts in any way. These are called interactive graphics because all the components for producing them are available for manipulation at the keyboard. Video character generators, line generators, and graphics keyers are also available for design and modification of the graphic results. Dynamic video graphics are digitally based.

FIGURE 9–6
Delivery Media for Presentation Graphics

Static Video Graphics
Prepared graphics in microcomputer memory
Prepared graphics in main computer memory
Use of slides, transparencies, and opaque documents

Dynamic Video Graphics
Variable graphics in computer memory
Interactive graphics
Video character generators and graphics keyers

Prerecorded Playback Graphics
Videotapes and disks
Prerecorded presentations in transportable memory
Store of cataloged electronic frames

Prerecorded playback graphics are the finished product of edited and produced presentations. They may be on videotapes or videodisks for duplication and easy transportation. They can be played on a television set or on sophisticated video-presentation equipment. They are prerecorded shows in a transportable memory, and their use is as familiar as commercial video cassettes. They even can be a mixture of motion pictures and digital graphs. For management presentations, they are a store of cataloged electronic frames, available in fixed sequence. These are storage-based graphics.

Presentation graphics have been studied professionally and artistically by many competent people. An amateur should not try to produce them without first reviewing what has been found from experience and analysis. There are preferred methods that can help focus the viewer's attention and get the message across more readily. Some useful points are listed in Figure 9–7. They are guidelines to the proper use of presentation graphics. The essence of good graphics is to make the data clear and easy to read, and the principal points obvious and understood. The purpose of the graphics is to attract and hold the attention of the audience and to transmit specific pieces of information in a way that will be accepted and retained. Common sense is the foundation of good graphics. Following proven graphics methods makes sense.

In particular, the axis annotations on a graph (the labels and numbers) must be made large enough to be read easily throughout the audience. If the audience is large, hearing and sight will be diminished, and the writing on the charts must be **bold** to be useful. Simplicity is a key factor. Whenever the audience takes longer to read the charts than the speaker takes to go over them, there is confusion, the message is distorted, and the charts are less effective. There are simple standards to follow: points must be summarized, charts must not appear ''busy,'' and the main emphasis or idea must be clear.

What actually is produced will depend on the subject, the audience size, the clarity of the screen, and the technical level of the audience, but graphs should follow an accepted art and architectural adage: less is more.

A word of warning about graphics. There is one obvious advantage to tabular data on charts or spreadsheets, particularly if they are controlled, balanced, and totaled: they represent the best numbers available without distortion. Insofar as statistics and accounting figures are true, the numbers can be assumed to be true. With charts and graphics, however, the numbers can be ambiguous or even distorted. If the considerations listed in Figure 9–7 are not followed or are inverted, graphics can misrepresent the data. Data can be obscured or slanted to make a particular point, giving the effect of an outright lie. This can be done in a number of ways:

- Colors can be used to emphasize the wrong points.
- Coordinates can be used that are widely different on the X axis and Y axis, distorting the slope.

FIGURE 9–7

Considerations for Presentation Graphics

No.	Item	Yes	No	N/A	Comments
			Responses		
1.	Are the axis annotations (labels and numbers) large enough to be read easily?	___	___	___	
2.	Are the axis scales easily interpolated?	___	___	___	
3.	Are the axis annotations outside the chart lines?	___	___	___	
4.	Are all data sets labeled?	___	___	___	
5.	Is the same scaling used on multiple charts for ease of comparison?	___	___	___	
6.	Are the grid lines, if any, lighter than the axis lines?	___	___	___	
7.	Is a zero value included for reference wherever possible?	___	___	___	
8.	Is the zero in the same position on multiple charts for ease of comparison?	___	___	___	
9.	Is the notation on the graph:				
	a. clear to a new reader?	___	___	___	
	b. adequate to cover all variables?	___	___	___	
	c. the minimal amount necessary?	___	___	___	
10.	When bar charts are used:				
	a. are they wide enough to clearly define the bars?	___	___	___	
	b. are they sorted roughly by magnitude to avoid "saw teeth" in each section?	___	___	___	
	c. are the shading patterns neither confusing nor distracting?	___	___	___	
11.	When logarithmic scales are used, is their interpretation clear to the audience?	___	___	___	
12.	When color is used:				
	a. are contrasting color combinations used?	___	___	___	
	b. are the color combinations nonvibrant?	___	___	___	
	c. are the labels and titles in dark colors?	___	___	___	
	d. is there consistent color-coding of lines, axes, and labels?	___	___	___	
	e. do the colors reflect the popular conception of their denotation?	___	___	___	
	f. do the colors reflect the relative importance of the information; i.e., stronger colors for more important information?	___	___	___	

- Zeros can be omitted from the scales, helping falsify the level.
- Small numbers and notations can confuse the audience.
- Lack of color contrasts can blur images.
- Unsupported projections can appear as data.
- Confusing patterns can obscure issues completely.

There are guidelines for good graphics, but there are no strict rules. If a manager wants to have graphics accepted by higher management and to make a convincing point more than once, then these warnings must be taken into consideration. In most organizations, the obligation is on the analysts to sell the advantages of graphics. This requires developing confidence in such representations.

Selection of Optimal Graphics System Features

There are many excellent graphics systems and system components on the market. An optimally effective computer graphics operation usually will be a mixed-vendor environment. IBM is widespread in the field, and its Enhanced Graphics Adapter card and Enhanced Color Display have assured that more usable high-resolution graphics software will be the standard everywhere. This new hardware firmly establishes the requirement for higher-resolution graphics in monochrome and color and standardizes the display of more colors at each available level of resolution. There are many vendors who are not only meeting and matching these standards, but are surpassing them in specific features that may be important to an organization.

The only reasonable approach to the selection of graphics systems is, first, to review the general considerations regarding the system, the vendor, and the software; and, second, to study the functional requirements of the application and determine the output media required, degree of quality desired, and which features are necessary, merely desirable, and unnecessary. The analysts then can turn to the checklists provided in Figures 9–8 through 9–12 to compare each system considered for acquisition. Those systems that have all the necessary features in place can be compared as to their cost and the number of desirable features they have.

Many features are listed in these checklists; all of them may not be needed for any given application. Thus the checklists should be scanned first for the appropriate questions. Other questions may be added, and the questions that address necessary features should be highlighted. The checklists then are used to compare two or three different systems. There is no need to consider a full system package at one time, but various system and software components can be separated out and compared individually.

FIGURE 9–8

Features of Graphics Systems: Graphics Computer System Features

No.	Feature or Characteristic	System	System	System
1.	What is the minimum microcomputer configuration requirement?			
	a. Memory required (128K, 256K, or other)?	——	——	——
	b. Memory recommended?	——	——	——
	c. Number of diskette drives recommended?	——	——	——
	d. Hard disk recommended?	——	——	——
	e. Dot-matrix printer recommended?	——	——	——
2.	Can the system be used without a knowledge of programming?	——	——	——
3.	Is the system compatible with the operating system being used?	——	——	——
4.	Can the user copy, delete, or rename files without returning to the operating system?	——	——	——
5.	Are directories of charts and data files provided?	——	——	——
6.	Is the program menu-driven?	——	——	——
7.	Does the system integrate with a spreadsheet program or data manager program?	——	——	——
8.	Does the system have multiple fonts?	——	——	——
9.	How many fonts can be used?	——	——	——
10.	What is the screen resolution (e.g., 512×512)?	——	——	——
11.	How many bits are there per pixel (e.g., 8 or 16)?	——	——	——
12.	For color, is there a requirement for:			
	a. color/graphics adaptor?	——	——	——
	b. color driver board?	——	——	——
	c. color graphics board, medium resolution?	——	——	——
	d. color graphics board, high resolution?	——	——	——
13.	Is the system sufficiently portable to work on any computer system that will be required in your organization?	——	——	——
14.	Is the system sufficiently device-independent to work on any plotting device that will be required in your organization?	——	——	——

FIGURE 9–8   *(concluded)*

No.	Feature or Characteristic	System	System	System
15.	Does the system have a sufficient set of options for the types of graphs that will be required?	——	——	——
16.	Is a co-processor (such as the 8087) required to increase your microcomputer's instruction set:			
	a. to use the graphics system?	——	——	——
	b. to speed the operation of the graphics system?	——	——	——
	c. to handle required statistical or mathematical routines?	——	——	——
17.	Is the combination of configuration, memory size, and disk size of the object microcomputer sufficient for the programs and data being considered?	——	——	——
18.	Is there a software requirement for IBM compatibility that can be met?	——	——	——
19.	Can system files be transferred between the central mainframe computer and the microcomputer that will be used?	——	——	——
20.	Does the system handle a sufficient number of variables?	——	——	——
21.	Is there an error-correcting file-transfer program available (such as Kermit)?	——	——	——
22.	Does the system have comprehensive user's documentation that is sufficiently easy to learn and use?	——	——	——

Notes:

FIGURE 9–9

Features of Graphics Systems: Graphics Data Input Features

No.	Feature or Characteristic	System	System	System
1.	Are there simple statements for the search for and selection of data from the database?	____	____	____
2.	Is there a data query capability, whereby data can be:			
	a. selected from a file?	____	____	____
	b. manipulated after selection?	____	____	____
	c. handled statistically and summarized?	____	____	____
3.	Can data be entered from a keyboard, as well as from data files?	____	____	____
4.	Can data be entered interactively during a session:			
	a. from the keyboard?	____	____	____
	b. using a mouse?	____	____	____
	c. using another digitizer?	____	____	____
5.	Does the system tie into the available database:			
	a. on the central mainframe computer?	____	____	____
	b. on the microcomputer?	____	____	____
6.	Does the system interface with the desired spreadsheet or other analytical program files?	____	____	____
7.	Does the system accept data from:			
	a. DIF data format files?	____	____	____
	b. IBM BASIC files?	____	____	____
	c. VisiCalc files?	____	____	____
	d. Lotus 1–2–3 files?	____	____	____
	e. Multiplan files?	____	____	____
	f. SYLK files?			
	g. other proprietary files? _____	____	____	____
8.	Can the available data be selected, reorganized, and recoded automatically for new, defined variables?	____	____	____

Notes:

FIGURE 9–10
Features of Graphics Systems: Business Graphics Design Features

No.	Feature or Characteristic	System	System	System
1.	Are all the desired chart types available in the system?	——	——	——
2.	Are all the desired statistical and mathematical functions available in the system?	——	——	——
3.	Are there adequate features and choices for:			
	a. formatting the graphics?	——	——	——
	b. scaling?	——	——	——
	c. size of finished graph?	——	——	——
	d. patterns desired?	——	——	——
	e. orientation of the graph?	——	——	——
	f. color selection?	——	——	——
	g. printing font selection?	——	——	——
	h. symbol selection or generation?	——	——	——
4.	Does the system automatically scale the graphs?	——	——	——
5.	Does the system aid in the design of the graphs by:			
	a. placing the labels and legends?	——	——	——
	b. developing patterns and pattern sequences?	——	——	——
	c. selecting color combinations?	——	——	——
	d. selecting letter fonts and font sizes?	——	——	——
6.	Does the program have single-keystroke commands?	——	——	——
7.	Does the program allow and aid calculation of scales, lengths, and areas?	——	——	——
8.	Can the program automatically scale the graphics?	——	——	——
9.	Does the system support automatic and forced scaling?	——	——	——
10.	Can combinations of different types of plots be produced from the same data at the same time?	——	——	——
11.	Can the system overlay plots?	——	——	——
12.	Does the system allow labeling:			
	a. on the X and Y axes?	——	——	——
	b. on the Z axis in three-dimensional figures?	——	——	——
	c. on plotted lines?	——	——	——
	d. on pie segments?	——	——	——
13.	Is labeling permitted anywhere on the plot?	——	——	——

FIGURE 9–10 *(continued)*

No.	Feature or Characteristic	System	System	System
14.	How many line graphs can be displayed on a single set of axes?	___	___	___
15.	Does the system allow:			
	a. graph overlays?	___	___	___
	b. mixed charts?	___	___	___
	c. chart overlapping for comparison?	___	___	___
	d. cut-and-paste?	___	___	___
16.	Does the system produce color plots?	___	___	___
17.	Can the user change the colors?	___	___	___
18.	Can the user create new symbols?	___	___	___
19.	Can the user write in different fonts in text?	___	___	___
20.	Can the system display:			
	a. grid lines in varied thickness?	___	___	___
	b. data values wherever required?	___	___	___
	c. tick points on the axes?	___	___	___
21.	Are there comprehensive error-checking routines?	___	___	___
22.	Are all prompts, responses, and error messages clear and easily understood?	___	___	___
23.	Is the system considered user-friendly in design work?	___	___	___
24.	Can screen menus be created by means of ordinary text files?	___	___	___
25.	Can lists of screens be edited, changed, and saved on disk?	___	___	___
26.	Does the system build and retain a standardized format for frequently used graphs?	___	___	___
27.	How many data points can be charted at one time?	___	___	___
28.	Can summary statistics be generated automatically, as the graph is being built, including:			
	a. counts and percentages?	___	___	___
	b. totals and running totals?	___	___	___
	c. averages?	___	___	___
	d. regression analyses?	___	___	___
	e. forecasting analyses?	___	___	___
29.	Can combinations of different types of plots, such as line charts, bar charts, and pie charts, be produced on a single page?	___	___	___
30.	Can any screen be customized by the user?	___	___	___
31.	How many colors are supported (8, 16, or other)?	___	___	___

FIGURE 9–10 *(concluded)*

No.	Feature or Characteristic	System	System	System
32.	How many colors can be displayed simultaneously? (Over 8 simultaneously viewable pure colors from a palette of 256 is minimal. 16 simultaneously viewable from a palette of 4096 is preferable.)	____	____	____
33.	Does the system plot in color with:			
	a. medium resolution?	____	____	____
	b. high resolution?	____	____	____
34.	What is the resolution of the system? (500 elements horizontally on a raster display to 15" is usually sufficient. 1000 horizontal elements are needed for color screen photography. 4000 horizontal elements may be needed for complex plots.)	____	____	____
35.	What is the screen size? (15" is popular for most work, 19" is preferable for higher raster resolution.)	____	____	____
36.	Are the screens erasable in an alphanumeric mode?	____	____	____
37.	Is the brightness, or light output, of the terminal adequate for use in an office environment?	____	____	____
38.	Does the system support:			
	a. pen plotters?	____	____	____
	b. impact printers?	____	____	____
	c. printer plotters?	____	____	____
	d. CRT copiers?	____	____	____
	e. camera systems?	____	____	____
39.	Is color hard copy available via:			
	a. impact ribbon printers?	____	____	____
	b. ink-jet printers?	____	____	____
	c. xerographic printers?	____	____	____
	d. thermal transfer printers?	____	____	____
	e. photographic systems?	____	____	____
40.	Is the system compatible with the communications facilities available in the office?	____	____	____

Notes:

FIGURE 9–11
Features of Graphics Systems: Types of Business Plots and Charts

No.	Feature or Characteristic	System	System	System
1.	Are the following types of business plots and charts available in the system?			
	a. Line charts?	____	____	____
	b. Point charts, including:			
	1. X-Y plots?	____	____	____
	2. X-Y-Z plots in 3-space?	____	____	____
	3. scatter charts?	____	____	____
	4. dot graphs with variable symbols?	____	____	____
	c. Bar charts or columns, single- and double-sided?			
	1. Horizontal?	____	____	____
	2. Vertical?	____	____	____
	3. Clustered or stacked?	____	____	____
	4. Hatch and line patterns?	____	____	____
	5. Shaded and unshaded?	____	____	____
	6. Multiple bars?	____	____	____
	d. Pie charts, including:			
	1. labeled segments?	____	____	____
	2. shaded segments?	____	____	____
	3. exploding segments?	____	____	____
	e. area charts, with area shading (maps)?	____	____	____
	f. histograms?	____	____	____
	g. tick charts?	____	____	____
	h. pyramid charts?	____	____	____
	i. high-low-close charts?	____	____	____
	j. bubble charts or tree structures:			
	1. for organizational structure?	____	____	____
	2. for PERT diagrams?	____	____	____
	k. Gantt charts?	____	____	____
2.	Do most of the plot types allow for 3-D graphics?	____	____	____
3.	Do most of the plot types allow for hatching, shading, and line patterns?	____	____	____
4.	Are mix-and-match chart combinations allowed on the same sheet?	____	____	____
5.	Are combinations with charts, words, and tables available?	____	____	____

FIGURE 9–11   *(concluded)*

No.	*Feature or Characteristic*	*System*	*System*	*System*
6.	Are the following chart uses possible?			
a.	Statistical data display.	——	——	——
b.	Word placement or insertion.	——	——	——
c.	Logical flow indications.	——	——	——
d.	Time periods noted.	——	——	——
e.	Critical ratios displayed.	——	——	——
f.	Relative strength indicators noted.	——	——	——
g.	Project and schedule displays.	——	——	——
7.	Can the full plotted output be obtained:			
a.	on the CRT screen?	——	——	——
b.	on the desired width of paper?	——	——	——
c.	transferred to transparencies?	——	——	——
8.	Are the following plotting functions available?			
a.	Linear.	——	——	——
b.	Constant.	——	——	——
c.	Moving average and smoothed moving average.	——	——	——
d.	Data points.	——	——	——
e.	Data points modified arithmetically.	——	——	——
f.	Logarithmic.	——	——	——
g.	Exponential.	——	——	——
h.	Parabolic and distribution.	——	——	——
i.	Sine and cosine.	——	——	——
j.	Cumulative addition and subtraction.	——	——	——

Notes:

FIGURE 9–12
Features of Graphics Systems: Statistical Analysis Features

No.	Feature or Characteristic	System	System	System
1.	Are standard statistical numbers available for plotting and printing, including:			
	a. counts and percentages?	___	___	___
	b. totals and running totals?	___	___	___
	c. averages?	___	___	___
	d. moving averages?	___	___	___
	e. oscillators?	___	___	___
	f. mean-line calculations?	___	___	___
2.	Are specialized statistical functions integrated with the system, including:			
	a. scatter diagrams with correlations?	___	___	___
	b. linear regression analysis?	___	___	___
	c. nonlinear or curvilinear regression analysis?	___	___	___
	d. distributions and characteristic curves?	___	___	___
	e. forecasting methods, including seasonal and exponential smoothing?	___	___	___
	f. optimization analysis, such as Box-Jenkins?	___	___	___
3.	Are numerical analyses available for calculation and plotting, including:			
	a. solution of simultaneous equations?	___	___	___
	b. Fourier series and transforms?	___	___	___
	c. simulation functions?	___	___	___
	d. simulation linkages?	___	___	___
4.	Do the types of plots include:			
	a. linear plots, with variable axes?	___	___	___
	b. logarithmic or semi-logarithmic plots?	___	___	___
5.	Can both simple and cumulative counts be produced and printed on the plots?	___	___	___
6.	Can relative-strength indicators be calculated and printed on a real-time, tick-by-tick basis?	___	___	___

Notes:

MICROCOMPUTER NETWORKING AND LOCAL AREA NETWORKS

Microcomputers (PCs) have become an indispensable tool in management support systems. Their capabilities have surpassed the expectations of a few years ago, and they clearly have proven themselves for rapid access to organized data, improving professional productivity, and replacement of all other types of corporate calculation, by hand or by machine calculator. Their power now exceeds that of the large computers of the last generation.

The Profitability Problem

The advantages and profitability of microcomputer networking and local area networks have presented a few obvious problems:

- How can an individual or a group input enough data to reasonably utilize the raw, data-hungry power of these small machines?
- How can complex solutions and data files be quickly and accurately shared among different individuals and groups?
- How can departments maximize the analytical efficiency of their staff while maintaining at least minimum necessary controls?
- How can the costs of the proliferating, ever-larger PCs be contained?

As PCs have become widely accepted and produced the capabilities that were anticipated, users have rightly demanded more functional capabilities, more add-on equipment, and more access to data. Most users started with single applications, such as spreadsheet analysis, then looked for extensions of their applications and sharing of data at indeterminate times. They have requested access to mainframe data, help in enhancing their applications, and means to communicate with other users. Managers, on the other hand, have perceived the limitations of individual processing and the problems of controlling information and the results generated from it. Initial advances in productivity and efficiency have been diminished by difficulties in proving and comparing results. The timeliness of data exchanged by manual sharing of floppy disks has become suspect. The inability to obtain rapid iterations between a number of analysts has slowed the initial progress in management support systems.

Some small user groups have extended and added to their microcomputers until they have reached the powerful-minicomputer class, with no increased capability of data control. Others have carried and shared floppy disks until they have become unusable. Managers have been concerned about the limited opportunities for review, checking, revision, and verification of data files. The cost of peripheral add-ons, such as high-speed printers, plotters, and storage devices, has mushroomed in the shadows. The loss of data, the unreliability of floppy disk data files, and the lack of documentation of data have reached serious proportions.

These are all problems that must be considered, but they have been so outweighed by the advantages and profitability of the use of micros that they have been handled loosely, until the possibilities of direct data interchange between micros have become a common reality.

Now individuals and groups can access data from other micros as well as from the mainframe to meet the large data requirements for their more sophisticated applications.

Now solution methods and data files can be quickly and accurately shared between PCs, with some guarantee of uniformity of data, completeness of files, and timeliness of updates.

Now department heads can manage the analytical efforts of their staff by cross-checking and controls, and increase overall staff effectiveness.

Now the costs of expensive peripherals and communication devices can be shared across a number of units, and standards can be realistically imposed.

PCs can be integrated in a variety of ways and thereby become more effective, efficient, and productive. Specific solution methods apply to different circumstances, but the general direction is obvious. Analysis of requirements for PC networking, some possibilities and varieties, and the development of controllable networks will be discussed in the following pages. Analysis of the telecommunications and technical details that must be worked out will not be discussed, but management considerations will be reviewed. It is clear that there are organizational objectives that can be advanced by the integration of PCs. If the analysis is approached systematically, their networking can be justified readily.

Three Types of PC Networking

Microcomputer networking generally can be accomplished by three different approaches. None is inherently superior to the others, but for specific applications, and in specific circumstances, any one of them may be clearly preferable. The three generic approaches are:

- *Micro-to-mainframe links* are two-tier networks where the PCs are all directly connected to a central mainframe computer.

- *Departmental computers* are three-tier networks where a group of PCs are connected to a central mainframe through a powerful minicomputer that serves as an intermediary.

- *Microcomputer peer networks* are single-tier networks where a group of PCs are interconnected, usually in an array called a local area network (LAN). The LAN frequently has gateways to the central computer and to external networks or other LANs.

In the micro-to-mainframe link, the considerable power of a central mainframe computer is used to manage internal PC networks, intracompany and external networks, and large central databases. Several architectures are available. The general operational control can be strong, but the security of the central files may be difficult to maintain if the PCs that are connected are powerful. This approach is particularly suited to large, transactional applications and to very large data files that may be accessed with sufficient control. It is usually tightly controlled by Information Services.

The micro-to-mainframe link is a host network that supplies shared processing. The host computer is the most intelligent device in the system and will store the largest data files. In cases where the terminals attached to the host are "dumb" terminals, control is relatively easy to maintain. Where intelligent PCs exist, control may be complex. The architecture is hierarchical, because the communicating components are unequal.

In the use of departmental computers, three levels of computer power are intertwined and balanced. A powerful minicomputer is connected between a central mainframe and the many PCs. The approach has many advantages. The balance between the operational functions of the three tiers can be adapted and adjusted. Ready access is available to large central data files, yet strict security controls can be imposed, with the departmental processor acting as the data "gate" and controller. Departmental PCs normally will communicate with each other through the departmental processor, which introduces both more control and more complexity to the operation.

The departmental computer, or departmental processor, comes close to the classical concept of distributed data processing. Connection is maintained to the central computer, but processing power is distributed. This is particularly advantageous when frequent access to a variety of data in large data files is required, but the files themselves must be securely maintained. This type of setup thus is indicated for analysis of financial information by people with different access requirements and clearances. Frequently, application programs also can be easily managed by this approach.

The departmental computer, with its micro-to-mini connections, provides the capability of having many management support applications resident on the large disk drives of the departmental mini. This material becomes a shared resource with a relatively low cost per PC for the storage of programs and related data. The powerful departmental mini allows a smooth and simple transfer of data, either up to the central mainframe or down to the PCs. It is able to offer excellent and varied PC connectivity at the departmental level. It also provides much greater user access to corporate data resources, because the mini has data selection, screening, and security provisions that are necessary in supplying access to the controlled central files. The most common functions designed into the departmental minicomputer are:

Gateways to information in the mainframe memory.

Central data files and file backup.

Shared database and management of the DBMS.

Central control of office automation functions, such as electronic mail, word processing, and departmental files.

Software server for the PCs.

Some departmental minicomputer arrangements use the minicomputer strictly as a file server for departmental PCs. The mini supplies access to the central mainframe and essential controls and security. It then downloads requested files to the PCs on demand. Other departmental minicomputer arrangements put more power in the mini and reduce the PCs essentially to the position of on-line terminals, which are micro-to-mini in the same category as the micro-to-mainframe operation methods. At the end of the spectrum where the mini is basically a file server, the typical applications are analyses of data. At the end of the spectrum where the mini is the departmental controller, the typical applications are on-line operational systems.

Microcomputer peer networks or local area networks are rapidly being introduced into all sizes of organizations. These are networks where personal computers in departments and buildings are linked for efficient sharing of information and common connection to a central computer or external networks.

Microcomputer peer networks are systems of data communication among a relatively small number of intelligent machines. The machines may not be equal in processing power or function, but they can communicate information readily among their peers in the system. They can share any number of peripherals, such as special printers and storage devices, together with file servers or other specialized servers, which may be micros, minicomputers, or mainframes. They also can share gateways to other networks and external data services. Because all the machines in a local area network are intelligent computers, processing can take place in any one of them, at any level that the computers are capable of performing. Local management controls and security methods can be imposed. Data consistency, validity, and timeliness can be expected within the department or grouping. All the advantages heralded for distributed data processing (DDP) can be realized.

Microcomputer peer networks can satisfy many management support processing requirements:

- They can operate as individual computers with occasional sharing of data files.

- They can do parallel processing on a number of parts of a single application and bring the results together whenever that is required.

- They can be run under the control of a group or departmental manager independently of the rest of the organization, if that is desired.
- They can operate as a group on common data files with consistent updating and maintenance.
- They can have the controlled access to central data files offered by the departmental computer approach.
- They can operate on their local work cooperatively and independently, yet have complete access to the entire corporate network and all available data.
- They can share expensive peripherals and other computing devices.

In brief, LANs, or microcomputer peer networks, can make efficient use of shared resources, and differing levels of group, departmental, and central control that are appropriate may be implemented. They can satisfy the great and increasing demand for organizational data at the PC level while optimizing the use of hardware and software resources.

It should be remembered that departmental minicomputer-controlled networks and microcomputer peer networks are compatible and may be mixed and matched. First, LAN groupings of micros frequently have gateways to external networks. These are often connections to a midrange computer, such as a departmental mini, that provides all the normal functions of a departmental processor to the LAN rather than to separate micros. Second, individual micros constantly are becoming more powerful. Software for the new 386-based micros is being produced and marketed rapidly to put it into multiprocessing environments that are more similar to larger minicomputers than to PCs. The significance of this is that such highly functional micros will be able to sit in a LAN network, yet supply most of the capabilities of the departmental mini.

The effect of this ever-changing hardware market and more integrated PC software is that the categories of departmental processor and local area network should not be considered as separate and distinct ways of computing, but rather as functional types of computing that may be used independently, but also can be used together in the same system.

In most PC LANs, one of the PCs is equipped with more memory and more peripherals and acts as a file server, or print server. It may also be the point of connection to other networks and thereby acts as a communications server and a database server. Over time, this PC usually is built up and extended to the point that it may become a super-micro or a small mini. There is no defined boundary to distinguish between such equipment. There always will be departmental minicomputers controlling a number of PCs. There always will be peer networks of PCs in which one or more may be more powerful than the others. And there constantly will be more combinations of these two architectural arrangements that defy simplistic classification. The three types of networking are described here simply to show generic approaches. They are in no way limiting or exclusive.

Integration Objectives

It may appear to be obvious why PCs should be networked, but, in reality, there are many different reasons. Effort and money are involved, and limitations are put on individual analysts, so it can be helpful to management to clearly state the objectives for the integration of PCs. Integration, by itself, is not necessarily a desirable objective. It has connotations of control and an extra layer of management. The objectives that may be achieved by integration, however, probably can be profitable to an organization.

Some of the integration objectives that should be examined for profitability are:

- Cooperative information processing.
- Sharing of costly peripherals and input/output devices.
- Increased information made available to users.
- Flexible user access to distributed data files.
- Linking together of multivendor products.
- High-speed and high-volume data transfers.
- Better management and control of office computer functions.
- Efficient use of the information in a database.
- More effective statistics, graphics, modeling, and other output.

There is clear potential for return by moving toward any of these objectives, but each of them has its own problems of planning, installation, and management. A few can be taken together and accomplished. There are a number of different approaches involved, however, and concentration on only a few objectives can be most effective. Some comments on these possible objectives follow.

Cooperative information processing is a frequent objective of smaller, departmental LANs. If several analysts or engineers are working on the same project and frequently exchanging data or physically exchanging floppy disk files of data where their analyses interface, then accuracy, speed, and timeliness all can be obtained by networking.

Facilities should be provided to make cooperation as smooth as possible. If there have been occasional discussions or sharing of calculation results between individuals in the past, there may be considerably more profitable interaction if appropriate means are provided to electronically switch programs, screens, and results between them. New ways to share calculation tasks quickly spring up if it is possible to do so. There should be no artificial limit set on the ways parties can talk to each other simply because there was no apparent business reason for it to happen up to now. It is hard to forecast who will need connectivity. Integration of PCs should be planned so that almost anyone can get the connectivity he or she desires in the future. Of course, the initial steps may give that connectivity to only a small group.

Sharing of costly peripherals and input/output devices is frequently one of the main objectives for connectivity in groups that want high-speed laser printers or specialized I/O equipment, and in engineering and technical groups that have computer drafting equipment and specialized computers. Other brands of computers that serve particular functions may be joined in the LAN and made available to all the users. Test equipment with digitizers may be set up to pour information into a shared memory device. Large and expensive hard disks may be connected to hold great quantities of information that will be available to every PC in the LAN.

The effect of sharing such peripherals and devices is to justify their acquisition more readily. A single user may not be able to justify an expensive device, but several users together may be able to meet purchase criteria. The result is that more equipment becomes available to everyone, and it is available on demand. The users do not have to go to a central location and wait in line for its use. They simply dial it up on the LAN. This ease of use will itself supply some justification for the installation. Users will waste less time waiting to use needed equipment.

Increased information made available to users is often the original objective of departmental computers and LANs. Most PC users quickly reach the point where they need to have more data than they possibly can input manually for their analyses. The information is available in the organization, but it simply is not feasible for an individual to handle it or else there are strict security controls on it that defeat access. For an individual user, it would not make sense to set up a structure to access data. For a number of users in a department, it makes a lot of sense. The more people who want files of information, the more system capability that can be justified to obtain it for them, because the same method and equipment is used to access all data files. Networking of PCs, either in a LAN or to a central mainframe, has become necessary to provide information that can be used profitably.

Flexible user access to distributed data files is a particular aspect of making more information available to users. It has been shown that there are a number of tiered methods of giving users access to central data files. The approach will depend upon the volume of data required and the controls that must be imposed. But now organizations are being faced with appreciably large data files that are not on the central mainframe. Departmental minicomputers and large PCs can have substantial files of data assembled on them as analytical work proceeds. Files anywhere in a large organization may be helpful and appropriate for use in almost any department. While the files on the central mainframe will be structured in a relatively uniform manner, however, the distributed data files may be structured in any number of ways. The problem, then, is not simply to have access to them, but to have flexible means of accessing a variety of files.

Linking together of multivendor products is a problem that is difficult to handle on a individual PC basis. There are too many variations and combinations of hardware and software, and links between incompatible products can be expensive to set up. LANs, however, are particularly useful for bringing together a series of completely different multivendor products. An organization may have an IBM PC, a Xerox, an Apple, a Macintosh, a DEC VAX, a Hewlett-Packard, and an IBM host. There are good, cost-effective solutions currently available for those kinds of linking requirements. Thus a lot of specialized functionality can be gathered in a department, and users who prefer the functions of a particular piece of equipment need not be forced to fit in with the rest, but can be integrated in the LAN without changing.

High-speed and high-volume data transfers obviously are practical with integrated PCs. Any individual case will have to be analyzed according to its requirements and the network arrangements that are possible. In many cases, a PC LAN network can provide much higher-speed data transfer than can be obtained through the departmental minicomputer arrangement. It depends upon many technical factors, which must be checked out in detail.

Better management and control of office computer functions is a prime objective for networking PCs. At present, departmental processors are more effective for processing office functions than are PC LANs. The reason is that most office applications software profits from central control. Accounting, inventory query, and similar applications need tight audit control and management, and a centralized system in the department offers the most control features. Such applications are database-oriented and readily handled on a minicomputer. They usually require the attention of a data administrator to keep them under reasonable control.

Efficient use of the information in a database is a common objective for PC integration. Any useful database requires management, control, and regular updating. Databases that are generated by small groups of individuals for specific projects tend to be well maintained only during the problem analysis phase, then are left to degrade. Multiple databases that overlap in a single department tend to have data that varies originally and is updated at different times. If effort is being put into entering controlled data into any database in a department, it is profitable to make that data readily available to others, because if it is useful once, there are likely to be other uses for it.

More effective statistics, graphics, modeling, and other output are possible through integration. Such programs are usually costly, and they frequently require specialized plotting equipment and engineering-oriented computers. In any engineering or statistical analysis, the objective is to have everyone coordinated with the same data, calculation programs, and controls, and with shared results. The combination of costly equipment and the need for tight coordination points directly toward networking and integration.

Management Considerations

Obviously, there are many management considerations that must be balanced when considering microcomputer networking, particularly the establishment of LANs. The approach is proven and attractive, and experience in many companies has shown that requests will multiply rapidly once a few users have had a satisfactory experience with a LAN. Figure 9–13 is a general checklist of indicators favoring a LAN, user concerns that can be addressed by a LAN, considerations when reviewing existing communications capacity, and requirements for planning a LAN. This is a management rather than a technical checklist, designed to point out many of the issues that must be considered by management. It is useful to review what bases have been touched by the analysts, and what areas require further study.

FIGURE 9–13
Local Area Networks

No.	Item	Yes	No	N/A	Comments
			Responses		
		Yes	*No*	*N/A*	*Comments*
	Indicators favoring a local area network				
1.	Are there requirements to access multiple applications from one terminal?	——	——	——	
2.	Have cabling and associated equipment proliferated to a point where they are difficult to maintain?	——	——	——	
3.	Is there extensive growth or constant change in communications requests from users?	——	——	——	
4.	Have cable lengths become a limitation to desired organizational communications?	——	——	——	
5.	Have the costs of extending communications lines multiplied rapidly?	——	——	——	
6.	Is there a need for high communications speed for peripheral sharing and transferring of files?	——	——	——	
7.	Is there a need to interface with a remote LAN through a wide area network?	——	——	——	
8.	Does management want to administer the communication of data more efficiently?	——	——	——	
9.	Does management want to monitor the hardware and software performance of a number of small computers?	——	——	——	

FIGURE 9–13 *(continued)*

No.	Item	Yes	No	N/A	Comments

User concerns that can be addressed by a LAN

10. Do users want guarantees of acceptable response times on on-line terminals? ____ ____ ____

11. Do users require access to another vendor's hardware and software in performing their assigned tasks? ____ ____ ____

12. Do users want guarantees of access to the network? ____ ____ ____

13. Has user management requested superior local data communications? ____ ____ ____

14. Do users want increased access to information to strengthen the organization's competitive position? ____ ____ ____

15. Will more flexible communications improve the organization's ability to respond to challenges? ____ ____ ____

16. Will modern communications methods facilitate a desire to enter new fields of activity? ____ ____ ____

Review of existing communications capacity

17. Are users prepared to cooperate with a detailed communications review? ____ ____ ____

18. Can all communications users in the organization be identified, including:

   a. data communications? ____ ____ ____

   b. voice communications? ____ ____ ____

   c. wire services? ____ ____ ____

   d. office services? ____ ____ ____

19. Will the potential users of a LAN cooperate in a survey to determine functional needs? ____ ____ ____

20. Is a competent analyst available to survey all the present requirements for communications functions, and to gather future projections? ____ ____ ____

21. Can a survey team be assembled to identify:

   a. equipment now in use in the organization? ____ ____ ____

   b. the number of devices installed? ____ ____ ____

   c. the terms and commitments under which equiqment is used? ____ ____ ____

   d. present vendor relationships? ____ ____ ____

Requirements for planning a LAN

22. Are future projections of communications functions assembled? ____ ____ ____

FIGURE 9–13 *(concluded)*

No.	Item	Yes	No	N/A	Comments
23.	Has the required anticipated access rate that users can expect from the network been analyzed, including:				
	a. the access rate for different periods during the day, including the peak-load period?	——	——	——	
	b. three- and five-year projections of demand?	——	——	——	
24.	Have you reviewed the following technical concerns in the requirements?				
	a. If video is a requirement, are baseband and twisted-pair systems eliminated?	——	——	——	
	b. If the organization has a large investment in a PABX, might the twisted pair prove feasible?	——	——	——	
	c. If the organization has a commitment that would be costly to abandon, must the solution fit that commitment?	——	——	——	
	d. Will numerous long runs sharply increase the cost of baseband and twisted-pair systems?	——	——	——	
	e. Will file transfers and peripheral sharing require speeds greater than twisted pairs can handle?	——	——	——	
25.	Are the factors present that indicate a proprietary network?				
	a. All equipment is compatible, and there is no intention to acquire other equipment.	——	——	——	
	b. It is desired to stay within a specific vendor's product line.	——	——	——	
	c. A turnkey solution is preferred.	——	——	——	
	d. The vendor will supply knowledgeable support staff.	——	——	——	
26.	Are the factors present that indicate an open network?				
	a. High-capacity products are needed for a wide range of systems.	——	——	——	
	b. Flexibility is desired in the selection of connected systems.	——	——	——	
	c. Noncompatible foreign devices need to be connected to the network.	——	——	——	
	d. It is desired to leave future connection options open.	——	——	——	
	e. A turnkey solution is not necessary, as support staff is available.	——	——	——	

When PCs are to be networked to any extent, the technical problems may be more straightforward than the business problems. The operations of the business will be enhanced, but only so far as desired results are obtained and sufficient control is exercised. Network management becomes tied to business functions instead of residing in some technical area. Network management and control must become part of the normal management process in the organization. The LANs and the larger network connections become an intimate part of running the business. Networks and their processes can be designed by outside consulting firms, but ongoing network management must be built into the organization. Network management must become an accepted philosophy in departments that previously did not know it existed. It must be built policy by policy, procedure by procedure, tool by tool, and person by person. The analyses of many of the points in Figure 9–13 may be technical, but the understanding of their meaning and use must be absorbed by the management involved.

In today's environment, for effective use of support systems, managers need to arm themselves with information about the network. This includes details of telecommunications expenditures and the resources that are used. Central to the problem is reliance on multivendor environments and the issue of system versus component integrity. Integrated communications systems thus require network management to be tied into business functions as distinct from the often-discussed network control, which is the technical aspect.

DOCUMENT IMAGE PROCESSING AND OPTICAL DISKS[2]

Document image processing using optical disks is a relatively new technology that will play a key role in large organizations for management information distribution and decision support. Most computer output is in the form of lists, graphs, and stylized figures. Document image processing provides the capability of storing and rapidly producing documents as they actually appear in hard copy. There are many areas of management support that require such information.

The problem is that a number of large organizations are being buried in paper. This has been well-documented and widely discussed. It could be a result of office automation. Look at the statistics. Each day, systems produce 600 million pieces of computer output. Each year, volume of output increases at a rate of 20 to 22 percent. Forty-five new sheets are filed per office worker per day. The existing paper files cost about 25 cents per page per year to store. Any company having a large number of files has a very strong opportunity for cost savings.

---

[2]Michael R. Alsup, manager, Arthur Andersen & Company.

The second problem is that the information stored in these files is not really accessible by more than one search criteria. For example, it could be filed by policy-holder or customer. Sometimes you might want to go back into those files and find the information by shareholder, by employee, or by date or type of transaction, and the physical nature of the files makes that very difficult.

Computer-Assisted Retrieval: Microfilm

A document on a microfilm screen has an image of high-enough quality to view it adequately. In some situations microfilm does a good job in storing and retrieving records, and many companies have large-scale microfilm systems. When microfilm is combined with computer-assisted retrieval, there are a number of additional advantages. Storage compaction is one advantage where the amount of space needed to file the material can be reduced. Computerized index maintenance is another. You are able to maintain an index and retrieve it on more than one key. File integrity and file security are additional important characteristics of these systems.

Computer-assisted retrieval has several drawbacks. These drawbacks indicate the important benefits of a modern image processing systems.

- *Manual intervention by a user.* Somebody has to go and physically pick up a cartridge and insert it into a reader before viewing a microfilm image.

- *Single-thread access and image locking* due to the physical storage characteristics. If one person is looking at an image on a cartridge, nobody else is able to access images on the same cartridge.

- *Access limited by location.* The users have to be close to the cartridges to load them into their systems.

- *The reference to images is not integrated* with the clerical routine. This is perhaps the most important problem. The objective has been to deliver document images to a clerk, who probably also has a CRT, without the clerk having to get up from the desk or break his or her routine by waiting an hour or longer to have that image retrieved.

Optical Disk: A Developing Technology

A developing technology based on optical disks will enable us to address many of these problems. On a single optical disk you are able to store 25,000 or more high-quality document images. Optical disks store images digitally. This means that the page is divided into little squares and the entire image is stored as a series of ones and zeros. Current systems divide a page into 400 pixels per square inch so that the system is able to reproduce images with the approximate quality of a good copier.

Image processing systems offer several advantages. One is the storage savings of microfilm. Second, the images can be integrated with data-processing applications. A third advantage is integration into normal work flow. A clerk is able to retrieve an image to the desk and view it without interrupting the main line of activities. A fourth is that there can be multiple access to the same image at the same time. Finally, we are able to achieve a number of areas of automated work management that were never really possible before.

Briefly, that is the background of image processing, why Arthur Andersen & Company thinks it is important, and why, in a number of organizations, the potential benefits are significant.

Image Processing System Components

The components of image processing systems are listed in Figure 9–14. These components are storage, workstations (high-resolution screens), networks to communicate the images from storage to workstation, input devices, output devices, image controllers, and index management software.

Figure 9–15 is a schematic of a research and development image-processing architecture that United Services Automobile Association, 3M, and Arthur Andersen are developing. To start it off there is a user's workstation and a clerk's desk. On that desk is a 3278 CRT. The CRT is attached to an IBM mainframe with an IMS database. The index for all the indices is stored on the IMS database and, when the system is in a production mode, will be integrated with a policyholder database. For example, a clerk retrieves an image by indicating it on an index on the screen. The command goes from IMS to a storage controller, where the image is retrieved and sent along a local network to an image mode controller, and then to a high-resolution CRT. Other image processing systems have different architectures, but the overall objective is to index images, transmit them along the local area network, and put that image onto a CRT.

The storage components and the central focus are optical disks. Optical-disk products are new, but currently they are a viable product. The products are still

FIGURE 9–14
Image Processing System Components

Storage
Workstations
Networks
Input devices
Output devices
Image controllers
Index management software

FIGURE 9–15

Integrated Image Processing Architecture

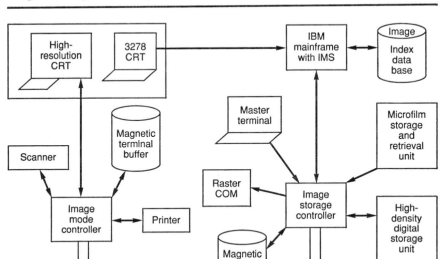

being developed in the marketplace, and large-scale production has not yet been achieved. Early optical disks had high error rates. There have been some developments in the area of technology that we call DRAW technology—direct read-after-write—which enables the optical disk information to be approximately as accurate as magnetic technology (it has the same error rates). There are a number of legal issues around the admissibility of images stored on optical disks that have yet to be resolved. We believe that the non-updatable nature of optical disks will enable images stored on optical disks to have approximately the same legal status as microfilm, which generally is coming to be accepted by the courts.

An optical disk drive is analogous to the floppy disk drives of personal computers. The difference is that approximately 1000 times as much information can be stored on a optical disk drive as on a floppy disk drive. These would be rack-mounted, and you would be able to communicate with them in the same way as you do with magnetic disks. The optical disk jukebox inside of the drive stores up to 100 optical disks, so that in one device you are able to retrieve information from a large number of optical disks.

It is important to remember that magnetic storage also plays an important role in these systems. However, there are severe storage limitations; for example, ten megabytes of magnetic storage stores twenty uncompressed documents. You can easily imagine how quickly you would run out of hard disk space when trying to store a million documents. However, magnetic storage is useful for buffering images, and for pre-fetching images, so you are able to improve the overall response time. Additionally, magnetics are not really acceptable as a legal version of a document because of the updatable and erasable nature of magnetic storage. There has been some talk that, in image processing, costs for magnetic storage will continue to drop so that they will always be lower than the cost of optical disk storage. Image processing is best understood from a functions perspective. If the legal issues of the updatability of magnetic storage can be resolved, a functions perspective will be helpful. You want to be able to store the images and retrieve them, and whatever technology is used to do that, so much the better.

For users of an image processing system, a workstation is their access device, the way they get into the system. The resolution of the images on the screen is the key user feature. In the IBM DISOSS demonstrations, images are demonstrated at approximately 70 pixels per inch, and the resolution is really not good enough for image-viewing applications. Whether there will be two screens or one on the desk is an important question for the user and the designers of these systems. We opted in one case for two terminals. FileNet opted for one terminal. On the image screen you would be able to clearly view handwriting and possibly open a window for data processing on the same screen.

The third area of components is networks. There is a great deal of information communicated in the image delivery subsystem of an image processing system. It is important to distinguish between the two types that exist. One is controller traffic, where you are handling index information and making requests for a particular image to be retrieved. The other type is the image traffic, which consists of very large messages; a compressed image in the neighborhood of 50,000 bytes. Local area networks are required to handle messages of that size, so most of the image processing systems in the near future will be located within a single building. There has been some work done in the area of image delivery over a wider area.

Architectural Alternatives

Image processing components are tied together in several architectural alternatives. The first of these is a mainframe architectural alternative (Figure 9–16). The image storage peripheral is tied into the mainframe computer, which drives the terminal controller and the multifunction workstation. This is the IBM DISOSS approach. There are a number of advantages. It builds on the current vendor environment and allows use of an unintelligent terminal if you are able to do software decompression of the images in the mainframe. It has disadvantages. It requires a lot of main memory to map images. It also requires quite a bit of channel capacity if you are handling a large volume of images. Additionally,

FIGURE 9–16
Mainframe Architecture for Image Processing

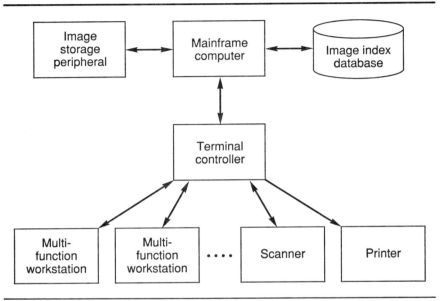

resolution is an issue, and there is a question of whether you want to pay $1 million for the 3083 to act as a switch.

A second architecture is the local area network, Figure 9–17. An image manager communicates with the workstation over a local area network. The user workstation also communicates with the index manager over the same local area network. An advantage of the LAN is that it makes sense from the perspective of having a simple, understandable architecture in which it is easy to know where the pieces fit. It also provides peer-to-peer communications, and the capacity is limited only by the bandwidths of the local area network. A disadvantage is that it requires an intelligent workstation with multitasking operating systems, because the workstations need to communicate with two different devices at one time. Also, integration occurs at the workstation.

The third of these architectural alternatives addresses the limitations of the mainframe and the local area network architectures (Figure 9–18). The advantage of this approach is that it offers an appropriate use of mainframe computer capacity and local area networks. It can be integrated well with data processing applications. It can offer relatively unlimited capacity, and in some large orga-

FIGURE 9–17
LAN Architecture for Image Processing

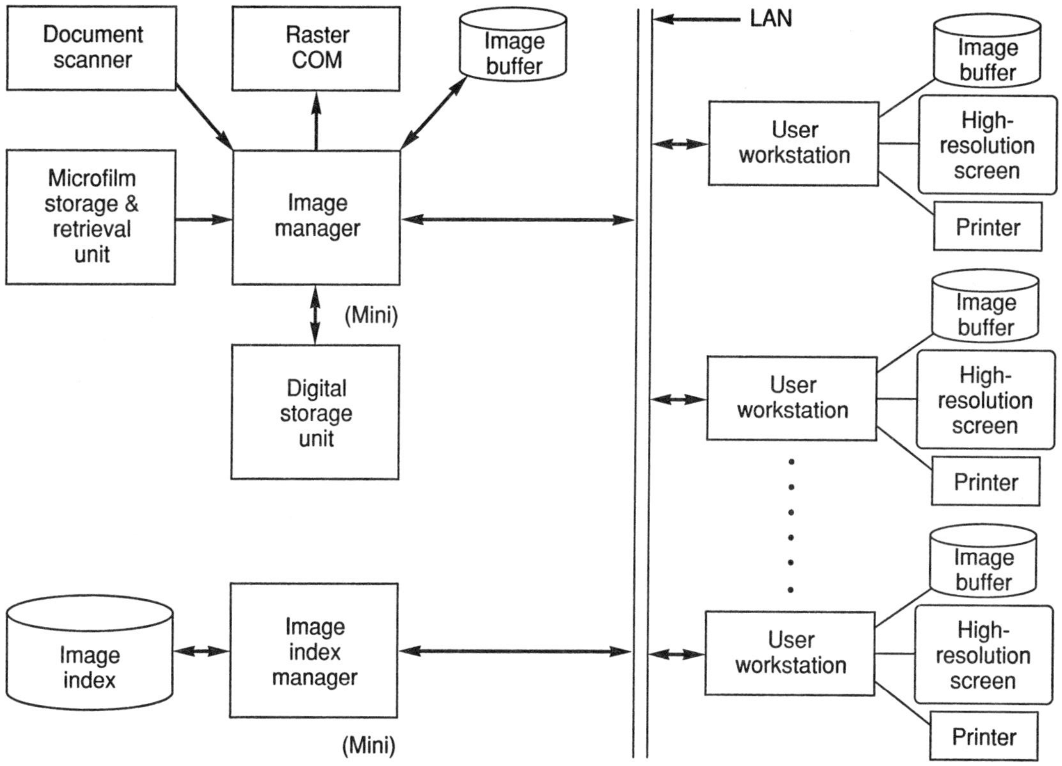

FIGURE 9–18
Integrated Image Processing Architecture

Advantages:
   Appropriate use of mainframe and LAN.
   Well-integrated with DP applications.
   Unlimited capacity.
   Cost-effective.
Disadvantages:
   Leading-edge technology.
   High cost of smallest system.

---

nizations it is cost-effective. The disadvantages are its leading edge in aggressive technology and the high cost of the smallest system, which will probably cost over a quarter of a million dollars.

Planning and Design Issues

There are a few planning and design issues that are important to discuss in order to put these systems in some perspective. First, a hierarchy of storage media is used in an image processing system. Magnetic storage is the fastest storage, and it is the most expensive. Micrographics might be tied in; the Kodak Kim system, for example. You might have multiple categories of optical disk storage in that system. As for intermediate speed of retrieval, access time of rack-mounted drives may be less than a second. A lower speed would be the jukebox devices where there are up to 100 optical disks in a box. It takes longer to retrieve because you have to bring the optical disk to a head and get it spun out before you are able to retrieve a particular image. The access time might be two to eight seconds. Finally, there is slow-speed retrieval. The person in the room where you are storing your optical disks might be out for coffee and might not be back for 20 minutes, so you need to pull the optical disk off the shelf and load it into the drive. There are a number of images that will always be stored on paper. There are oversized images, old documents, and for one reason or another you do not want them in the system. So there is hierarchy of storage with its own costs and economics and access-time characteristics.

   The second design issue is index design (Figure 9–19). It is important to spend some time thinking about and planning for the types of items that will be viewed in the index. It is necessary to consider carefully the pros and cons of an internal versus an external index. The external index is that information given to the clerk who is retrieving images. The internal index is for the system only. The description of an image is a good example of index information in which there are

FIGURE 9–19
Design Issues: Index Design

- Types of items in index.
- Internal versus external index.
- Description of image.
  - Time to prepare.
  - Space requirements.
  - Need to access image.
- Logical groupings of images.

FIGURE 9–20
Design Issues: File Conversion

- Critical issues for design.
- Volume of files might be impossible.
- Dual paper flow: A problem.
- Develop a conversion approach.
  - By department.
  - By document type.
  - By cutover date.

trade-offs. The time to prepare a quality index has to be traded off against the need to access the image, because if you are able to produce a high-quality description of the image, frequently you will not need to look at the image itself. A high-quality description of the image usually will require more space than a brief description of the image. In a very large system, the space requirement for 10 million images with 100 bytes of index information can get into a billion bytes of storage. Finally, for the efficiency of the system, you would want to be able to group images logically. One way to do this, especially at the initial phase, is to convert your files to have the images logically grouped.

Figure 9–20 addresses a critical issue to be considered in design because many organizations that will want to use image processing systems will have such a large volume of files that it will be a very intensive effort to convert them. The files for an organization such as the IRS, which has massive old paper files, might be impossible to convert. The other side of that is to have some paper converted and some not converted. A dual paper flow can create problems of its own for administration of the system.

Figure 9–21 shows the last issue. In image processing systems, if you look at retrieving image when focusing on the technology, you miss a lot of the point

FIGURE 9-21
Design Issues: Workflow Management

Workflow management components:
  Routing
  Queues
  Priorities
  Assignment
  Load balancing
  Annotation
  Audit trails
  Management reports
  Redefine flow of work to improve overall productivity

---

of these systems and some of the most important benefits. Figure 9–21 lists several workflow management components that image processing systems can address directly. These include routing of images, queues of images, prioritization of images, assignment of these images, load balancing, and annotation of images so you can track anybody who has looked at an image and what they have done with it. You can create very sophisticated audit trails and management reporting on the handling of documents that is far superior to the manual systems that traditionally have been used in organizations. These new systems have dramatic potential to redesign the flow of work to improve the overall productivity of an organization.

These systems will require a broad base of skills to be successfully implemented. These include image processing skills, industry and functional skills, and experience with strategic planning, information systems, implementation, and telecommunications. There are other skills that will be necessary, many of which we do not know about because this is a new, developing area.

A number of industries will be able to make particular use of these systems, including large financial services organizations, government, manufacturing, and oil companies. There is a profitable opportunity in many of these organizations.

USE OF TELECONFERENCING AND CORPORATE VIDEOTEX

There are many methods of electronic communication available, and the field is being developed rapidly. Such communication has special value for management support and group decision support. The ability to transmit computer output and printed lists of numbers and graphs to managers on request, and to regularly interchange documents by electronic mail and similar arrangements, has great significance for executive information systems.

Central to the new methods are corporate videotex, electronic mail, document image processing, and image transmission. Excellent systems are available for all of these. The structure and methods of teleconferencing form the vehicle for group decision support systems of many types, whether they are computer-centered or simply management discussions.

Teleconferencing, or telemeeting, is the method by which three or more people in two or more locations communicate electronically. The technology covers activity from a simple telephone conference call to a sophisticated videoconference, utilizing two-way video transmission, color, graphics, and multiple locations. Teleconferencing, a rapidly evolving technology, offers a wide range of services between these two extremes.

Originally thought of as a means of reducing travel costs and unproductive travel time, teleconferencing has been adapted to a number of other applications, and has enabled users to involve a larger number of skilled individuals in essential meetings. Improvement of video capability has enhanced its use for product development and display.

Every teleconferencing system is a custom assemblage of several subsystems, all of which must interact to enhance each other. The principal elements of a teleconferencing system are:

- One or more of the four teleconferencing modes: audio, audiographic, video, and computer conferencing. The choice among them is determined by such factors as the type of information that users need to exchange, the duration and frequency of user interaction, and user evaluation of the importance of the presence that videoconferencing adds to a meeting.

- One or more of the possible transmission channels: public telephone lines, data circuits, dedicated leased land lines, microwave and satellite transmission circuits. Cost, convenience, and equipment requirements are the chief determinants.

- A special teleconferencing facility, the need for which is determined by the number of potential conferees at any one location, system acoustics and illumination requirements, and the availability of suitable space (portable equipment is often used when a dedicated facility cannot be made available).

- Ergonomics, or human factors, including advance preparations, user training, selection of user-friendly equipment, group dynamics and the need for a facilitative moderator, and a facility environment that minimizes eyestrain and fatigue.

Teleconferencing media.   Teleconferencing media fall into categories as follows:

Function	Form	Description
Voice	Audio	In its simplest form, a telephone conference call. Multipoint communications utilizing voice amplification and transmission options.
Writing (drawing)	Image processing telewriting	Transmission of handwriting or drawing over an electronic circuit.
Document	Image processing, videotex, fax	Transmission of page-size copies over normal voice lines.
Typing	Electronic mail, computer conferencing videotex	Exchanges generated through a computer with a typewriter keyboard.
Video	Still video (freeze-frame or, slow-scan)	Snapshot picture, updated periodically and displayed on a television screen.
	Motion video	Full-motion television.

Each mode of teleconferencing has options to adapt it to a range of applications of varying complexity. In general, more complex applications require broadband transmission media (T-1 data circuit), a private microwave system, or satellite communication. However, the simpler and most frequently used applications of each mode of teleconferencing use the public telephone transmission network.

An overview of transmission applications and requirements is given in Figure 9–22. Microwave, cable, and satellite systems can accommodate any information that can be transmitted over public telephones lines or full-duplex circuits. However, these transmission media are vastly more expensive than the public telephone network. They generally are used only when required for full-motion video, when justified by an exceptionally high rate of utilization, or when they are already available because of other communications needs.

Modes of Teleconferencing

Audio teleconferencing.   This is the most common, simple, and widely used form of teleconferencing. Its main advantage is that it uses the well-understood telephone system and can reach nearly every business telephone in North America and many throughout the world.

FIGURE 9–22

Teleconferencing Modes and Transmission Options

Teleconferencing	Transmission Media			
Mode And Options	Public Telephone Network (2-Wire)	Full Duplex 4-Wire Circuit	Private Microwave or Cable System	Satellite System
Audio teleconferencing	C		A	
Audiographics teleconferencing				
Analog equipment	C2		A	A
Digital equipment	C2	AR	A	A
Video teleconferencing				
Slow-scan video	C2	AR	A	A
Compressed video		C	A	A
Full-motion video			C	C
Computer conferencing	C	AR	A	A
Corporate videotex			C	C

Key: C Most common transmission mode.
     C2 Two 2-wire circuits generally used, one for each direction.
     A   Alternate transmission mode.
     AR Required alternate for some equipment.

Capabilities for audio teleconferencing depend on the particular telephone equipment installed. Manual dialing of the group can set up a conference of four telephones with the aid of call transferring. Teleconferencing also can be set up through PBX or Centrex switching with a normal limit of six stations. There is a loss of voice volume level as more stations are added.

In dial-out (or dial-up) bridging, a telephone company operator calls each location to link it to the conference. Theoretically, 58 locations can be bridged, but because each location has to be called manually, the bridging is typically up to 5 locations. Enhancement is sometimes available to minimize the deterioration of voice quality. Dial-up conferences generally are limited to the public telephone network, which may not be the most cost-effective method.

With meet-me (or dial-in) bridging, conferees call a predetermined number at a designated time. Incoming calls are linked either automatically or by an attendant operator. A high degree of audio quality control is generally available. Dial-in bridges can link up to 25 sites and can be used in tandem to link 200 locations. WATS can be used to lower costs. A major advantage of meet-me or dial-in bridging is that conferees need not be at a specific location. Salespeople and traveling executives can dial-in at the prearranged time from any convenient telephone.

Meet-me bridges generally are owned or leased on-premise installations, or are obtained from vendors (such as the Darone Connection, Connex International, and Kellogg Telephone Conferencing Service) on a contractual or per-conference basis. Northwestern Bell in Minnesota is testing a teleconferencing service called Direct Dial Conference. The system requires only that the user have a touch-tone phone. It soon may become available through other Bell companies.

An alternative to audio teleconferencing through the public telephone network is a dedicated system of leased transmission circuits to fixed locations. Dedicated networks also can be used for data transmission and other communications. They can be cost-effective for high-use applications.

Audio teleconferencing is widely employed and has proven very useful. Conference calls can be greatly extended at each location by using amplifier systems or speaker phones. It has the same limitations of any telephone call, however. Participants cannot simultaneously exchange graphics or use telewriting systems.

Audiographic teleconferencing.   It has been estimated that up to 40 percent of business meetings involving travel can be replaced with audiographic teleconferencing. These systems can be handled with interrupt on a single line, or they can have separate communication lines. A variety of graphic transmission methods are used.

• *Facsimile.* Facsimile devices can be used for exchanging detailed documents during a teleconference and prior to it. Because they are installed in many locations, they can be used easily to increase the content of a teleconference exchange. Newer facsimile equipment has reasonably fast transmission, and documents can be sent at breaks in the discussion without great loss of contact.

• *Telewriting.* Telewriting systems consist of an electronic writing pad and pen, a graphics processor, and a color television monitor. Telewriting is a conversational graphics system. Conferees use the pen to write or draw figures and diagrams in two colors (red and green) on a pad. Parts or all of the image can be erased. The material appears on the local television monitor and on the television monitors at the conferencing stations. Any conferee can add to or delete material on the "common" screens. A video printer can be used to obtain a hard copy of the material on the screens. Telewriting operates at 200 band simultaneously with the voice conversation, although it requires two communications channels to do so. Telewriting therefore, can be used to expand, detail, or enrich a subject. It also can be used to keep points at issue or highlights before the conferencing group.

• *Electronic mail.* Computer systems can be used with audio teleconferencing to provide graphics, tabular data, and previously prepared computer-drawn diagrams, schematics, and presentation "slides." This real-time, interactive use of computer systems to supply a graphics enhancement to audio information exchange places the system in the realm of audiographic teleconferencing. True computer conferencing, as explained later, lacks an audio exchange and is generally not used in the real-time mode.

• *Electronic blackboard.* This is a Bell System graphic aid called Gemini 100 or Electronic Blackboard. It consists of a 42" × 56" writing surface that the conferees use to draw or write on with ordinary chalk. Whatever is on the blackboard is transmitted to a television monitor at the other location. Material can be erased, and the erasure is transmitted. The blackboard operates in black and white by mail or message. It also allows a recording of the teleconference to be kept for study or backup records or to enhance future conferences.

• *Recording devices.* Material can be recorded on audio cassettes or videotape before and during a conference, and then transmitted.

Video teleconferencing. If it is desirable to have more interpersonal communication in teleconferences, where participants can view each other and a variety of visual materials can be seen, then video teleconferencing may be preferred. It allows for viewing three dimensions, objects and people, and simultaneous multiple projection and transmission. Clearly, it requires a wideband network. Several methods are in use.

• *Slow-scan video.* This involves a television camera scanning a person or object and transmitting that scan to a receiving monitor at another location. The rate of scan varies, but some units do the scanning in sixty seconds. This approach is relatively inexpensive because of the simple equipment involved and the ability to transmit on conventional dial telephone lines. Slow-scan television cannot handle movement. If there is any motion during the scan, a blurred image will be transmitted. It is best for the transmission of detailed diagrams.

• *Freeze-frame video.* This technique involves "freezing" a rapidly scanned single frame from the camera, then transmitting the frame to other locations. The frozen picture can be viewed before it is transmitted. The frame can be transmitted over conventional dial or dedicated telephone circuits. Pictures of people, things, and diagrams can be transmitted readily, even if there has been motion. It limits interaction to some extent, however. Evolving technology is blurring the distinction between slow-scan and freeze-frame, and the terms often are used interchangeably. Other common terms are still-frame and captured-frame video.

• *Compressed video.* This system uses a telephone data circuit, a T-1 carrier of 1.5 or 3 million megabits, for video and voice transmissions. A picture processor, or codec, reduces the original video signal of 100 million bits to 1.5 or 3 million bits (depending upon which T-1 carrier is used). Compressed video provides full color and near-motion. Rapid motion appears jerky or blurred. Transmission costs are far lower than for full-motion video, but codec costs range from $150,000 to $180,000. Technological advances soon may lower costs and improve image quality.

• *Full-motion video*. This technique provides the most realistic interpersonal communication by transmission of live, full-motion video and audio. Conferees can have full face-to-face communication. They can watch gestures and see body language to some extent. They can get a good feeling for the way the meeting is progressing. This approach cannot be used on dial telephone lines. It requires wide bandwidth circuits and relatively expensive video equipment.

(Note: For any type of video transmission, the cost of basic site equipment will be fairly similar. The cost of the video processing equipment and the transmission charges will vary greatly, however. Analog video transmissions will have relatively low equipment cost and high transmission cost. Digital video transmissions will have high equipment cost and lower transmission cost. Digital video transmission requires a lesser amount of bandwidth than analog transmission.)

• *Holography*. A future development, holography utilizes lasers to project lifelike images. In the teleconferencing center, the holographic images will be indistinguishable from the genuine item. If a participant leaves his seat and walks around the room, he will see the side and back of the remote participants. Of course, if he attempts to pat one on the back, his hand will go right through the image.

Computer conferencing. Computer conferencing consists of communicating through computer terminals that are linked to a central computer, usually by a telephone line. Conferees can communicate simultaneously or asynchronously at their own convenience. The central computer maintains a permanent record of all proceedings. This generally can be accessed by a key word, data, or source. Although computer conferencing lacks an audio component, it has a number of advantages, including:

The economy of using telephone lines.

In the asynchronous mode, there is no limit to the number of conferees.

Conferences can (and do) last months or longer, yet there are no travel costs, and demands on the conferees' time are minimized.

Conferees can interact with one, several, or all other conferees.

Conferees can control their degree of participation and choose to interact anonymously.

New information can be gathered between participations.

Problems of scheduling and different time zones can be overcome easily.

Off-peak transmission times can be used to reduce costs.

Figure 9–23 summarizes some of the positive and negative impacts of teleconferencing.

FIGURE 9–23
The Impact of Teleconferencing

Positive

Reduces travel time and expenses.

Facilitates attendance at meetings, which eliminates mistakes due to missing key personnel.

Eliminates duplication of effort at separate sites.

Shortens business decision and project cycle times.

Opens meetings for attendance by all concerned personnel.

Facilitates business continuity when outside turmoil might otherwise cause interference.

Enables new internal communications paths.

Enhances preparation for or follow-up of face-to-face meetings.

Enhances reaction to emergencies.

Increases management control over communications.

Increases management control over remote sites.

Provides enhanced access to dispersed "people" skills.

Enhances personnel relations.

Opens meetings to additional personnel.

Increases employees' sense of participation.

Makes job assignments less dependent upon employee location.

Provides opportunities for personnel to form beneficial working relationships.

Encourages consideration of alternative solutions.

Negative

May increase nonproductive time in meetings.

Enables management to "over-control" operations.

Encourages overspecialization.

Decreases sense of personal contact.

Dependence on technology subject to breakdown or sabotage.

Applications Suitable for Teleconferencing

Management communications and training. Teleconferencing can be used for rapidly called meetings or for holding meetings when travel is difficult. It can be used for increasing personal emphasis in communications and for reaching several people at the same time with identical communications for policy dissemination. It can reduce the expense of training and education by increasing the number of participants in a course or briefing with wide interest. Examples include:

- Administrative and staff meetings.
- Sales and marketing.
- Crisis management (computer conferencing was developed specifically as an aid in crisis management).
- Board meetings.
- Stockholder meetings.
- Press conferences.
- Training sessions.
- Personnel interviews.

Planning and control. Teleconferencing enables planning personnel to discuss issues or ask questions of a group and to get all the answers in a similar context. It helps reduce the time frame of fact-gathering for planning, increases management coordination in project control, and brings together all of the inputs in the coordination of design, construction, and system development. Examples include:

- Project reviews.
- Budget and finance meetings.
- Planning sessions.
- Reports and presentations.
- Scheduling.
- Sales meetings.

Technical exchanges and problem solving. Teleconferencing allows analysts, engineers, or other technical personnel to have a formal discussion among several knowledgeable people on technical subjects. It also helps get all participants to a similar level of technical understanding. Also, it is used for an interactive discussion of problems in which all who have valid contributions are present. It helps participants reach conclusions rapidly in the analysis of failure or other problem areas. Examples include:

- Technical consultation.
- Information exchanges and updates.
- Problem solving.
- Engineering design.
- Document review.
- Generating ideas/brainstorming.
- Committee meetings.

- Contract negotiations.
- Architectural design.

The best types of meetings for teleconferencing are:

- Low in conflicts, not requiring face-to-face and body-language communication.
- Briefing and policy dissemination meetings where there is some interaction.
- Emergency communications, where time is of the essence.
- Project review meetings, when information is needed but travel is not warranted.
- Ad hoc problem solving, where quick solutions are helpful.
- Training, to increase coverage and reduce costs.

Teleconferencing Rooms

The need for special teleconferencing rooms depends upon the type of teleconferencing system and the number of conferees at each site that the system is designed to accommodate simultaneously. Audiographic and video teleconferencing systems need dedicated rooms with special lighting and equipment. Audio teleconferencing systems that accommodate only a small number of conferees at each site can take place in offices with speakerphones or similar equipment. However, as the number of audio conferees at any one site increases, so does the need for a dedicated facility that provides an acoustically controlled environment and high-performance audio equipment.

If a specialized teleconferencing facility is deemed necessary, careful consideration should be given to the location, construction or renovation, and furnishing of the room. An inadequate facility can defeat the advantages of even the best audio and visual equipment and generate considerable reluctance to use the system. Unless experienced technical experts are available within the organization, it is advisable to secure the assistance of experienced specialists for facility planning and design. The major considerations include:

- A location that is convenient. People are reluctant to use rooms that are out of the way or in ''off-limits'' territories —such as among or near the executive offices.
- A location as free as possible from external sources of noise; that is, not near exterior walls, bathrooms, elevators, busy corridors, shops, loading docks, etc.
- A visual environment designed to minimize eye fatigue and eliminate glare. This is achieved by a combination of lighting design and a selection of appropriate surface textures for the room's furnishings and fix-

tures. Diffused lighting is adequate for audiographic applications. Spectral lighting is preferred for video teleconferencing. Spectral lighting produces the crisp shadows needed to provide detail and give form to three-dimensional objects, especially people.

- Enough space to seat the participants comfortably, to allow cameras, projectors, and other equipment to be moved into place or to be housed discreetly, and to provide for the control panel and operators. The controls can be in a separate room.

- Soundproofing, carpeting, and nondistractive walls with no windows, except to an operator's room. Clear sound transmission is crucial, and the room must be well constructed acoustically.

- Table arrangements for a clear view of all participants. This may be a chevron arrangement or a trapezoid with the long side toward the camera. Square or round tables are not advisable unless the particular equipment is designed specifically designed for them.

- Capability of producing charts, diagrams, etc., rapidly and smoothly in view of the cameras and the participants.

- Sufficient monitors so that the participants do not have to strain to see the materials being viewed.

General Considerations

There are several general factors to consider in planning equipment and facilities for a teleconferencing installation.

Compatibility.   Equipment must be end-to-end compatible, preferably with existing communications methods. It must co-exist with PBX's networks, controllers, terminals, and other technology already in use.

Flexibility.   The field is changing rapidly, and the use of teleconferencing equipment will increase dramatically if it is effective and meets real needs. It must be flexible to adapt to future needs.

Training.   This is a new way of communicating, a giant step past the simple use of the telephone. Planned and ongoing training is necessary for its effective use.

User friendliness.   People are asked to change their patterns of communication. They also are asked to interject technology into the middle of their communications. The system must be user-friendly and easily handled.

Use of graphics. There are systems available for integrated graphics. Some videographic teleconferencing systems contain shared-graphic workspaces. Advanced systems create fully integrated, simultaneously shared graphics that can be annotated by one group member and then transmitted to all of the other participants. With this type of device, the user can observe and annotate an image in real time, while it is being discussed. Soon to become reality will be the ability to combine, store, and manipulate personal computer graphics, animation, spreadsheets, text, and video images. Somewhat further off is the ability to share a video image among more than two interactive sites.

Applications in Large Corporations

Atlantic Richfield Company (ARCO) initiated Arcovision, a $17 million upgrade of its in-house communications network. The video system, built from components by ARCO to its own specifications, allows videoconferencing among special conference rooms at company headquarters in Los Angeles and major facilities in Denver, Houston, Philadelphia, and Anchorage. Additional rooms in Washington, D.C., and Dallas are expected to be added in the near future.

Arcovision forms a part of the Arconet enhancement project, a satellite-circuit expansion and upgrade of what the firm believes is already the nation's largest single-firm private telephone network. The basic Arconet system connects data centers and 23,000 telephones through leased and company-owned terrestrial microwave links from Los Angeles to Dallas, Chicago, Houston, and Philadelphia.

To enhance the network, ARCO took a 10-year lease on an entire transponder in the Alascom satellite. The network has 36 MHz of bandwidth for digital transmissions of up to 70 megabits per second. Arcovision uses about one-fourth of the satellite channel's capacity. Another one-fourth is used for internal ARCO data transmission. The remaining half of the bandwidth is used for voice transmission in the daytime and batch data transmission at night. Two-thirds of the $17 million cost of the project went for earth stations and digital microwave equipment.

The initial Arcovision rooms cost $700,000 each. However, the company expects the cost of additional rooms to drop to $500,000 now that it has experience in building them.

Each room is the size of a normal conference room and seats 12. Each contains equipment for full-motion color video transmission. The rooms are designed so that only two microphones are needed to accurately capture voices from anywhere within them. Each room also contains a facsimile system and an electronic blackboard for videographics transmissions.

The facsimile system, called Nefax, was custom built by NEC of Japan. The system operates at 56 kilobits per second and takes between 4 and 30 seconds to transmit a document. The system allows a choice of resolution of 200 or 400 dots per inch.

One of the goals of the Arcovision system is to eliminate some travel expenses. A 1980 study found that ARCO's 55,000 employees took 52,000 trips that year at a cost of $60 million. Currently, an average of 600 ARCO employees travel by air every day, half on company planes and half on commercial flights. If Arcovision can replace 15 percent of all corporate travel, the firm could save $9 million annually in travel expenses.

More that 1100 employees, including more than 100 senior executives, were interviewed before work on the development of the system began. The research formed the basis of such decisions as appropriate room size, equipment, and cities to be served. Before full implementation, Arcovision was tested on a group of employees for six months. Early user preference led to the selection of a video system that produces life-size images by means of rear projection. Users felt this system to be more natural than systems that use monitors. Feedback from the early users was used to design a training course for other system users.

Microcomputers associated with each conference room both control the room's equipment and gather statistics on its use. The statistics can be used by the firm to apportion the system's cost among its users.

The Boeing Company has an in-house microwave network with full-duplex (two-way simultaneous) color videoconferencing that links twelve rooms at four sites in the Renton, Washington, area. The video portion of the conference signal is transmitted by a terrestrial microwave relay network (the longest distance between any two conference rooms is 40 miles). The audio portion is sent over ordinary dial-up telephone lines. Industrial security is provided by separating the two signals during transmission.

Although the sites are close to each other, the chief incentive for the installation of the system was to reduce man-hours lost to travel time. In the first year of operation (with only ten rooms at three locations), the company's records show that the system saved 21,057 conferees from driving 177,260 miles to attend 981 meetings. Most of the meetings were short; the 981 meetings consumed a total of 1135 hours. Although the cost savings are estimated to be large, they are not readily identifiable because of the wide variation among conferee salaries.

The service costs $23,000 per month to operate and it is sold to the user divisions at $65 per room-hour, or $130 per hour for a two-way conference. Each Boeing division provides its own origination room and any unique transmission equipment, including color TV cameras, that it requires.

Within each origination room there is a studio camera, a small camera for the moderator, and a camera mounted on a photo-enlarger stand for graphics. Conferees sit at long, narrow tables arranged in chevron formation. All conferees face the front of the room. Each table has a nine-inch black-and-white monitor and two voice-activated microphones. Large color monitors are available in the front of each origination room, but Boeing employees have found that the local monitors stimulate participation.

Typical conferences have 15 to 30 participants at the origination end and 5 or 6 at the other end. Most conferences are for engineering design problems. However, the convenience of the conference rooms allows management to sit in and stay abreast of activity, something busy managers tend to do less of when the conferences require additional time for travel.

Among the interesting findings Boeing made in using its system were the following:

- Moderators are an absolute must.

- Participants require training to use the system effectively. Engineers tend to put as much information as possible in a single diagram. Videoconferencing works best with simple drawings that focus on one aspect of a problem at a time.

- While the chevron arrangement works well, participants need training and moderator assistance to refrain from turning around to address participants within the conference room (which turns their backs to the camera and projects their voices away from their microphones). Other behaviors that training must overcome are tendencies to shout at participants on the monitor instead of at the cameras.

At J.C. Penney Company installation of a videoconferencing system resulted from two years of successful utilization of a high-quality audio system. Although used extensively by a number of groups, the audio system proved inadequate for the needs of the merchandising staff who wanted to "see" the available merchandise.

Although J.C. Penney leases a private network from Satellite Business Systems, the video gets a free ride because the network is justified by its main use—voice and data transmission.

The most important contribution to J.C. Penney's investment in the video system came from the merchandising operation. Normally, 65 market merchandisers traveled to New York every month from all over the country to make sure that the retailer delivered the latest fashions to more than 800 stores in 50 states. At these meetings, the merchandisers would take orders for fashions that corporate buyers had selected from designer showrooms. Videoconferencing eliminated the need for the monthly trips.

In application tests of videoconferencing, a number of things were learned. It became readily apparent that merchants required the highest possible picture quality, with accurate color reproduction and good motion handling, so they would get an accurate picture of the merchandise. It was also necessary for Penney to find a substitute for touch, because the merchants were accustomed to handling the fabric. This was overcome by training the buyers to emphasize the "feel" of the article on display.

Figuring that merchandisers meet 12 to 14 times a year at a cost of $40,000 in travel expenses and meals per week, this application justifies the expense for the system, with a savings of about $160,000. This does not include the savings in management time or the increase in field merchandisers' productivity.

FUTURE CD ROM AVAILABILITY

Technological advances that aid in management information retrieval for decision support are appearing with regularity. Some of the more immediately useful advances are coming from the vendors of management support systems to increase the differentiation of their products. For example, touch-screen systems are used frequently now, and new types of mouse control of the screen are popular. These are fairly simple techniques.

One of the most promising of the new approaches from product developers is the use of CD ROM (compact disk read-only memory) for useful retrieval from large volumes of data. The initial applications look promising, and it is likely that this medium will be a significant part of future management information systems. The speed of development is being aided by the rapid commercial successes of CD audio and video.

The purpose of many CD ROM applications is to simplify the management of archival materials. It can make accessible unwieldy volumes of corporate text—both administrative and technical. The CD ROM approach can be justified by displacing the present costs of printing, distributing, and storing volumes of data alone. Files like multiyear parts catalogs, personnel histories, and policies and procedures manuals are good candidates for CD ROM. A particularly useful candidate is the documentation for large projects, which sometimes requires a computer alone.

A large part of the cost for CD ROM is in transferring the data from existing tapes and disks, indexing it, compressing it, and designing logical search and retrieval for it. There are commercial systems available to handle these functions effectively. Initial costs for large systems are not excessive, however. They may be less than $100,000. If the information and the system for keeping track and retrieving it are important, the investment may be justified readily. The point to remember is that the technology is still in its infancy. If the application is particularly suitable, however, it is ready to be used today.

One of the better-known CD ROM applications is the Grolier Electronic Encyclopedia, from Grolier Electronic Publishing, New York. This mechanizes Grolier's 20-volume Academic American Encyclopedia and lists for under $200. With a CD ROM player, the cost is under $1,500, and yearly updates are available for $25. This application uses hypertext links to make the information available in the form of interrelated screens. A Key work system was used to select the references in the hypertext. KnowledgeSet Corporation of Monterey, California, developed a sorting algorithm to locate and index the links that were referenced in the text. The hypertext links then were entered into three tables.

The first Grolier hypertext table is for searching for a reference and keying onto it. Linked subjects then appear on the screen, and other references can be keyed, which will open other screens, and so on. The reference path is maintained, so that the user always can return readily if a path has proved to be fruitless.

The second Grolier hypertext table contains a summary of all the references made within a given entry. The user can key into an item in the collected references and proceed to an item of interest.

The third Grolier hypertext table is an inversion table that lists all the links according to their relationship with other links. The user can move horizontally in reference to topics, instead of moving vertically in single topic.

The Grolier Electronic Encyclopedia is an example of an excellent static hypertext. The text links are set, and there are excellent results in sorting through the text. Hypertext is a relatively new idea for efficient searching for related information in a large file. Hypertext approaches data storage and retrieval associatively. The file of information is referenced by its content within itself, rather than to an outside directory. This differentiates it from the normal file directories in computers for magnetic files that would be too wordy and time-consuming for large files. Hypertext tries to solve the storage-and-retrieval problem by using a 3-D network of logical data links. The hypertext approach is being improved rapidly as new application systems are released.

In the use of hypertext, links are picked by selecting words in a document. Each word pulls out a menu of related topics. Choosing items from one menu leads to another menu, and so forth. This process is continued until the desired item is reached.

A promising area for the improvement of searches in CD ROM files is the use of artificial intelligence principles. With these, meaningful heuristics are used to establish search patterns. These heuristics are based on the type of approach that a librarian would use. Relationships can be found that will help enter the text at points that improve the efficiency of subsequent searches.

One of the leaders in CD ROM work for technical documentation has been Northern Telecom. The company has found that using CD ROM is much faster than leafing through a book, or even downloading the information from a computer. Also, the distribution of CD ROM disks is easier, faster, and cheaper than binding and mailing computer printouts, or transmitting it over a telephone line. Other companies have found that these same economics are available with CD ROM.

Microsoft is publishing the Microsoft Bookshelf on CD ROM. This is a set of ten databases in a condensed reference library for professional and business writers. In a single disk it files: Houghton Mifflin's Roget II Thesaurus, Usage

Alert, and Spelling Verifier and Corrector, Bartlett's Familiar Quotations, The World Almanac, The Chicago Manual of Style, The American Heritage Dictionary, the U.S. Postal Service's ZIP Code Directory, the University of California Press's Business Information Sources, and Microsoft's own compendium of common business letters.

The Microsoft Bookshelf can be used as a stand-alone program or as a background program with any application. It can be linked to a word processor. It also supports Microsoft's graphics mode and some RAM-resident utilities. It has help and option menus at the top of the screen, and pulldown menus and dialog boxes to help define search criteria, perform the search, and insert data into an active word processing document. It communicates primarily through dialog boxes. Boolean operators allow a search of databases with full-screen browsing. The search structure is relatively simple.

Other CD ROM disks are being sold, distributed, and routinely updated, and it appears that there will soon be many of them. It is an excellent way to get hundreds of millions of items of information distributed and available for ready search. CD ROM clearly will be used for management information extraction, and there will be more ways of interfacing the information to analytic programs.

Some of the companies currently marketing CD ROM drives, applications, services, and information are in the following list. Their particular products are not described because the market is changing rapidly.

Financial Information

Compact Disclosure, Version 2.0.   Database of text and financial information on 11,000 public corporations. Disclosure Information Group, 5161 River Rd., Bethesda, MD 20816, (301) 951-1300.

CD/Corporate.   Four disks containing financial information on 10,000 publicly traded industrial, technology, consumer, and service companies in the United States. Datext Inc., 444 Washington St., Woburn, MA 01801, (617) 938-6667.

CD/CorpTech.   Profiles, product descriptions, and key-executive information for 14,000 high-technology companies. Datext Inc., 444 Washington St., Woburn, MA 01801, (617) 938-6667.

One Source.   Nine financial databases, including Compustat, Value Line, Daily Stock Price History, and Disclosure II. Lotus Development Corp., 55 Cambridge Parkway, Cambridge, MA 02142, (617) 577-8500.

PC Plus. Compustat database containing 20 years of financial information on 6500 U.S. companies. Standard & Poor's Compustat Services, 7400 S. Alton Ct., Englewood, CO 80112, (800) 525-8640.

Your Marketing Consultant. Database of demographic information for U.S. states, counties, metropolitan areas, and television markets. Bill Communications, 633 Third Ave., New York, NY 10017, (212) 986-4800.

Reference Material

BiblioFile. Catalog of the Library of Congress. The Library Corporation, P.O. Box 40035, Washington, DC 20016, (800) 624-0559, (304) 725-7220.

Books in Print. Annual bibliography of all books published in the United States. R.R. Bowker Co., 205 E. 42nd St., New York, NY 10017, (212) 916-1605.

Dissertation Abstracts on Disks. Database of 900,000 doctoral dissertation titles dating from 1861; abstracts start from June 1980. University Microfilms International, 300 North Zeeb Rd., Ann Arbor, MI 48106, (313) 761-4700.

ERIC. Bibliographic database developed by the U.S. Department of Education containing education-related research and journal articles. Dialog Information Services, 3460 Hillview Ave., Palo Alto, CA 94303, (415) 858-3785.

Grolier Electronic Encyclopedia. Grolier's 20-volume Academic American Encyclopedia. Grolier Electronic Publishing, 95 Madison Ave., #1100, New York, NY 10016, (212) 696-9750.

Optext. Full text of the Code of Federal Regulations. VLS Inc., 5215–11 Monroe St., Toledo, OH 43623, (419) 882–8819.

Ulrich's International Periodical Directory. International bibliography of regularly issued periodicals, updated quarterly. R. R. Bowker Co., 205 E. 42nd St., New York, NY 10017, (212) 916–1605.

Wilsondisc. Ten-disk set of periodical indexes including Reader's Guide to Periodical Literature, Business Periodicals Index, and Applied Science

& Technology Index. H. W. Wilson Company, 950 University Avenue, Bronx, NY 10452, (212) 588–2266.

Science and Medicine

Aquatic Sciences and Fisheries.   Database of abstracts on the biology and ecology of marine and freshwater environments. Cambridge Scientific Abstracts, 5161 River Rd., Bethesda, MD 20816, (800) 638–8076.

Life Sciences Collection Version 1.0.   Citations from 5,000 journals, books, monographs, conferences, and patents in various fields of the life sciences, including microbiology, neurosciences, biochemistry, and ecology. Cambridge Scientific Abstracts, 5161 River Rd., Bethesda, MD 20816, (800) 638–8076.

The McGraw-Hill CD ROM Science and Technical Reference Set. Collection of 7,300 articles from the McGraw-Hill Concise Encyclopedia of Science and Technology and 98,500 terms from the Dictionary of Scientific and Technical Terms. McGraw-Hill, Inc., 1221 Avenue of the Americas, New York, NY 10020, (212) 512–3474.

Medline Version 1.0.   Biomedical database of abstracts from 3,500 medical, dental, and nursing journals. Cambridge Scientific Abstracts, 5161 River Rd., Bethesda, MD 20816, (800) 638–8076.

PsycLIT.   Information on psychology and behavioral sciences from the American Psychological Association. SilverPlatter Information Inc., 37 Walnut St., Wellesley Hills, MA 02181, (617) 239–0306.

Service: Database Transfer to CD ROM

Batelle Software Products Center, 505 King Ave., Columbus, OH 43201, (614) 424–7387.

Knowledge Access, 2685 Marine Way, #1305, Mountain View, CA 94043, (415) 969–0606.

Reference Technology, Inc., 5700 Flatiron Pkwy., Boulder, CO 80301, (303) 449–4157.

Reteaco, Inc., 1051 Clinton St., Buffalo, NY 14206, (800) 387-5002.

Service: CD ROM Disk Replication

Digital Audio Disk Corp., 1800 N. Fruitridge Ave., Terre Haute, IN 47805, (812) 466–6821.

Discovery Systems, 555 Metro Pl. N., Columbus, OH 43017, (614) 761–2000.

3M Optical Recording Project, 3M Center, Bldg. 225–4S-09, St. Paul, MN 55144, (612) 736–9581.

CD ROM Drives

Hitachi Corp., OEM Division, 1200 Wall St., Lyndhurst, NJ 07071, (201) 935–5300.

KnowledgeSet, 2511 Garden Rd., Ste. C, Monterey, CA 93940, (408) 375–2638.

Laser Magnetic Storage International, 200 Park Ave., #5501, New York, NY 10166, (212) 578–9400.

Panasonic Industrial Co., 2 Panasonic Way, Secaucus, NJ 07094, (201) 392–4602.

Sony Corporation of America, Optical Memory Group, 675 River Oaks Pkwy., San Jose, CA 95134, (408) 280–0111.

Toshiba America, Inc., Disk Products Division, 3910 Freedom Circle, #103, Santa Clara, CA 95054, (408) 727–3939.

CD ROM Books

CDI and Interactive Videodisc Technology. Howard Sams & Co., 4300 W. 62nd St., Indianapolis, IN 46268, (317) 298–5400.

CD ROM Vol. I: The New Papyrus. Microsoft Press, 16011 N.E. 36th, #97017, Redmond, WA 98073–9717, (800) 638–3030.

CD ROM Vol. II: Optical Publishing. Microsoft Press, 16011 N.E. 36th, #97017, Redmond, WA 98073–9717, (800) 638–3030.

Essential Guide to CD ROM. Meckler Publishing, 11 Ferry Lane W., Westport, CT 06880, (203) 226–2967.

CD ROM Publications

CD Data Report. Langley Publications, Inc., 1350 Beverly Rd., #1151–324, McLean, VA 22101, (703) 241–2131.

CD ROM Review. CW Communications, Inc., 80 Elm St., Peterborough, NH 03458, (603) 924–9471.

The DDRI CD ROM Sourcebook. 6609 Rosecroft Pl., Falls Church, VA 22043, (703) 237–0682.

Optical Information Systems. Meckler Publishing, 11 Ferry Lane W., Westport, CT 06880, (203) 226–2967.

Optical Memory News. 256 Laguna Honda Blvd., San Francisco, CA 94116–1496, (415) 681–3700.

The Videodisc Monitor. Future Systems, Inc., P.O. Box 26, Falls Church, VA 22046, (703) 241–1799.

Evaluation and Selection of Management Support Systems

Management support tools are designed for senior decision makers. Properly chosen, MSS software can be one of the most beneficial purchases a corporation can make. The selection process should be systematic and should include business and technical considerations. A nine-step software selection process is outlined.

Checklists can be valuable in assisting in the selection of software packages. Their use is reviewed. Fourteen management and technical areas are discussed; they should be covered by routine examination each time a package acquisition is considered. A detailed checklist is given for comparative evaluation of software packages in each of these areas. The use of metrics in software comparision also is described, with a useful form for weighted comparison of packages.

The use of a request for proposal (RFP) is described. A detailed features list is provided for the types of questions that could be asked of vendors. It is pointed out that the answers simply may be found in the vendor's literature.

Vendor presentations can be a vital phase in the evaluation process; some ground rules for them are described. Reference query forms are provided to give to the vendor for general and specific questions about support. Another form helps evaluate the vendor's software enhancement history.

The cost justification of such a purchase is described. The handling of product performance benchmarks and the design of benchmark prototypes are reviewed.

Finally, control of the evaluation, testing, and selection of the primary product is emphasized, and a typical evaluation control document is provided.

DEFINING OBJECTIVES AND NEEDS

Management support tools are aimed directly at that segment of the corporation most responsible for decision making. Properly chosen, MSS software can be one of the most beneficial purchases a corporation can make. Improperly chosen, these tools can drain the very processes they were intended to enhance. The cost of the software is minimal compared to the potential impact on the corporation.

The Selection Process

Most corporations seek to marry the diverse disciplines of data processing professionals and end-users when evaluating MSS software. The typical user understands his or her business needs, but lacks the knowledge to translate those needs into appropriate technology. Conversely, the data processing professional understands hardware issues and concepts such as data dictionaries, security, and data integrity, but is unfamiliar with important end-user requirements. Rather than complementing each other's strengths, such unions often result in compounding each other's weaknesses.

A company may purchase a hundred thousand dollars worth of software based on an advertisement or a demonstration. Few firms view the use of the software as successful. However, a vast majority of companies understand the importance of the MSS purchase and seek to reflect this in their selection process. The software selection process should consist of nine steps:

1. Determine the primary buying motivation.
2. Select the evaluation committee.
3. Develop a criteria checklist.
4. Conduct a preliminary evaluation.
5. Attend vendor presentations.
6. Review product performance benchmarks.
7. Select the primary product.
8. Test the software.
9. Make the final selection.

Some of these steps may be considered optional. However, the evaluator actually does touch on each activity. Each step in the evaluation process must be reviewed, not as an end in itself, but as a necessary means of achieving the ultimate objective.

The Objective

An obvious but oft-missed point in beginning the software evaluation is to establish the ultimate objective before proceeding with the evaluation. There are three commonly stated objectives:

1. *Acquiring the perfect package.* It is surprising how often an organization will conduct an evaluation of MSS software with just such an end in mind. True, one rarely expresses such an impractical target explicitly, but a close look at the stated actions and criteria will reveal that perfection is indeed the goal. At the risk of belaboring the obvious, there is no perfect package. All software is fundamentally flawed, if not for one user, then for another.

2. *Acquiring the best package.* This approach certainly has the ring of reason. Indeed, taken in context, there is nothing wrong with it. However, can an evaluation that leads to the best package be viewed as totally successful? Should we be asking anything more of the evaluation process?

3. *No surprises.* When viewed in the corporate context, all software is a compromise. There inevitably will be significant groups and/or applications that become disenfranchised.

Even in selecting the best package, it is necessary to understand *all* weaknesses and strengths. This extends beyond the search for the best. With this understanding, implementors and supporters of MSS can plan for any weaknesses. Only by minimizing surprise can the success of MSS be ensured. The theme for this treatment on evaluating MSS, therefore, will extend beyond merely finding the best package to also minimizing surprise.

Understanding Needs

Most corporations seek to purchase MSS software as a means to solve problems. Few can afford the luxury of making a purchase merely to "round out" their software offering. Yet the majority of software evaluations are independent of the problems (applications) for which they are intended.

Sometimes the MSS purchase is driven by one major application. Under this circumstance, the success or failure of the evaluation is related directly to the needs of this critical application.

At the opposite end of the spectrum is the generic motivation. This type of evaluation is found most often in the Information Center (IC). Under this circumstance, the users and applications are not identified yet. Success, therefore, is judged not on the basis of the user's needs, but by those of the IC itself. Because most IC management personnel purchase software during the early phases of development, success is measured primarily in the popularity, or growth in use, of the software by the user community. Such motivation usually emphasizes ease-of-use as the critical criterion, reasoning that user-friendly leads to popularity, which increase the IC client base.

There is no right or wrong reason to purchase an MSS. Each corporate motivation is different, from a single application to generic IC requirements. The success of the evaluation, however, is directly contingent on early identification of the primary motivational factor. Literally, every subsequent step in the evaluation process is impacted by the identification of the primary buying motivation.

What are some typical buying motivations? A list might include:

- *Single application.* Projects such as establishing an automated budget, cost control, executive workstations, and reporting systems are popular here.
- *Multiple applications.* Usually due to cost-justification considerations, multiple applications are grouped together. These often revolve around accounting and/or finance, but may include marketing or sales.
- *Application-driven Information Center.* Under this scenario, the IC has been wanting to purchase an MSS but has been unable to muster the appropriate budgetary support. A significant cost-effective application is identified and sold to management as the justification for the IC purchase.
- *Generic Information Center.* Least frequent among motivations. IC management has not identified any major need for the MSS purchase.

When Faced with Trade-offs

Figure 10–1 illustrates the trade-off that should occur between functionality and ease-of-use as the purchase motivation moves from single application to generic acquisition. Such trade-offs do not occur with all software. There is no law of science that dictates that a package cannot be both easy to use and functional. If forced to choose, however, buyers in search of a single application should always lean toward applied functionality: "What do I need to succeed in this project?"

Faced with a more generic motivation, one might wonder whether functionality is important at all. Certainly it is, but using a different standard. Most management support systems are intended to satisfy a broad range of needs. Few will offer statistics comparable with SAS. Graphics products like TELEGRAF will also not be challenged from this sector. It is reasonable to expect an MSS to provide the user with 80 to 90 percent of the functionality normally required, and to do so in a user-friendly and consistent manner. In a corporate context, any remaining unfulfilled needs should be justified separately and filled by either time-sharing or discipline-specific software.

FIGURE 10–1
The Functionality/Ease-of-Use-Trade-Off

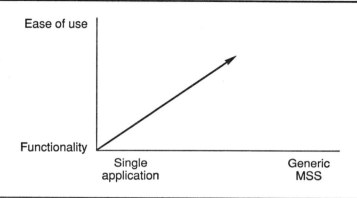

As obvious as this motivation-based approach may appear, many single-application evaluators pay only lip service to the importance of applied functionality. John Bear observes that most people first purchase the software, then figure out what they wanted to do. He concludes, correctly, that buyers should conduct an assessment of needs before addressing the software-decision issue:

> It is safe to say that if you can really assess your own needs, and articulate clearly exactly what you would ideally like to do with, and learn from your data, you will find . . . software that can handle your needs.[1]

Ironically, most prospective buyers do conduct some form of needs assessment. However, the vital follow-through to reflect those needs in the evaluation process is lacking. An exploration of the subsequent steps in the evaluation will continue to return to the critical issue of primary motivation.

THE SELECTION COMMITTEE

The selection committee is usually a group of part-time evaluators charged with the reponsibility of selecting appropriate MSS software. There are several valid reasons for establishing such a committee:

---

[1]John Bear, "Software: What to Do Before You Do What You Were Going to Do." *Business Week,* September 17, 1984.

- *Safe selection.* Good performance in the selection of software rarely brings fame to the evaluator. A poor selection, however, can bring swift and deadly visibility to a well-intentioned individual. Given the impact software selection can have on corporate resources, most employees desire to blend their accountability among others.

- *Group wisdom.* There is a belief among many corporations that, when it comes to decision making, many is better than few. Whether minimizing risk or maximizing wisdom, the committee process is often standard operating procedure.

- *Diverse backgrounds.* Diversity of backgrounds can enrich cross-functional decision making. Since most DSS software will be used by groups from different functional backgrounds, many companies seek to reflect this mix in the makeup of the committee itself.

- *Continuity.* Evaluating DSS software is rarely a full-time activity. Vacations, leaves of absence, closing the books, and special projects are just a few of the many distractions experienced by individual evaluators. Safety in numbers means that if one "drops the ball," there is always another to carry the responsibility.

Forming the Committee

In forming the committee, the two fundamental questions that must be answered are *how many* and *who serves*. The selection of the committee is directly related to the primary motivation of the purchase. The less generic the primary usage, the fewer and more specialized the participants.

Does this imply that a single-application purchase precludes the use of the software as a generic MSS tool? Definitely not! Long wish lists of features can still be considered, and ease of use can still play a large role in the decision. Early identification of the primary motivation provides an essential method for prioritizing performance requirements and for ensuring that the tone of the evaluation process remains consistent with the original goals.

What factors tend to maximize the effectiveness of the evaluation committee beyond establishing the primary motivation? There are four major characteristics of a well-functioning committee:

1. *I/S-end-user cooperation.* Conflicting orientations can often push these two camps into confrontation. This atmosphere can stall the best-intentioned efforts.

2. *I/S responsiblity.* I/S retains ultimate responsibility for the effective use of the corporation's computing resources. Ranging from volume purchases of micro software to single purchases of mainframe software, most I/S groups correctly feel that they will have to bear the consequences of a poor decision. This same fear sometimes is shared by the

Information Center, often siding with I/S in attempts to bridle end-user automony.

3. *End-user leadership.* The end-users should provide the committee leadership because they will have to bear the consequences of a poor decision forced on them by I/S or the Information Center.

4. *Mutual understanding.* The mission of the committee, the responsibilities of the participants, and the evaluation process should be well understood from the beginning.

USE OF CHECKLISTS IN EVALUATION

The use of checklists in the evaluation of software packages can be most helpful to assure that personnel of different levels of experience all will have a similar, proven base of information from which to work; apply some objective criteria to the comparison of different packages; and maintain a record of the items and issues that were considered in the evaluation of various packages.

The checklists provided in this section are the key to enhancing the user's capability when considering and selecting a software package. Careful analysis of each checklist in its specific area will provide the user with a most valuable tool.

The information obtained from the use of these checklists can aid in determining whether the packages under consideration meet the functional requirements that have been specified and would be useful in your own operational environment. The conclusions from these checklists can be combined with analysis of systems' costs, the legal considerations, and any overriding management considerations to reach a documented, objective conclusion as to the preferred package acquisition. Each self-appraisal checklist is organized so that the prospective purchaser of a package can select the elements deemed most important, copy the most-useful pages for the review and analysis, and follow the evaluation procedure. One of the results will be a package of working papers in the analysis that can be reviewed by others or audited.

The purchase or lease of a software package represents not only a considerable financial commitment, but also an operational commitment to a relatively rigid procedure. It therefore behooves the purchaser to use the self-appraisal checklists carefully before reaching a decision. They can go a long way to help see that the users' desires and functional requirements are met. A package acquisition decision should never be made on price alone, but also on all critical considerations. Many an EDP group has lived for years with package difficulties because it did not analyze its choice of packages in a sufficiently objective manner.

The checklist is not a mechanism to resolve differences, merely to air them. Because of its end-user orientation, an MSS package can never be confined merely to a list of existing features.

Most evaluators would be hard pressed to make a confident selection based only upon a checklist. No matter how encompassing, few lists leave the evaluators with a clear selection at the end of the process. The checklist is a good mechanism to reduce the total number of options to a manageable level and to highlight differences.

It is important to maintain a sense of the primary buying motivation and those features required to ensure success. But even here, the choices may not be simple. In trying to weigh trade-offs, keep in mind that the solution may not be to decide between one package and another. One corporation had a basic need for a large number of financial functions, as well as a request that all MSS results be communicated to management through the use of high-quality graphics. This provided quite a problem, as no package it evaluated offered both financial functionality and presentation graphics. It was only after exhausting all options that it realized it did not need to satisfy both needs with the same package. It already owned a powerful graphics package with which executive management was quite satisfied. This shifted its needs to a financial package with good software-interfacing capabilities that met its needs.

Faced with what appears to be an overwhelming choice of packages, checklists provide an opportunity to drastically reduce the number of packages being considered. Following this phase, many users feel they now know what products they do not want, but still are not sure which product they do want. Completion of the checklist phase may be unsatisfying from a decision perspective, but most evaluators would be thankful their checklist reduced the field down to just three before soliciting vendor presentations. Think of the agony of having to sit through 15 vendor presentations!

The checklists also help evaluators consider trade-offs and priorities. Most organizations have one person who insists that the Box-Jenkins trade-off technique is essential to the performance of their job. When forced to choose, however, graphics usually come up the winner.

AREAS OF SOFTWARE PACKAGE EVALUATION

There are a number of management and technical areas that should be routinely examined each time a software package acquisition is considered. These are listed below and are followed by more detailed checklists of items to consider in the evaluation. The areas of concern are:

End-user ease-of-use features.   Software packages for end-users must be selected primarily for their applicability to the problems at hand and the simplicity of their use. Efficiency of operation and technical excellence simply are not as important as the ease and rapidity of learning the systems, and their smooth operation in the hands of end-users. The appearance of the systems on the CRT screen, the way the menus are presented, the variety of HELP features, and the aids for troubleshooting are of prime importance.

Controls and data protection. Few end-users are aware of the need for tight controls and effective data protection in the systems on their small computers. These computers often are used to handle sensitive organizational information, however, and they are rapidly being directly tied in to tightly controlled mainframe databases.

Adequate input, output, and processing controls must be given high priority in the selection of software packages. Data can be readily manipulated, distorted, or stolen in powerful microcomputers. Controls must be examined realistically, and confidential data files must be guarded by sophisticated software and hardware means.

Equipment requirements. Because many applications packages are designed for Apple or IBM systems, users of these computers normally will have the greatest choice in package selection. Many other producers of microcomputers have designed their systems so that they are compatible, in varying degrees, with IBM PC systems.

Every software package has minimum equipment configuration requirements. These must be examined closely by any prospective purchaser as a key to some of the design qualities of the package. The scope of a package may be better on a larger computer, but it may be designed intentionally to appeal to the upper end of the personal computer market.

Software packages are usually developed for specific computers, operating systems, peripherals, and utilities. Clearly, the system control language can be changed for differing operating systems and environments, but the purchaser should be aware that this may alter the advertised efficiency of the application.

Programming language. The majority of microcomputer system application packages are programmed in BASIC or Assembler for efficiency of operation. Clearly, the programming language used must be considered before a package is purchased. It is of interest from the viewpoint of efficiency, modifiability, maintenance, and internal control.

Generality. Generality relates to the scope of the package, and to how completely various situations may be handled by changes in parameters only, rather than by extensive modification. A package with considerable generality provides the purchaser with the flexibility to alter certain procedures and continue to use the package with a minimum of effort. A negative factor in some packages is that they are aimed at a broad range of applications, and a purchaser might be better off with a package aimed at a particular application.

Input/output methods and efficiency. Input methods should be efficient, with provisions for obtaining input via an interface with another system. This would provide a purchaser with the benefits of shared access to data files. Output capabilities vary greatly with packages. The purchaser should examine these as they pertain to the intended use of the package.

Modifiability. Even if the modifiability of a package is not immediately critical to a purchaser, it might be important over time as the users of the package demand more capability. All packages are not designed to be readily modifiable. If a packaged program is developed with each program consisting of several carefully contained modules (so that a specific module is replaceable by a rewritten module without necessitating any significant alterations), then the package can be considered a modifiable one. The purchaser should give considerable importance to this characteristic. In order to assess modifiablility, the purchaser must request that the supplier review in detail with the purchaser the technical aspects of the package.

Expandability. Expandability refers to whether or not the software package can be expanded to have more capability, or if it is to handle larger files. This quality is a function of the package's design. Taking advantage of a package's expandability depends on the present and planned size of the purchaser's computer configuration. Additional data may be added to the recordings within existing files, thereby increasing the length of the file. Additional alternative procedures within a program may need to be provided, thereby increasing main memory requirements unless certain other alternatives are removed.

The ease with which such expansion can be accommodated is an important consideration. Selection of a package that has a very limited expansion capability will shorten the potential life of the package, requiring the purchaser to accomplish major modifications or acquire a new package. Also, the purchaser's present or planned computer configuration should have a reasonable amount of expansion capability if the purchaser is to benefit from an expandable package.

Package installation experience. The vendor's experience regarding previous installations of a package can be most helpful. It should be given definite consideration in the selection process, yet it should not override the more critical consideration of the package meeting operational requirements. If the vendor has installed only a few of the software packages, then installation may be a more time-consuming and complex procedure than it would be if the vendor has had considerable experience with the package.

It is particularly important that the purchaser confirm the exact operational status of the package. being considered. After a newly developed package becomes operational, a minimum of six months is usually required before the worst of the errors are detected and corrected. Accounting applications should have a full year of operation, since a number of reports are produced only annually.

The more installations in which the package is performing satisfactorily, the more confidence the purchaser will have that the package will perform properly when installed. Therefore, the number of locations in which the package is operating successfully is an important measure of package quality. The purchaser should require the supplier to provide a list of purchasers where the package is operational. Several of these purchasers should be contacted with specific questions regarding the performance of both the supplier and the package. In addition, the purchaser should visit at least one or two locations where the package is operational to obtain a first-hand demonstration.

Pricing.   Vendors generally base the prices of software packages on development costs, anticipated sales volume, the prices of comparable products, and the price that prospective purchasers are willing to pay. Development costs can vary greatly, depending upon the complexity of the various programs, the detail by which the package is defined initially, and the experience of the development group. Applications may contain many programs.

The prices of comparable packages may show great variations. A new, unproven package marketed by a new, unproven company may go on the market initially at $500, while an established supplier may price its package initially at $5,000, anticipating that the supplier's name and the improved features of the package over competition will enable the package to sell.

Processing rates.   The design characteristics discussed earlier and the programming language used have a very direct bearing on the processing rates. Easily modifiable and highly expandable packages have these characteristics at the expense of reduction in processing rates.

Quality of documentation.   Most software package suppliers attempt to provide adequate documentation with their packages, although there are some who do not do a credible job with documentation. The purchaser should be careful not to judge the documentation on nontechnical criteria, such as the volume or weight of documentation binders or the quality of the printing.

While these points may be indicative of the thoroughness of the supplier, the purchaser must delve into details of the written documentation before an adequate evaluation can be made. If the purchaser does not obtain adequate documentation with the software package, he or she will be dependent upon the supplier for modification assistance throughout the life of the package. Some package types, such as utility packages, require a minimum of documentation, while an application package such as accounts receivable requires a large amount of documentation.

The purchaser should be aware of the various types of documentation problems that may exist. For example, the documentation may be vague and ambiguous. Incompleteness is also a frequent problem. As changes are made to the package, there may be lengthy delays prior to corresponding changes in the documentation. Consequently, the purchaser may receive an installed package containing the most current changes, while the documentation the supplier delivers still supports an earlier version of the package.

Estimated package life. Application software packages generally will have a longer life than system software packages, utility packages, or programmer efficiency packages. Software package life refers to the length of time the purchaser can use the package effectively, though perhaps modified, before it must be replaced. A good application package, under normal circumstances, should be expected to have a life of approximately five years.

If the purchaser concludes that the design characteristics of an application package are good, then a reasonable estimated life of the package can be expected, provided there are not specific indications that the package will last less than five years. Other types of packages should be expected to have a life of 24 to 30 months, with variations as a consequence of special conditions regarding the purchaser, the package, and equipment changes.

Contract terms. Contract terms for the software package must be carefully considered before any commitment is made. The contract itself should be approved by legal counsel, but there are a number of terms that should be reviewed carefully by the systems people who handled the negotiations before it is considered for legal review. These are terms such as:

- The price of the basic system, extensions, modifications, installation, and support.
- The purchase of lease arrangements and their fit with projected budgets.
- The number of copies of the package that may be used.
- The timing on the agreement for the system to be operational and the start of payments.

- The price of future options or extensions and the handling of further developmental support.
- Any limitations or conditions on the use of the package and its handling or modification by internal personnel.
- The cost of customer assistance, training, and other help.
- How much is provided in the way of programs on magnetic media, program listings, and documentation.
- Responsibility for system maintenance and the handling of errors.

CHECKLISTS FOR COMPARATIVE EVALUATION OF SOFTWARE PACKAGES

A number of software packages being considered for acquisition can be compared and evaluated readily by using the checklist provided in Figure 10–2. All of these questions are based on experience in different circumstances, and all may not apply in specific circumstances. The persons selecting the software packages should review all the questions first, pick those that appear to be appropriate, then mark a few of them that are critical to the selection process at hand. When the choice has been narrowed down to the very few packages that satisfy the critical questions, the responses to the rest of the questions can be qualitatively reviewed. At that point it usually becomes obvious which package best fits the functional requirements of the end-users who have been defined previously.

The systematic use of checklists is not only a superior process to simply listening to salespeople or getting a general impression of packages, it is also an excellent documentation of the reasons for the choice of a particular package. It can be reviewed readily by the concerned end-users, management, and auditors. Figure 10–2 will be helpful as an initial overview of a package and the approach being taken for its acquisition. The questions cover the field generally and may be modified to enable more specific judgment of particular packages.

For microcomputer application packages, the technical staff first should analyze all possible candidates for the application needed. After the preliminary selection of two or three of the better candidate systems, the final contenders may be evaluated thoroughly by using the checklist approach.

FIGURE 10–2

Comparative Evaluation of Software Packages

No.	Characteristics to Consider	A	B	C
		Software Packages		

Ease-of-use features for end-users

No.	Characteristics to Consider	A	B	C
1.	Is the program menu-driven? (an organized list of options on the screen from which the user can make a selection)	____	____	____
2.	Does the menu have pictures or icons?	____	____	____
3.	Are commands that drive the system:			
	a. single-key functions? (best)	____	____	____
	b. multiple-key functions?	____	____	____
4.	Are there satisfactory on-screen HELP messages?	____	____	____
5.	Can the HELP messages be turned off if desired?	____	____	____
6.	Is status information displayed on the screen for reference?	____	____	____
7.	Is there a standard assumption of common pitch, margins, and tabs set by default?	____	____	____
8.	Does a register line show margins, tabs, and decimal tabs graphically?	____	____	____
9.	Are resettable format controls available?	____	____	____
10.	Are document line numbers displayed if desired?	____	____	____
11.	Are there special screen effects, such as highlighting and blinking?	____	____	____
12.	Are there forgiveness interrupts for any command that would markedly change the file?	____	____	____
13.	Are there simple, nondestructive EXIT methods?	____	____	____
14.	Are there simple, nondestructive GO BACK methods to review the steps that have been taken?	____	____	____
15.	Are there clear READY prompting messages to inform the operator that another task may be entered?	____	____	____
16.	Is there fixed-screen data entry available, where each data name and item stays on the screen until a section of the data entry is complete?	____	____	____
17.	Are numbers accepted from the numeric pad?	____	____	____

FIGURE 10–2 *(continued)*

No.	Characteristics to Consider	Software Packages		
		A	B	C
18.	Is there a message that anticipates an approaching disk-filled condition?	____	____	____
19.	Is the user's manual organized for ready access to troubleshooting suggestions?	____	____	____
20.	Is a self-teaching program available for rapid introduction to the program?	____	____	____
	Controls and data protection			
21.	Is the program source code:			
	a. protected from tampering?	____	____	____
	b. available for permitted modification?	____	____	____
22.	Are backup copies of the source code available, or can they be prepared?	____	____	____
23.	Does the vendor have a disk replacement policy for necessary backup?	____	____	____
24.	Are there sufficient, documented error messages or error codes?	____	____	____
25.	Are there adequate and sufficient controls on the input?	____	____	____
26.	Are there means of handling batch controls and run controls?	____	____	____
27.	Are there standard procedures to follow when any input controls fail?	____	____	____
28.	Are there sufficient controls on deleting or changing records in the files?	____	____	____
29.	Are there methods of identifying and controlling input hard copy?	____	____	____
30.	Is type-ahead buffering available to match typing speed to system input speed?	____	____	____
31.	Is there periodic automatic storage of workspace to save large amounts of entered data?	____	____	____
32.	When the memory space is filled, is the operator allowed to retain control and recover the work?	____	____	____
33.	Do the file deletion commands give a notification or short grace period?	____	____	____
34.	Will the program survive most wrong single key-strokes, except possible RESET?	____	____	____
35.	Will batch processing resume without changes after interruptions?	____	____	____

FIGURE 10–2   *(continued)*

No.	Characteristics to Consider	Software Packages		
		A	B	C
36.	Are there adequate controls on the output reports?	____	____	____
37.	Is the combination of data entry control, program checking, error messages, and change control handled adequately and efficiently?	____	____	____
38.	Is there sufficient protection from power failure:			
	a. by recommended frequent storage of data?	____	____	____
	b. by the storage of new data on disk as soon as it is processed?	____	____	____
	c. with a disk directory or table of contents on each disk, allowing for a restore-directory utility?	____	____	____
	Equipment requirements			
39.	Does the package run on the present or planned microcomputer systems?	____	____	____
40.	Does the package run on another micro-computer in the same manufacturer's series?	____	____	____
41.	Has a guarantee of conversion or the cost of conversion been considered?	____	____	____
42.	Has the vendor stated in writing that the present equipment configuration is adequate?	____	____	____
43.	Has the cost of equipment configuration upgrade been included in the estimate?	____	____	____
44.	Will an equipment configuration upgrade markedly improve the capacity relative to the system being considered?	____	____	____
45.	Does the package operate under both your present and planned operating systems?	____	____	____
46.	Has the vendor verified that your release of the operating system is sufficient for the application?	____	____	____
47.	Does the vendor supply any system-control language programs required?	____	____	____
48.	If the vendor does not supply the system-control language programs, have their costs of development been considered?	____	____	____

FIGURE 10–2 *(continued)*

No.	Characteristics to Consider	Software Packages		
		A	B	C

Programming language used

49. If the source language is unavailable in the contract, are there sufficient assurances that vendor personnel will be available to make modifications and extensions during its natural life? ____ ____ ____

50. Has the vendor made clear what the costs will probably be for any necessary modifications and extensions? ____ ____ ____

51. Is the program written in a standard version of a higher-level language? ____ ____ ____

52. Is the staff experienced in the language in which the program is written? ____ ____ ____

53. If parts of the program are tightly written in assembler code, are there sufficient routines written in a higher-level language so that programmers can make modifications or add extensions? ____ ____ ____

Generality

54. Is the package flexible and driven by parameter tables? ____ ____ ____

55. Can the package handle a change in organizational structure without extensive recoding? ____ ____ ____

56. Can the package handle future requirements that have been foreseen by systems analysts? ____ ____ ____

57. Have you listed all your likely systems requirements and checked them against the package? ____ ____ ____

Input/output method and efficiency

58. Does the system readily interface with other existing systems you are using regarding data formats and data files? ____ ____ ____

59. Are the input formats sufficiently flexible for the variety you anticipate? ____ ____ ____

60. Can input be on CRT and tape cassette as required? ____ ____ ____

61. Are there satisfactory data element codes and sufficient space for expansion? ____ ____ ____

FIGURE 10–2 *(continued)*

No.	Characteristics to Consider	Software Packages		
		A	B	C
62.	Are there sufficient user or customer codes and sufficient space for expansion?	___	___	___
63.	Are standard coding forms part of the documentation?	___	___	___
64.	Can data elements be identified and accessed on the file?	___	___	___
65.	Is the combination of data entry and control, program checking, error messages, and subsequent changes handled efficiently?	___	___	___
66.	Are the CRT screens easy to use efficiently?	___	___	___
67.	Are the CRT screens effective and user-friendly?	___	___	___
68.	Is the output readily adapted to the printing system?	___	___	___
69.	Are all the reports produced that were determined as required in the systems analysis?	___	___	___
70.	If more reports need to be produced, have they been discussed with the vendor to include a satisfactory plan of production?	___	___	___
71.	Are sufficient edit reports produced for the control personnel and the users?	___	___	___
72.	Is sufficient information reported for all reconciliations and audit checks that are required?	___	___	___
73.	Are sufficient options available with each report?	___	___	___
74.	Can the formats of the reports be varied to handle the needs of different organizational groups?	___	___	___
75.	Are the reports sufficiently flexible to handle the future needs that have been determined by your analysis?	___	___	___
	Modifiability			
76.	Have the possibilities of system modification been discussed with the vendor?	___	___	___
77.	Does the package appear to be designed to be readily modifiable in the future?	___	___	___

FIGURE 10–2   *(continued)*

No.	Characteristics to Consider	A	B	C
		Software Packages		
78.	Is the package modularized and well-documented?	___	___	___
79.	Can anticipated modifications be handled without significant alterations of the base package?	___	___	___
80.	Was the package designed in the structure it now has, or was it retrofitted from an older package?	___	___	___
81.	If it was retrofitted, does the base logic allow for even further modification?	___	___	___
	Expandability			
82.	Has there been an analysis of the largest possible files expected in the life of the package?	___	___	___
83.	Will the package and microcomputer configuration handle these largest possible files without substantial modification?	___	___	___
84.	Does the package allow for increasing the number of fields of data within a record?	___	___	___
85.	Does the package allow for increasing the number of records within a file?	___	___	___
86.	Does the package appear to be realistically expandable without too much difficulty?	___	___	___
	Package installation experience			
87.	Has the package been proven in operation?	___	___	___
88.	Has it been in commercial operation at least a year?	___	___	___
89.	Are there several satisfied users of the package?	___	___	___
90.	Are the users willing to talk about their experiences with the package?	___	___	___
91.	Are there any customers with accessible installations who are willing to demonstrate the package and discuss their experiences?	___	___	___
92.	Is the package in actual use in the customer installations, or has it merely been installed?	___	___	___
93.	How do other users compare the package with competitive packages?	___	___	___
94.	Did the supplier readily supply a list of other customers?	___	___	___

FIGURE 10–2   *(continued)*

No.	Characteristics to Consider	Software Packages		
		A	B	C
	Pricing			
95.	Is the price competitive with similar packages when modifications and extensions are considered?	___	___	___
96.	Does the price offer a reasonable rate of return on the package installation?	___	___	___
97.	Has the installation of the package been analyzed as to its value to the organization?	___	___	___
98.	If the package has a base price with extra charges for features on an optional basis, is the total price likely to remain within budget limitations over a three-year period?	___	___	___
99.	If the price appears to be set to allow the seller to establish a sale, are there guarantees that the total package can be installed on time by the supplier?	___	___	___
100.	Are all details of purchase, additional features, documentation, training, installation, and future support spelled out in the contract price statement?	___	___	___
	Processing rates			
101.	Has it been carefully estimated how long it will take the package to process the programs that are needed?	___	___	___
102.	Is it possible to speed up the most-used subroutines?	___	___	___
103.	Are the program linkage and memory organization conducive to good processing rates?	___	___	___
104.	Have present users of the package been contacted as to their experience with processing rates?	___	___	___
105.	Is it possible to make test runs at an installation to observe the processing rates?	___	___	___
106.	Is the systems analysis definitive as to the processing rates and response times that will be required from the system?	___	___	___
107.	Does the system apparently meet those rates and response time?	___	___	___
108.	Does the vendor guarantee any response time under defined conditions?	___	___	___

FIGURE 10–2 *(continued)*

No.	Characteristics to Consider	Software Packages		
		A	B	C
	Quality of documentation			
109.	Has the level of documentation that is provided been spelled out by the vendor?	____	____	____
110.	Are you able to examine samples of the documentation?	____	____	____
111.	Is there an introduction and overview that is usable for distribution to managers?	____	____	____
112.	Is the documentation logically organized and indexed for ease of use?	____	____	____
113.	Is there a tutorial section that is usable for self-teaching of the system?	____	____	____
114.	Does the documentation include, for the users:			
	a. detailed descriptions of the functions and commands?	____	____	____
	b. clear description of the error messages, and the actions to take?	____	____	____
	c. samples of all the screens that are in the system?	____	____	____
	d. samples of all the output reports from the system?	____	____	____
	e. data input and control information?	____	____	____
115.	Are sample data input forms or form design guides supplied?	____	____	____
116.	Are potential problems with input and output discussed?	____	____	____
117.	Does the documentation precisely specify the required activities of the users that must be performed for the package to function smoothly?	____	____	____
118.	Are there charts showing the sequence of operations?	____	____	____
119.	Are there quick-reference summaries or pocket reference cards for experienced users?	____	____	____
120.	Does the documentation sufficiently describe the data input, operations, and report output controls on the system?	____	____	____
121.	Is the audit trail specifically addressed and sufficiently described?	____	____	____
122.	Is there a keyboard function chart supplied?	____	____	____

FIGURE 10–2   *(continued)*

No.	Characteristics to Consider	A	B	C
		Software Packages		
123.	Is there an installation guide for the system?	___	___	___
124.	Is the documentation packaged in usable form?			
	a. In loose-leaf binders?	___	___	___
	b. Softbound with loose-leaf pages?	___	___	___
	c. Hardbound, but readily copied for use?	___	___	___
	d. Tabbed pages keyed to functions?	___	___	___
125.	Does the documentation appear to be satisfactory and done in a professional manner?	___	___	___
126.	Does the documentation sufficiently address the needs of:			
	a. end-users?	___	___	___
	b. support analysts?	___	___	___
	c. management and audit control?	___	___	___
	Estimated package life			
127.	Have your systems analysts made an estimate of the package life that is required to obtain a suitable return on investment?	___	___	___
128.	Are there any anticipated equipment or system changes that may preclude the package from being used for its required life?	___	___	___
129.	Does the operating life appear to be 5 years if an application package, or up to 30 months if a system software package?	___	___	___
130.	Is the package close to the midpoint of its life cycle for the vendor and not approaching its end?	___	___	___
131.	If the package has been installed for several years, will the vendor give a written guarantee that it will be enhanced in the near future to extend its life cycle?	___	___	___
	Contract terms			
132.	Are the contract terms clear as to method of acquisition and price, including limitations and conditions?	___	___	___
133.	Has the contract been reviewed by legal counsel for the purchaser?	___	___	___

FIGURE 10–2 *(concluded)*

No.	Characteristics to Consider	Software Packages		
		A	B	C
134.	Have the systems analysts made clear to the legal counsel what their specifications and requirements are?	___	___	___
135.	Does the contract clearly state what is provided relative to the programs, documentation, maintenance, and support?	___	___	___
136.	Does the contract appear to be consistent with the representation of the package made by the supplier?	___	___	___
137.	Does the contract make clear the degree of supplier contact and support that can be expected during installation and use of the package?	___	___	___
138.	Is it clear how many copies of the software package will be received or authorized to be duplicated?	___	___	___
139.	Is there reference to the need for a backup copy of the software for security or disaster recovery?	___	___	___

Notes:

FIGURE 10–3

Comparison of Software Packages

Category	Package	Package	Package
Software package cost Software modifications System installation System maintenance Special peripheral equipment Other devices **Total estimated costs**			

Special considerations:
    Ease-of-use rating
    Vendor training materials
    Vendor-sponsored user groups			

Notes:			

Final selection of a package, if the decision has been made to purchase one of the candidate systems, should be summarized on Figure 10–3. Note that this summary has space for special considerations. These considerations might be notations regarding the vendor, special features of the packages, vendor training materials, or other particulars. Based on this review, a clear recommendation can be made to management.

USE OF METRICS IN SOFTWARE PACKAGE COMPARISON

If the project team assembled to search for a software package and make a selection is not large, and the packages being considered are quite different, then a reasonable technical analysis of the alternatives and a few discussions will result in a clear decision as to which package to select. On the other hand, many cases of software selection involve six or more people on the project team from different groups, two or more departments in the organization interested in the outcome, two or three packages quite similar in quality but differing in details, complex packages and interrelated programs, and outside consultants involved in the selection.

If any of these conditions exist, it is simply not enough to "get a good feel" for the packages. It is best to state the variables involved as objectively as possible and to apply some sort of measuring scale; that is, use a *metrics approach*. Discussions then will tend to center on specific numbers assigned to definable points. The final outcome will arise from the sum of all the smaller agreements that were made. A metrics approach cannot be undertaken without considerable initial discussion of the software package characteristics under review, and agreement on which characteristics are necessary and which are merely desirable. There must be discussion of the weighting factors being employed and a willingness to rework them until most participants are satisfied with the scale. Finally, everyone must understand that the numbers that fall out are only comparisons on a relative scale and, for example, cannot be extended to expected costs.

If all members of the project team agree that a metrics approach is the best way to assign values and solve differences, it will be an efficient and economical way to compare alternatives. It tends to bring people to the more important points and center discussions on issues that matter to the particular users.

Figure 10–4 is one of the better types of form sheets that can be used in a metrics approach. The steps to be taken and the use of the form sheet are as follows:

Preparing the comparison worksheet. Gather the project team and discuss the characteristics of the software package under consideration. List all the characteristics that come up in the discussion and place them in approximate

FIGURE 10-4

Weighted Comparison of Software Packages

Necessary Package Characteristics	Weighting Factor *	Vendor/Package		Vendor/Package		Vendor/Package	
		Rating **	Score	Rating **	Score	Rating **	Score
User requirements (3 or less)							
Computer/operating system/language compatibility							
Is package acceptable or not acceptable?	///////						
Desirable Package Characteristics	///////						
Total Score	///////	///////		///////		///////	
Software package cost summary: 1. Base package 2. Modifications 3. Maintenance Total First-Year Cost	///////						

* Weight on a scale of 1 to 10.   ** Rate on a scale of 1 to 5.
Score = (rating) x (weighting factor)

order of importance. Decide which three or fewer of the characteristics are absolutely necessary to have in the package. These normally will be the key specified user requirements. Decide what level of computer/operating system/ software language compatibility is necessary. Note that sometimes compatibility can be obtained only at extra cost.

Decide on four to twelve characteristics of the software package that are clearly desirable (as opposed to necessary) and should enter into the analysis. Reject the other characteristics, but not until the team compares their importance, individually, against the characteristics already chosen. Do not hesitate to change the list several times as the discussion proceeds, but the chairperson must get decisions on these characteristics. List the selected characteristics in Figure 10–4 in order of importance or in an order that makes sense technically or operationally.

Assign weighting factors on a scale of 1 to 10 for the characteristics. The assigned numbers may be duplicated, and all numbers from 1 to 10 need not be used. Most of the necessary characteristics should have weighting factors close to 10. The other factors will vary according to the feelings of the team. Characteristics will vary greatly in importance, and there should be some low weighting factors in the list.

Applying package ratings.   Have the team, or smaller groups, study the alternative packages and assign ratings for each package for each of the characteristics. Use a scale of 1 to 5 for the ratings. These are arbitrary numbers, and in no sense are they ''real'' numbers. That is, they cannot be used for extensive arithmetic manipulation because they do not follow the laws of mathematics. One person's 2 may be another person's 4. A scale of 1 to 5 is controlled fairly readily as follows:

5   Excellent or completely acceptable.

4   Good or acceptable.

3   Average or passable.

2   Below average or barely meets requirements.

1   Poor or requires modification.

A scale of 1 to 10 for ratings cannot be controlled between different groups of people or even with one group at different times. The gradations of the numbers become meaningless.

In all cases, when several packages are being considered, give only *one* package a rating of 5 for each characteristic. Select the best package for that particular characteristic and declare it the winner. The ratings for the other packages need not be unique, such as 4, 3, 2, 1, however, because trying to line up all packages for all characteristics can be difficult and time-consuming. The team simply should give the other packages ratings according to its feelings about the approximate position the packages would have on the arbitrary scale of 5 to 1. Thus they would seldom be rated 5, 4, 3, but more likely would be rated 5, 4, 2, or 5, 2, 1, or 5, 3, 3.

Developing the scores.   Multiply each rating by its weighting factor and enter the result in the Score column. That is,

score = (rating) × (weighting factor)

Sum all the scores in each column, both the necessary and the desirable characteristics scores, and enter the sums in the Total Score spaces.

Software package cost summary.   Summarize the cost information obtained from Figure 10-4—comparative costs for the base package, any required modifications to the package, and maintenance costs for the first year. This will give a rough comparative figure to aid in screening of the packages.

Determining "go/no go."   Review the ratings for the necessary package characteristics. If any one of these characteristics has ratings of 2 or 1 (below average or poor), or if any of the necessary characteristics is not met by the package, write "Not Acceptable" in the column. If all the necessary characteristics are met and the ratings are reasonable, write "Acceptable" in the column. Determine whether modification or payment for extra features could make the package acceptable. If the package cannot be made acceptable, mark it as such and remove it from further consideration.

Review of ratings, scores, and costs.   Reproduce the worksheet and give it to all members of the project team. Have the team review the validity of the scoring and make a recommendation to accept the package with the highest score if there are no extenuating circumstances. If extenuating circumstances or organizational considerations might affect the outcome of the score, state them objectively. Repeat the weighted comparison of the packages that are acceptable, introducing other considerations that have been brought into the discussion.

Package Selection Report

When the project team has made a decision on the acquisition of a software package, possibly using this metrics approach, a package selection report should be written and distributed to interested management for concurrence and approval. This report should contain a summary of:

- Advantages and disadvantages of the selected package.
- The vendor selected and the reasons for the selection, possibly including a copy of the weighted comparison worksheet covering the packages in the final selection decision.
- The costs and benefits of the particular package recommended.
- The installation plan with dates of key milestones.
- A recommendation for approval of the report by management.

Example of a Weighted Comparison

Figure 10–5 is an example of a completed weighted comparision, with the types of entries and numbers that may possibly appear in such a selection. In this example, three vendors are designated as X, Y, and Z and rated. Descriptions of their packages should be attached.

Vendor Y's package received reasonable ratings under user requirements. In fact, it was the best package under reports produced. It only received a rating of 1 for computer compatibility, however, and this rating made it not acceptable. If the package is attractive, discussions with the vendor may show that the package can be made compatible at a certain cost. If there is any interest in the package, this avenue should be explored further, then another weighted comparison made in which that rating might be better, but the cost of the package would be higher.

On the total score, the vendor X package was higher. Note, however, that the difference between vendor X and vendor Z on the total score is less than 5 percent, not a significant difference in rating schemes with estimated numbers such as this. The difference should be greater than 10 percent to show a significant difference. On the other hand, the vendor X package is nearly 10 percent less expensive than the vendor Z package. The combination of the better score and the lower cost make it very reasonable to select vendor X in this case.

If the cost differential had been the other way around, further study would be required to distinguish between the packages. In the example shown, however, the selection probably still would go to vendor X because of its higher ratings in the very significant category of necessary user requirements.

Use of the Metrics Approach

It should be clear that, when using the metrics approach, the result does not necessarily fall out automatically and finally. Frequently, much discussion is still needed. On the other hand, the value of such an approach is great when there are several parties involved in the selection with different objectives in mind. The

FIGURE 10-5
Weighted Comparison of Software Packages

Necessary Package Characteristics	Weighting Factor *	Vendor X		Vendor Y		Vendor Z	
		Rating **	Score	Rating **	Score	Rating **	Score
User requirements (3 or less)							
Examples:							
Functions handled	10	5	50	3	30	3	30
Reports produced	8	4	32	5	40	3	24
Computer/operating system/language compatibility	10	4	40	1	10	5	50
Is package acceptable or not acceptable?		Acceptable		Not acceptable unless modified		Acceptable	
Desirable Package Characteristics							
Examples:							
Vendor support & service	5	4	20	2	10	5	25
Ease of modifying system	8	5	40	2	16	3	24
System expandability	8	5	40	3	24	2	16
System reliability	7	3	21	5	35	4	28
User opinions	4	3	12	2	8	5	20
Desired requirements:							
• Input devices	8	4	32	2	16	5	40
• Inquiry capability	3	5	15	1	3	3	9
• Report generation	3	2	6	3	9	5	15
Ease of conversion	5	5	25	2	10	4	20
Audit & control features	7	3	21	5	35	3	21
Security features	6	2	12	4	24	5	30
Total Score			366		270		352
Software package cost summary:							
1. Base package		$65,000		$35,000		$58,000	
2. Modifications		15,000		30,000		28,000	
3. Maintenance		5,000		13,000		7,000	
Total First-Year Cost		$85,000		$68,000		$93,000	

* Weight on a scale of 1 to 10. ** Rate on a scale of 1 to 5.
Score = (rating) x (weighting factor)

metrics approach gives a clear description of how the packages were rated, for what reasons, and how the selection decision was reached. At any later time, others can enter into the same discussion and know what principal points were considered, and why certain packages were rejected and others considered. In one sense, this approach leaves a clear audit trail of the route taken in the decision process of the project team and states its thinking objectively.

Despite some of its problems, the metrics approach to package selection is undoubtedly the superior method of reaching a final decision objectively, and of documenting the decision clearly and succinctly.

REQUEST FOR PROPOSALS

A request for proposal (RFP) is a formal request from the evaluating company for information concerning a targeted vendor's product or product line. It can vary in length from several pages to the size of a small book. It is usually sent one to two months prior to the time vendors actually are invited to present their products.

An RFP is not always necessary. In fact, the majority of evaluations occur without formal requests. The process of collecting and sorting the firm's needs, however, does contribute to the effectiveness of the entire process. If the RFP process seems appropriate for a particular situation, Figure 10–6 should prove helpful in forming the nucleus of such a document. It should be noted, though, that use of the RFP features checklist is not always requisite to a successful evaluation.

Having completed an assessment of the organization's MSS requirements, the next step is to isolate the architectural requirements from the feature requirements. Architectural means the hardware, communications, and software interface needs specific to the firm's environment.

Separation of architectural from utilization requirements is critical. This concentrates attention on those things of fundamental importance to corporate decision support. Such attention should not be seen as minimizing the value of specific user requests. To do otherwise could lead to the evaluation of packages that might not fit into the corporate environment. To consider a package that only runs on PRIME computers, for example, when an organization has a stated reliance on IBM, would not be fruitful for either evaluator or vendor.

Another important part of the RFP is the review of product capabilities. This includes all the critical functions, as well as the "bells and whistles," offered by each vendor. Despite the potential misuse of the features checklist in Figure 10–6, it does provide several quite helpful functions.

The majority of the questions on this checklist normally will be answered in the vendor's literature, in context. The vendor should be asked to supply such literature and give easy references to the sections where the question is answered.

FIGURE 10-6
RFP Features Checklist (For Vendor Response)

No.	Item	Responses

Technical and system support

1. Is your software compatible with our environment as described?
2. Is your philosophy to support the latest version of the operating system?
3. Can you demonstrate this commitment with past performance?
4. Does your system require any modifications to use on our operating system? If so, please describe.
5. How many of the proposed systems are currently installed in an environment similar to ours?
6. Is your proposed system primarily batch or interactive?
7. What is the source language for your system?
8. Is the source language available to us?
9. What is the frequency of maintenance updates?
10. What technical modifications can be made without voiding the warranty?
11. Are there:
    a. documented user exits?
    b. undocumented user exits?
12. What are the number, type, and size of files required for normal operation of your system? What could the extremes be?
13. What provisions have been made to provide data integrity in the event of a system failure (hardware systems, operating system, your system)? Can you recover or do you rebuild?
14. Will you demonstrate your system on our computer?
15. Do you have a users group for the proposed system? Can we attend prior to the purchase or commitment to your system?
16. What type of technical assistance is available?
    a. If by telephone, what are the coverage hours?

FIGURE 10-6 *(continued)*

No.	Item	Responses

b. What kind of crisis support are you prepared to provide?

c. Is on-site support available?

d. At what cost?

e. Is the cost waived if the problem is in your system?

17. What training is available to our personnel?

    a. How much and what type is included in the purchase price?

    b. What options are available for additional education and at what price?

18. Describe the documentation provided with the system.

    a. How many copies are provided at no charge?

    b. What are the charges for additional copies?

19. Does your usual contract provide for on-site installation assistance?

20. Given our environment, what level of performance should we expect:

    a. with a lightly loaded system?

    b. with a heavily loaded system?

21. Are there any rules of thumb to predict system resources usage?

22. What growth capabilities are designed into your proposal?

    a. Do we currently have the facilities to utilize the growth potential?

    b. If not, what additional facilities would we require?

23. What operating system products and/or features are required or recommended (e.g., VM/CMS, RSS, GDDM, etc.)?

24. What software interfaces are currently supported (e.g., SQL, SAS, etc.)?

25. What interfaces are currently under development?

26. What is the frequency of major enhancement software releases? Please highlight the major enhancements in the last four releases.

FIGURE 10–6   *(continued)*

No.	Item	Responses
27.	What output devices (printers, plotters, CRTs) are supported?	
28.	How many installations of the proposed software are you supporting?	
	a. How many of them were installed within the past year?	
	b. How long has the oldest user been installed?	
29.	What resource accounting facilities are provided?	
30.	Is it possible to allocate all resource usage by user?	
31.	Can inactive files be easily archived and retrieved from tape using standard facilities such as VM/BACKUP?	
32.	What type of administrative work, such as table maintenance, is required to support the system?	
33.	Do we need a full-time, part-time, or no system administrator?	

System history

34.	Describe chronologically the development of your system from its inception. Address any changes in corporate ownership of the system.	

System architecture

35.	Outline your system architecture. How do you differentiate your system architecture and capabilities from your competitor's products?	
36.	Define your system's maximum model size.	
37.	State the maximum number of variables your system can accommodate.	

Data access

38.	Describe the capabilities of your foreign file interface (FFI).	
39.	Does your FFI have accumulation capabilities, which allow the user to accumulate a series of numbers and pass only one number onto the MSS model?	

FIGURE 10–6   *(continued)*

No.	Item	Responses

40. What report output, COBOL output, and other output formats does your system accommodate?

41. How does your FFI treat "bad" data records? Please include sample error reports.

42. Does your FFI dynamically adjust the model? For example, if a new product code is added to the production system and then later passed on to the MSS model, will the FFI alter the model to accommodate the new product code? Explain how your system accomplishes this.

43. Identify the efficiencies of your FFI as documented at your client sites. These sites should be similar to ours.

44. Describe the data management component of your system. Address the data management structure, data access capabilities, data manipulation features, and analytical capabilites of this component.

Software interface

45. What mainframe end-user software can your system access (e.g., SAS, Easytrieve)?

46. What micro software can your system access (e.g., Lotus, dBase III, Chart)?

47. Which software can be accessed by your modeling software without exiting MSS and then having to reenter MSS? Describe how this is accomplished.

Procedurality, syntax, and editing

48. Define procedural versus nonprocedural versus procedural with forward referencing. Describe the procedurality of your system. What are the pros and cons of your system's procedurality?

49. If you offer a "micro MSS" product, describe the procedurality of that product. Contrast the differences, if any, with your mainframe product.

FIGURE 10-6   *(continued)*

No.	Item	Responses

50. Describe the code syntax of your system.
    For example, what is the maximum length of
    variable names? Are code lines numbered or
    not numbered? Can variable name and/or
    line numbers be used in specifying an equa-
    tion, etc.? Discuss the pros and cons of your
    system's code syntax. Provide example mod-
    eling problems and the code used to solve
    the problems.

51. Describe the screen editor capabilites of your
    system—for example, line-by-line editor,
    full-screen editor, split screen capability,
    other capabilities.

52. Does your system have the capability to uti-
    lize an editor other than its own; for exam-
    ple, VM-Xedit? If so, how do you accom-
    plish this?

*Multidimensional and hierarchical
capabilities*

53. Describe your system's multidimensional
    capabilities and differentiate your sys-
    tem's capabilities in this area from your
    competition.

54. How many dimensions can your system
    handle?

55. Break out by percent the estimated number
    of client applications on your system that are
    two-, three-, four-, etc., dimensional.

56. Is your system capable of goal seeking and
    solving simultaneous equations across many
    multidimensional spreadsheets? Provide ex-
    amples from your client base.

57. Describe your system's hierarchical capabili-
    ties. Contrast your system's capabilities with
    your competitors' products.

58. Describe your system's consolidation capa-
    bilities. Contrast your system's capabilities
    with your competitors' products.

Statistical and financial functions

59. List and define the statistical and financial
    functions built into your software.

FIGURE 10–6 *(continued)*

No.	Item	Responses

60. Does your system provide users the facility to create user-defined functions? How is this accomplished?

61. Is there a limit to the number of user-defined functions that can be created? If so, how many?

62. Can user-defined functions be cataloged in a library? How is this accomplished? Please provide examples of user-defined functions created by your clients.

Investigation capabilities

63. Describe the "what if" capabilities of your system. Address step-function "what if" capabilities in your answer.

64. Describe the goal-seeking capabilities of your system. Identify the number of variables that can be addressed in the backward iteration of a goal-seek.

65. Describe the risk-analysis techniques available with your system.

66. Describe the optimization capabilities of your system.

67. Describe how your system solves simultaneous equations.

68. Does your system solve circular equations?

Graphics

69. Describe the graphics capabilities of your system.

70. What other graphics software can your system utilize? Explain how it would be accessed and used.

Security

71. Does your system allow the user to secure and control security and access to data?

72. How and at what levels does your system restrict access to data?

FIGURE 10-6 *(concluded)*

No.	Item	Responses
	Micro MSS products	
73.	For your micro MSS modeling package, contrast the micro functions and capabilities with your mainframe product.	
74.	Are the commands and syntax of the micro package comparable to your mainframe software?	
75.	Describe the graphic capabilities of your mainframe product.	
76.	Describe the communication and data access capabilites of your micro MSS package.	
	Training and documentation	
77.	Describe your MSS system training program. Identify the training classes offered and the subject matter covered in each class.	
78.	How many days is your first introductory class? What subject matter is covered in this class? Please include a copy of your introductory class workbook.	
79.	Describe the documentation of your system. Address your documentation approach— for example, how-to approach, example approach, etc. Provide samples of your documentation.	

VENDOR PRESENTATIONS

There has been relatively little written on the art of participating in vendor presentations. Most corporate views on this topic range from "a commercial to be endured" to "a waste of time to be avoided." Yet, properly controlled, vendor presentations can be a vital phase in the evaluation process.

At this point in the evaluation, the choice of products should have been reduced to no more than three or four. Most heads are still swimming with a legion of features and the vague feeling of hopelessness in ever being able to distinguish between packages. The committee is facing the prospect of an in-depth examination of software alternatives. This is an excellent time to pause and gain some insight into the character of each product as well as the respective vendors.

The secret to productive vendor presentations is control. The committee must decide what information is needed from the vendors and then present a list of required topics and ground rules. Some issues to consider include:

- *Duration.* It is rare indeed to find a group of people who can carve three half-days out of their schedules, and rarer to find any that can stay alert for four hours. Find the committee's time tolerance (two hours?) and limit all vendors to this.

- *Participation.* Beyond the committee, who should be invited to the show? The general rule is, the more the better. Broad participation usually ensures a good foundation of questions and reinforces the feeling of ownership instilled by the checklist process. The only exception to the principle of participation is executives. Most executives appreciate being presented with a decision, but not with all the options to be considered. Expecting an executive to sit through hours of presentations on a "for your information only" basis is usually not realistic.

- *Place.* The most desirable setting for these presentations is in the vendor's own facilities, if there is a local office. This is off-site, away from distractions, and offers the added benefit of enabling the committee to gain insight into the local support facilities. If these facilities are not adequate, ask the vendor to reserve appropriate space at a local hotel. The benefits of being off-site far outweigh any inconvenience resulting from the nonresident location.

- *Demonstrations.* Whether live demonstrations are given at this time can be left up to the vendor. If they are to be included, however, make it understood that they should support and not detract from the topics to be covered.

- *Topics.* Although shaped by the needs of the company, the topics generally should include history of the vendor, genealogy of the software, MSS philosophy, major product characteristics, vendor support, and future development plans.

Finally, the committee should not be overly concerned about duplication of topics among vendors. Listening to four definitions of MSS can be helpful, since the way the vendor defines MSS helps shape the committee's image of the corporate philosophy and product direction.

Making the Most of References

At some point in the evaluation process, the question of references will arise. For many companies, the process of checking the vendor's references seems about as productive as checking the references of a prospective employee. One evaluation committee chairperson has remarked:

I know we probably should contact the vendor's references, but let's be realistic. Are they honestly going to provide names that will be anything less than glowing? Why go to the trouble of talking to someone who will do nothing more than confirm the vendor's hype? I just do not think it is very productive.

Despite the popularity of such an attitude, references can provide valuable insight into the performance (good and bad) of the products in question. Figure 10–7 provides a guideline for the productive use of references. The following comments should enhance the evaluator's understanding of the reference interview process.

When did you purchase this product?   If the software was purchased many years ago, the vendor's customer might not be aware of recent advances in MSS technology. On the other hand, a long-term association with the vendor would provide valuable understanding relevant to support issues. Having recently purchased the software, the reference would be well versed in the competitive technologies and would be an excellent source of comparative information. Occasionally, however, the vendor provides references so recent that they have yet to actually employ the software for even one significant development project. Thus knowing the date of purchase does not automatically qualify the reference as appropriate, nor does it potentially invalidate the reference. It does provide a framework within which the subsequent questions can be considered.

Why did you decide on this product?   Companies (people) buy MSS software for many reasons. Some look for a generic product, while others primarily desire a single application solution. Still other companies seek a product that will offer a compromise between end-user computing and application development. As with the first question, there is not necessarily a right or a wrong answer here. Views on support, strengths, and weaknesses can have different meanings depending on the response to the question.

What other software did you consider?   It is not always easy to identify the real reason a company made a purchase. If the competitive products considered were fourth-generation languages, for example, it might indicate a desire on the part of the company to satisfy application development and MSS at the same time. Understanding the other products considered also can serve as confirmation that the products being evaluated represent the key products for the need. Not infrequently, this question brings up at least one MSS overlooked during the preliminary evaluation.

What applications are currently in use?   As discussed earlier, ease of use is significantly less important when the purchase is motivated by single

FIGURE 10–7
Reference Query Form

Name of Software Package _____ Date _____

1. Date of purchase _____

2. Why did you decide on this product? _____

   _____

3. What other software did you consider? _____

   _____

4. What applications are currently in use? _____

   _____

5. Is this employed as a tool for end-user development? _____

   _____

6. What is the ratio of users versus coders for implementing applications? _____

   _____

7. How do you rate the software's performance on your computer? _____

   _____

8. What do you consider the software's strengths? _____

   _____

9. What do you consider the software's weaknesses? _____

   _____

10. How would you rate the vendor's support? _____

    _____

11. What other companies (contacts) could you recommend?

    _____

applications. It follows, therefore, that the fewer the applications, the less critical the reference's need for ease of use.

Knowledge of the applications is also vital in assuring that the reference is appropriate to the committee's needs. To coin a phrase, "A budget is not a budget is not a budget." Some companies treat budgeting as a simple consolidation and reporting exercise. Others conduct scenario planning, execute cost control programs, and implement executive performance reviews, all in the name of budgeting. Obviously, a reference's expressed satisfaction over the software's budget performance means little unless the application demands are comparable.

Is this employed as a tool for end-user development?   A popular consultant once recounted an experience with a reference in this way:

> I was told that the MSS was quite favored among the end-users. Everyone praised the product's ease of use and commented on the great help it had been in their jobs. It took me three days to realize that *not one* of the users had actually ever created an application in the software. They had been using programs written by their Information Systems support representative. It seems that the only thing they could really attest to is her ability to black-box applications. Needless to say, I had to ask for other references.

Often overlooked, every reference must be validated as to the nature of the MSS usage.

What is the ratio of users versus coders for implementing applications?   This question is similar in orientation to the prior question. Employing MSS software as an application development tool is not inappropriate. Failure to uncover the usage pattern, however, can lead to significant distortion when evaluating the reference's responses.

How do you rate the software's performance on your computer? It is common to ask the reference about the software's resource performance. Out of context, however, the response can be meaningless at best, misleading at worst. Understanding the applications also contributes to one's ability to appreciate the validity of the reference's experience. Hearing that the product is a "machine hog," for instance, can be alarming to the uninitiated evaluator. If the reference is running enormously complex and/or large systems, however, such information takes on new meaning.

Remember also that some companies strive for broad applicability when purchasing software. Within that range of applications, therefore, one might expect some singularly inappropriate uses of the MSS. Such potential misuse of the product cannot be identified without a thorough understanding of the applications and their hardware environment.

What do you consider the software's strengths?   This also is a popular question asked of references. It also can be the source of considerable misunderstanding. The knack is in reading between the lines. Many vendors, for example, tout their MSS's ease of use. Not surprisingly, asking about the product's strengths will get the same response. The trick is to ask for specific examples indicating the strengths listed by the reference.

The evaluator also should remember that any strength (or weakness) is only meaningful when considered within the framework of the qualifying questions. Productivity means less when the frame of reference is performing the process manually. Ease of use is less impressive when the user is an I/S professional. If the software's power is compared with Lotus 1-2-3, it will not lead to a high-probability selection of a powerful MSS.

What do you consider the software's weaknesses?   This question is far more interesting than it would first appear. Even when references genuinely like the product, they are almost always psychologically unprepared to appear too "unsophisticated" as to not be able to identify a few shortfalls. The identification of weaknesses always should be given its full weight. Although a product characteristic might not be important to the reference, the implications for the specific environment under consideration may prove critical.

How do you rate the vendor's support? Why?   Support, like the perfect product, is always easier to promise in the future than to deliver today. The vendor's stated commitment to its customers can be reinforced by receiving the assurances of its customer base.

What other companies (contacts) could you recommend?   It is quite natural for the vendor to direct attention to customers who will speak highly of the product and related services. The committee may feel frustrated at being limited to this valuable resource. One method to avoid these limitations is to ask the reference for the name of other companies using the product in question. Be certain to ask for specific contacts within those companies as well. Also, consider asking for companies the reference knows to be critical of the software. While such a perspective is not adequate in isolation, it will give the evaluator an enhanced feeling of control over the evaluation process.

Vendor Support of the Package

Software support by the vendor is often just as critical to the success of the MSS project as is the software itself. Unfortunately, the issue of support often is given far too little importance on the part of the evaluator. Even the most judicious use of references will not mitigate against the need to thoroughly understand the vendor's commitment to support. Achieving such an appreciation is not, however, an easy matter. Figure 10–8 reviews some support questions that need to be asked of the vendor. It contains a vendor support evaluation to help in arriving at this important assessment. In assessing the vendor's ability to deliver support now and in the future, a number of issues must be explored.

What is the frequency of new releases?   The concept of "what you see is what you get" in MSS evaluation speaks to the objective of minimizing surprise. This is the least that should be desired when taking on the selection process. Ideally, however, what you see will be *less* than what you get. The product's ability to keep pace with technology is critical to every organization's need to retain the value of its investment.

FIGURE 10–8
Vendor Support Services Form

Name of Vendor _____ Date _____

1. What is the frequency of new releases? _____

2. What is your financial stability?   <u>Recent Year</u>   <u>3-Year Average</u>

        Sales

        Profit

        Number of Employees

3. What is your approximately installed base for this package? _____

4. How many years have you been in business? _____

5. Do you have a customer service hot line? Include restrictions. _____

_____

_____

_____

6. How large a staff is working on:

    a. customer support? _____

    b. package enhancements? _____

    c. new package development? _____

As will be seen below, the measure of a vendor's ability to stay state-of-the-art is *delivered R & D*. That is, neither the availability nor the expenditure of funds for research and development actually reflects the potential of the DSS to grow. What actually matters is the frequency and quality of new releases.

Financial stability.   In most cases, the investment in software is actually far less than the ultimate investment in the applications themselves. Once committed, the buying organization becomes extraordinarily dependent upon the long-term reliability of the vendor. One critical indicator of the vendor's reliability is its financial stability. The greater the question of its long-term health, the greater the risk involved in committing to that vendor.

Caution is indicated when evaluating the financial stability of a vendor. Relied upon too heavily, such a criterion would preclude new entries into the marketplace. After all, even the most popular, financially stable vendors had to start somewhere. In addition, many vendors are privately held. This limits the ability to evaluate. Some companies take the attitude that lack of an available financial statement equates to nonreliability. Others limit their assessment of financial stability to publicly held vendors. This gives an unfair advantage to those software vendors providing financial information.

Despite the practical problems inherent in this assessment, it bears so greatly upon the vendor's ability to deliver support that every evaluation should make an earnest attempt to measure financial stability.

Years in business.   Like the above criterion, this question is biased in favor of established MSS software vendors. Unfortunately, the question of the risk associated with the software purchase is still quite relevant to many buying organizations.

Hot line (include restrictions).   The need for direct support varies from organization to organization. Some offer national support (out of one central location). Others offer local support, operating out of cities within close proximity. Still others offer hot-line support (telephone assistance), with restrictions ranging from the number of hours support is offered to the number of individuals supported from any one organization. As with so many other measurements, the specific support required, as well as the value placed on support, varies with each organization.

Size of staff working on package.   As mentioned earlier, the concept of delivered R & D is fundamental to evaluating a vendor's ability to enhance its offering in the future. Most evaluators are quite skeptical in regard to promises of future enhancements. This skepticism is quite natural. It is, after all, incredibly difficult to appraise a company's real commitment and ability to deliver what is promised. It seems the only commitment anyone can be sure of is that required to prepare the color slides flashed during a presentation. As one vice president of MIS maintains, ". . . beyond that, it's vaporware." Yet the evaluating organization can make such assessments. The knack is in knowing what to ask and being prepared to evaluate the replies.

Evaluating the Vendor's Product Enhancement

To begin evaluating the future potential of R & D, it must be recognized that one of the best assurances of a company's commitment to the future is their proven commitment in the past. Figure 10–9 is a form with which such a track record can be evaluated. Care must be taken when judging the results. Only those capabilities that truly represent an enhancement to the existing product line should be included. The vendor should be asked whether such features make the software more state-of-the-art or whether they merely fix existing weaknesses in the MSS. A track record of frequent, significant enhancements does not guarantee future commitment, but should be viewed with a much higher sense of certainty.

Another step is to understand the terms normally used (and confused) when addressing product enhancement since a vendor may include any one of these in qualifying the investment in the future.

• *Bug fixes* involve fixing the problems that exist in the software. This is accomplished by changing the actual code (the source of the problem) or by creating a new feature (Band-Aid) to provide the user the means to minimize the damage. By including bug fixes in R & D, a vendor may appear to be committed to product investment, when, in fact, its investment level may actually measure the relative weakness of the software itself.

• *Operating system translation* measures the vendor's investment in supporting the many operating systems on which its software resides. Naturally, the greater the number of operating systems, the greater the investment.

Whether this sort of investment is of benefit to an organization largely depends on the number of operating systems residing within the end-user computing facility. If the product is expected to run on many different operating systems, then its portability (as measured by the translation investment) can be vital. Regardless of the importance of portability, however, confusing operating system translation with R & D does little to advance understanding as to the growth potential of the MSS software.

• *Research* is the product investment for which there exists no specific delivery timetable (usually deliverable in excess of 18 months). Such investment is the best indicator of the strategic direction of the vendor.

• *Development* includes that product investment targeted for specific delivery timetables. A low development budget translates into an inability to respond to

FIGURE 10–9
Evaluating the Vendor's Product Enhancement

Product Enhancement Analysis

Software Product _____

Release No. _____

Release Date _____

Date	Enhancement	Benefit
———	———————	———————
		———————
———	———————	———————
		———————
———	———————	———————
		———————
———	———————	———————
		———————
———	———————	———————
		———————
———	———————	———————
		———————
———	———————	———————
		———————

---

requests for implementation (RFI) submitted by the customer base. One MSS vendor largely funds its development with contributions from its customer base: "If a new capability is important to a customer, they pay us in advance. That then becomes the means through which we set development priorities."

• *Customer support* is not normally included in R & D. Yet there are still a few vendors who classify expenditures so as to confuse the two, and many vendors are hesitant to disclose detailed R & D information. Since no software is perfect, however, an evaluation often comes down to weighing product trade-offs. Comparing relative merit, therefore, may involve not just evaluating today's performance, but the ability to improve tomorrow's as well. Measuring true R & D is not easy. Most evaluators, however, find it is well worth the effort.

JUSTIFYING THE PURCHASE

Sooner or later, most MSS advocates will have to address the challenge of justifying the software purchase. Rarely will vague claims of improved decision making be persuasive enough to sway the skeptical manager. Unfortunately, MSS advocates are ill-prepared for the problem. The difficulty is not in determining whether MSS is of value, because the value is quite real, as shown in Figure 10–10. Rather, the problem lies in the methodology by which software value is traditionally judged.

Under most circumstances, the decision to make any computer-related purchase is one of dollars and cents. For most companies, this involves the following steps:

- *Calculate* the labor currently required to complete the task or application. Typically, this involves the summing of man-hours, -days, -weeks, or -months.

- *Estimate* the anticipated (hopefully lower) labor requirements following implementation of the system.

FIGURE 10–10
Cost Justification

Cost	
Software	$100,000
Maintenance	75,000
Training	5,000
Extra disk memory	5,000
Miscellaneous hardware	15,000
Systems development	60,000
Total Cost	$260,000
Savings	
Consolidation & reporting	$180,000
Budgeting	135,000
Sales analysis	45,000
Inventory analysis	45,000
Total Savings	$405,000

Payback: 1.5 years
Traditional cost justification conservatively based on five years' cost, four years' savings.

- *Multiply* the difference between steps one and two (labor savings attributable to computerization) by the total cost of labor (including benefits).

Expenditures, of course, are far easier to calculate. Included in expenditures are such items as software cost, maintenance, training, development, incremental hardware, and so forth. Compare known outlay with projected savings and arrive at the financial viability of the software investment (usually measured by internal rate of return or payback).

So goes traditional cost justification methodology. But as pointed out by one manager struggling to scrape together extra labor savings, "This is a *decision support system*. How do you measure the value of a good decision?" Captured in this question is the fundamental problem with this orientation. Traditional cost justification methodology (Figure 10–10) is designed to address traditional data processing applications. These are almost exclusively labor-intensive, high-volume activities closely associated with the basic survival of the firm.

There is a subset of MSS applications that matches the characteristics of low-level "life-support" applications. The justification process for these applications quite naturally conforms to the traditional cost/benefit approach. The value of supported strategic decisions, however, is not nearly as easily measured.

Perhaps the best method of measuring the strategic value of an MSS is to measure not merely the labor-hour savings, but the value of enhanced strategic decision making itself. Figure 10–11 describes the approach used in measuring strategic value:

1. Ask the responsible executive to provide his or her estimate of the value of "perfect" knowledge regarding a critical component of his or her field (inventories, taxes, etc.). This can be called the potential savings of MSS.

FIGURE 10–11
Strategic Cost Justification

Strategic savings based upon the interview approach			
	Potential	*Probability*	*Expected*
Inventory control	$4,000,000	10%	$400,000
Acquisition analysis	2,500,000	5%	125,000
Tax planning	600,000	10%	60,000
Capital construction	500,000	20%	100,000
			$685,000

2. Briefly describe the concept of MSS and ask with what probability the executive believes the system would achieve the desired perfect knowledge. This captures the probability that potential savings will be realized.

3. The expected savings are calculated by multiplying the potential savings by the expected savings. What the expected savings actually represents is an estimated value for *improved* knowledge in this strategic field. That is, it is an attempt to quantify the generally recognized fact that there is some value in accessing more information targeted to high-value needs.

Naturally, any one individual value for expected savings will be suspect. The total expected savings, however, represents an overall measure of the strategic value of MSS.

It should be noted that the potential value of perfect knowledge in strategic fields is so great, almost any probability, regardless of how small, will justify the MSS purchase. For this reason, it is not recommended that the above approach be employed in isolation. When used in concert with traditional methods, however, it offers a powerful measure of the value of MSS to a firm.

There is one final point to be made regarding the strategic value of MSS. As noted above, strategic applications almost always represent a value to an organization many times that of traditional development projects. Consider, therefore, that over 80 percent of all uses for MSS are in the areas of operational and managerial control. While some software packages are definitely superior to others in terms of their appropriateness for strategic applications, the limited scope of MSS is less a reflection of technological limitation than of linear thinking on the part of the user community. Decision support systems must be used strategically to break out of the mold.

Finally, when justifying the software purchase, there is one group of benefits derived from MSS for which financial equivalents cannot be found. This is the political (nontechnical) value of MSS. These organizational contributions can in themselves justify the cost of the software. Examples include:

- Forty percent reduction in the information float (the time between closing the books and getting the critical reports to management).

- Improved deployment of technology (analysis of patent and licensing options, allocation of R & D, etc.).

- Faster response to executive's questions.

- Executive access to critical information.

Certainly, only on rare occasions will a mainframe software buying decision be made on the basis of a single justification. More frequently, a composite of motivations would be used. What is important is that the expectations regarding the uses of MSS be expanded and the trap of limiting this powerful technology to only the most tangible of applications be avoided.

PRODUCT PERFORMANCE BENCHMARKS

Benchmarking software involves objective performance measurements of specific characteristics for one or more products.

There are three basic groups of characteristics to be considered when evaluating management support software: functionality, ease of use, and machine efficiency. In order to measure success against the *primary buying motivation* (PBM), all three must be evaluated consistent with the PBM.

Traditional data processing software is vigorously tested for efficiency, loosely considered for functionality, and rarely evaluated for user-friendliness. This benchmarking approach make sense when considering production applications (large, high-transaction, batch, and inflexible). Unfortunately, many committees give little attention to ensuring that benchmarks accurately reflect software performance in the environment in which it will be used.

Because the PBM is company-specific, no single approach is appropriate for all situations. Certain guidelines should be employed when preparing to benchmark MSS products. These guidelines cover both designing a prototype application and reviewing benchmark methodology.

Designing a Benchmark Prototype

Performance cannot be measured in the abstract. Benchmark results are only of value when measured against consistent and realistic requirements. The best measure of realism is found in the PBM. In short, performance should be measured against the most pressing software requirements. Naturally, such specific requirements do not always exist, such as with a generic PBM. But even here there is a consensus of system requirements. These can be used to construct a successful fictitious benchmark application.

It rarely makes sense to entirely duplicate an application, especially when comparing three or four products. For reasons of time and effort, a *prototype* is constructed. A prototype is a scaled-down but representative version of the ultimate application. This should form the cornerstone of the benchmark.

The concept of benchmarking is not unfamiliar to most companies. Ironically, it is specifically due to this familiarity that many MSS benchmarks fail. To better appreciate these problems, the following section outlines the benchmarking efforts of a large West Coast retail chain.

A Benchmarking Case History

This retail company had just completed a major evaluation of an important database production application. The project involved sorting more than a million records. It developed a prototype of the application, benchmarking software against a database of 50,000 records, and felt pleased with its selection following the tests. In approaching the MSS benchmark it employed similar techniques.

The MSS application consisted of a profit performance mode. With it the company planned to evaluate store performance, analyze regional and national trends, and project the impact of key environmental factors on future performance. The prototype seemed reasonable. It consisted of a trimmed-down income statement and cash-flow projection and required several key reports to be generated. Based on the results of the benchmark, a product was chosen.

Problems developed almost from the start. The data needed for the application resided on a different database. Access was programmer-intensive, slow, and inefficient. After long delays, the users completed the system, only to realize that much of the organizational structure had changed. The system proved inflexible in dealing with that change, causing further delays in implementation.

What a Benchmark Should Do

The key element in a prototype's success is in its ability to simulate the system requirements. Scaling down does not mean scaling out. If, for example, fast and flexible data extraction on large volumes is needed, then the prototype should simulate the extraction of large volumes of data. Similarly, if the application requires 200 products and 15 locations, the prototype should reflect a significant number of products and locations. To do less will risk the prototype being nonrepresentative of the application.

Who should construct the prototype for benchmarking? Contrary to common practice, it is usually not necessary (and often inadvisable) for the users or committee members to participate in the preparation for several reasons. First, it is difficult to motivate people to learn a software package with the understanding that there is a high probability it will not be chosen. Also, users will exert only a part-time effort at best becoming familiar with the package. This leaves evaluators unsure if poor product performance is the result of the software or the user. Finally, strict comparability of results is essential to any benchmark. Differences in personal backgrounds, abilities, and perceptions compromise comparability.

If the evaluators have the time, an alternative is to prepare a prototype and subsequently review it with the respective vendors. If time and/or motivation is a problem, similar results can be achieved by assigning the prototype creation to the vendors. If this option is chosen, the committee can be sure the results represent the best the product has to offer. This does not relieve the evaluators of responsibility, since they must prepare a clear, detailed, and written explanation of the prototype specifications, including:

- Time frame for completion.
- Explanation of how the application will be used.

- Description of the prototype organization.
- Rule specifications.
- Input data, including foreign (nonresident) file formats and descriptions of source files.
- "Hostile" (other vendor) software to be interfaced.
- Ouptut requirements, including sample reports and graphics.

Conducting a benchmark. Having constructed the prototypes, the next step is to put the software through its paces. The critical strategy in conducting a successful benchmark is to simulate reality. Production applications traditionally are run in batch, which is consistent with this strategy because such applications normally are not run on-line. Such methods are rarely appropriate, however, when using an MSS support.

How will the MSS most likely be used? Usage is characterized by active rather than passive interactivity. For instance, users' knowledge of a problem is often incomplete, either because of the iterative process or business dynamics. Such change usually is unforeseen, and sometimes dramatic and fundamental. Most MSS applications demand changes in reports, rules, and the very organization of the business itself.

One of the popular uses of an MSS is in temporarily alternating data and logic. Such game-playing as "what if," "goal-seeking," or "sensitivity" analysis is an unpredictable yet essential ingredient in real-world use.

How does this translate into the benchmark itself? The evaluators should establish a standard set of usage patterns against which the benchmark will run. It is essential that these patterns be known to the prototype developers, because they would be unknown in real life. The benchmark is run then not just on the basic prototype, but against the appropriate usage patterns as well.

In running the benchmark, it is advisable to maintain a record of all activity for later review. Most operating systems make provisions for this through spooling techniques. With the help of this documentation, the entire committee can make performance comparisons.

Evaluating the benchmark. The ideal MSS is *concurrently* functional, easy-to-use, and efficient relative to other high-level languages. The environment within which concurrent performance is measured must reflect the real-world usage of the software (spreadsheet, hierarchy, and/or multidimensional).

Measuring functionality. The measurement of MSS functionality has two sides. As the evaluators review the checklist, they usually will find several capabilities missing from a product. These are fairly straightforward, because they either exist or they do not. Does the mere existence of features, however, sufficiently guard against the software becoming little-used? The measurement of any capability is rarely one-dimensional. For example, in an evaluation of a tool's ability to cut, many tools would seem to satisfy that need. If performance is measured against the range of cutting needs (wood, glass, and steel), far fewer tools would satisfy the requirements.

The existence of any feature (particularly modeling capabilities) should be evaluated not only in spreadsheet mode, but across the full range of the company's usage patterns. If consolidation is required, how does the feature perform across consolidation levels? If there are multiple dimensions to an application (product, division, market, etc.), how does performance alter when applied across those dimensions? Only by including such considerations can the MSS evaluator be sure he or she does not end up with an unused product.

Once the products have performed across a range of applications, their true functionality can be assessed by evaluating the answers to such questions as:

- Did the basic prototype generate the correct answers?
- Did all data entry, hostile software interfacing, and peripheral connections work?
- Did temporary changes work effectively?
- Did all evaluated features work (regression, depreciation, graphics, etc.)?

Efficiency.   While efficiency is not the critical criterion of an MSS, it can become important under some circumstances. If the organization charges users for access, then extraordinarily low efficiency can diminish usage of an application. In the extreme, inefficient software can degrade hardware performance and make it economically impractical. To measure such performance, evaluators might ask:

- How does efficiency compare for the basic prototype?
- As the prototype is put through its usage patterns, does this comparative efficiency change?
- How does efficiency compare when accessing foreign data?
- How does incremental usage impact efficiency?

MSS efficiency is not a simple consideration. The points mentioned in Figure 10–12 are particularly relevant when attempting as MSS resource perspective.

Ease of Use.   Perhaps the best method of evaluating ease of use is to ask, "What does this software procedure add to my understanding of the business or the problem?" As the prototype performance is measured for both spreadsheet and non-spreadsheet uses, do users find they are spending more

FIGURE 10–12
Efficiency Is Relative

Running cost is just one piece of the total cost picture

	Intelligent MSS	Programming MSS
People cost to develop	low	high
Machine cost to develop, debug	medium	medium-high[1]
Elapsed time to develop	low	medium-high
People cost to run	low	low-medium[2]
Machine cost to run	medium	medium
People and machine cost to maintain	low	medium
People cost to get data	low	high
Machine cost to get data	low	medium[3]
People cost to change	low	high
Machine cost to change	low	high[4]
Elapsed time to implement	low	medium

[1]Debugging is much more involved due to more lines of code and typical file manipulation.
[2]Depends on how rigidly "black-boxed" the application is.
[3]Assumes quality data interface.
[4]If the change is sufficiently structural, the programming model will have to be rewritten.

time satisfying the computer than their own business needs? If they do, then the software is high in overhead.

To help identify such problems, the evaluators might ask:

- How much overhead was required to create the prototype?
- Were the required techniques covered in the introductory software class, or is more advanced training required?
- How easily was the prototype modified? Did the software provide for documentation of those changes?
- Did the ease of using the system change as complexities were introduced?
- How much documentation did the software provide?

It should be noted that benchmarking products is not always necessary. There will be times when the software decision is so clear that the evaluators may wish to move directly to a trial. As long as such a commitment is unanimous, a benchmark will only delay the implementation process. Lacking universal accord, however, conducting the benchmark will help keep the evaluation process uncontentious.

SELECTION AND TEST OF THE PRIMARY PRODUCT

In most cases, a thorough benchmark as described in the previous section will highlight the significant differences between products. If the choice is still unclear, requesting a presentation on product comparisons from the contending vendors might prove helpful. In the final analysis, such considerations as the vendor's future company direction, planned product enhancements, and support capabilities are often used as tiebreakers.

One useful selection approach that several writers have advanced is the construction of a "product priority grid" to visually see which product is preferable. The first step is to agree on what critical points of functionality will be used for comparison, possibly assigning priorities.

The second step is to produce a product priority grid, as shown in Figure 10–13, as a working document. This will be the base to help sort out the relative appropriateness of the software for individual environments. Beneath the grid, write the most critical MSS requirements. As an aid to prioritizing, first list those capabilities that are absolutely essential, without which the product is likely to fail. Once on the grid, place the products in the position that most closely matches their performance. Place the easiest-to-use products toward the top. Naturally, the "perfect" MSS would be placed in the upper right (see Figure 10–14).

This approach is a simple way to visualize a large number of software products. While it is an oversimplification, it can be used to weigh trade-offs meaningfully and reduce the number of choices.

Testing

Most vendors offer the intial 30 to 60 days as a trial period during which the product may be used without obligation. For the evaluators, this is the final opportunity to confirm that the software performs as expected.

As previously discussed, during the benchmark it is not always necessary to participate in training on the MSS product. During the trial, training is a critical and necessary first step. It is only through knowledge and thorough use of the product that the evaluators can make the purchase decision confidently.

Once again, the application is of prime importance during this phase in the evaluation. Lacking a significant application, the trial often lapses into several unrelated and nonchallenging uses. These rarely provide a confident trial for the software. This danger can prove of particular concern for the generic PBM. Thus it is suggested that, lacking a specific application as the buying motivation, the committee identify a major application for use during the trial period.

FIGURE 10–13
Product Priority Grid

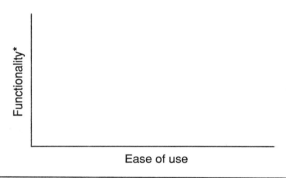

*Selected functionality

FIGURE 10–14
Sample Product Priority Grid

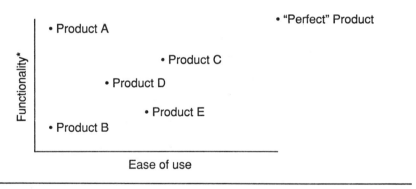

*Ease of use by novice
*Data access (MSA, VSAM, MVS)
*Flexible and maintainable
*Micro version
*Handles complex allocations
*Powerful statistical functions

MAKING THE FINAL SELECTION

After the software trial is completed, the evaluation committee must make a final decision based on all available information. Either the MSS software that was chosen initially will be retained or the software will be rejected and another software package will be tested. In either event, if the prescribed selection process has been followed, the evaluation committee will have conducted a logical, well-documented procedure to justify its decision.

Figure 10–15 is a sample evaluation control document (ECD). Its purpose is to provide solid guidelines as to how to appropriately establish and implement an MSS software trial. The ECD is actually an agreement between the evaluation committee and the MSS vendor and consists of six parts:

1. Purpose.
2. Objectives.
3. Trial applications.
4. The vendor team.
5. The evaluation team.
6. The trial calendar.

FIGURE 10–15
Sample Evaluation Control Document

Prepared by: _____

Prepared for: _____

Date: _____

I. Purpose

This document is intended to outline in specific terms the criteria that have been established for the acquisition of MSS software.

In addition, it identifies the process and applications by which the specific objectives will be measured to ensure that each one is addressed successfully. This will ensure that the trial will result in a clear understanding of the software and, more importantly, an appreciation of its value.

II. Objectives

A. Select a user-oriented package with nonprocedural language syntax that supports:

1. database management
2. modeling and analysis
3. reports generation

B. Select a package that will access detailed data from other internal systems and provide capability to manipulate and analyze various summaries of the data.

C. Select a package that is able to upload/download data through remote interface with IBM microprocessor.

FIGURE 10–15 *(continued)*

III. Trial Applications

Application	Initial	Date
A. Savings activity report	_____	_____
B. Fixed-rate loan analysis	_____	_____
C. Budgeting (allocation of corporate expenses)	_____	_____
D. Micro version evaluation	_____	_____

A. Savings Activity Report

_____

(Responsible Assignee)

Process

A sample of savings data, initially one branch's transactions for the week of 8/30 to 9/5, as well as the previous weekend balances will be extracted, loaded to tape, and read into the package. The data will be processed to produce the Savings Activity Report. A key objective is to enhance the report by showing movement of funds between accounts. Although the initial report will include only a small sampling of data, a more ambitious "stress test" could be processed toward the end of the trial.

Trial objectives addressed

This application will satisfy objectives A and B.

Comments:

Signatures: _____

Completed as of: _____

(Date)

Evaluator: _____

User Services: _____

Vendor: _____

FIGURE 10–15 *(continued)*

B. Fixed-Rate Loan Analysis

_____

(Responsible Assignee)

Process

The fixed-rate loan porfolio will be extracted, loaded to tape, and read into the package. The data will be analyzed on an ad hoc basis to produce various groupings of loans. Additional fields will be created as required.

Trial objectives addressed

This application will satisfy objectives A and B.

Comments:

Signatures: _____

Completed as of: _____

(Date)

Evaluator: _____

User Services: _____

Vendor: _____

FIGURE 10–15 *(continued)*

C. Budgeting (Allocation of Corporate Expenses)

_____

(Responsible Assignee)

Process

A model will be developed to handle allocation of corporate expenses to each of the branches. This application will be done if time is available after application A is completed.

Trial objectives addressed

This application will satisfy objectives A and B.

Comments:

Signatures: _____

Completed as of: _____

(Date)

Evaluator: _____

User Services: _____

Vendor: _____

FIGURE 10–15   *(continued)*

D. Micro Version Evaluation

_____

(Responsible Assignee)

Process

This evaluation will include the data input, modeling, and reporting capabilities of the vendor's micro version as well as communications between mainframe and micro. This communication capability includes data as well as models.

Trial objectives addressed

This application will satisfy objective C.

Comments:

Signatures: _____

Completed as of: _____

                                                         (Date)

Evaluator: _____

User Services: _____

Vendor: _____

FIGURE 10–15 *(continued)*

IV. Vendor Team

Primary contacts are: _____

Technical questions: _____

Information requests: _____

Name: _____ Title/Department _____

V. Evaluation Team

Trial Coordinator: _____

Alternate: _____

Data Processing: _____

Name: _____ Title/Department _____

FIGURE 10–15   *(concluded)*

VI. *Trial Calendar*

Month Day	Task	Responsibility
1	Overview of trial and objectives; training	Joint
2	Training	Joint
3–7	Design and prototyping	Joint
	Review of progress and advanced topics*	Joint
8–12	Development phase	
13–17	Evaluation phase	
18–20	Review of objectives and evaluation of results	Joint
	Executive review	

*Regular weekly meetings

While requiring a minimum amount of paperwork, the ECD provides several valuable benefits. It establishes documentation that provides the basis upon which management can review the evaluation process. It ensures that all products evaluated are subject to the same hurdles. Finally, it provides a timetable by which the vendor and the evaluator can plan the necessary commitment.

Figure 10–15 includes sample applications based upon an evaluation of a banking MSS. These applications naturally should be modified to apply to particular situations.

Chapter Eleven

Microcomputer MSS Software

Model-based management support software on microcomputers can take various forms: versions of the mainframe package; packages created specifically for microcomputers; decision-structuring packages; or cell-based spreadsheet packages. The usual limitations of micros compared with top mainframes are discussed, together with reasons for using microcomputer-based packages. The spreadsheet package is described briefly, with an example of use. The usefulness of windows is noted. The use of integrated MSS packages is reviewed, with a comment on the value of mainframe spreadsheets. A checklist is provided for evaluating spreadsheet packages.

MSS MODELING PACKAGES ON MICROCOMPUTERS

Three major types of model-based management support software are available for microcomputers:

1. *Financial modeling packages* created specifically for microcomputers, such as ENCORE! from Xerox Microsystems.

2. *Decision-structuring packages* designed to help managers organize decision problems to manageable levels. These packages are useful for decisions that involve qualitative as well as quantitative aspects. An example of a decision-structuring package is Expert Choice.

3. *Cell-based spreadsheet packages,* such as Multiplan and Lotus 1-2-3, that can be used for small financial DSS applications. The main difference in capability between spreadsheets and other modeling packages discussed below is that the modeling packages allow the user to see the logic and relationships being followed, whereas formulas are hidden within the spreadsheets. For large models, with many cells, spreadsheets can become very tedious to define and difficult to understand.

The large, mainframe-based MSS modeling software packages available on the market use large amounts of core storage (random access memory) and rely on the availability of the corporate database as an input to the MSS. Microcomputers are typically storage-limited. Because of their small size, microcomputers are usually slower than mainframe machines for solving specific problems. Most microcomputer-based MSS modeling packages have some limitations on what they can do. In general, the microcomputer versions are restricted to handling much smaller problems than their mainframe counterparts. One important example is in risk analysis. Whereas many mainframe packages provide Monte Carlo simulation capabilities for risk analysis, the microcomputer packages do not.

With the growth of microcomputer use in large firms, MSS package vendors have responded to a potential market by creating versions of their products that run on small machines. Several approaches have been taken. One is to provide a communications link between the microcomputer and the mainframe. The link permits downloading information in a form that can be manipulated by conventional microcomputer packages such as Lotus 1-2-3, or Multiplan spreadsheets, or databases such as dBase II. Data also can be uploaded to the mainframe to be used by the mainframe MSS package. This is the approach followed by Management Decision System's Express. It is, at best, an interim solution that eventually will be replaced by a full-scale microbased version.

Another approach is to create a subset of the mainframe system that can work on its own and also be used in an upload/download mode with the mainframe version. Two examples of such systems are IFPS/Personal from Execucom Systems Corporation and Micro/W from Comshare. These microcomputer packages usually give up some major capabilities available in the mainframe version. For example, IFPS/Personal does not have risk analysis capabilities, and Micro/W at this time does not have stand-alone graphics or data-handling capabilities. Moving mainframe MSS packages to the microcomputer has also resulted in some upgrades. For example, IFPS/Personal is menu-driven and has color graphics, windows, and on-line help capabilities as standard features, none of which are available in the mainframe version.

A third approach is to create a complete version of the mainframe MSS software for the microcomputer. These micro versions involve systems that do not have any data management capabilities. An example of such a conversion is Foresight, by Information Systems of America.

In evaluating the suitability of the various microcomputer MSS modeling packages for an organization it is important to check what computers they run on and how much memory they require. Most packages are designed for the IBM PC and usually will run with a two-disk system. However, the majority of systems require 256K or more of random access storage, and some, such as IFPS, require 512K. A hard disk is desirable. In the case of Micro/W (which is offered on five disks), a hard disk is mandatory because of the large amount of disk swapping required in a two-disk system.

Although microcomputer-based systems are limited when compared to mainframe versions, there is a strong incentive to use them because the microcomputer does not take up mainframe computing time. MSS packages may incur high computer charges because they use up a large amount of resources. This is particularly true for organizations that buy MSS packages from time-sharing services. Decoupling avoids this problem. Also, the high-resource use slows down the mainframe computer for all users. Offloading large portions of MSS use in effect creates additional computer resources. Finally, the microcomputer software is portable and may be used on a home computer.

An effective way to use the microcomputer versions of mainframe MSS software is to have staff do its development work on the micro version. For small models, results can be obtained directly on the micro. For large models, when production runs are required, the models can be moved to the mainframe.

THE SPREADSHEET PACKAGE

The spreadsheet, perhaps more accurately named "the electronic tablet," has been at the heart of most commercially offered MSS mainframe software since the late 1960s. It was little wonder, then, that the electronic tablet was one of the first microcomputer-based pieces of MSS software. The appearance of VISI-CALC, developed by two Harvard graduate students who founded Software Arts, in many ways changed the microcomputer market from one directed to hobbyists and computer hackers to one directed to business users. Depending on whom one talks to, VISICALC was directly responsible for selling 10,000 or 50,000 or 100,000 Apple II computers.

The original electronic tablets would perform "what if" calculations (which is the characteristic that allows them to support decision making) and permitted a limited amount of data formatting for management output in printed reports. As the limits of the available capabilities were reached and, at the same time, microcomputers with more storage reached the market, it became clear that the electronic tablet was interacting with other software functions. However, these functions had to be obtained separately and were generally not compatible with the outputs of the spreadsheets. The next step forward was the integrated package, of which Lotus 1-2-3 is the best known. In these integrated packages, several functions were available within the same software package. Lotus 1-2-3, for example, includes a graphical capability and a database query capability. The graphical capability permits showing selected results in simple business chart form, in color. The database capabilities allow treating the spreadsheet data as if it were a database, providing the ability to sort, query, and do simple distribution analysis.

The trend to integration continues with additional capabilities being added to the basic spreadsheet program, including communications, word processing, and graphics capability. Widely sold products that provide multiple functions are Symphony, an expanded version of 1-2-3 from Lotus, and Framework from Ashton-Tate, which started with dBase II and expanded into a multifunction package with electronic spreadsheet capabilities.

A major contribution of the spreadsheet developers was the definition and use of standardized data formats. The Data Interchange Format (DIF) associated with VISICALC was either adopted by other packages that came on the market or the others provided the ability to move between this format and their own. The advantage of standard formats is that they make it possible to move data sets from one spreadsheet package to another.

Spreadsheets have been used principally for financial analysis where the rectangular spreadsheet output format is familiar. As people have started working with the tablets, however, they have found that many other problems can be represented easily in this format. For example, decision trees used in decision analysis can be nicely represented visually and the needed computations performed.

When the software is initially invoked, a blank spreadsheet appears on the screen (Figure 11–1). The rows typically are given numbers and the columns are labeled with letters (two-letter combinations such as AE are used once the original 26 letters are exhausted). The maximum size of the spreadsheet available depends on the tablet's design and the memory available in the particular

FIGURE 11–1
Blank Spreadsheet

	A	B	C	D	E	F	G
1							
2							
3							
4							
5							
6							
7							
8							
9							

microcomputer being used. Other products provide the ability to give names to the rows and columns and to refer to them by name.

The basic element of the tablet is called a *cell* and is referred to by its row and column coordinates. Thus, for example, the cell in the third row of column two is referred to as B3. Figure 11–2 shows a completed spreadsheet denoting a simple profit statement for the first quarter of the year. Notice that two types of information appear: text information (labels) and numbers. The text information is designed to help the decision maker understand the numbers shown in the tablet. It is entered once and, unless specifically overwritten, does not change. The numeric information, on the other hand, is either entered in fixed form or in relational form.

In the example of Figure 11–2, rows 1 and 2 and column A contain text information that label the spreadsheet. Many of the numerical values are inputs; for example, sales and direct and other costs. Some, however, are computed. For example, sales for first quarter (Q1) are computed using the formula

Sales: B3 + C3 + D3= E3

The user inputs either a numerical value or a formula for each cell. The formulas are given in terms of cell location. A number of functions are provided by most spreadsheets. These include:

- Mathematical functions (e.g., sine, cosine, exponential).
- Logical functions (e.g., if, and, or, true, false).

FIGURE 11–2
Sample Completed Spreadsheet

	A	*B*	*C*	*D*	*E*	*F*	*G*
1				*Title*			
2		JAN	FEB	MAR	Q1		
3	Sales	100	125	110	335		
4	Direct cost	70	80	75	225		
5	Gross profit	30	45	35	105		
6	Other cost	20	25	25	70		
7	Profit	10	20	10	40		
8							
9							

- Statistical functions (e.g., average, minimum, maximum, standard deviation).
- Financial functions (e.g., net present value, internal rate of return, future value).

Logical operations and arithmetic operations (add, subtract, multiply, divide, etc.) can be performed. Of the various functions, the financial functions are of greatest use in business because they provide measures of effectiveness by which alternatives can be judged.

Spreadsheets work on the principle that they always present current values. Thus when the user changes a value or a formula in a spreadsheet, the entire tablet is recomputed to present values based on the current information. This recomputation makes it possible to undertake "what if" analyses to explore the effects of changes. The major attractiveness of the electronic tablet as a decision support tool is the ability to obtain instant feedback on the effects of altered assumptions.

Although it is possible to copy items from one cell to a group of other cells, using electronic tablets requires defining each cell to be used. This can prove to be a chore, particularly for very large spreadsheets. Large spreadsheets with many formulas in them also are prone to errors that can be difficult to locate, or even to recognize that they exist.

A particularly useful feature provided on most microcomputer spreadsheets is *windows*. A window divides the screen into two or more parts. In the simplest form, each window contains a copy of the same information, and it is possible to move the information in each window independently. Thus the user can make a change in one place in the spreadsheet and observe its effects on some other place in the spreadsheet. This is particularly useful when doing sensitivity analysis, in which it is desirable to observe the effects of a change in some assumption (e.g., anticipated sales volume) or on a measure of effectiveness (e.g., net present worth).

INTEGRATED MSS PACKAGES

Although the spreadsheet provides the core of the decision support function, it is not sufficient by itself. The major thrust in spreadsheet-based microcomputer software has been toward integrated packages that provide a multiplicity of functions. The major reasons for using integrated software packages are ergonomic; that is, the human interface involved. Integrated packages allow one to move back and forth between different kinds of computing and to see the same formats and use the same instructions in each kind of computing. As a result, the software is easier to learn and to use.

A second important consideration is that integrated packages share data and data format, thereby making data compatible from one application to another.

How Integration Is Achieved

The strategies followed for integration fall into three broad categories:

- *Creating different packages* that share a common data format and a common user interface. This is the strategy followed by the pfs family (pfs:file, pfs:report, etc.). The idea is that once one is familiar with a member of the family, learning the others is easier.
- *Creating a single disk* (or set of disks) with all the programs on it. This is the approach of Lotus 1-2-3, Lotus Symphony, and Ashton-Tate Frameworks. In these systems, one application (e.g., spreadsheet or database) serves as the foundation for all the others. The advantage is that there is no need to convert files or switch disks. The disadvantage is that not all functions are done equally well. The foundation function is often done best, while some of the others are satisfactory but mediocre.
- *Creating a "shell"* that can run a variety of applications. This approach is followed by Vision, DesQ, GEM from Digital Research, and Topview from IBM. Each application runs in a separate window, and it is possible to share and move information among windows.

What Integrated Packages Do

Integrated packages provide a number of compatible functions. Following is a list of functions provided by integrated packages. The specific functions vary from package to package.

- *Spreadsheet.* These are usually cell-oriented.
- *Database management.* The type of database varies. For example, Framework provides a relational database while Symphony is forms-oriented. The database environment allows searching, sorting, extracting, and editing in the spreadsheet.
- *Forms manager.* Used together with the database system, the forms manager allows creation of forms that are tied to the spreadsheet information.
- *Word processing.* The program allows text creation and the ability to insert spreadsheet data in the middle of the text.
- *Business graphics.* Spreadsheet data can be graphed in a variety of forms.
- *Telecommunications.* A micro-mainframe link is provided that allows data to be transferred, including text and spreadsheets.

- *Command language.* For window management. Command strings can be created that allow a single instruction to perform a series of operations either within a window or between windows. The term "macro" is often used to refer to these command strings.
- *Miscellaneous functions.* Because there are no standards for integrated packages, different vendors provide different functions. Various combinations of the ones listed above are found in several packages. Some functions are idiosyncratic to a particular package. For example, Framework provides an outline organizer.

Mainframe Spreadsheets

Thus far, our discussion of spreadsheet packages has centered on microcomputers. However, there are a few spreadsheet packages available on mainframes. Three examples of these are MegaCalc, OmniCalc, and Supercomp/20. These packages will run on IBM, DEC, Data General, and similar minis and mainframes. Although the licensing costs for the mainframe versions will be higher, they become economically viable for multiterminal environments when the user base grows large. These products usually are spreadsheets only.

CHECKLIST FOR EVALUATING SPREADSHEET PACKAGES

Figure 11–3 is a helpful checklist for examining the key factors in the evaluation of spreadsheet packages, or the spreadsheet portion of larger MSS packages.

FIGURE 11–3
Evaluating Spreadsheet Packages

No.	Item	Yes	No	N/A	Comments
			Responses		
	User interface				
1.	Is the package easy to use compared to others on the market?	___	___	___	
2.	Is the complexity of commands within the ergonomic limits of the expected users?	___	___	___	
3.	Do the prompts provided by the package lead to predictable results?	___	___	___	

FIGURE 11–3 *(continued)*

No.	Item	Yes	No	N/A	Comments
4.	Does the prompt simply give the user what is expected when it is followed?	___	___	___	
5.	Is the display easy to read?	___	___	___	
6.	Is the information on the display not overly cluttered or complex?	___	___	___	
7.	If the package contains graphics, can the user readily create the graphics that are desired?	___	___	___	
8.	Are the graphics clear and understandable?	___	___	___	
	Technical features				
9.	Are the desired functions built in, including:				
	a. internal rate of return?	___	___	___	
	b. net present value?	___	___	___	
	c. other desired financial functions?	___	___	___	
	d. desired statistical functions?	___	___	___	
	e. desired mathematical functions?	___	___	___	
	f. desired logical functions?	___	___	___	
10.	Is the spreadsheet the size desired, such as:				
	a. matrix of 53 by 256 cells?	___	___	___	
	b. matrix of 1,000 by 1,000 cells?	___	___	___	
	c. other desired size?	___	___	___	
11.	Does the size of the matrix readily fit on the microcomputer being used?	___	___	___	
12.	Can spreadsheets be combined to produce:				
	a. consolidated reports?	___	___	___	
	b. variance reports?	___	___	___	
	c. other desired reports?	___	___	___	
13.	Do the spreadsheets work as fast as required?	___	___	___	
14.	Has the speed of computing the spreadsheet been tested against typical end results?	___	___	___	
	Compatibility				
15.	Are the files produced compatible with:				
	a. the central database?	___	___	___	
	b. existing micro files?	___	___	___	
16.	If there is not complete compatibility, which is likely, can the spreadsheet be used without a massive conversion effort?	___	___	___	

FIGURE 11–3 *(concluded)*

No.	Item	Yes	No	N/A	Comments
17.	Can files be exchanged with other programs?	——	——	——	
18.	Can files be moved between the micro and the mainframe?	——	——	——	
	User support				
19.	Is the documentation easy to read and understand?	——	——	——	
20.	Does the documentation describe the operation of the package adequately?	——	——	——	
21.	Are tutorials provided as:				
	a. help screens obtained through a function key?	——	——	——	
	b. printed tutorials to help in hands-on sessions?	——	——	——	
	c. specialized tutor programs?	——	——	——	
22.	Are tutorial disks provided as part of the software?	——	——	——	
23.	Does the software vendor provide a telephone hot line?	——	——	——	
24.	Is the quality of the help provided considered adequate?	——	——	——	

Chapter Twelve

Some Final Thoughts

Where is all this going to lead? Is it just a matter of time until everyone will be able to generate information systems? In many kindergarten and first-grade classes in the United States, children are learning how to use computers. Many have them in their homes. Soon, if it has not already happened, every U.S. business of any measurable size will not be able to operate without a computer. Basic business information and decision support systems will be a necessity.

The only executives who will not be users of executive information systems by the end of this decade will be very old, very stubborn, and probably very rich.

In closing this book, let's examine some of the key considerations and issues relevant to our topic.

SECURITY CONSIDERATIONS

At the top of the list is security. This needs to be addressed at the front end. It may not be a consideration at all in your case, but you should decide whether it is or not only after giving the matter due consideration. You may want to go back and review the portion of Chapter Eight that deals with security.

The microcomputer is one of the most significant inventions of modern times. Plastic is the only other modern invention that can cover as many areas. Microcomputers enable us to do many things never before possible. It will probably take many more years to cover all areas where they have applicability. That's the good news. The bad news is that the opportunities for misuse and abuse, to say nothing of ignorance and stupidity, are rampant.

Think of the things that microcomputers have made possible!

You can make a fortune. You can lose a fortune.

You can steal a fortune.

You can run a company. You can ruin a company.

You can design complex semiconductor circuits. You can design and lay out buildings. You can do a building layout for a burglary.

You can protect your home from intrusion. You can have your microcomputer call the police if someone intrudes illegally.

You can produce wonderful animated pictures for children.

You can control a huge "scoreboard" or video screen.

You can read other people's mail.

You can scan/read and transmit/receive any paper document to/from anyplace in the world.

You can run factories.

You can compute and submit your income tax.

You can scan a human body and produce video images highlighting diseased areas.

You can maintain your client list whether you have two or two million customers.

You can play a game that simulates the Civil War.

Your child can learn his/her ABCs.

You can have on-line access to the recipe for making PCP.

You can write a book like this one.

EIS FOR USE BY TOP EXECUTIVES

A recent trade publication article stated that about 70 percent of the CEOs in corporate America have some degree of computer literacy. The degree of literacy was not discussed, but most MIS professionals would agree that it is becoming common for top executives to have microcomputers on their desks. This will, increase, no doubt, and when the current generation passes on and the next generation is in control, the computer literacy rate will approach 100 percent.

What about now? Here are a few dos, don'ts, and other considerations.

Top executives should be literate in and have access to:

• Hot screen with limited number of menus or icon-driven capabilities.

• Electronic mail.

• Electronic bulletin boards.

• External services (e.g., Prodigy, Dow Jones).

• Corporate financial databases containing the latest information.

When the executive has mastered the above, only then should you consider putting spreadsheet and word processing software on the machine. Put the identical software on the executive suite secretaries' machines. They may well have other packages, but the executive's secretary is his or her first-line computer consultant. An IC or MIS consultant should be readily available to provide assistance to the executive and relevant secretaries.

Do not make unedited operational data available to the executive. To do so would, at some point, result in the executive jumping on an operations manager, which in turn will trigger a whole chain of events. These events will generate recriminations that will be totally disruptive, time-consuming, and unconstructive. A word to the wise should be sufficient.

Do not build a grandiose custom-made executive information system for a particular executive, who:

1. Will be gone before it is finished.
2. Will not use it.
3. Will misuse it.
4. Will need six analysts to feed, maintain, and modify it.
5. Will end up hating computers.
6. Will end up hating you.
7. Will have a secretary who will hate you in all cases.
8. Will find out how much it costs, and you will be gone.

At best only two of the above items will occur. At worst seven out of eight will happen.

COMPUTER HARDWARE AND NETWORK CONSIDERATIONS

The goal of the provider should be to make the environment as transparent as possible to both end-users and user-developers of support systems.

The communications system should keep track of and handle all protocol and routing considerations. Every element should have a simple and unique ID. The worldwide telephone system is a good example of this. Imagine the confusion that would exist if you had to be knowledgeable about the local exchange, central office, satellite transponder, and more before you could make a phone call. Your organization may not yet be at this point. If the communications network plays a role in your information or support system, *make no assumptions*. Check it out in advance.

Components of computer systems provided by a single vendor are often incompatible. Mainframe or microcomputers provided by different vendors are usually incompatible. Some systems are advertised as compatible, but they may not be. There are more systems in the world today that are *almost* compatible than actually *are* compatible.

The PC world has fared much better than other areas, because the majority of systems are built around the same Intel chip design. But even in the PC world, the Apple MacIntosh is a "different breed of cat," as are Commodore, TRW, and a host of lesser-known systems. The software for various incompatible PC systems is also incompatible in most cases.

SOFTWARE TOOLS

A vast array of excellent software tools is available for executive information and decision support systems developers. There are packages available for almost every kind of business, discipline, application, degree of complexity, degree of comprehensiveness, and degree of ease of use. Finding the best software available for a particular job can be very difficult. Most end-users learn one or several of the well-known general-purpose packages, such as WordPerfect, Lotus, and Ventura. It gets a little more complicated when you add a database package (often DBASE 2) to your repertoire. Shortly, you have learned more than you can remember, and by the time you add FOCUS or some other reporting-system package to your skill set, your brain is bulging and you have forgotten all but what you have used in the last two weeks.

If you can match a single software package to your problem and use it on a regular basis, you can become an expert in the use of that package. Equally important, the skill can be maintained. There are few, if any, software packages that are so easy to use that you can retain the skill indefinitely even if you do not use it. It continues to be a case of use it or lose it.

After you have run through the top 100 most popular software packages, it can get very difficult and cumbersome to locate the best, or even a very good, software package for a specific job. Once you get into the "trivial many" searching for a package, the search may be anything but trivial. In many cases, even after selecting a candidate package, a considerable amount of effort must be expended to determine if there is a good package/job fit.

Even if you are developing your own system, consider this: For *your* particular application is DBASE 2 better than DBASE 3, 4, 5, 6, or 99? Is RBASE better than ABASE, BBASE, or ZBASE? Is ASKSAM better than ASKJOE, BOB, OR SALLY? And so on. Pretty soon it starts to sound like the Abbott and Costello routine, "Who's on First?"

The best place to start a random search is probably the software trade publications. They continually have software write-ups and comparison charts that are very good. Computer stores—not Walmart!—can frequently help. Public and corporation technical libraries are also a good source.

When you have gone through these choices, "Let your fingers do the walking." Before you start, be sure you have a comfortable chair and a full cup of coffee, because you may be busy for a while. In some cases, a bedroll will also be needed.

DATABASE CONSIDERATIONS

The hub of the wheel for information and support systems is the databases that serve as the source of raw information used by the system. These databases may come from a variety of sources; the most common are I/S production databases, a user's own databases, databases owned by another user/developer, and commercially available databases. Each of these sources is discussed in some detail below.

I/S Production Databases

This is the most common source of data for user/developers in companies with I/S departments and host computers. Many key corporate production databases are developed by the I/S department and maintained by ongoing operation of the relevant production system. Examples are payroll, general ledger, payables, receivables, purchasing, order entry, and shipping.

Executive information and decision support systems normally do not access production databases directly. Summarized and tailored extracts are usually provided by the I/S department for the end-user population. See your I/S department regarding the use of this data.

User's Own Databases

The advice here is, "Don't bite off more than you can chew, or you will choke." The purpose is not to discourage the design, use, or accessing of end-user designed and maintained databases. There are disk drives, even for microcomputers, that hold hundreds of millions of bytes. There are numerous excellent software packages with great capabilities that are easy to use. Everything needed to do a wonderful database job exists at all levels of computing. But no matter who does it or where it is done, if proper controls and security procedures are not exercised, you have a potential disaster just looking for a place to happen.

One of the best techniques for microcomputer users attached to hosts is to use the host as a repository for your key PC databases. You immediately have host back-up, control, and security procedures available. This also provides a convenient way to allow other authorized users to gain access to the database without them getting in your "playpen."

Databases Owned by Another User/Developer

The comments in the previous paragraph apply here. Before becoming dependent on another user's database, ask yourself these questions:

Are the controls and security procedures adequate?

Do I know the exact content of the files?

How are they maintained?

What is the frequency?

Do adequate back-up procedures exist?

What happens if the owner leaves the company?

Commercially Available Databases

"There's gold in them thar hills!" Fortunes are being made selling data. We have seen just the tip of the iceberg. Hardly a day goes by that some new "information" cannot be obtained by computer. Customer lists, prospect lists, mailing lists, and every conceivable list containing names, addresses, and phone numbers are available. Dow Jones, Computer Source, and Prodigy already contain everything from games and shopping information to stock market results and airline fares and reservation data.

At some point with your microcomputer, you will most likely be able to obtain every item of public information known to humanity, and a good bit that is not public. You will probably be able to get the recipe for manufacturing your own nuclear bomb or make a reservation to the moon. Only carefully guarded business and personal data will escape the persons who pilfer and purvey information for profit.

ROLE OF STANDARDS

In companies that contain multiple organizations and locations, a degree of standardization is required to facilitate any information or support system that hopes to utilize data from different systems, databases, or locations. Utilization of different codes and naming conventions can make it very difficult, even impossible, for a developer to utilize data from multiple entities.

Distributed systems often have this drawback. A particular system may do an excellent job of serving the area for which it was designed. However, if it was done locally with no plans for higher-level access and use, great difficulties may arise when some future executive information system attempts to utilize data from this system. Frequently, extra effort results, and mapping of formats and codes from one form to another is required. Hardware, software, and telecommunications standards (or lack thereof) can also be a factor any time there is a need to transmit or utilize data between entities. The opportunities for incompatibilities are endless. Something as simple as printing a report that was generated by someone else designed for use with a printer different from the one you are using can be a time-consuming and frustrating experience.

The purpose here is not to write a treatise on standards and incompatibilities. The intent is to give a forewarning so potential problems can be addressed in advance. In mathematics, quantities equal to the same quantity are equal to each other. In information technology, this may not be true.

ROLE OF MIS OR THE I/S ORGANIZATION

The I/S organization should be the greatest ally of user-developers of information support systems. Since it typically owns and operates the production or basic systems of an organization, it is in the best position to provide data and knowledge regarding those systems. As pointed out earlier in this chapter, the database is the hub of the wheel. Most major corporate databases are the result of I/S systems. When any user of information or support systems needs to utilize data from I/S databases, the I/S department is usually the source.

For databases having widespread user interest, data extracts may be provided by the I/S department. Sensitive data may be filtered out or custom extracts may be run that will pull only the data needed by the requestor.

In many companies, the I/S department provides consulting assistance to users seeking to develop information or support systems. It can be an invaluable source and may be able to save these developers a lot of time and effort. Frequently, the I/S organization can provide information on standards, hardware and software tools, communications, equipment, and protocols that may apply to a particular situation or developer.

In many cases, the more advanced I/S organizations have set up end-user repositories of data for use by the user-developers. The MIS group responsible for financial systems, for instance, will provide financial information for departmental users in Lotus spreadsheet format. This can be downloaded to the PC by the authorized user for that department for manipulation, reporting, or other PC analysis.

THE END

Maybe our next book will be titled *Using Computers for Fun and Profit.* On the other hand, maybe we should call it *Microcomputers—The Curse of the Damned!*

If you have been in the computing field for very many years, you have seen both sides of the coin. The 1980s saw microcomputers proliferate in U.S. companies. Information and decision support systems developed by end-users have become commonplace. The 1990s will see a continuation of this, and the computers will become more comprehensive and sophisticated. The 1990s also will see the microcomputer expanding to become commonplace in homes across the continent.

Do not be afraid to jump into the microcomputer waters. Proceed at a reasonable pace, and do not believe all the hype. Proper use of microcomputers can make the rest of 1990s even more productive, fun, and interesting for both companies and individuals.

Index

Academic American Encyclopedia, 306
Access, 182
  and availability, 53–54
  to corporate data, 206–7
  modes of, 29
  requirements, 139–44
Action, 20–22
Active database, 131
Ad hoc models, 161–62
Administration, and database, 144–46
Administrative services, of information center, 67
ALGOL, 45
Allocations, 118
American Psychological Association, 310
Analyses, 4, 8, 28, 29, 61–64, 66, 82, 95–96, 125, 172, 178, 255, 271
Analysis graphics, 255
Application
  and application prototyping, 4, 44, 231–45
  of expert system, 251–54
  and purchase applications, 242
  selection and development, 67
Application-generation programs, 238
Application models
  delivery of, 240–41
  and GDSS design, 83–84
Application prototyping, 4, 44, 231–45
Aquatic Sciences and Fisheries, 310
Architecture, 110–12
  design, 94
  and document image processing, 287–90
  for MSS, 32–33
Arthur Andersen & Company, 15
Artificial intelligence (AI), 4, 19, 25, 245–54
Assessment, and self-assessment checklist, 221–22
Assumptions, and DSS, 122–23
Atlantic Richfield Company (ARCO), 303–4
Attitudes, and culture, 11–14
Audiographic teleconferencing, 296–97

Audio teleconferencing, 294–96
Audit, and audit control, 55, 217
Automatic documentation, 238
Automation, 79–80
Availability
  and accessibility, 53–54
  of corporate information and shared data, 37–39
  of systems, 42–43

Backup, 151–52, 227–28
Backward iteration, 178
BASIC, 237, 242
Believing, 123
Benchmarks, and product performance benchmarks, 363–67
BiblioFile, 309
Bland data, 103
Boeing Company, 304–5
Bold, 260
Books in Print, 309
Brainstorming, 82
Briefing rooms, 68–73
Budgeting systems, 118
Business application models, delivery of, 240–41
Business graphics, 73, 254–58
By-product approach, 101, 103

CAD/CAM, 73
Calculation rules, 164
Capabilities, 100
Carnegie-Mellon University, 85
Carnegie Tech, 17
Causality, 179
CD/Corporate, 308
CD/CorpTech, 308
CD ROM, 4, 230, 306–12
Cell-based spreadsheet packages, 377, 379–82
Center for Information Systems Research (CISR), 90, 108

Central Corporation, 90
Centralized computing, 187–89
Centrex, 295
Challenging, 123
Charts, and plots, 269–70
Checklist for evaluating spreadsheet packages, 384–86
Chrysler Corporation, 20
COBOL, 18, 25, 45, 232, 237, 240, 242, 243
College on Information Systems, 10
Color graphics, 118
Communicating, 123
Communication graphics, 73–74
Communications, 66
    and GDSS design, 83–84
    and network compatibility, 41–42
    and telecommunications groups, 78
    with information services, 55
Compact Disclosure, 308
Comparative information processing, 277
Comparisons, 122
Complex models, 122
Compressed video, 297
CompuServe, 75
Computations, 122
Computer-assisted retrieval, 284
Computer conferencing, 298–99
Computer graphics, and GDSS design, 86–87
Computer modeling, 4, 159–79
    and data for model, 172–74
    and debugging and documenting the model, 175–78
    and initiating model development, 162–64
    and model development, 170–72
    and model development time, 167–70
    and model investigation, 178–79
    and study reports, 174–75
    types of, 161–62
    use of, 159–61
    and viewpoint modeling, 164–67
Computer resource management, 180–89, 198
Computers, and briefing rooms, 70–71
Computerworld, 77, 90
Comshare, 115, 117
Conferencing technology, 84–86
Confidentiality, 16, 209
Consolidations, 118, 165
Consulting, 52–53, 67, 79, 80
Contract, terms of, 324–25

Control, 3, 29, 55, 217
    and data protection, 321
    of information, 202–3, 204
    and interactive control, 74
    and process control groups, 78–79
    of staff, 53–54
    and teleconferencing, 300
Control graphics, 255
Controllable variables, 163
Corporate culture, and individual attitudes, 11–14
Corporate data, 205–7
Corporate functional staff groups, 63
Corporate information, availability of, 37–39
Corporate library, 79
Corporate records, 79, 80
Corporate videotex, and teleconferencing, 4, 292–306
Costs, 16
    and cost-effective operation, 39–40
    and information, 203–4
    justification of, 360–62
    and software, 323
Cost-to-correct curve, 47
Crandall, Richard L., 115, 117
Critical success factors (CSF), 3, 60, 62, 89, 99, 100, 101, 102, 105–12
    approach, 105–8
    and data access, 110–12
    tracking, 108–9
Cullinet, 192
Culture, and attitudes, 11–14

Data
    access, 110–12, 139–44
    acquisition, 101–8
    architecture, 94, 110–12
    availability of, 37–39
    backup, 227–28
    controls and protection, 321
    corporate and noncorporate, 205–7
    integrity, 55, 209–11
    management. *See* Data management
    for model, 172–74
    ownership of, 14, 197–211, 227
    processing trends, 46
    public and private, 208–9
    resources management, 67
    security of, 146–52, 153–55, 225–27
    sharing, 197–201, 211–14

Data—*Cont.*
  structure, 164
  and subject perspective, 134–37
  usage standards, 214–16
  user responsibility for data protection, 226
  validation, 209–11
  and volume of requests, 133–34
  warehouse, 194–95
Database, 131, 391–92
  administration, 144–46
  and end users, 144
  and GDSS design, 83–84
  of information, 74
  management system, 95
  and relational database systems, 189–97, 196–97
  and staging database, 135–36
  transfer to CD ROM, 310, 311
DATACOM, 192
Data encryption standard (DES), 150
Data engine, 194
Data extractor, 194
Data file manipulation, 166
Data interchange format (DIF), 380
Data management, 4, 128–58
  alternatives, 130–32
  and data access requirements, 139–44
  and database administration, 144–46
  and data security, 146–52, 153–55
  and disaster preparedness and recovery, 152–58
  for DSS and EIS, 128–30
  issues, 128–58
  principles and practices of, 37–38, 130–32
  responsibilities and roles in, 137–39
  and subject perspective, 134–37
  trends, 189–97
  and volume of data requests, 133–34
Data Query, 192
Data systems analysis, 125
DB Dictionary system, 192
Debugging of model, 160
Decision making, 119
  graphics, 74
  improvement of, 54
  process, 91
Decisions
  environment of, 81–82
  structured and unstructured, 17–20
  structuring packages, 377
  support graphics, 255
  types of, 19–20

Decision support systems (DSS), 2, 3–4, 6, 7, 24, 27, 28, 29, 54, 61, 115–27, 128–30
  building blocks for, 123–24
  comparisons of, 26–31
  data management for, 128–30
  integrated view of, 117–20
  level of support provided by, 120–22
  and organizing for MSS, 77–80
  primary aspects of, 29
  review of activities, 125–27
  role of assumptions in, 122–23
  technical uses of, 125
  when to use, 115–17
Delivery, of business application models, 240–41
Delivery systems, and organizations, 59–88
Delivery tools, 194
DeLong, David W., 14
Delphi technique, 82
Departmental, distributive-system concept, 183–84, 187–89
Departmental computers, 273
Departmental control of staff, 53–54
Departmental processor, 35–36, 37, 39, 40, 42, 43, 52, 53, 54, 55, 57, 183–84, 187–89
Dependent variables, 163
DeSanctis, Geraldine, 82
Desirable measures, 157–58
Development
  and heuristic development, 244
  management for, 50–57
  of model, 160, 162–64, 167–72
  for MSS, 44–47
  and research and development, 358–60
Dialog Information Service, 75
Differentiation, 16
Direct access trunk lines (DATL), 112
Direct read-after-write (DRAW), 286
Disaster, preparedness and recovery, 152–58, 224–29
Discounted cash flow (DCF), 214
Discovery, and exploration, 93
DISOSS, 287
Dissertation Abstracts on Disks, 309
Distributed data processing (DDP), 275
Distribution models, 125
Distributive-system concept, 183–84, 187–89
Diversity, 13

Documentation
  automatic, 238
  of model, 160
  quality of, 323–24
Document image processing, and optical disks,
  4, 283–92
Domain, 249
Dow Jones News Retrieval, 75
Du Pont Corporation, 72
Dynamic access, 182
Dynamic video graphics, 259

Ease, 29
Economic modeling and forecasting, 25
EDP Analyzer, 87
Effectiveness, 88
Efficiency, 87, 367
Electronic blackboard, 297
Electronic data processing (EDP), 63
Electronic mail, 296–97
Enablers, 64
Encryption, 150
End-user computing (EUC), 24, 28, 60–64
  and business graphics, 257
  consulting, 67
  and database, 144
  movement toward, 60–64
Enhanced Color Display, 262
Enhanced Graphics Adapter, 262
Enhancement of support capabilities, 10–11
Entrepreneurial graphics, 255
Environment
  defining, 160
  of group decisions, 81–82
Equipment requirements, 321
Erasure, 151
ERIC, 309
Estimation of model development time, 169
Evaluation
  checklists and MSS, 319–43
  of MSS, 5
  of software packages, 320–43
  of spreadsheet packages, 384–86
Evaluation control document (ECD), 370–76
Everyone's Support Systems, 2
Evolutionary systems, 242
Executive action, implications for, 20–22
Executive decision-making process, 91
Executive expectations, molding of, 94
Executive information briefing rooms, 68–73

Executive Information Service, 75
Executive information support systems, 24
Executive information systems (EIS), 3, 6, 7,
  19, 24, 27, 28, 60, 61, 63–64, 89–114,
  128–30, 388–389
  comparisons of, 26–31
  components of, 95–96
  and data access challenges, 110–12
  data management for, 128–58
  implementation of, 96–101, 102
  implications for executive action, 20–22
  and individual needs, 90–92
  and information requirements and data ac-
    quisition, 101–8
  and micro-to-mainframe connections, 112–14
  organizational impact of, 92–94
  primary aspects of, 29–30
  and top executives, 388–89
Executive support, 100–101
Executive support systems (ESS), 24, 27, 90
Expandability, 322
Expectations, molding of, 94
Expert, 250
Expert systems, 4, 25, 245–54
Exploring, 93, 123
Extended features, 75
External files, 137–39
Externalizing, 123
Extract databases, 25
Extract files, 131

Face-to-face, 82
Facilitator, 83–84
Facsimile, 296
Feigenbaum, Edward, 248
Fifth-generation languages, 244
Files
  conversion, 291–92
  internal and external, 137–39
  management, 95
Finance
  analysis, 66
  information, 308–9
  modeling packages, 377
  planning, 125
Fire protection, 150, 161–62
FITS, 192
Flexibility, 29, 72
Flexible systems, 113
FOCUS, 16, 121, 192

Ford, Henry, 94
Forecasting, 25, 118, 164, 173
Foreign file interfaces (FFI), 112, 173–74
FORTRAN, 45, 237, 242
Fourth-generation languages, 4, 25, 28, 44, 230, 231, 242–45
Freeze-frame video, 297
Frequency of information use, 141
Full-motion video, 298
Functional models, 241–42
Future management issues, 180–229
Future technology issues, 230–312

Gallupe, Brent, 82
Gantt charts, 256
Gatekeepers, 34
Generality, 321–22
Geodata systems analysis, 125
Gleason, David, 15
Goals
    of executive information briefing rooms, 69–70
    and goal seeking, 4, 118, 178
Golden Gates, 192
Graphics, 4, 29, 95, 96, 118
    advanced use of, 254–71
    and business graphics, 73–74, 254–58
    and GDSS design, 86–87
    and hard-copy graphics, 68, 76–77
    optional graphics systems features, 262–71
    and plots and charts, 269–70
    and statistical analysis, 271
    systems, 262–71
    and terminal graphics, 68, 73–76
Grolier Electronic Encyclopedia, 309
Grolier Electronic Publishing, 306, 307
Group decision environment, 81–82
Group decision support systems (GDSS), 3, 59, 80–87
    design of, 83–84
    environment types, 81–82
    example, 84
    implementing, 80–87
    optimum balance, 87–88
    process types, 72
    technology, 84–87
Groups
    and corporate functional staff groups, 63
    implementing GDSS, 80–87
    and organization for MSS, 78–80

Growth, and planning, 33–35
Gulden, Gary K., 13, 26

Hard-copy graphic production, 68, 76–77
Hard measures, 106
Hardware, and networking, 389–90
Harvard Business Review, 99
Harvard University, 91, 104
Heuristic, and heuristic development, 244, 250
Hierarchy of consolidation, 165, 166, 167
High-quality systems, and software, 36–37
Holography, 298
Hybrid strategies, 241

IBM, 24, 99, 101, 123, 181, 182, 183, 262, 287
IDEAL, 192
Ideas, open marketing of, 57
IDMS, 192
Image processing, and optical disks, 283–92
Implementation, of EIS, 96–101, 102
Implications for executive action, 20–22
Important records, 150
Index design, 290–91
Index Group, Inc., 26
Index Systems, 13
Indicators, 107–8
Individual attitudes, and corporate culture, 11–14
Information
    availability of, 37–39
    briefing rooms, 68–73
    control of, 202–3, 204
    and costs, 203–4
    database, 74
    delivery systems and organization, 59–88
    display for executives, 68–77
    and financial information, 308–9
    ownerships of, 201–2
    processing, 277
    reporting of, 66
    requirements and data acquisition, 101–8
    resources, 39–40, 198
    retrieval, 121
    systems, 24, 393
    types of, 140
Information Center (IC), and support for MSS, 64–68, 79, 80
Information resource management (IRM), 198
Information Services, 7, 55
Information systems (I/S), 24, 393

Information technology (IT), 1
Infotech, 122
Innovation, 16
Inquiry and analysis functions, 66, 95–96
Installation, of briefing room, 72
Installation phase, of EIS, 97
Institute of Management Science, 10
Integrated data dictionaries, 238
Integrated MSS packages, 382–84
Integrated systems, 113
Integration, 94, 277–79
Integrity
  and data, 55, 209–11
  and report, 214
Intelligent assistant, 250
Interactive control, 74
Interactive screen-generation programs, 238
Interactive systems, 113
Interactive workstations, 238
Interlocking support, 26
Internal files, 137–39
Intersystem data sharing, 212–14
Interview, 106–7
Intrasystem data sharing, 212
Investigation of model, 160, 178–79
ISPS, 192

J.C. Penney Company, 305–6
Jokiel, Richard A., 44

Keen, Peter G. W., 10, 116, 122
Key external factors (KEF), 3, 62, 89,
  109–10
Key indicator approach, 101, 104–5
Key success factors (KSF), 108
Kiester, Sara, 85–86
KISS, 172
Knowledge, 250
Knowledge base, 250
Knowledge engineering, 250
Knowledge representation, 250
KnowledgeSet Corporation, 307
Knowledge systems, 250

Legal considerations, 228–29
Levinson, Eliot, 97
Library, 79
Life cycle, for MSS. See System development
  life cycle (SDLC)
Life Sciences Collection, 310

Local area network (LAN), 4, 41–42, 129,
  272–83, 288, 289
Local data management, 131
Location hierarchy, 166
Location models, 125
Lockheed, 75
Logic, 175–76
Lowest common denominator (LCD), 168,
  171

McGraw-Hill CD ROM Science and Technical
  Reference Set, 310
Machiavelli, Niccolò, 11
Magnetic media storage, 150–51
Mainframe, 35–36, 37, 39, 40, 42, 43, 51,
  52–53, 54, 55, 56, 57, 112–14, 147–50,
  161, 181–83, 384
Mainstream integration, 94
Management
  baseline, 7
  of data resources, 67
  and MSS. See Management support systems
    (MSS)
  relations and distinctions in, 218–19
  reporting applications, 117
  special and future issues, 4, 180–229
  study models, 122
Management control systems (MCS), 24, 27,
  28
Management information systems (MIS), 24,
  27, 393
Management science/operations research systems (MS/OR), 24, 160
Management support systems (MSS), 2, 3, 4,
  5, 6, 23–58, 313–76
  benefits of, 57–58
  comparison of, 26–31
  and ECD, 370–76
  and evaluation checklists, 319–20, 325–43
  evaluation and selection of, 313–76
  information center support for, 64–68
  and management for development, 50–57
  and microcomputer MSS software, 377–86
  need for, 7–11
  and objectives and needs, 314–17
  organizing for, 77–80
  and product performance benchmarks,
    363–67
  and RFP, 313, 343–50
  and selection committee, 317–19

Management support systems (MSS)—*Cont.*
  and selection and test of primary product, 368–89
  and software package evaluation, 320–43
  spectrum of, 23–58
  strategic value of, 14–17
  system development for, 44–47
  and technology, 32–44
  terms used for, 23–25
  and vendor presentations, 350–60
Mandatory measures, 157
Marketing of ideas, 57
Market models, 125
Market segment, 16
Massachusetts Institute of Technology (MIT), 28, 90, 108
Mead Data Central, 75
Media, and teleconferencing, 294
Medicine, and science, 310
Medline, 310
Meilach, Dona, 86
Memory aids, 66
Messaging technology, 84–86
Metrics approach, and software package comparison, 337–43
Microcomputers
  computing, 161
  and control of information, 204
  and microcomputer-to-mainframe connections, 112–14, 147–50, 273
  MSS software, 377–86
  networking and LAN, 272–83
  peer networks, 273
Microfilm, 284
Mission statement, 223
Mode, and EUC, 60
Modeling, 4, 25, 29, 118, 125, 159–79
  and data for model, 172–74
  and debugging and documenting the model, 175–78
  and delivery of business application models, 240–41
  and functional models, 241–42
  and GDSS design, 83–84
  and initiating model development, 162–64
  for management study, 122
  and model-based analysis, 29
  and model-based management support software on microcomputers, 377–86
  and model development, 170–72

Modeling—*Cont.*
  and model development time, 167–70
  and model investigation, 178–79
  and multidimensional modeling, 168, 179
  and study reports, 174–75
  support, 95
  types of, 161–62
  use of, 159–61
  and viewpoint modeling, 164–67
Modes of access, 29
Modes of teleconferencing, 294–99
Modifiability, 322
Monitoring, 8, 27, 66, 67
Montgomery Ward, 20
Morton, N. S. Scott, 24, 116
Multidimensional modeling, 168, 179
Multiple file management, 95
Multiple hierarchies, 167

National Computer Graphics Conference, 87
National Fire Protection Association (NFPA), 150
Necessary measures, 157
Needs, and MSS, 314–17
Networking, 4, 214, 272–83, 288, 289
  and communications, 41–42
  and hardware, 389–90
NewsNet, 75
Nexis and Lexis, 75
NOMAD, 92
Nominal face-to-face, 82
Noncorporate data, 205–7
Nonessential records, 150
Nonprocedural query, 238
Nonprocedural report writers, 238
Null approach, 101, 104

Objectives
  of executive information briefing rooms, 69
  of integration, 277–79
  and MSS, 314–17
Office automation systems (OAS), 24, 79–80
Old data, 103
One Source, 308
On-line active database, 131
On-line extract files, 131
Open marketing of ideas, 57
Operational decisions, 19–20
Operational phase, 97
Operational policies, 224–25

Operational support systems (OSS), 24, 27
Operations, 3
    cost-effective, 39–40
    groups, 78
    and information center, 67
Operations research (OR), 24, 116, 160
Optext, 309
Optical disks, and document image processing, 4, 283–92
Organization
    and information delivery systems, 59–88
    for MSS, 77–80
Organizational phase, 97
Overlapping support, 26
Ownership of data, 14, 197–211, 227
Owning, 123

Paper strategy, 192
PASCAL, 45
Pattern recognition, 121–22
PBX, 295
PC Plus, 309
PCs, 35–36, 37, 39, 40, 42, 43, 52, 53, 54, 55, 57, 185–86, 272–83
Peak-period support, 72
Peer networks, 273
People, and EUC, 60
Performance, and briefing rooms, 71–72
Performance benchmarks, 363–67
Personal analysis, 29, 61–64
Personal support staff, 63
Personnel productivity, 54
PERT charts, 256
Pilot Corporation, 15
Pilot project, 99–100
Planning, 8, 66, 125
    and briefing room, 72
    and growth, 33–35
    and teleconferencing, 300
Playback graphics, 259, 260
Plots, and charts, 269–70
Policy
    and data ownership, 203, 207
    and data and software backup, 228
    and operational policies, 224–25
    and review of data usage, 216
    and security measures for data ownership, 227
    and standards of data usage, 215
    and user responsibility for data protection, 226

Portfolio management systems, 125
Prerecorded playback graphics, 259, 260
Presentation graphics, 255, 258–62
Presentations, and vendor presentations, 350–60
Prespecification, and prototyping, 233–39
Price, and software, 323
Prince, The, 11
Priorities, realignment of, 93–94
Priority, and product priority grid, 369
Privacy legislation, 229
Private data, 208–9
Problem diversity, 13
Problem solving, and teleconferencing, 300–301
Procedures function, 222, 223
Process control groups, 78–79
Processing rates, 323
Product hierarchy, 166
Production models, 162
Productivity, of personnel, 54
Product performance benchmarks, 363–67
Product priority grid, 369
Product support, 67
Professional support systems, 24
Profile, and modeling, 163
Profitability, 272–73
Profit Oriented System Planning Program, 1
Pro forma consolidations with allocations, 118
Programming language, 321
Projection, 122
Proposal, and RFP, 313, 343–50
Prototyping, 44, 47–50
    and application prototyping, 4, 44, 231–45
    approaches to, 241–42
    fourth-generation languages in, 242–45
    and prespecification, 233–39
    requirements definition by, 235
PsycLIT, 310
Public data, 208–9
Purchase applications, 242

Quality assurance (QA), 4, 216–24
Quality control, 217
Quality management, 218–19
Quality of documentation, 323–24
Query form, 353

RAMIS, 192
Rand Corporation, 97
Real Decisions Corporation, 192

Realignment of priorities, 93–94
Records, 79, 80, 150, 153–55
Records management, 150, 153–55
Recovery, 152–58, 224–29
Reference query form, 353
References
  material, 309–10
  and presentations, 351–55
  and reference query form, 353
Relational database systems, 189–97, 238
Reports and reporting
  applications, 117
  graphics, 255
  information, 66
  integrity, 214
  and report-writing functions, 95, 96
  specifications, 164
  and study reports, 174–75
Report-writing functions, 95, 96
Request for proposal (RFP), 313, 343–50
Research and development, 358–60
Resource management, 180–89, 198
Responsibility
  and data management, 137–39
  of user for data protection, 226
Retrieval, 66, 121, 284
Reuss, Robert, 90
Reviewing, 67, 216
Rickeman, Norman F., 15
Risk analysis, 4, 178
Rockart, John F., 14, 20, 24, 28, 58, 62, 108
Roles, and data management, 137–39

Sample screens, 241
SAS, 192
Scheduling, 66
Science and medicine, 310
Search, 66
Sears, 20
Security, 55, 111, 387–88
  and briefing rooms, 71
  of data, 146–52, 153–55, 225–27
  and data ownership, 227
  and disaster recovery requirements, 224–29
  and security control, 217
  and software, 148–49, 153–55
Selection
  of MSS, 5, 317–19
  of primary product, 368–69
  and selection committee, 317–19

Self-assessment checklist, 221–22
Sensitivity analysis, 4
Series forecasting, 118
Seventh International Conference on Decision
    Support Systems, 10
Sharing of data, 37–39, 197–201, 211–14
Simon, Herbert, 17
Simplicity, 112
Sloan School of Management, 15
Slow-scan video, 297
Soft measures, 106
Software, 5, 390–91
  backup, 227–28
  and high-quality systems, 36–37
  and microcomputer MSS software, 377–86
  package evaluation, 320–43
  and software security, 148–49, 153–55
Source, The, 75
Special management issues, 180–229
Special technology issues, 230–312
Spreadsheet packages, 377, 379–82
Spreadsheet reporting, 175
Stability of information, 140
Staff, 63
  and briefing rooms, 71
  departmental control of, 53–54
Staging database, 135–36
Stand-alone personal computers, 185–86
Standard & Poor's Compustat, 110
Standards, 55
  role of, 392–93
  and procedures function, 222, 223
  of data usage, 214–16
Stanford University, 248
Static video graphics, 259
Stations and users, 43–44
Statistical analysis, 271
Statistical methods, and briefing rooms, 70
Status access, 27, 29, 61–62
Step-function what if, 178
Storage, and magnetic media, 150–51
Strategic decisions, 19, 20, 119
Strategic information systems, 14
Strategic planning, and growth, 33–35
Strategic systems, 15
Strategy
  and hybrid strategies, 241
  and MSS, 14–17
Structured decisions, 17–20
Structured query language (SQL), 192

Structured resolution models, 162
Study reports, 174–75
Subject perspective, 134–37
Support, 2–3, 6–22
  interlocking and overlapping, 26
  and practical consultation, 52–53
  staff, 63
System development, for MSS, 32, 44–50
System development life cycle (SDLC), 32,
  44, 45, 46–50, 233–39
  comparison of prototyping and prespecifica-
    tion, 233–39
  comparison of traditional and prototyping,
    47–50
System modeling, 4, 159–79
  and data for model, 172–74
  and debugging and documenting the model,
    175–78
  and initiating model development, 162–64
  issues, 159–79
  and model development, 170–72
  and model development time, 167–70
  and model investigation, 178–79
  and study reports, 174–75
  types of, 161–62
  use of, 159–61
  and viewpoint modeling, 164–67
Systems
  availability of, 42–43
  characteristics of, 193–94
  high-quality, 36–37

Tabulation, 29
Tactical decisions, 19, 20
Technical analysis, 66
Technical assistance, 67
Technical exchange, 300–301
Technology
  and data access, 112
  and EUC, 61
  and GDSS, 84–87
  new and old, 32–44
  special and future issues, 230–312
Telecommunications, 3, 78
Telecommunications groups, 78
Teleconferencing
  applications for, 299–301
  and corporate videotex, 4, 292–306
  impact of, 299
  and media, 294

Teleconferencing—Cont.
  modes of, 294–99
  rooms, 301–2
Telegraf, 192
Telephone tag, 85
Telewriting, 296
Terminal graphics, 68, 73–76
Testing, of primary product, 368–69
Test management function, 222, 223–24
Throwaway models, 162
Timeliness, 111–12
Timeliness of information, 140
Time-series forecasting, 118
Timing, 99
Total study approach, 101, 105
Trade-off, 316–17
Training
  efficient and effective, 51–52
  of end users, 67
  packages, 66
  and teleconferencing, 299–300
Treacy, Michael E., 58
Trends
  analysis, 8
  in data processing, 46

Ulrich's International Periodical Directory,
  309
Uncontrollable variables, 163
Understanding, 123
Unstructured decisions, 17–20
Useful records, 150
User
  control, 29
  orientation, 113
  responsibility, 226
  and station, 43–44

Validation, and data, 209–11
Validity, and GDSS, 87
Value-added elements, 35
Value analysis, 82
VanOpdorp, John, 15
Variables, and modeling, 163, 164–67
VAX, 192
Vendor
  presentations, 350–60
  relationships, 42–43
  support services form, 356
Vendor support services form, 356

Video, 297–98
   graphics, 259–60
   teleconferencing, 297–98
Videotex, 4, 292–306
Viewpoint modeling, 164–67, 175
VISICALC, 379, 380
Visioning, 215
Vital records, 150
Volume of information, 140

WANG, 192
WATS, 295

Weighted comparison, 341, 342
What if analysis, 4, 28, 178
What if modeling, 118, 164
Wilsondisc, 309–10
Windows, 382
Workflow management, 291–92
Workstations, 238, 285
Writing, 66, 95, 96
Wrong data, 103

Yourdon, Edward, 45
Your Marketing Consultant, 309

Also of interest to you from Business One Irwin . . .

MANAGING MICROCOMPUTER SECURITY
Chantico Publishing Company, Inc.
Dr. Robert S. Snoyer and Glenn A. Fischer, Editors. Co-published by
Chantico Publishing Co., Inc./Business One Irwin

Protect your company's systems from security threats! This essential reference offers strategies to increase security awareness among all workers. You'll understand how to identify and eliminate internal and external system vulnerabilities for hardware, software, databases, and communications systems with the book's real-world examples, helpful checklists, and a comprehensive reference of security products. (400 pages)
ISBN: 1-55623-875-4

CORPORATE INFORMATION SYSTEMS MANAGEMENT
The Issues Facing Senior Executives, Third Edition
James I. Cash, Jr., F. Warren McFarlan, and James L. McKenney

Updated for today's executive, this guide shows you how to use recent advances to identify and turn business opportunities into strategic advantages. The authors describe how you can implement these innovative organization, planning, and management control ideas to improve operation efficiency. You'll gain a clearer insight into the challenges and opportunities that are posed by the latest technological advances, ways to overcome the unique IS problems that multinational companies face, and much more. (301 pages)
ISBN: 1-55623-615-8

THE BUSINESS ONE IRWIN HANDBOOK OF TELECOMMUNICATIONS
Second Edition
James Harry Green

Over 17,000 copies sold in the first edition! Now, this popular guide is expanded to include the most current equipment updates, new technologies, and emerging trends so you can stay abreast of—and profitably use—these latest developments. This essential resource shows you how to get up to speed quickly and easily using practical information on prevailing telecommunications technology. (1,119 pages)
ISBN: 1-55623-333-7

NEW LIFE FOR OLD PCs
How to Keep Your Company's Computers from Becoming Obsolete
Alfred E. Poor

Effectively salvage, convert, and upgrade your PCs so you can receive the maximum value from your investment! This informative guide gives you the strategic tools to keep your system productive—within your organization, inside of your home, or within the community. Includes a user-friendly hypertext disk with practical checklists and decision trees to help you update and recycle your machine. (222 pages, paper)
ISBN: 1-55623-427-9